Napoleon
A Biographical Companion

Napoleon
A Biographical Companion

David Nicholls

ABC-CLIO

Santa Barbara, California
Denver, Colorado
Oxford, England

Library of Congress Cataloging-in-Publication Data
Nicholls, David, 1949–
    Napoleon : a biographical companion / David Nicholls.
      p.   cm. — (ABC-CLIO biographical companion)
    Includes bibliographical references and index.
    Summary: Describes the life, achievements, rise to power, and influences of the military leader who crowned himself Emperor of the French and established dominance over Europe.
    ISBN 0-87436-957-6 (alk. paper); 1-57607-191-X (UK only)
    1. Napoleon I, Emperor of the French, 1769–1821. 2. France—Kings and rulers Biography. 3. Napoleonic Wars, 1800–1815—Campaigns. 4. France—History—1789–1815. [1. Napoleon I, Emperor of the French, 1769–1821. 2. Kings, queens, rulers, etc. 3. Napoleonic Wars, 1800–1815. 4. France—History—1789–1815.] I. Title. II. Series.
DC203.N53   1999
944.05'092—dc21
[B]   99–22535
                                            CIP

04   03   02   01   00   99   10 9 8 7 6 5 4 3 2 1

ABC-CLIO, Inc.
130 Cremona Drive, P.O. Box 1911
Santa Barbara, California 93116–1911

Typesetting by Letra Libre, Inc.

This book is printed on acid-free paper ∞.
Manufactured in the United States of America

ABC-CLIO BIOGRAPHICAL COMPANIONS

Benjamin Franklin, by Jennifer L. Durham
Thomas Jefferson, by David S. Brown
Susan B. Anthony, by Judith E. Harper
Napoleon, by David Nicholls

————————————————

ABC-CLIO Biographical Companions are encyclopedic guides to the lives of
men and women who have had a significant impact on the social, political, and
cultural development of the Western world. Each volume presents complete
biographical information in an easily accessible format. An introduction and a
chronology provide an overview, while the A-to-Z entries amplify a myriad of topics
related to the person. A collection of documents and extensive illustrations give the
reader an acute sense of the individual's life and times.

CONTENTS

PREFACE

There are innumerable biographies of Napoleon, of all sizes, in all languages, and written from widely different points of view, and the stream shows no sign of running dry. Bonaparte has divided historians as much as he divided and excited his contemporaries, and political and national prejudices, as well as particular interests, continue to color assessments of his extraordinary life and his place in history. For every admiring or heroic account of the "greatest general in history" or the glorious emperor there is a belittling attack on the upstart Corsican nobody. This situation will never change, nor should it. Napoleon's career and personality are so intimately connected with the circumstances that produced him and the consequences of his actions and ambitions that no bland consensus can ever do justice to them.

No consideration of Napoleon can ignore his relationship to the French Revolution, a cataclysmic event that, despite unconvincing attempts to deny its significance, continues to divide opinions far outside the small world of professional historians. Nor can it gloss over neutrally the horrors of the years of warfare on an unprecedented scale that he unleashed in Europe and beyond. The unparalleled rise and fall of Napoleon Bonaparte belong to the histories of France, Europe, and the world, and historians of Right and Left, French and non-French, whose principal interests are political, military, social, cultural, or religious, will continue to provide readers with a complex and sometimes bewildering variety of different perspectives.

The alphabetical entries in this volume have been conceived to provide readers with an understanding of Napoleon as politician, ruler, soldier, revolutionary, administrator, dynast, and myth. They therefore cover a wide range of topics in several categories: the principal events of Napoleon's multifaceted life; the broader events, movements, and institutions that helped to shape his career; particular aspects of his styles of government and waging war; his family and the numerous other major personalities whose lives crossed that of Napoleon in significant fashion; the impact of Napoleon in different countries and of Napoleonic rule in Europe; and the construction and components of the Napoleonic myth. While the main focus is firmly on Napoleon himself, the attempt is made to place him in the broadest possible context, in terms of his place in the making of modern France and the reshaping of Europe. Where specific achievements, whether in domestic reform or on the battlefield, are associated with Napoleon, his personal contribution is placed in perspective and due credit given to other figures, whose names are perhaps less well known outside specialist circles.

The entries, then, allow the reader to view Napoleon from various angles. For example, he looks very different when viewed from Spain or from Poland, from within the *Grande Armée* or from the salons of Paris, from the French provinces or from the chancelleries of the European powers. The views of some notable contemporaries may also be found in the entries and documents. No final assessment is given, nor can the picture pretend to be complete. But the comprehensive nature of the entries, with suggestions for further reading indicated for each entry, should guide readers toward a rounded view of one of the towering figures of European history in the context of the continent during one of the most crucial and fertile periods of its history.

INTRODUCTION

The figure of Napoleon Bonaparte has always sharply divided opinions and elicited strong emotions. As he himself said with a characteristic lack of reserve: "I am not a man, I am a historical figure." He created his own legend and legends were created about him. The story of his rise to power and his dominance in Europe exerts a kind of fascination which was felt at the time even by his most determined opponents and which has extended into the twentieth century in film and popular fiction. As we approach the twenty-first century the Napoleon web site (http://www.napoleon.org) receives 20,000 hits a month. "The worldwide interest in Napoleon is staggering," says its editor-in-chief, who adds, probably going to the heart of the matter: "I don't think anyone really knows how he was so successful."

Napoleon's influence can still be seen in contemporary France and beyond, whether it be in providing the basis of French law and the law of other European countries and former French colonies, in the centralization of French government, or in the tourist sites of modern Paris. Napoleon has been and still is held responsible for many things, including the political unification of Germany and Italy and every authoritarian turn and movement in French history. National and ideological prejudices are still to be found in historical writing about him. Napoleon was the man who imposed order on revolutionary chaos and led his country to greatness, or he was the oppressive despot who imposed tyranny, bloodshed, and suffering on Europe. Napoleon's relationship with the great movements of the nineteenth and twentieth centuries—nationalism, democracy, imperialism—will forever be controversial and ensure that the fascination will continue.

The author of one of the greatest novels ever written, based around Napoleon's invasion of Russia, was a determined member of the anti-Bonaparte camp. Leo Tolstoy in *War and Peace* called Napoleon "that most insignificant tool of history who never anywhere, even in exile, displayed human dignity" (Tolstoy 1982, p. 1285). For Tolstoy the flow of historical events "depends on the combined volition of all who participate in those events," and "the influence of Napoleon on the course of those events is purely superficial and imaginary" (p. 932). So-called great men "are merely labels serving to give a name to the event, and like labels they have the least possible connection with the event itself" (p. 719). Napoleon was the contemptible instrument of the movement of peoples that makes up what we call history.

The opposite view would emphasize the exertion of Napoleon's will for good or ill, the shaping of events by the force of personality. His downfall becomes a satisfying punishment for hubris, but with a tragic dimension. It was another great French soldier, though of more modest ambition, Marshal Ferdinand Foch, who observed of Napoleon: "He forgot that a man cannot be God" (Herold 1983, p. 407). Or as one of his most notable intellectual adversaries, Germaine de Staël, expressed it, "'He wanted to put his gigantic self in the place of mankind" (Herold 1983, p. 7). "The force of his will," she wrote, "consisted in the imperturbable calculation of his egoism: he was an able chess-player for whom the human race was the opposite party" (Kafker and Laux, eds. 1989, p. 18). For Tolstoy's fellow Russian, Alexander Herzen, "It is possible to lead astray an entire generation, to strike it blind, to drive it insane, to direct it toward a false goal: Napoleon proved this" (Best 1982, p. 203). Whether Napoleon was a mere tool of history or a colossus imposing his will upon it, his life represented the extraordinary culmination of an extraordinary age, the "Age of Revolutions." The principle of hereditary monarchy, still dominant over the vast majority of the world's population, had been challenged first by the Americans then by the French Revolution. Out of the latter emerged a man leading a nation who carried the revolutionary challenge to the autocracies of continental Europe and the constitutional monarchy of Great Britain and who set himself up as the equal of the emperor of Austria, the tsar of Russia, or the king of Prussia, exposing the illusions of their absolute power. The question of how this happened bound to fascinate even those who find it repulsive or dangerous.

For many of those in other countries who had welcomed the French Revolution, Napoleon represented the ultimate disillusion. But for strong minorities in Germany, Italy, Spain, Poland, Holland, and elsewhere he maintained the hope brought by the armies of the Revolution, at least for a while. Yet for all he embodied something unique and unforeseen. Even Tolstoy, many years later and from the depths of his contempt for Napoleon, could not help testify-

ing, despite himself, to the remarkable nature of his appearance on the scene of French and European politics: "A man of no convictions, no habits, no traditions, no name, not even a Frenchman, emerges—by what seems the strangest freak of chance—from among all the seething parties of France, and, without attaching himself to any one of them, is borne forward to a prominent position" (Tolstoy 1982, p. 1344). How had this happened? "Why, how," writes Alistair Horne, "could this little Corsican nobody have climbed from nowhere to the top of the world and have achieved so much?" (Horne 1996, p. xx).

Napoleone Buonaparte was born on 15 August 1769 in Ajaccio, the capital of Corsica, as the second of the eight children of Carlo Buonaparte and Maria Letizia Ramolino Buonaparte. The moment was a crucial one in the history of his native island. Napoleone's parents had been supporters of the Corsican patriot, Pasquale Paoli, and the pregnant Letizia had carried Napoleone in her womb as she and her husband fled from Paoli's defeat by the Genoese rulers of Corsica. However, Genoa ceded Corsica to France, and Napoleon was born a subject of King Louis XV. The Buonaparte family had their claim to noble status confirmed by the French, but they were far from rich. Until his death in 1785 Carlo made a sometimes precarious living as a lawyer and cultivated connections with the new French rulers, which enabled him to send his children to be educated in France.

Accordingly, in January 1779 Napoleone and his elder brother Giuseppe (later Joseph) were sent to school at Autun, but in April the nine-year-old who now called himself Napoleon entered the military school at Brienne. During his five years there he was distinguished chiefly by a fierce Corsican nationalism and an aptitude for mathematics. In October 1784 he moved to the *École Militaire* in Paris, graduating as a sublieutenant of artillery in September 1785. Reports from his schools describe the young Napoleon as "reserved and hard-working," "extremely egotistical," and "extremely ambitious" (Schom 1997, p. 7), indicating possibly a sense of superiority compensating for his outsider status as a relatively poor provincial, speaking French with a strong Corsican accent.

Napoleon spent the years between 1785 and 1791 first with the La Fère Artillery Regiment at Valence and then at the Artillery School at Auxonne. He therefore observed the early dramas of the French Revolution at a distance. The monarchy of Louis XVI, facing the last and most serious of the interminable financial crises that afflicted the ancien régime like a recurring cancer, had been forced to call the representative Estates General, which met for the first time since 1614 on 5 May 1789. The storming of the Bastille on 14 July 1789 marked the symbolic beginning of the Revolution. Under popular pressure the Estates General, transformed into the Constituent Assembly, created a constitutional monarchy with the king as "the first citizen of France." The abolition of noble privileges in the army was to open the path to promotion to many an ambitious junior officer.

As the new revolutionary regime slipped toward war with monarchical Europe, Napoleon was promoted to first lieutenant in April 1791, lieutenant colonel in April 1792, and captain in May 1792. But this was no orderly progress. Napoleon's boyhood hero, Pasquale Paoli, had returned to Corsica in 1791, but soon showed that he was prepared to shelter Corsican independence under either French or British protection. Napoleon and his brother Lucien, on the other hand, had embraced Jacobinism, standing for popular government and centralization. Napoleon was in Ajaccio in April 1792, where the Second Battalion of Corsican Volunteers of the National Guard, of which he was lieutenant colonel, was involved in rioting.

As France declared war on Austria, Napoleon returned to Paris in time to witness the overthrow of Louis XVI when a revolutionary crowd invaded the Tuileries palace on 10 August 1792. The king's feeble behavior in the face of popular unrest made a lasting impression on Napoleon. "If Louis had shown himself on horseback," he wrote to Joseph, "he would have won the day" (Herold 1983, p. 40). By September Napoleon and Lucien were back in Corsica, actively agitating against Paoli in the Jacobin clubs, but the veteran patriot still enjoyed majority support on the island. While in Paris the French Republic was proclaimed on 22 September 1792, the situation in Corsica continued to deteriorate, culminating in open revolt against France in March 1793. In June the entire Buonaparte family fled to the mainland, arriving in Toulon on the thirteenth.

The events in Corsica had prevented Napoleon from being involved in the remarkable victory of the Revolutionary army over the invading Prussians at Valmy on 20 September 1792. Now he returned to duty with his regular rank of captain as the Jacobins, dominated by Maximilien Robespierre, tightened their grip on power in Paris. The beginning of the Terror in July 1793 sparked the federalist revolt against Parisian rule. In September Napoleon was assigned to the army besieging Toulon, the biggest French naval base in the Mediterranean, where the federalist rebels were being supported by a British fleet. When the French artillery commander was wounded, Napoleon, on the initiative of his fellow Corsican, Antonio Cristoforo Saliceti, took his place and drove out the British fleet, enabling the recapture of Toulon. At the age of twenty-four, Napoleon got his first taste of military glory and popular acclaim, and was promoted to general of brigade.

But if the mass armies of the Revolution gave unprecedented opportunities to ambitious soldiers, politics could still make the life of a general difficult if not precarious. Assigned to the staff of the Army of Italy in February 1794, Napoleon needed political protection, principally from Paul Barras, when after the overthrow and execution of Robespierre on 28 July 1794 (10 Thermidor Year II) he was briefly imprisoned at Antibes as a Jacobin. Back in Paris in May 1795 Napoleon refused an assignment to fight against the royalist and Catholic rebels in the Vendée and was instead transferred briefly to the Topographical Bureau.

His next opportunity for fame was again provided by the internal opposition. Unrest in Paris, arising from economic problems, turned in a royalist direction, aimed against the ruling Convention. When dangerous revolt spread through the streets on 13 Vendémiaire Year IV (5 October 1795) Napoleon saved the Convention with his whiff of grapeshot, leaving up to four hundred dead. A grateful but nervous Barras secured his promotion to general of division and commander of the Army of the Interior.

At the age of twenty-seven Napoleon was a Republican hero but in grave danger of becoming an overmighty general. His ambitious nature was evident for all to see. "It is said that I am an ambitious man," he wrote later, "but that is not so: or at least my ambition is so closely bound to my being that they are one and the same" (McLynn 1997, p. 286). But what direction would this ambition take? The new government of the Directory, installed in November 1795, inadvertently provided the answer. On 2 March 1796 he was appointed commander of the Army of Italy. In the continuing war with Austria France had suffered some embarrassing and potentially very serious defeats in the Rhineland. Part of the response would be to seize the initiative from the Austrians in Italy. Young General Buonaparte could be the man to achieve this, serving the Directory while being kept at a suitable distance from Paris.

Napoleon wrote to Talleyrand in September 1797: "All great events hang by a single thread. The clever man takes advantage of everything and neglects nothing that may give him some added opportunity" (Herold 1983, p. 72). He now made use of his extraordinary ability to inspire his troops and the willingness of the revolutionary French to ignore the "rules" of eighteenth-century warfare to seize the opportunity handed to him by his uneasy political masters. Before setting off for Italy, Napoleon married Joséphine de Beauharnais, the Creole widow of an aristocratic planter from the West Indies executed during the Terror, and one of Barras's numerous mistresses. Hurrying from his wedding to Nice to take over his command, he changed his last name from Buonaparte to Bonaparte.

The Italian campaign of 1796–1797 made Napoleon the military hero of France and alerted Europe to the new name of Bonaparte. Faced by superior Austrian forces, he fought a war of maneuver across northern and central Italy, preventing the enemy from ever concentrating his forces and imposing a series of resounding defeats on separate Austrian armies. Napoleon entered Milan in May 1796, after the battle of Lodi, and brought the campaign to an end by finally securing Mantua in February 1797. Striking north out of Italy toward Vienna, Napoleon, showing a haughty disregard for the hesitations of the Directory, forced Austria to sign the Treaty of Campo Formio, which ended the First Coalition against France, leaving only Great Britain still at war.

To the French people Napoleon seemed to bring glory in war and strength in peace, and for the first time he made use of army bulletins to promote his image. With his stirring speeches to his troops (some probably concocted after the event) and exaggerated if not downright fictitious accounts of his own bravery, soon to be immortalized in prints and paintings, Napoleon re-created himself as the incarnation of all the military virtues. More usefully for the Directory, he created the Cisalpine Republic in northern Italy as a "sister," that is subordinate, Republic to France and sent millions in treasure to replenish French coffers. For as long as he could, he would continue to make conquered peoples pay for their own subjection.

With only Britain left at war with France, plans were mooted for an expedition against England, but cooler heads, including Bonaparte's, prevailed. Instead Napoleon, together with the Directory's Minister of Foreign Affairs, Charles-Maurice de Talleyrand, urged an expedition to Egypt as a way of disrupting British relations with India and possibly even invading the colony. Here again we may possibly detect the Directory wishing to dispatch the threatening general as far away as possible. The Revolution's obsession with the classical past made the Directors nervous about a possible new Julius Caesar.

Napoleon's Egyptian adventure prefigured the later Napoleonic Wars in that while he won victory after victory on land, the British established domination of the sea. While Napoleon defeated the army of the Mameluke rulers of Egypt in the Battle of the Pyramids on 21 July 1798, the British under Horatio Nelson destroyed the French fleet at the Battle of the Nile on 1 August. And while Napoleon busied himself with completing the conquest of Egypt and reorganizing the country along French lines, a new Coalition, including the Ottoman Empire, nominal ruler of Egypt and Syria, was formed against France. The days of the Directory were numbered.

In Paris a purge of the Directory on 18 June (30 Prairial) 1799 had consolidated the position of Barras while promoting the veteran revolutionary Emmanuel Sieyès. These two and other conspirators were convinced that a change of regime, strengthening the executive power, was necessary. Napoleon too, whose sense of his own destiny was swelling, was persuaded that he could "save France." Leaving his army in Syria he sailed for France, landing at Fréjus on 9 October. The events of 18 Brumaire (18 November 1799) which overthrew the Directory started as a parliamentary coup and ended as a military coup. Napoleon's personal conduct did not show the sublime confidence that he doubtless wished, and he had to be rescued by the quick thinking of his brother Lucien and Joachim Murat's grenadiers. But his trump card with the people was that he could pose as a "savior above party," putting an end to factional strife. Sieyès and others may have wanted a new balanced constitution for the new Consulate regime; what they got was dictatorship.

The Constitution of the Year VIII, proclaimed on 12 December 1799 and subsequently approved by questionable plebiscite, created a complex governmental system, but First Consul Bonaparte ruled. An amended Constitution of the Year X in 1802, similarly approved by popular vote, made him consul for life. But first he needed a general peace in Europe to consolidate his power, and that meant another campaign against the Austrians in Italy. Napoleon crossed the Alps again in May 1800, and within a month the battle of Marengo assured what the royalist agent Hyde de Neuville described as "the baptism of Napoleon's personal power" (Furet 1992, p. 218). Now, he was later to claim, he fully saw his destiny stretching out before him.

Peace was finally achieved with Austria by the Treaty of Lunéville in February 1801 and with Britain by the Treaty of Amiens in March 1802. As war staggered toward peace, Napoleon and his supporters started the work of reforming France. Almost all of Napoleon's constructive work, the influence of which is to be felt in France to this day, was either completed or commenced in the years before the declaration of the empire in 1804. His purpose and historical role as he saw it was to bring the Revolution to an end, to draw a line ending the turbulence of the revolutionary decade and place French government on new, stable ground under his overall control.

Napoleon applied his own peculiar idea of the democratic legacy of the Revolution: "My policy is to govern men as the greater number wish to be governed. That, I think, is the way to recognize the sovereignty of the people" (Wright 1984, p. 26). His rule was authoritarian but inclusive: careers were open to the talented, and most royalist *émigrés* were invited to return to France, with only the royal family and the most irreconcilable excluded. The final amnesty of April 1802 excepted only about a thousand *émigrés*. The administration was centralized, with prefects appointed for all departments in March 1800. Work on new law codes began in August 1800, and the final Civil Code, known as the Code Napoléon, ensured that those who profited most from the Revolution, the peasants and bourgeois who had acquired confiscated noble and church lands, held onto their gains. The various Napoleonic codes are still the basis of French law today.

The most urgent act of reconciliation achieved under the Consulate was a new religious settlement. The Catholic Church had been persecuted under the Revolution, and a short-lived attempt had been made to replace Christianity with a new cult of the Supreme Being. The imposition of the Civil Constitution of the Clergy had created an underground refractory Church, and Catholicism was one of the main driving forces behind counterrevolutionary revolt in western France, principally in the Vendée. The Revolutionary calendar had even abolished Sunday as a day of worship and rest. However, within a few weeks of the coup of 18 Brumaire, on 28 December 1799, churches were reopened on Sundays, and in November 1800 Napoleon began negotiations with the newly elected Pope Pius VII for a fresh agreement with the papacy. The signing of the Concordat in July 1801 established a close relationship between church and state which was to last

for over a century and reconciled the Catholics, the overwhelming majority of the population, to the regime.

The Church had, however, permanently lost its monopoly control over French education. A new state system, designed to inculcate young people with antimonarchist values and create a new governing elite for France, was initiated by the law on public education of 1 May 1802. It was to be six years before a monopoly of teaching was vested in the new Imperial University, and the new centralized education structure never functioned fully under Napoleon. But here again Napoleon's scheme laid permanent foundations. The new elite secondary schools, the *lycées,* are still the lynchpin of the French educational system.

By the middle of 1803 Napoleon was consul for life and had taken the major steps in creating a new regime in his own image. There was no doubt that the Revolution was over. But there was no guarantee that the new order, resting in essence on the life of one man, would last any longer than its predecessors, nor that relations with the rest of Europe could be anything other than an armed truce. Napoleon's stance remained aggressive. He became president of the Republic of Italy, formerly the Cisalpine Republic, in January 1802, annexed Elba and Piedmont to France later in the same year, and interfered with British trade.

War between Britain and France resumed in May 1803. French troops occupied Hanover, Britain's only possession in continental Europe, and in December the French army encamped on the Channel coast near Boulogne was given the title of Army of England. But hostilities remained at a low level in 1804, as Napoleon took the final step in consolidating his personal power by declaring himself emperor of France.

The discovery in February of a royalist plot, involving Generals Jean Moreau and Charles Pichegru, to kidnap First Consul

Bonaparte revealed both the vulnerability of the regime and the personal nature of Napoleon's power. Napoleon became hereditary emperor of the French in May 1804, proclaiming himself the heir of Charlemagne, the great early medieval king of the Franks and Holy Roman Emperor. The full extent of his overreaching ambition stood revealed to the world.

Napoleon's coronation in December 1804 was a particular affront to the Holy Roman Emperor Francis II, head of the house of Habsburg and by tradition successor to Charlemagne. As Napoleon assumed the title of king of Italy in May 1805, annexed Genoa to France, and appointed Joséphine's son, Eugène de Beauharnais, viceroy of Italy, a new Coalition of Austria, Britain, and Russia was signed on 9 August 1805. Napoleon abandoned the invasion of England, and the Army of England became the *Grande Armée* and marched into Germany.

In his campaigns of 1805 and 1806 Napoleon transformed the map of Europe. After his victories at Ulm (20 October) and Austerlitz (2 December), he could impose his terms on the defeated Habsburgs and give a free rein to his dynastic ambitions. His elder brother Joseph was made king of Naples, and a new kingdom of Holland was created with another brother, Louis, as king. The Holy Roman Empire was dissolved and most of Germany reorganized as the Confederation of the Rhine under Napoleon's tutelage.

All this provoked Prussia into action, but the belated entry of the largest German state besides Austria into the fight against him only succeeded in raising Napoleon to the height of his power. The Prussians allied with Russia, but Napoleon acted with typical speed, defeated the Prussians at the battles of Jena-Auerstädt on 14 October 1806, and on 27 October entered Berlin, the Prussian capital. However, this was not the end of Prussian resistance. On 7–8 February 1807 Napoleon fought the bloody but indecisive battle of Eylau against the Prussians and Russians before on 14 June finally crushing the Russians at Friedland. He could dictate his own terms to the other powers in the Treaty of Tilsit (July 1807), which allowed him without fear of contradiction to call himself master of Europe. His youngest brother, Jérôme, became king of Westphalia, and a new duchy of Warsaw was created from lands held by Prussia in Poland. At a famous meeting on a raft anchored in the river Niemen, Tsar Alexander I of Russia was forced into an alliance with Napoleon which was destined to last until 1812.

But even at the summit of his glory, Napoleon's empire was vulnerable to erosion from two sources, soon to be combined: Great Britain and Spain. Even before his triumph at Austerlitz, Horatio Nelson's destruction of the French and its allied Spanish fleet at Trafalgar on 21 October 1805 had confirmed British mastery of the seas. Having abandoned all plans for an invasion of England, Napoleon's only weapon against his irreconcilable island enemy, the principal trading nation on the oceans, was economic warfare. The Continental System, inaugurated by the Berlin Decrees of 21 November 1806, was meant to prohibit all trade, even by neutral countries, with Britain, thereby sealing it off from continental Europe. A reluctant Alexander was forced at Tilsit to commit Russia to the blockade.

Although industry in some areas of Europe, notably Belgium and the Rhineland, was to benefit from the ending of British competition, the System was doomed to fail in its goal of bringing Britain to its knees by ruining its finances and provoking social unrest. Smuggling and other methods of avoidance, often connived at by French officials, were rife; some countries, including Louis Bonaparte's Kingdom of Holland, effectively ignored it; and its consequences served to heighten the unpopularity of Napoleonic rule in Europe. Napoleon was forced first to strengthen then eventually to grant exceptions to the ban. Britain replied with its own Orders in Council against French trade, and in a commercial trial of strength there could in the long run be only one winner.

Britain's strategy in the struggle against Napoleon was based on providing subsidies to his opponents and harrying France on the seas and in its colonies, but without committing British ground forces to fighting on the Continent. The only exception was in the Iberian Peninsula. French intervention in Spain and Portugal began in late 1807, and when on 30 November General Junot's forces occupied Lisbon, it marked the beginning of the draining and bloody Peninsular War, Napoleon's "Spanish Ulcer," which was to last until June 1813. His decision to include the peninsula in his dynastic plans was a necessary consequence of the Continental System: Napoleon could not allow the vast gap in his blockade represented by an independent Spain and Portugal, free to trade with Britain, to go unplugged.

Napoleon deposed the Spanish Bourbons and installed his brother Joseph as king of Spain, but the rising of the people of Madrid against Joachim Murat's French occupation forces in May 1808 signaled the start of a war which was to cost France dearly in blood and money and badly weaken Napoleon's empire. When he briefly took personal command in Spain between November 1808 and January 1809, he left the country convinced that it was pacified. But neither the emperor nor his *Grande Armée* could be everywhere at once. Further victories and the extension of his power in Germany and Italy had to be paid for by an ever increasing burden of taxes and conscription imposed on the peoples of the empire. Almost everywhere, this burden came to outweigh the liberating effects of Napoleonic rule embodied in the law codes and the abolition of outdated social regulations and constraints.

Austria resumed hostilities against Napoleon in April 1809, seeking to capitalize on popular discontent with his imperial rule by proclaiming the German War of Liberation. In a momentous few months between April and July, Napoleon defeated the Austrians in the campaign culminating in the battle of Wagram on 5–6 July, a British army under Arthur Wellesley, the future duke of Wellington, landed in Portugal, Pope Pius VII excommunicated Napoleon, France annexed the Papal States, and the pope was arrested.

Napoleon was now in a position to attain the summit of his personal and family ambitions: to gain for the Bonapartes a permanent place among the ruling dynasties of Europe. He may have been master of Europe, but his power was still personal, a heartbeat away from destruction. He needed an heir, and the Habsburgs, humbled once again by his military prowess, could be his instruments. There can be no doubting Napoleon's genuine affection and respect for Joséphine, but such human considerations could not be allowed to influence or to dim the glory of the self-styled successor of Charlemagne.

The divorce of Napoleon and Joséphine was pronounced on 15 December 1809, and in February 1810 Rome was annexed to the French Empire. Napoleon's heir was to bear the title of king of Rome, the same borne by the heirs of the defunct Holy Roman Empire. On 1 April 1810 Napoleon married the eighteen-year-old Marie-Louise, daughter of the former Holy Roman Emperor, now retitled Francis I, emperor of Austria, and their son, known to history as Napoleon II or the king of Rome, was born on 20 March 1811. But Napoleon's hope that the established monarchs of Europe would recognize his heir was not to be fulfilled. From the Austrian point of view the match with Marie-Louise had been a marriage of convenience. The oldest ruling house in Europe would never consider the Corsican upstart as an equal.

Meanwhile Napoleon's system of satellite kingdoms ruled by members of his family was beginning to crumble. Napoleon's displeasure at Louis Bonaparte's too independent behavior as king of Holland, especially in circumventing the Continental System, led to his deposition and the annexation of the kingdom to France in July 1810. His brother Joseph was merely a shadow king of Spain, where the tide of war ebbed and flowed between Napoleon's marshals on the one hand and British, Spanish, and Portuguese forces supported by Spanish guerrillas on the other. Napoleon's military strategy had always been based on concentrating his own and the enemy's forces to his advantage and delivering a decisive blow, as at Austerlitz or Wagram. Such an approach was completely inapplicable in Spain, where even at the moments of greatest French power the rebels always held some territory, however little, and the guerrillas could never be decisively subjugated. Napoleon's usual strategy was to prove equally inapplicable in Russia.

Napoleon's invasion of Russia in 1812, eternalized in Tolstoy's *War and Peace,* has become a byword for the nemesis of overreaching power. Like Charles XII of Sweden before him and Adolf Hitler in the twentieth century, Napoleon was to face destruction in the endless reaches of the East. Contrary to one popular misconception, Napoleon's Russian adventure was well planned and supplied. Preparations began in January 1811, immediately after Alexander I had signaled the end of his unwilling alliance with Napoleon by breaking the Continental System, and continued throughout the year.

A secret alliance between Russia and Sweden in March 1812 was followed by the formal declaration of the Sixth Coalition against France, in which the two northern powers were supported by Britain and indirectly by rebel Spain. In May Napoleon took command of the multinational *Grande Armée,* assembled in East Prussia and Poland, and on 24–25 June crossed the Niemen into Russian territory. Although presented to the French people in grand terms as motivated by the desire to destroy the permanent threat to Europe posed by Russian power, Napoleon's vast enterprise was above all meant to punish the tsar for leaving the continental blockade. It was far from being the crazy or impossible enterprise it may appear with the benefit of hindsight. But the refusal of the Russian army to engage in the one big battle Napoleon always sought rendered all his plans worthless. The only major battle of the campaign, at Borodino on 7 September 1812, was fought to a bloody stalemate.

The Russian refusal to talk peace while his army remained on their soil eventually forced Napoleon into the harrowing and disastrous retreat from Moscow, less than a month after his occupation of the ancient capital of Russia in September 1812. His vulnerability was exposed to the world, and his reluctant allies and satellites would not be slow in abandoning him. Napoleon left his army on 5 December to hurry back to Paris, where the conspiracy led by the half-mad General Malet had spread the news of his death in Russia. In the early months of 1813, Prussia broke from its alliance with Napoleon and joined Russia against him; northern Germany rose against Napoleonic rule; Sweden, ruled by Marshal Bernadotte, reinforced the coalition; Austria broke the French alliance but remained neutral until August; and the French finally evacuated Madrid.

All Europe was now united against Napoleon. The final Grand Alliance was completed in August 1813 when Austria abandoned its neutrality to take part in driving Napoleon's forces from Germany. Although he showed all his old expertise and daring in the campaigns of Germany in 1813 and France in 1814, it was now acknowledged, not least by his marshals and his legislators in France, that Napoleon's cause was lost.

The "Battle of the Nations" at Leipzig on 16–19 October 1813 led to the collapse of the Confederation of the Rhine and the Kingdom of Westphalia and Napoleon's retreat from Germany. With Wellington's advance through northern Spain to the Pyrenees, Napoleon was having to fight on two fronts at once, and could rely on nothing but his own boldness and rearguard actions by his commanders. As the Allies crossed the Rhine in January 1814 and Joachim Murat, king of Naples, defected in a desperate attempt to retain his throne, Napoleon stubbornly refused all offers of peace. But even his brilliant series of actions in eastern France in February could not stop the Allied advances from east and south.

Wellington entered Bordeaux on 12 March; Marshals Marmont and Mortier surrendered Paris to the Allies on 31 March; the marshals refused to continue the fight; and after a final attempt to preserve the dynasty by abdicating in favor of his son, Napoleon abdicated unconditionally on 11 April 1814. Marie Louise and the king of Rome were placed in the custody of Francis I of Austria, and Louis XVIII became king of a France restored to its frontiers of 1792. Napoleon began his exile on the island of Elba on 4 May.

Napoleon's empire was thus reduced to a small island off the coast of Italy, but even here he kept up the illusion of power, with a court and a tiny army. He was denied any access to his wife and son, and was saddened by the sudden death of Joséphine at her château of Malmaison on 29 May 1814. Meanwhile the powers of Europe met to decide the future political shape of the Continent at the Congress of Vienna, which opened in September 1814. It was to last until June 1815. Die-hard conservatives might delude themselves that the clock could simply be turned back to the ancien régime, but the effects of the Napoleonic "episode" had been too profound. The Congress had to struggle toward a new concept of the balance of power, with a new order guaranteed by the great powers, including France. The erstwhile Allies each pursued their own interests in the comfortable but fallacious belief that Napoleon had been dealt with once and for all.

The difficult negotiations at Vienna were interrupted in March 1815 by the astonishing news that Napoleon had sailed from Elba on 25 February, landed in France near Cannes on 1 March, and was marching toward Paris picking up soldiers on the way. The adventure of the Hundred Days, a gamble that seemed as if it might succeed, shows Napoleon's awareness of the divisions among his enemies. He could still count on considerable support in the army, whose officers and men were threatened with loss of pensions and unemployment. Disillusion with the restored Bourbons and their reactionary and vengeful supporters was widespread, and peasants in particular feared the restoration of the ancient rights and privileges of the nobility. As far as one can tell, however, among the bulk of the population Napoleon's return engendered neither great enthusiasm nor great hostility. People were prepared to wait and see how things turned out.

By the time Napoleon arrived in Paris on 20 March and the Hundred Days, properly speaking, began, Murat had already attacked the Austrians in Italy. An Additional Act to the Constitutions of the Empire (usually referred to as the *Acte Additionnel),* drawn up by Benjamin Constant, hitherto an opponent of Napoleon, created a new theoretically liberal empire, guaranteeing basic freedoms and a stronger representative element in government. But even if Napoleon was serious about his new democratic feelings, he was denied the opportunity to put them into practice. His return forced the Allies to put their quarrels aside and organize new united action against the resurgent usurper.

Acting quickly, on 13 March the Congress of Vienna declared Napoleon an outlaw, banished from the empire. The Austri-

A

Abdication, First (April 1814)

Napoleon's first abdication was forced upon him by the Allies and his own marshals after the surrender of Paris on 31 March 1814 by Marshals Louis Marmont and Joseph Mortier. Napoleon blamed Joseph Bonaparte for leaving Paris and authorizing Mortier to treat with the Allies, exclaiming: "He lost me Spain, now he has lost me Paris!" But the key players were Tsar Alexander I and Charles-Maurice de Talleyrand.

Napoleon, installed at Fontainebleau, decided to march on Paris, but on 1 April Talleyrand formed a provisional government in Paris with the support of the tsar and on 3 April persuaded the Senate to depose the emperor. On 4 April Napoleon's marshals refused to march, and he reluctantly abdicated in favor of his son, Napoleon II, king of Rome. However, his attempts to secure the continuity of the Bonaparte dynasty were doomed to failure. Marmont and his corps had gone over to the Allies on 3 April, and the tsar and Talleyrand backed the restoration of the Bourbons in the person of Louis XVIII. Marmont was blamed by Napoleon's supporters for the seeming restoration of the ancien régime, the order that had provoked the Revolution.

Napoleon vowed angrily to march on Paris, but the marshals again refused to follow him, and on 6 April he abdicated unconditionally. By the Treaty of Fontainebleau (11 April 1814) Napoleon was given sovereignty over the island of Elba, with an annual income of two million francs from France. The Empress Marie-Louise was to be duchess of Parma, Piacenza, and Guastalla, and generous pensions were provided for all the Bonapartes. The empress's feelings about possibly following Napoleon into exile are unclear, but her fate was decided by her father, the Emperor Francis I, who took her and her son to Vienna. Napoleon was never to see them again.

On the night of 12 April Napoleon apparently tried to commit suicide, taking a poison capsule which he had carried with him for two years, but he soon recovered. Nothing was left for him but to proceed to his new tiny island empire. On 20 April he bade an emotional farewell to the soldiers of the Old Guard in the White Horse court of the château of Fontainebleau, and on 4 May was installed on Elba.

Related entries: Alexander I, Tsar of Russia; Louis XVIII, King of France; Marmont, Auguste Frédéric Louis Viesse de; Marshals; Talleyrand-Périgord, Charles-Maurice de

Suggestions for further reading:
Arnold, Eric A., ed. 1994. *A Documentary Survey of Napoleonic France.* Lanham, MD: University Press of America, pp. 326–327.

Hamilton-Williams, David. 1994. *The Fall of Napoleon: The Final Betrayal.* London: John Wiley.

Mackenzie, Norman. 1982. *The Escape from Elba: The Fall and Flight of Napoleon, 1814–1815.* New York: Oxford University Press.

Petre, F. Loraine. 1994. *Napoleon at Bay, 1814.* London: Greenhill.

Abdication, Second (22 June 1815)

After his defeat at Waterloo on 18 June 1815, Napoleon hurried to Paris, arriving on 21 June. Great crowds greeted him, shouting their support outside the Elysée Palace, where he was lodged. "The voice of the Nation speaks through them," he declared to Benjamin Constant, but this was reckoning without the Chamber of Representatives established by the *Acte Additionnel* of 22 April 1815. Napoleon's brother Lucien and Marshal Louis Davout, minister of war, urged him to declare the nation in danger, dissolve the legislature, and assume dictatorial powers to continue the war, but at the same time the Chamber met and passed a decree making it treason for Napoleon to dissolve them.

On 22 June Napoleon abdicated in favor of his son: "I offer myself as a sacrifice to the hate of the enemies of France" (Arnold 1994, p. 357). But the Senate voted against Napoleon II, while the Chamber of Representatives, led by Marie-Joseph de Lafayette, appointed a provisional governing council headed by Joseph Fouché. Fouché immediately contacted Charles-Maurice de Talleyrand and arranged the restoration of Louis XVIII, who reentered Paris on 8 July. Napoleon, meanwhile, had retreated to Malmaison, where he bade farewell to members of his family, and from there to Rochefort, where his brother Joseph urged him to flee to the United States. Napoleon, refusing to sneak away like a thief in the night, surrendered to Captain Maitland of HMS *Bellero-*

phon and appealed for refuge in England. His appeal was denied, and he was exiled to Saint Helena.

The result of the second abdication was the second restoration of Louis XVIII and a partial return to the ancien régime under the Bourbons.

Related entries: Fouché, Joseph; Louis XVIII, King of France; Talleyrand-Périgord, Charles-Maurice de

Suggestions for further reading:
Arnold, Eric A., ed. 1994. *A Documentary Survey of Napoleonic France.* Lanham, MD: University Press of America, pp. 356–358.

Brett James, Antony. 1964. *The Hundred Days: Napoleon's Last Campaign from Eyewitness Accounts.* New York: Macmillan.

Hamilton-Williams, David. 1994. *The Fall of Napoleon: The Final Betrayal.* London: John Wiley.

Mackenzie, Norman. 1982. *The Escape from Elba: The Fall and Flight of Napoleon, 1814–1815.* New York: Oxford University Press.

Thornton, M. J. 1968. *Napoleon after Waterloo: England and the Saint Helena Decision.* Stanford, CA: Stanford University Press

Aboukir Bay, Battle of

See **Nile, Battle of the**

Acte Additionnel (1815)

Drawn up by Benjamin Constant, the Additional Act to the Constitution of the Empire, usually referred to as the *Acte Additionnel,* was meant as the new constitution of the empire following Napoleon's escape from Elba during the Hundred Days. It guaranteed equality before the law, individual liberty, freedom of religion, and liberty of the press. Executive power rested with the emperor, who named and removed ministers, but was limited by the Senate and a Chamber of Representatives elected by electoral colleges composed according to the Constitution of the Year X. Promulgated on 22 April 1815 and approved by referendum (but with a huge number of abstentions), the new constitution was only applied for two months, in the period leading up to the battle of Waterloo. Meant to be the basis of a new, liberal empire, it satisfied few: republicans were angered by the limited franchise and liberals by the extent of the emperor's powers.

Related entries: Constant, Benjamin; Hundred Days

Suggestions for further reading:
Arnold, Eric A., ed. 1994. *A Documentary Survey of Napoleonic France.* Lanham, MD: University Press of America, pp. 348–356.
Mackenzie, Norman. 1982. *The Escape from Elba: The Fall and Flight of Napoleon, 1814–1815.* New York: Oxford University Press.
Schom, Alan. 1992. *One Hundred Days: Napoleon's Road to Waterloo.* New York: Oxford University Press.
Wood, Dennis. 1993. *Benjamin Constant.* London and New York: Routledge.

Ajaccio

Napoleon's native town is situated on the west coast of Corsica, overlooking the Gulf of Ajaccio, the largest gulf on the Corsican coast. In 1793, on Napoleon's advice, Ajaccio was made capital of the new department of the Liamone, and in 1811 when Corsica was united as one department Napoleon made Ajaccio the capital, which it remained until 1975, when the island was once again divided into two departments. It is now capital of Corse du Sud (southern Corsica). Napoleon's birthplace, the Maison Bonaparte, has been a museum since 1923, while the Napoleonic Museum exhibits artifacts relating to the Bonaparte family, including Napoleon's baptism certificate and the death mask made at Saint Helena.

Related entries: Corsica

Alexander I, Tsar of Russia (1801–1825)

Born in 1777, son of Paul I and grandson of Catherine the Great, Alexander's seemingly kaleidoscopic character has led biographers to dub him "the enigmatic tsar" and "the sphinx of the north." He was educated in the ideals of the Enlightenment by his tutor, the Swiss philosophe Frédéric-César de La Harpe, but also inherited a love of all things military and what turned out to be an unfortunate respect for German military planning from his father. This dual inheritance left him "ever torn between the classroom and the parade ground" or, in the words of his reforming minister Mikhail Speranski, "too feeble to rule and too strong to be ruled."

Alexander came to the throne as a result of the overthrow and murder of his father in 1801. According to his friend, Adam Czartoryski, Paul's murder, to which Alexander seems to have assented, "settled like a vulture on his conscience, paralyzed his best faculties at the commencement of his reign, and plunged him into a mysticism sometimes degenerating into superstition at its close" (Saunders 1992, p. 9). His youthful idealism for reforming his vast and backward empire came to little because of his own character, the immensity of the problems involved, and the war against Napoleon, which occupied most of his time from 1804 onward.

At first Alexander pursued a policy of peace, dealing impartially with France and Britain, but by 1803, with the influential Czartoryski arguing that Russia could not stand aside from Europe, he was preparing for war with Napoleon. The murder of the duke of Enghien and Napoleon's assumption of the title of emperor in 1804 personally offended Alexander, and he determined to oppose French expansion in alliance with Austria. Alexander commanded the Austro-Russian army at the battle of Austerlitz (2

December 1805), where, ignoring the advice of the experienced Mikhail Kutuzov, he was partly responsible for the disastrous defeat. Austria made peace, but Alexander continued the war in alliance with Prussia, only suing for peace after the Russian defeat at Friedland in June 1807.

Peace with Napoleon was sealed by the controversial Treaty of Tilsit in July 1807. Although Russia lost little by the alliance with Napoleon, she was threatened by Napoleon's gains in Germany and the creation of the Duchy of Warsaw. Above all, Russia was forced to join the Continental System, while vague plans were laid for the dismemberment of the Ottoman Empire. Whatever the reality of Tilsit, Alexander's subjects saw it as abject surrender. The tsar had abandoned Prussia to its fate; French principles were anathema to the Russian nobility: the Continental System had an extremely adverse effect on Russian commerce; and the plans to divide the Ottoman Empire, if they had ever been serious, came to nothing. At the end of 1810 Alexander withdrew from the Continental System, opening Russian ports to British trade, and war became inevitable.

Alexander could claim little personal credit for the failure of Napoleon's Russian campaign of 1812, but by pushing forward beyond the boundaries of Russia he gained enormous prestige in Europe and became the anchor of the coalition against Napoleon. His final contribution to European diplomacy was the creation of the Holy Alliance with Austria and Prussia to impose a new Christian order upon Europe. He was now under strong religious influence, but it is doubtful whether his partners knew what Holy Alliance was supposed to mean. He had, however, played a key role in the restoration of monarchy, not only in France but throughout Europe.

Related entries: Abdication, First; Austerlitz, Battle of; Bagration, Pyotr Ivanovich, Prince; Barclay de Tolly; Mikhail Andreas, Prince; Borodino, Battle of; Caulaincourt, Armand Augustin Louis, Marquis de; Coalitions; Continental System; Erfurt, Congress of; Kutuzov, Mikhail Ilarionovich; Ottoman Empire; Paul I, Tsar of Russia; Poland; Quadruple Alliance; Russian Campaign; Suvorov, Alexander; Tilsit, Treaty of; Vienna, Congress of

Suggestions for further reading:
Cate, Curtis. 1985. *The War of the Two Emperors: The Duel between Napoleon and Alexander, Russia, 1812*. New York: Random House.
Hartley, Janet. 1994. *Alexander I*. London and New York: Longman.
Niven, Alexander C. 1978. *Napoleon and Alexander I*. Washington DC: University Press of America.
Palmer, Alan. 1974. *Alexander I, Tsar of War and Peace*. London: Weidenfeld and Nicolson.
Ragsdale, Hugh. 1980. *Détente in the Napoleonic Era: Bonaparte and the Russians*. Lawrence, KS: Regents Press.
Saunders, David. 1992. *Russia in the Age of Reaction and Reform, 1801–1881*. London and New York: Longman.

Amiens, Peace of (1802)

Negotiated following the collapse of the second coalition and the fall of William Pitt and signed on 27 March 1802, the peace of Amiens brought peace between France and Britain for the first time since 1793, and along with the peace of Lunéville marked the end of the revolutionary wars. But it was the product of exhaustion, not reconciliation, and only brought a brief respite. France pledged to respect the independence and integrity of Naples, Portugal, and the Batavian Republic, while Britain agreed to restore its conquests of possessions of France and its allies, except Ceylon and Trinidad, and to evacuate Elba and Malta. Malta was restored to the Knights of St. John. But the discussions surrounding the treaty had convinced British ministers of Napoleon's inordinate ambition, and with French hegemony in Europe left intact and no commercial agreement, there was little hope that the peace would be lasting.

Related entries: Coalitions; Great Britain

James Gillray's satirical cartoon **The Plum Pudding in Danger** *(1803) shows Napoleon and William Pitt slicing up the globe between them. Bonaparte takes the continent of Europe and Britain takes the oceans, an accurate enough view of what was to happen over the next four years. (The Trustees of the British Museum, London)*

Suggestions for further reading:
Arnold, Eric A., ed. 1994. *A Documentary Survey of Napoleonic France.* Lanham, MD: University Press of America, pp. 104–114.
Deutsch, Harold C. 1938. *The Genesis of Napoleonic Imperialism.* Cambridge: Harvard University Press.
Mowat, R. B. 1924. *The Diplomacy of Napoleon.* London: Edward Arnold.
Ross, Steven T. 1981. *European Diplomatic History, 1789–1815.* Malabar, FL: Krieger.

Arcola, Battle of (15–17 November 1796)

One of the most celebrated engagements of Napoleon's Italian campaign, Arcola played a significant part in the creation of the Napoleonic legend, notably through Jean Antoine Gros's dramatic but fanciful painting of *Bonaparte at Arcola.* In order to defeat the Austrian army commanded by General Josef Alvintzi, which was attempting to relieve the siege of Mantua, Napoleon moved to cut Austrian communications at Villanova, seize their supply train, and prevent Alvintzi from joining with a second Austrian force that was advancing down the river Adige. On 14 November Generals André Masséna and Charles Augereau crossed the Adige at Ronco and attacked the Croat forces defending the village of Arcola, but were thrown back from the wooden bridge over the river Alpone.

Napoleon arrived and personally led another attack. This was also turned back, but General Jean Guieu seized Arcola from the rear. Alvintzi's troops escaped, and that night the French were inadvertently withdrawn from Arcola. Two days of additional fighting were necessary to secure control of the village and bridge for the French. In the three days of fighting the Austrians lost 7,000 men and eleven guns, while French casualties amounted to over 4,500. The French victory made the fall of Mantua inevitable. Alvintzi's army was defeated and driven back to Montebello, and Napoleon occupied Verona.

Related entries: Italian Campaigns; Napoleonic Legend

Suggestions for further reading:
Burton, Reginald George. 1912. *Napoleon's Campaigns in Italy, 1796–97 and 1800.* London and New York: G. Allen.
Jackson, Sir William Godfrey Fothergill. 1953. *Attack in the West: Napoleon's First Campaign Re-read Today.* London: Eyre and Spottiswoode.
Phipps, Ramsay Weston. 1926–1939. *The Armies of the First French Republic and the Rise of the Marshals of Napoleon I.* London: Humphrey Milford. 5 vols.

Armed Neutrality

The League of Armed Neutrality was formed in December 1800 on the initiative of Tsar Paul I as a result of British insistence on searching neutral shipping for contraband cargo destined for France. Russia, Denmark, and Sweden were joined by Prussia in an attempt to keep British merchant ships out of the Baltic. The League halted shipments of corn to Britain at a time of poor harvests and dearth and cut off British supplies of Baltic timber and hemp for use in shipbuilding. It was dissolved after the British victory over the Danish fleet at the battle of Copenhagen (2 April 1801) and the assassination of Paul I.

Related entries: Denmark; Paul I, Tsar of Russia

Suggestions for further reading:
Feldbæk, Ole. 1980. *Denmark and the Armed Neutrality 1800–1801.* Copenhagen: Akademisk Forlag.

———. 1986. "The Foreign Policy of Tsar Paul I, 1800–1801: An Interpretation." *Jahrbücher für Geschichte Osteuropas* 30, pp. 16–36.
Ragsdale, Hugh. 1980. *Détente in the Napoleonic Era: Bonaparte and the Russians.* Lawrence, KS: Regents Press.

Army

Napoleon inherited his weaponry from the armies of the French ancien régime and his basic tactical formations from those of the Revolution. The Revolutionary army, however, had come to see itself as an autonomous force standing apart from civilian society and dedicated to fighting against everything backward and feudal in Europe. The army was dominated by its generals; hence the importance Napoleon gave to securing their personal devotion to him. His originality lay in organization—detailed staff planning to concentrate the greatest possible numbers of men at the probable site of battle—and in his personal tactics, which were different for each battle. After 1805, under the empire, the standing army numbered between 500,000 and 600,000 men. Napoleon usually took the field with 200,000 French, reinforced in the course of a campaign by foreign contingents raised by conscription in the conquered territories. For example, about half a million Italians served in the armies of the Directory and empire, of whom about one quarter were volunteers. The *Grande Armée* of 1812 was 611,000 strong, but two-thirds non-French. The ranks were augmented, when necessary, by conscription: Napoleon called up 500,000 during 1811 and 1812 and 1 million in 1813 and 1814. All officers and NCOs were regulars, though many had begun as members of the National Guard or as conscripts. The Napoleonic army was probably at its peak of effectiveness in 1805 and 1806: thereafter there was little time to train troops and massive avoidance of conscription. After 1812 recruits were lucky to get more than a week's training.

Napoleon's greatest innovation was in making the corps, numbering 20,000 to 30,000 men, usually commanded by a marshal, and capable of giving battle alone, the basic unit of the army. A corps would ideally consist of two or more infantry divisions, a brigade of cavalry, six to eight companies of artillery, and a company of engineers. A division, commanded by a major general, comprised two brigades of two infantry regiments, one or two companies of artillery, and a company of engineers. Each infantry regiment numbered nearly 4,000 men all told, comprising four battalions of six companies, together with its headquarters, medical detachment, and band. Each battalion included in its numbers a company of *grenadiers,* used as shock troops, and *voltigeurs* or *tirailleurs,* used as skirmishers.

The cavalry was of two sorts, heavy and light. The light cavalry, comprising dragoons, hussars, and *chasseurs,* were distinguished by wearing no armor, though, like the heavy cavalry, they were armed with carbine, pistol, and saber. Cavalry regiments numbered 1,200 to 1,800 men, with light cavalry divided into four squadrons of two companies each and heavy into three squadrons of two companies each. The light cavalry used faster horses, like modern hunters and thoroughbreds, usually European stock bred with Arabians. Reserve troops mostly came from the Imperial Guard.

Related entries: Conscription; *Grande Armée;* Imperial Guard

Suggestions for further reading:
Bertaud, Jean-Paul. 1986. "Napoleon's Officers," *Past & Present,* no. 112, pp. 91–111.
Chandler, David G. 1979. *Dictionary of the Napoleonic Wars.* London: Arms and Armour.
Lachouque, Henry. 1997. *The Anatomy of Glory: Napoleon and his Guard.* London: Greenhill.

Lynn, John A. 1989. "Towards an Army of Honour: The Moral Evolution of the French Army," *French Historical Studies,* 16, pp. 152–182.
Rogers, H. C. B. 1974. *Napoleon's Army.* London: Allen.

Art of Warfare, Napoleon and

Napoleon's tactics in war were unpredictable, one reason for his success and his reputation as a commander. He made no real innovations, building upon the "revolutionary warfare" of 1793 based on mass attack with fixed bayonets. Napoleon exploited the divisional system, originally introduced during the Revolution, so that he could concentrate his army, by a few hours' march, at any point that he wanted to take or that was in danger. He took calculated risks in order to be stronger than the enemy at the decisive point: "All fire must be concentrated on one point: the breach once made and the balance broken, everything else is unnecessary. The place is taken." Showing an unrivaled capacity for improvisation, Napoleon engaged, held back a large reserve, and waited for the enemy to make a mistake or expose a weakness; then he struck hard with infantry followed by massed cavalry, preparing the way with artillery fire. Napoleon's genius lay in knowing when and where to strike, and this, he said, could not be learned; it came from instinct.

Related entries: Artillery; Danube Campaigns; Germany, Campaigns in; Italian Campaigns

Suggestions for further reading:
Chandler, David G. 1974. *The Campaigns of Napoleon: The Mind and Method of History's Greatest Soldier.* New York: Macmillan.
Connelly, Owen. 1987. *Blundering to Glory: Napoleon's Military Campaigns.* Wilmington, DE: Scholarly Resources.
Epstein, Robert M. 1994. *Napoleon's Last Victory and the Emergence of Modern War.* Lawrence: University Press of Kansas.

Gates, David. 1997. *The Napoleonic Wars, 1803–15*. London: Edward Arnold.

Glover, Michael. 1980. *Warfare in the Age of Bonaparte*. London: Cassell.

Lachouque, Henry. 1966. *Napoleon's Battles.* New York: Dutton.

Marshall-Cornwall, Sir James. 1967. *Napoleon as Military Commander.* London: Batsford.

Muir, Rory. 1998. *Tactics and the Experience of Battle in the Age of Napoleon.* New Haven: Yale University Press.

Rothenberg, Gunther E. 1980. *The Art of Warfare in the Age of Napoleon.* Bloomington: Indiana University Press.

Suggestions for further reading:

Glover, Michael. 1980. *Warfare in the Age of Bonaparte.* London: Cassell.

Marshall-Cornwall, Sir James. 1967. *Napoleon as Military Commander.* London: Batsford.

Quimby, Robert Sherman. 1957. *The Background to Napoleonic Warfare.* New York: Columbia University Press.

Rothenberg, Gunther E. 1980. *The Art of Warfare in the Age of Napoleon.* Bloomington: Indiana University Press.

Auerstädt, Battle of

See **Jena-Auerstädt, Battles of**

Artillery

Napoleon introduced no real innovations in the use of artillery on the battlefield. Technology remained unchanged, and the average range of guns was no more than half a mile. But he used massed fire better than previous commanders had done. Senior artillery commanders were appointed at army, corps, and (usually) divisional level, each with his own small staff and in close touch with the formation commander he was supporting. For a time, also, guns were allocated permanently to battalions as a way of installing confidence into troops, especially, after 1805, the increasingly ill-trained conscripts. "The less good troops are," he said, "the more artillery they require." But this organization was not used in the Peninsular War or at Waterloo.

"Artillery," said Napoleon, "like other arms, must be collected in mass if one wishes to attain a decisive result." He always sought to concentrate his guns in large batteries with the purpose of overwhelming a selected section of the enemy's defense. He also used converging fire from several large batteries, which, as well as having a potentially devastating effect in its own right, also made countermeasures more difficult. But this tactic depended on suitable positions being available, which was not always the case.

Related entries: Army; Art of Warfare, Napoleon and

Augereau, Pierre François Charles (1757–1816)

Later given the titles of duke of Castiglione and marshal of France, Augereau was born of humble origins in the popular Faubourg Saint-Marceau of Paris. Augereau's early career as a soldier in various armies between 1774 and 1791 is obscure; he certainly fought in and deserted from the forces of several countries, but his own accounts of his exploits are unreliable. Back in Paris in 1792 he volunteered for the German Legion, the start of a genuine military career, which meant a rapid rise to prominence during the Terror and after. Augereau fought against the rebels of the Vendée as a divisional general and then with distinction against the Spanish.

In 1795 Augereau transferred to the Army of Italy and in 1796–1797 shared with André Masséna the position as Napoleon's leading subordinate, his most notable exploit being the defeat of the Austrians at Castiglione in August 1796. However, he also gained a well-deserved reputation for looting and personal profiteering, and Napoleon thought Masséna the better general. Between 1797 and 1804 Augereau filled a variety of posts, some of which at least were designed to keep him away from the centers of political intrigue. The year 1799 saw him as commander of the French forces in Holland, and he maintained a low profile during the coup of 18 Brumaire.

He was named a marshal of the empire in 1804, and the years between 1805 and 1809 were the days of Augereau's glory. As commander of the Seventh Corps he forced the Austrian surrender at Feldkirch in November 1805 and played a significant role in the victory of Jena in October 1806. He was wounded at Eylau in February 1807, but his appointment to command the Army of Catalonia in Spain was short-lived and he was replaced by Jacques Macdonald. He had finally overcome his freebooting tendencies, but from 1810 onward a decline in his abilities is evident.

During the invasion of Russia in 1812 Augereau remained in Prussia on occupation duty as commander of the Eighth Corps, and he saw his last significant action in 1813 as commander of the Sixteenth Corps at Naumberg. Appointed as commander of the Army of the Rhône, based at Lyon, in January 1814, he was again removed from the center of affairs. Augereau denounced Napoleon in April 1814, but during the Hundred Days tried to switch sides again. He was ignored by both sides and struck from the list of marshals in April 1815. He died at La Houssaye, reportedly of dropsy, in June 1816.

A contradictory and somewhat unstable character, Augereau undoubtedly performed great services to Napoleon from the turn of the century to 1809, but was struck by declining health during his last years and ended up as a virtual spectator during the dramatic events of 1814–1815.

Related entries: Castiglione, Battle of; Eylau, Battle of; Jena-Auerstädt, Battles of

Suggestions for further reading:
Elting, John R. 1987. "Augereau," in David G. Chandler, ed., *Napoleon's Marshals.* New York: Macmillan.

Phipps, Ramsay Weston. 1926–1939. *The Armies of the First French Republic and the Rise of the Marshals of Napoleon I.* London: Humphrey Milford. 5 vols.

Austerlitz, Battle of (2 December 1805)

The "Battle of the Three Emperors," fought on the first anniversary of Napoleon's coronation as emperor, was one of his most famous and decisive victories. A joint Russian and Austrian force was crushed on the plateau of Pratzen above the Moravian village of Austerlitz, forcing the Austrians to sue for peace and the Russians to withdraw behind their own frontiers.

The Allies outnumbered Napoleon's forces, with 84,000 men and 280 guns facing the French force of 73,000 men and 140 guns. But Tsar Alexander I, the Allied commander in chief, played into Napoleon's hands by attempting a flanking maneuver, weakening his center, while Napoleon, as always, was prepared to wait for the decisive moment to attack. Turning for advice to the Austrian chief of staff, Franz von Weyrother, rather than the more experienced and cautious Russian commander, Mikhail Kutuzov, Alexander committed both Austrian and Russian forces to an outflanking assault on the French lines of communication, starting at half past six in the morning. But a heavy mist shrouded the battlefield, and when the sun rose shortly before nine o'clock Napoleon ordered the cavalry under Nicolas Soult to attack the weakened Allied center. The tsar and his staff were forced to fall back, leaving the Allied vanguard isolated in an area of ponds and marshes covered by a deceptively thin layer of ice. Many Russians were drowned when they were forced back onto the ice. A Russian counterattack led by the Grand Duke Constantine was brave but disastrous: many more Russians were killed,

Napoleon ordered the triumphal Arc du Carrousel in honor of the Grande Armée after Austerlitz. It was erected between 1807 and 1809 between the Louvre and the Tuileries. (Art Resource)

and the Austrians were thrown into confusion as their northward line of retreat was cut off. By midday, when snow began to fall, the Allied armies were in total chaos, with only the Russian cavalry of Prince Pyotr Bagration managing to withdraw in good order.

Around a third of the Allied forces had been killed, wounded, or taken prisoner, and 180 cannon had been captured. The French lost some 1,800 killed and 6,500 wounded. Austria signed peace three weeks later by the Treaty of Pressburg, and the Russian army had been shattered. William Pitt is reported as having said after Austerlitz, "Roll up the map of Europe. It will not be wanted these ten years."

Related entries: Alexander I, Tsar of Russia; Austria; Danube Campaigns; Kutuzov, Mikhail Ilarionovich

Suggestions for further reading:
Chandler, David G. 1994. "Napoleon's Masterpiece: Austerlitz, 2 December 1805," in his *On the Napoleonic Wars: Collected Essays.* London: Greenhill.
Duffy, Christopher. 1977. *Austerlitz*. Hampden, CT: Archon Books.

Austria

What for convenience we call Austria represented the heart of the dynastic realm of the Habsburgs, who had ruled in Vienna since the thirteenth century. The Habsburg lands in central Europe included present-day Austria, Hungary, the Czech and Slovak lands, southern Poland, parts of western Romania, Croatia, Slovenia, northeastern Italy centered on Milan, and regions of the southern Ukraine. In addition the Habsburgs, as Holy Roman Emperors, held theoretical sovereignty over Germany and much of the rest of Italy.

Austria fought six wars with France between 1792 and 1815. Its participation in the First Coalition was ended by Napoleon's Italian victories at Arcola and Rivoli, resulting in the Treaty of Campo Formio (1797). Some successes during the Second Coalition were followed by defeats at Marengo and Hohenlinden and the Treaty of Lunéville (1801). In 1804 Francis I assumed the new title of Emperor of Austria and joined the Third Coalition in 1805. But after the French invasion of Austria, culminating in the disaster of Austerlitz in December 1805, he was forced to accept peace by the Treaty of Pressburg. The title of Holy Roman Emperor, which had long ceased to have much meaning, was finally abolished on Napoleon's insistence in 1806.

Seeking revenge for past humiliations, Austria again declared war on France, against Francis's better judgment, in 1809. But despite army reforms and the Tyrolean rising of Andreas Hofer, the Austrians suffered defeat once more at Wagram, and were forced to accept the harsh conditions of the Peace of Schönbrunn. Now, on the advice of his new foreign minister, Klemens von Metternich, Francis became a nominal ally of France, forming a dynastic link through the marriage of his daughter Marie-Louise to Napoleon in April 1810. An Austrian auxiliary force took part in Napoleon's invasion of Russia in 1812, but Francis concluded a separate peace with the tsar at the end of the year and again declared war on France in August 1813. Austrian troops took part in the battle of Dresden and Leipzig and in the invasion of France. In 1815 an Austrian army crossed into France five days after the battle of Waterloo and participated in the second occupation of France.

The skilful diplomacy of Metternich ensured that Austria played host to the Congress of Vienna, where the Habsburgs, though they lost Belgium, regained almost all their Austrian lands and gained territory in Italy, including direct rule over Lombardy and Venice, and the Dalmatian coast. The Austrian Empire was now second in population only to Russia in Europe, and the lands lost to Napoleon had been regained. Austria emerged from the Napoleonic Wars as a great power and enjoyed a flourishing cultural life in the age of Beethoven and Schubert, but the hopes of its subject peoples had been raised during the wars, planting the seeds of revolt and dissension for the future.

Related entries: Austerlitz, Battle of; Belgium; Campo Formio, Treaty of; Charles, Archduke of Austria; Coalitions; Danube Campaigns; Francis I, Emperor of Austria; Germany, Campaigns in; Hohenlinden, Battle of; Illyria; Italian Campaigns; Leipzig, Battle of; Lunéville, Treaty of; Marengo, Battle of; Marie-Louise von Hapsburg, Empress; Metternich, Klemens Wenceslas Lothar, Fürst von; Pressburg, Treaty of; Schönbrunn, Treaty of; Wagram, Battle of

Suggestions for further reading:
Brauer, Kinley, and William E. Wright, eds. 1990. *Austria in the Age of the French Revolution, 1789–1815*. Minneapolis: Center for Austrian Studies, University of Minnesota.
Kohn, Hans. 1967. *Prelude to Nation States: The French and German Experience, 1789–1815*. Princeton: Van Nostrand.
Kraehe, Enno Edward. 1963. *Metternich's German Policy, Vol. 1: The Contest with Napoleon, 1799–1814*. Princeton: Princeton University Press.
Langsam, Walter C. 1930. *The Napoleonic Wars and German Nationalism in Austria*. New York: Columbia University Press.
Rothenberg, Gunther E. 1982. *Napoleon's Great Adversaries: The Archduke Charles and the Austrian Army, 1792–1814*. London; Batsford.

B

Bagration, Pyotr Ivanovich, Prince

Descendant of an ancient Georgian noble family, Bagration entered the Russian army in 1782 and distinguished himself in wars in the Caucasus and Poland, thereby attracting the attention of Alexander Suvorov, under whom he took part in the Italian and Swiss campaigns of 1799 against Napoleon. Widely regarded as Suvorov's heir, Bagration showed such tactical skill, charisma, and commanding presence that he earned the nickname of God of the Army.

During the Danube campaigns of 1805–1807 he proved his skill when his rear guard of 6,000 men held off the 30,000 commanded by Joachim Murat, so securing the retreat of Mikhail Kutuzov's main Russian army and suffering heavy losses in the process. Bagration fought with courage at the battles of Austerlitz, where he had command of 13,000 men on the Allied right, Eylau, Heilsberg, and Friedland. After the Treaty of Tilsit freed Russia's hands in eastern Europe, he played a major role in the conquest of Finland by leading a daring march across the frozen Gulf of Finland and capturing the Aaland Islands. He was promoted to full general and in 1809 commanded the Russian forces in Bulgaria in the war against the Ottoman Empire.

During the Russian campaign of 1812 the Russian effort was hampered by the bad relations between Bagration and Mikhail Barclay de Tolly. Tsar Alexander I declined to appoint a supreme commander, and Bagration was jealous of the fact that Barclay, though junior in seniority, commanded the First West Army while he had charge of the Second West Army, based on the Russo-Prussian border. At first Bagration advocated a counterinvasion, but was forced to retreat, evading the French forces of Louis-Nicolas Davout and Jérôme Bonaparte and joined forces with Barclay de Tolly at Smolensk. Alexander was wary of Bagration and divided command between him and Barclay. But Bagration moderated his previously vicious criticism of Barclay's policy and gradually came to espouse a similar strategy, acknowledging Barclay as effective commander in chief.

Bagration and Barclay overcame their animosity and cooperated fully in the crucial battle of Borodino. Bagration's Second Army was responsible for holding the Russian center and right engaged in bloody hand-to-hand combat. Bagration was wounded when his left shinbone was shattered by a bullet, but refused to leave the field. Three weeks later he died of his wounds at the age of forty-six. Twenty-seven years later his remains were returned to Borodino and buried there.

Related entries: Alexander I, Tsar of Russia; Austerlitz, Battle of; Barclay de Tolly, Mikhail Andreas, Prince; Borodino, Battle of; Russian Campaign

Suggestions for further reading:
Duffy, Christopher. 1972. *Borodino and the War of 1812*. London: Seeley.
Riehn, Richard K. 1991. *1812: Napoleon's Russian Campaign*. New York: John Wiley.
Tarle, E. 1942. *Napoleon's Invasion of Russia, 1812*. London: Allen and Unwin.

Bailen, Battle of (19 July 1808)

This early engagement in the Spanish uprising against French occupation decided Napoleon to assume personal command in Spain. The French corps in Andalusia, under General Pierre Dupont, was trapped near the town of Bailen by an army of 30,000 men commanded by General Francisco Castaños and forced to capitulate. Some 17,500 French surrendered, and, while senior officers were released, most of the men were imprisoned under harsh conditions and only one in seven survived. The defeat was a serious blow to French prestige and encouraged Spanish resistance. Joseph Bonaparte fled from Madrid, where he had recently arrived as king, and Napoleon decided to take matters into hand personally. The Spanish exaggerated the significance of Bailen: Castaños had enjoyed numerical superiority over Dupont's raw conscripts. This victory did not mean that the Spanish would be capable of engaging Napoleon's crack troops in open battle, but nothing like it had previously happened to any of Napoleon's armies, and it inspired people in Spain and elsewhere in Europe out of all proportion to its true significance.

Related entries: Spain

Suggestions for further reading:
Oman, Charles W.C. 1902–1930. *A History of the Peninsular War*. 7 vols. Oxford: Clarendon Press.

Bank of France

Established by statute in 1800 as the central financial institution of France, the Bank of France was a private stock company organized on Napoleon's orders by a group of Paris bankers headed by Jean Frédéric Perregaux, with the government as one stockholder among many others, and run by a board of fifteen directors elected by the biggest shareholders. The bank was given a monopoly on the issue of paper notes in 1803, but in 1805 its existence was threatened by the expenses of warfare. In 1806, therefore, Napoleon reorganized the bank, increasing its capital funds and assuming the right to appoint a governor and two assistant governors. Under the supervision of the new minister of the treasury, Nicolas François Mollien, the reorganized bank was now firmly established and by 1813 had opened branches at Lille, Rouen, and Lyon. It was retained by Louis XVIII and became a permanent institution. The lack of such a body had been a constant weakness of French finances under the ancien régime and during the Revolution, a weakness that Napoleon rectified once and for all.

Related entries: Finance; Mollien, Nicolas François

Suggestions for further reading:
Arnold, Eric A., ed. 1994. *A Documentary Survey of Napoleonic France*. Lanham, MD: University Press of America, pp. 39–45.
———. 1996. *A Documentary Survey of Napoleonic France: A Supplement*. Lanham, MD: University Press of America, pp. 58–63.
Bergeron, Louis. 1981. *France under Napoleon*. Princeton: Princeton University Press.
Holtman, Robert B. 1967. *The Napoleonic Revolution*. Philadelphia: Lippincott.

Barclay de Tolly, Mikhail Andreas, Prince (1761–1818)

The strategist behind Napoleon's defeat in the Russian campaign of

1812, Barclay was an experienced soldier who had first seen action in Russia's Turkish War of 1787–1791. A major general by 1799, he was in command of the Russian advance guard that failed to reach Austerlitz in December 1805, but distinguished himself as commander of the rear guard in the Russian retreat, struggling valiantly against the French at Frauendorf and Hof. During the campaign of 1806–1807 Barclay was wounded just before the battle of Eylau and remained an invalid for fifteen months. During his convalescence he was visited by Tsar Alexander I, and an immediate bond was created, giving Alexander an advisor who could be relied on for an honest assessment of the situation.

Following the disaster of Friedland in June 1807, Barclay became convinced that the only way to defeat Napoleon was to lure him deep into Russia and attack him in strength only when he was isolated and had used up his supplies. The Treaty of Tilsit in July 1807, however, deferred the opportunity to test his theory. He was promoted to full general following his success in the conquest of Finland in 1808, while as governor-general of the newly conquered country he showed himself an able administrator and persuaded many Finns to become loyal to Russia.

In 1810 Barclay was appointed minister of war and, convinced that war with Napoleon was inevitable, reorganized the ministry and almost doubled the size of the army. He imposed a simplified chain of command and defined the functions of the fifteen branches of the army more precisely. Barclay's contingency plan in the event of war consisted of defensive operations until Napoleon had been weakened through attrition and his supply lines had become vulnerable.

When war broke out in 1812, Barclay was given command of the First Western Army of 100,000 men. Outnumbered almost four to one, he immediately set in motion his planned withdrawal, denying

Napoleon the opportunity to force the decisive battle he always craved. But this policy attracted heavy criticism, reinforced by Russian chauvinist suspicion of Barclay's origins as a Livonian of Scottish descent. The tsar, giving in to ultranationalist pressure, appointed the thoroughly Russian Mikhail Kutuzov as supreme commander in chief. Barclay remained in the field as commander of the First Army, which fought resolutely at Borodino, convincing many of his critics that he was no coward or traitor. But friction remained with Kutuzov, and in September 1812 Barclay decided to go on leave, pleading reasons of health. His strategy was now blamed for the fall of Moscow.

As Napoleon retreated, Barclay was recalled and given command of the Third Western Army. Advancing into Germany he fought the battle of Bautzen in May 1813, after which Alexander appointed him commander in chief of the Russian and Prussian armies. And following the battle of Leipzig, the tsar raised him to the dignity of count. He led his forces into France and to Paris, where he was promoted to field marshal. Barclay accompanied the tsar to the victory celebrations in London and then led his troops triumphantly back to Russia.

The Hundred Days recalled Barclay to action. Leading a Russian army toward France, he had reached the Rhine when he received news of Waterloo. When he reached Paris for the second time he was granted the title of prince, a very rare honor. When he died three years later, he was still supreme commander of all Russian forces.

Barclay was most responsible for Napoleon's defeat in Russia. Despite the bad blood between them, Kutuzov on the whole followed his strategy. The historian David Saunders has written: "Most Russians thought Barclay pusillanimous, but the strategy which saved them was his" (Saunders 1992, p. 52).

Related entries: Alexander I, Tsar of Russia; Bagration, Pyotr Ivanovich, Prince; Bautzen, Battle of; Eylau, Battle of; Kutuzov, Mikhail Ilarionovich; Leipzig, Battle of; Russian Campaign

Suggestions for further reading:
Duffy, Christopher. 1972. *Borodino and the War of 1812*. London: Seeley.
Josselson, Michael, and Diana Josselson. 1980. *The Commander: A Life of Barclay de Tolly*. New York: Oxford University Press.
Saunders, David. 1992 *Russia in the Age of Reaction and Reform, 1801–1882*. New York: Longman.
Tarle, E. 1942. *Napoleon's Invasion of Russia, 1812*. London: Allen and Unwin.

Barras, Paul François Jean Nicolas, Vicomte de (1755–1829)

One of the most powerful figures in the Directory, Barras played a significant role, though not as important as he claimed, in Napoleon's rise to power. They met for the first time at the siege of Toulon in December 1793. Barras, as representative on mission to areas in revolt, ensured that Napoleon received due recognition for his part in the victory and was promoted from captain to brigadier general. After Toulon was regained, Barras showed his ruthlessness by ordering the execution of hundreds of people who had supported the British.

Barras held several important posts during the Thermidorian period, effectively commanding the Army of the Interior and the police. As such he employed Napoleon again in the suppression of the rising of Vendémiaire in Paris on 5 October 1795. This action allowed him to engineer elections to the Directory. He was the only director of noble birth and the only one to serve throughout the five years of the regime. As "king of the Directory" Barras followed the advice of Madame de Staël in sponsoring the appointment of Charles-Maurice de Talleyrand as minister of foreign affairs and was instrumental in removing Lazare Carnot from the post of director in September 1797. Royalist gains in the elections of 1797 impelled Barras to call once again on Napoleon, then in Italy. But Napoleon refused, instead sending Charles Augereau to help in purging royalists from the National Assembly, bringing Barras to the apex of his career.

When Napoleon returned from the Egyptian campaign in October 1799, Barras suggested to him that he should win more military glory and leave politics to the politicians. Napoleon had now come to detest Barras for his shameless profiteering and luxurious lifestyle, calling him a "rotten plank." During the coup of Brumaire Barras remained in his apartments, only signing a letter of resignation after he learned of Napoleon's success at the Tuileries. Napoleon's continuing suspicion of him led to his exile to Brussels in 1801. He returned to France in 1805 but was exiled again to Rome in 1813. At Napoleon's fall he failed to get the restored Bourbons to accept his support and spent the rest of his life on his magnificent estate at Chaillot, living on his ill-gotten gains and dictating his memoirs.

Barras possessed genuine abilities but lived a life of unashamed corruption and luxury. During his years in power he grew wealthy by extracting money from military contractors and bribes from foreign governments. Among his many mistresses was Joséphine de Beauharnais, and he claimed to have been instrumental in arranging her marriage to Napoleon. But his memoirs, in which he viciously attacked all those with whom he had fallen out, including Joséphine, are full of distortions. Carnot said of Barras that he "masked the ferocity of Caligula behind a carefully assumed casualness of manner" (Palmer 1984, p. 27).

Related entries: Beauharnais, Marie Rose Joséphine de; Directory; Toulon, Siege of

Suggestions for further reading:
Lefebvre, Georges. 1965. *The Directory*. London: Routledge and Kegan Paul.

Lyons, Martyn. 1975. *France under the Directory.* Cambridge: Cambridge University Press.
Palmer, Alan. 1984. *An Encyclopaedia of Napoleon's Europe.* London: Weidenfeld and Nicolson.

Bassano, Battle of (8 September 1796)

This engagement of Napoleon's Italian campaign was a disaster for the Austrians, opening the way for the French occupation of Vicenza and Padua. Napoleon trapped an Austrian force under General Würmser in the town of Bassano del Grappa, nineteen miles northeast of Vicenza. The forces of Charles Augereau surrounded the town to the east and those of André Masséna from the west, while Jean Lannes and the cavalry of Joachim Murat led a frontal assault on Bassano itself. Würmser himself escaped, but the French took over 3,500 prisoners, plus 35 cannon, 220 wagons and 2 pontoon bridge trains. On the following day Masséna occupied Vicenza and Augereau took Padua. The Austrian survivors rallied in Mantua, where Würmser assumed command of the defenses.

Related entries: Italian Campaigns

Suggestions for further reading:
Ferrero, Guglielmo. 1961. *The Gamble: Bonaparte in Italy (1796–1797).* London: G. Bell.
Jackson, Sir William Godfrey Fothergill. 1953. *Attack in the West: Napoleon's First Campaign Re-read Today.* London: Eyre and Spottiswoode.

Batavian Republic

This "sister" republic of the French Republic was proclaimed in 1795 following the conquest of the Netherlands, initially with considerable popular enthusiasm. Various political structures, centralized and employing universal male suffrage, were tried before Napoleon's seizure of power, but as first consul he wanted a compliant and less democratic regime. The legislature refused to bow to his pressure, and only in September 1801, after a purge of the executive and closure of the legislature, was a new constitution adopted.

The new Batavian Commonwealth possessed a weak one-house legislature and a twelve-man executive, with considerable powers returned to the traditional ancient provinces of the Netherlands. In 1805 another constitution was imposed, with a regime headed by Councillor Pensionary Rutger Jan Schimmelpennink, but this only lasted until May 1806, when Napoleon made his brother Louis Bonaparte monarch of the new Kingdom of Holland.

The Republic had been a notable democratic experiment: equality before the law had been established, church and state separated, and the once mighty East India Company dissolved, with its possessions going to the nation.

Related entries: Netherlands

Suggestions for further reading:
Kossman, E. H. 1978. *The Low Countries, 1780–1940.* Oxford: Clarendon Press.
Schama, Simon. 1977. *Patriots and Liberators: Revolution in the Netherlands, 1780–1813.* New York: Knopf.

Bautzen, Battle of (20–21 May 1813)

After checking the Russo-Prussian invasion of Germany at the battle of Lützen on 2 May 1813, Napoleon attempted to take the walled cathedral city of Bautzen in Saxony. His newly formed Army of the Elbe sought to engage the Russian and Prussian defenders of Bautzen in the marshes and woodland on the banks of the river Spree. Bautzen was then to be surrounded by forces under Michel Ney and Nicolas Oudinot. However, delays in deploying the French forces and their lack of cavalry allowed the defenders to slip out and retreat southward toward Silesia, and the French were unable to pursue them effectively. A brief armistice, secured by Austrian mediation, ensued between 2 June and 17 August.

Related entries: Germany, Campaigns in

Suggestions for further reading:
Petre, F. Loraine. 1974. *Napoleon's Last Campaign in Germany, 1813.* London: Arms and Armour.

Bavaria, Kingdom of

Throughout the Napoleonic period the large Catholic southern German state of Bavaria, traditionally under the Wittelsbach dynasty an ally of France in Germany, was ruled by Maximilian Joseph, first as Elector and after December 1805 as King Maximilian I. Bavarian troops had fought against the French in 1799–1800, but after the decisive battle of Hohenlinden Maximilian struck a lasting bargain with Napoleon. Bavaria hoped thereby to strengthen its own position at the expense of Austria. A Bavarian force of some 25,000 men fought with the French at Austerlitz, and as a reward Bavaria received, by the Treaty of Pressburg, the Tyrol, the Vorarlberg, and some ecclesiastical lands.

In 1806 Bavaria joined the Confederation of the Rhine, and the Franco-Bavarian alliance was strengthened further by the marriage of Maximilian's daughter Augusta to Eugène de Beauharnais. During the Wagram campaign of 1809 the Bavarians defeated the Austrians on the river Inn on 19–20 April, but thereafter were fully occupied with the revolt of Andreas Hofer in the Tyrol. By the Treaty of Schönbrunn Bavaria received Salzburg, Berchtesgarden, and further lands along the Inn.

Bavarian troops made up the bulk of the Sixth Corps of the *Grande Armée* in 1812, and fourteen squadrons of Bavarian cavalry fought under Eugène de Beauharnais at Borodino. Following Napoleon's defeat in Russia, however, Bavaria sought reconciliation with Austria, and by the Treaty of Ried of October 1813 Maximilian, in return for recognition of his royal title, withdrew from the Confederation of the Rhine. Bavarian troops now participated in the invasion of France in 1814. At the Congress of Vienna Bavaria was forced to give up Salzburg, the Tyrol, and the Vorarlberg to Austria, but Maximilian consolidated his kingdom's position in southern Germany as a Catholic counterweight to Prussia within the new German Confederation.

The Napoleonic years had been a period of important internal reform in Bavaria. A single chamber legislature was set up in 1808 and a legal code based on the Napoleonic model introduced in 1810. Serfdom was abolished by stages between 1802 and 1808, the activities of religious orders curbed in 1804, and the privileged influence of the Church over education reduced in 1809. In 1815 Bavaria had been transformed into a modernized kingdom capable of playing a considerable role in German affairs.

Related entries: Austria; Confederation of the Rhine; Pressburg, Treaty of; Schönbrunn, Treaty of; Tyrol, Revolts in

Suggestions for further reading:
Klang, Daniel. 1965. "Bavaria and the War of Liberation, 1813–1814," *French Historical Studies* 4, pp. 22–41.
Sheehan, James J. 1989. *German History, 1770–1866.* Oxford: Clarendon Press.

Beauharnais, Eugène Rose de (1781–1824)

Eugène, the son of Joséphine de Beauharnais by her first marriage to vicomte Alexandre de Beauharnais, began his military career at the age of fourteen as orderly to General Hoche against the rebels of the Vendée. When his mother married Napoleon Eugène became a loyal supporter of his stepfather: he was his aide-de-camp during the Egyptian campaign and served as a cavalry captain at the battle of Marengo. Given the title of prince in 1804, he served as colonel-general of the guard at Napoleon's coronation. In 1805 he was named viceroy of Italy and in 1806 married Augusta of Bavaria.

While he genuinely did his best to provide his kingdom in northern Italy with efficient and enlightened government, Eugène's principal service to Napoleon was on the battlefield. On the renewal of war in 1805, together with André Masséna, he kept the Austrians occupied in Italy while Napoleon overran Germany. In 1809 he played a crucial role in Napoleon's victory at Wagram, firstly by preventing the juncture of the Austrian armies of the Archduke John and the Archduke Charles and then as a cavalry commander in the battle itself. But Eugène distinguished himself primarily between 1812 and 1814. The opinions of historians may be divided about his capacities as a commander, but he learned much during the Russian campaign of 1812, putting the lessons to use in the defense of Italy in 1813–1814.

During Napoleon's retreat from Moscow Eugène and his Italian Royal Guard won the battle of Maloyaroslavets (25 October 1812), and he rescued Marshal Michel Ney and the French rearguard at Smolensk. Assuming command of the army after Joachim Murat abandoned his post and returned to his kingdom of Naples, Eugène succeeded in effecting a brilliant retreat across eastern Germany to the river Elbe, where he held the line until Napoleon appeared with a new army in April 1813. He then left for Italy where, with Napoleon occupied in Germany and France, he held the kingdom against the attacks of the Austrians and Murat, king of Naples. Eugène was still fighting when, on 16 April 1814, he heard of Napoleon's abdication and concluded an armistice with the Austrians, rejecting their tentative offer to retain his kingdom.

Eugène retired to Bavaria at the invitation of his wife's father, King Maximilian, and did not rally to Napoleon in 1815 because it would have placed his family in danger. He lived out the remainder of his life as duke of Leuchtenberg and prince of Eichstädt, though in 1818 he did appeal to Tsar Alexander I to improve Napoleon's conditions of confinement on Saint Helena. Eugène died at Munich at the age of forty-one, but his five children all married into European royal families. His eldest daughter, Joséphine, married Oscar, son of Jean-Baptiste Bernadotte, and was Queen Consort of Sweden from 1844 to 1859.

Related entries: Beauharnais, Marie Rose Joséphine de; Beauharnais, Eugénie-Hortense Cecile de; Italy, Kingdom of; Russian Campaign; Wagram, Battle of

Suggestions for further reading:
Connelly, Owen. 1965. *Napoleon's Satellite Kingdoms.* New York: Free Press.
Oman, Carola. 1966. *Napoleon's Viceroy: Eugène de Beauharnais.* London: Collins.

Beauharnais, Eugénie-Hortense Cecile de (1783–1837)

Daughter of Joséphine de Beauharnais by her first husband, Alexandre de Beauharnais, and sister of Eugène, the young Hortense was a favorite of her stepfather Napoleon. Naturally charming and talented, she sketched, painted, and composed music, including the marching song "Partant pour la Syrie," which was to become the national anthem of the Second

Empire under her son, Napoleon III, between 1852 and 1870.

In 1802 Hortense dutifully married Louis Bonaparte, becoming queen of Holland in 1806. Their marriage was not happy, though it did produce three children. Hortense only spent a few months in Holland, and even at the palace of The Hague the king and queen kept separate apartments. She returned to the Netherlands in April 1810, less than three months before her husband's abdication, and after Louis's departure from Holland the couple never saw each other again.

Hortense settled at Aix-les-Bains, where she became the mistress of the comte Charles de Flahaut, the natural son of Charles-Maurice de Talleyrand. The couple had an illegitimate son who, as the duke of Morny, was to hold influential posts under the Second Empire. She was with her mother at Malmaison during Joséphine's final illness in 1814, and during the Allied occupation of Paris became a favorite of Tsar Alexander I, who persuaded Louis XVIII to make her duchess of Saint-Leu on 30 May 1814. During the Hundred Days, however, she acted as First Lady of France and provided a refuge for Napoleon at Malmaison for five days after his defeat at Waterloo. This fidelity to her stepfather forced her into exile, and she settled at Arenenberg in Switzerland. She traveled widely in the company of her son Charles Louis, the future Napoleon III, with whom she visited London in 1831. She died at Arenenberg in 1837. Her fascinating memoirs, written between 1816 and 1820, were published in 1927.

Related entries: Beauharnais, Eugène Rose de; Beauharnais, Marie Rose Joséphine de; Bonaparte, Louis, King of Holland

Suggestions for further reading:
Beauharnais, Hortense de. 1927. *Memoirs of Queen Hortense.* 2 vols. New York: Cosmopolitan.
Wright, Constance Choate. 1962. *Daughter to Napoleon: A Biography of Hortense, Queen of Holland.* London: Alvin Redman.

Beauharnais, Marie Rose Joséphine de (1763–1814), Empress Joséphine

Napoleon's first empress was born Marie-Josèphe-Rose Tascher de la Pagerie to a family of minor nobility established as planters in Martinique. In 1779 at the age of fifteen she was married to the much older vicomte Alexandre de Beauharnais, an army officer, diplomat, and man of affairs whose constant traveling provided the occasion for real or alleged infidelities on his wife's part. Their son Eugène was born in 1781 and daughter Hortense in 1783. But the vicomte denied paternity of Hortense, and the couple were legally separated.

At the outbreak of the Revolution in 1789 Joséphine was in Martinique. But Alexandre supported the Revolution as a member of the Constituent Assembly and then as commander of the Army of the Rhine in 1793. In 1794, however, he was accused of treason, arrested, and sent to the guillotine. Joséphine was saved from the scaffold through the influence of Jean Tallien and his wife, a salon socialite known as "Our Lady of Thermidor." It was probably at Mme. Tallien's salon that Joséphine met Napoleon in the autumn of 1795, when the young general was the toast of respectable Paris after suppressing the rising of Vendémiaire. They were married on 9 March 1796 against the objections of the Bonaparte family, who considered Joséphine, then known as Rose, a dissolute woman. It was also thought that at the age of thirty-two she would be incapable of bearing more children.

Napoleon departed almost immediately to command the Army of Italy, and Joséphine returned to the fashionable life of Paris, only finally being persuaded to join her husband in July 1796. They were soon separated again by Napoleon's Egyptian campaign of 1798–1799, and this time

Joséphine's affair with a certain Captain Hippolyte Charles was too public to be denied. When Napoleon returned to Paris he was determined to divorce her, but Hortense and Eugène brought about a reconciliation just before the coup of 18 Brumaire.

From now on Joséphine devoted herself faithfully to her marriage, and in 1802–1803 accompanied First Consul Napoleon on lengthy inspection tours in France and the Netherlands. Just before Napoleon's coronation in 1804 he forced Pope Pius VII to marry the imperial couple in a religious ceremony, and Joséphine was crowned empress by Napoleon himself. She presided over the imperial court in impeccable style, but was never crowned queen of Italy even when Eugène was made viceroy. In 1809, however, Napoleon decided to marry Marie-Louise of Austria in order to produce a direct heir to the dynasty. The civil marriage of Napoleon and Joséphine was dissolved "by mutual consent" in December 1809 and Cardinal Fesch secured an ecclesiastical annulment in January 1810. The settlement was generous: Joséphine kept the château of Malmaison and received an annual income worthy of an empress.

Joséphine lived at Malmaison for the few remaining years of her life. In 1814 during the Allied occupation of Paris Tsar Alexander I paid a call on her and she entertained the cream of Russian military society. Joséphine died suddenly on 29 May 1814. After his defeat at Waterloo Napoleon visited Malmaison and walked sadly through the apartments where Joséphine had spent her last years.

Related entries: Beauharnais, Eugène Rose de; Beauharnais, Eugénie-Hortense Cecile de; Coronation; Fesch, Joseph

Suggestions for further reading:
Bruce, Evangeline. 1995. *Napoleon and Josephine: An Improbable Marriage.* New York: Scribner.
Cole, Hubert. 1963. *Josephine.* New York: Viking Press.
Epton, Nina. 1975. *Josephine: The Empress and her Children.* London: Weidenfeld and Nicolson.
Knapton, Ernest J. 1964. *Josephine.* Cambridge: Harvard University Press.

Belgium

Before the French Revolution the territory of modern Belgium had been ruled by the Habsburgs as the Austrian Netherlands. Conquered and annexed in 1794, it remained part of France throughout the Napoleonic period until 1814. The rule of the Directory had been harsh and unpopular, marked by heavy taxation and religious persecution of the dominant Catholic Church. The population had remained largely docile until 1798, when resistance to conscription sparked off the so-called Peasants' War, which was brutally repressed by the French. At the time of Napoleon's coup of 18 Brumaire, therefore, Belgium was emerging from a period of poverty, repression, and economic stagnation, and the long-suffering people greeted the change of regime with indifference.

The government of the consulate endeavored to restore order and to reorganize the administration using more diplomacy and understanding than had its predecessors. As in all occupied territories the prefects of the nine Belgian departments were all foreigners, but they chose their officials from among the former opposition as well as from supporters of the French. Public security and peace were gradually restored, and following the Concordat of 1801, Catholic worship was restored in 1802. Bishops appointed by Napoleon became fervent supporters of his rule, though a dissident group known as *la petite église* opposed the adoration of the emperor after 1804.

Under the empire Belgium was treated on an equal footing with other parts of France. The majority of former nobles continued to participate in public life, and Napoleon attained a peak of popularity that lasted until 1809. Annexation to the large French market and the ending of British competition by the Continental System allowed a degree of prosperity in the textile and metallurgical industries. The region of Verviers, for example, achieved "a precocious, fast, and perfect Industrial Revolution" (Crouzet 1964, p. 584) under Napoleon's rule. The downside of equality of rights with France, however, was an equal obligation to provide soldiers for Napoleon's armies, and the heavy burden of conscription created a seething hostility, which began to grow more serious in the later years of the empire.

In 1809 the French under Jean-Baptiste Bernadotte repulsed the British forces of the Walcheren expedition, and the construction of new defensive works in Antwerp provided another stimulus for the economy. But the breach between Napoleon and Pope Pius VII, resulting in the annexation of the Papal States, revived Catholic opposition to French rule. The fall of Napoleon in 1814 was greeted with rejoicing in Belgium, but the Treaty of Paris (30 May 1814) stipulated that Belgium was to be annexed to Holland under Prince William I of Orange-Nassau. After the battle of Waterloo, the liberation of Belgium from France was complete, only for it to become part of the enlarged Netherlands, designed as a buffer state against future French aggression. Belgium did not gain its independence until 1830.

Related entries: Austria; Continental System

Suggestions for further reading:
Craeybeckx, J. 1970. "The Beginnings of the Industrial Revolution in Belgium," in R. E. Cameron, ed., *Essays in French Economic History.* Homewood, IL: Irwin.
Crouzet, François. 1964. "Wars, Blockades and Economic Change in Europe, 1792–1815," *Journal of Economic History* 24, pp. 567–588.
Kossman, E. H. 1978. *The Low Countries, 1780–1940.* Oxford: Clarendon Press.

Berg, Grand Duchy of

Established in 1806 from Prussian and Bavarian possessions in the Rhineland, the Duchy of Berg formed part of Napoleon's Confederation of the Rhine, and was made a Grand Duchy in 1807. In 1806 Napoleon gave the new duchy to Joachim Murat, and by the Treaty of Tilsit added the territories of Nassau and Münster. In 1808 Napoleon raised Murat to the Kingdom of Naples and ruled Berg himself until March 1809, installing his four-year-old nephew Louis Napoleon as nominal ruler. Berg lost about one-fourth of its territory in 1810 when Holland and North German lands were annexed to France.

Düsseldorf was made capital of the Grand Duchy, and the imperial commissioners, first Claude Beugnot and then Pierre-Louis Roederer, appointed Germans in the administration and created modern financial and legal structures. Economically, however, French rule was a disaster for Berg. The Continental System brought trade to a virtual halt, and when a plea for economic integration with France was rejected, manufacturing enterprises relocated to the French left bank of the Rhine, adding to unemployment and the misery of the population. Economic destitution, conscription, and the hated tobacco and salt taxes caused the people of Berg to rise against French rule in 1813, when news of Napoleon's defeat in Russia filtered through. The rising was repressed without pity, but the end was near for the artificially created Grand Duchy. The territory was occupied by Prussian and Russian troops in 1813–1814 and the area annexed to Prussia in 1815.

Related entries: Confederation of the Rhine; Continental System; Murat, Joachim; Roederer, Pierre Louis

Suggestions for further reading:
Sheehan, James J. 1989. *German History, 1770–1866.* Oxford: Clarendon Press.

Berlin Decrees

*T*hese edicts of December 1806 mark the creation of Napoleon's Continental System. Following the French defeat at the battle of Trafalgar, it was clear that Napoleon could not challenge British naval dominance, and the Berlin Decrees recognized this by switching the struggle against Britain into the economic field. They declared Britain to be in a state of blockade by France and its allies and satellites, officially ending all trading contacts between them and the British. The British responded with the Orders in Council of January and November 1807, which obliged neutral ships to get British permission to trade with enemy ports. This action in turn forced Napoleon to respond with the Milan Decrees of November and December 1807 extending the Continental System to neutral shipping.

Related entries: Continental System

Suggestions for further reading:
Arnold, Eric A., ed. 1994. *A Documentary Survey of Napoleonic France.* Lanham, MD: University Press of America, pp. 226–231.
Hecksher, E. F. 1922. *The Continental System: An Economic Interpretation.* Oxford: Publications of the Carnegie Endowment for International Peace.

Bernadotte, Jean-Baptiste Jules (1763–1844)

*G*iven by Napoleon the titles of marshal of France, and prince of Ponte Corvo, and king of Sweden after 1818, Bernadotte was the son of a lawyer from Pau in Gascony. He joined the army in 1780 but was not commissioned until after the Revolution, rising from lieutenant in 1791 to general of division in 1794. In 1797 he was sent to reinforce Bonaparte in Italy and took part in the last phases of the Italian campaign. He was briefly and reluctantly ambassador to Vienna in 1798, and in the same year married Désirée Clary, so becoming Napoleon's brother-in-law.

Bernadotte was the Directory's minister of war between July and September 1799 and at first refused to support Napoleon's coup of 18 Brumaire. Nevertheless Napoleon made him a councillor of state and in 1800 gave him command of the Army of the West in preparation for the subsequently abandoned invasion of England. In 1804 he was appointed governor of Hanover and marshal of the empire. Bernadotte commanded the First Corps at Austerlitz in 1805, but in 1806 was blamed by Napoleon for his failure to reach the battlefield of Jena. Napoleon made him governor of the Hanseatic towns in 1807, but he returned to command of the First Corps in 1809. When his conduct at the battle of Wagram led to a new quarrel with the emperor Bernadotte resigned his command and returned to Paris.

With Napoleon's approval Bernadotte was elected crown prince of Sweden in October 1810, changing his name to Charles-John. But as effective ruler of the country he supported Sweden's reluctance to join the Continental System and signed a treaty with Great Britain in December 1812. As commander of the Allied Army of the North in August and September 1813 he defeated Nicolas Oudinot at Gross Beeren and Michel Ney at Dennewitz, before taking part in the Battle of the Nations at Leipzig in October, where he was again criticized for arriving late.

Bernadotte gained control of Norway for Sweden by the Treaty of Kiel in January 1814 and continued in the coalition against Napoleon until the emperor's abdication. He aspired to succeed Napoleon, but was regarded as a traitor by most French people, and the allies preferred Louis XVIII. His hopes in France thus dashed, Bernadotte now devoted himself to Swedish affairs, principally the occupation of Norway, and refused to join the new coalition of 1815 against Napoleon.

Bernadotte succeeded to the thrones of Sweden and Norway in 1818 as King Carl XIV and ruled as a cautious but capable and mostly popular monarch. He died in Stockholm in his eightieth year.

Bernadotte's fiery Gascon temperament was responsible for his constantly difficult relations with Napoleon, who frequently referred to him as too hotheaded or even mad. He cut a dashing figure on the battlefield, and his personal bravery was never in doubt, but his reluctance to commit his troops to the field until he thought the time was right caused extreme exasperation among his allies, whether he was fighting for or against Napoleon, and accusations of cowardice. He was a difficult subordinate. In supporting Bernadotte's aspirations in Sweden Napoleon had hoped to secure control of the Baltic to the exclusion of the British, but once installed in his adopted country Bernadotte pursued Swedish national aspirations, which meant conflict with Denmark over control of Norway, and his personal ambitions, which brought him into conflict with his brother-in-law.

Related entries: Austerlitz, Battle of; Clary, Bernadine Eugénie Désirée; Coalitions; Jena-Auerstädt, Battles of; Leipzig, Battle of; Wagram, Battle of

Suggestions for further reading:
Heathcote, T. A. 1987. "Bernadotte," in David G. Chandler, ed., *Napoleon's Marshals.* New York: Macmillan.
Palmer, Alan. 1990. *Bernadotte: Napoleon's Marshal, Sweden's King.* London: John Murray.
Scott, Franklin Daniel. 1933. "Bernadotte and the Throne of France, 1814," *Journal of Modern History* 5, pp. 465–478.
Scott, Franklin Daniel. 1935. *Bernadotte and the Fall of Napoleon.* Cambridge: Harvard University Press.

Bernier, Abbé Etienne (1762–1806)

*T*he versatile abbé Bernier went from being one of the inspirational leaders of the Vendée revolt to Napoleon's chief negotiator with Pius VII over the Concordat of 1801. As pastor of the parish of St. Laud in Angers in 1790 he refused to subscribe to the Civil Constitution of the Clergy; he then showed considerable ability and heroism as head of the supreme council directing the Vendée insurrection, earning the title of Apostle of the Vendée. By 1794, however, his independent attitude led to his losing the confidence of the other leaders of the revolt. But even as things went badly for the rebels Bernier remained as Louis XVIII's official agent in the Catholic and royalist armies. By 1799 he had come to realize the futility of the royalist cause, refused to join in the final uprising of that year, and after Napoleon's coup of 18 Brumaire switched his loyalties.

In January 1800 Bernier concluded the Peace of Montfaucon, securing religious liberty for the Vendéans, and went to Paris where he preached sermons and was received cordially by Napoleon. His talent for intrigue was of great use to Napoleon in negotiating the Concordat, but Bernier was playing a double game. He used all his diplomatic skill as intermediary between Napoleon's minister, Jean Portalis, and the papal legate, Cardinal Giovanni Caprara, all the time doing his best to defend the pope's interests. Bernier drafted the notes and responses for both sides until the treaty was finally signed on 16 July 1801, but his slippery behavior was viewed badly by Napoleon. Having been promised the bishopric of Paris as a reward for his diplomacy, he was assigned to the lesser see of Orléans.

Bernier was now used by Charles-Maurice de Talleyrand for a series of delicate missions with the Church: the Italian and German Concordats and Napoleon's coronation. Most notably he succeeded in getting Pius VII's acquiescence in the matter of Napoleon's crowning himself. Again frustrated in his ambition to be named papal nuncio to Germany, Bernier had to be content with running his diocese of Orléans until his death at the age of forty-four. The crafty cleric had received scant reward for his valuable services after abandoning the royalist cause.

Related entries: Concordat; Coronation; Pius VII, Pope; Vendée Revolt

Suggestions for further reading:
Hales, Edward Elton Young. 1962. *Napoleon and the Pope.* London: Eyre and Spottiswoode.
Tilly, Charles. 1976. *The Vendée.* Cambridge: Harvard University Press.
Walsh, Henry Horace. 1933. *The Concordat of 1801: A Study of the Problems of Church and State.* New York: Columbia University Press.

Berthier, Louis Alexandre (1753–1815)

Napoleon's invaluable chief of staff was born at Versailles, son of an officer in the topographical engineers, and joined the same service himself at the age of thirteen in 1766. His rise in the ranks was rapid during the last years of the ancien régime and the early days of the Revolution, from lieutenant of infantry in 1770 to brigadier general in 1792. He was Napoleon's chief of staff for eighteen years, from the first Italian campaign in 1796 to the first abdication in 1814. He also served as minister of war between November 1799 and April 1800 and again from October 1800 until September 1807.

Berthier was a professional of the highest order, whose loyalty and efficiency gave Napoleon an immediate advantage at a time when Prussia, Austria, and Russia had no general staffs. A workaholic who could grasp the essentials of any situation, his creation of a disciplined staff providing up-to-the-minute information allowed the emperor's commands to be translated into precise and detailed orders for specific army units. Berthier never criticized Napoleon, though as their personal relations deteriorated he could indulge in self-pity. Napo-

leon's judgments on Berthier varied widely, revealing one of the worst sides of his character. At one moment he could praise Berthier, saying that "as chief of staff, Berthier has no equal" (Connelly 1985, p. 65), at another call him "a gosling transmuted by me into some kind of eagle" (Raeuber 1987, p. 50). During their years of friendship Napoleon showered Berthier with honors: first marshal of France in 1804; senator and Grand Master of the Palace in the same year; sovereign prince of Neuchâtel in 1806; vice-constable of the empire in 1807; prince of Wagram in 1809. But Berthier's loyalty was sorely tried. Napoleon tricked him into marrying Princess Elizabeth-Marie, niece of King Maximilian of Bavaria, and abandoning his beloved Madame Giuseppina Visconti. And in 1809 he forced Berthier to take the blame for his own initial error in dividing his forces at the beginning of the Wagram campaign, knowing that he could be relied upon to preserve the imperial image of infallibility.

Berthier never visited his principality of Neuchâtel in Switzerland. But he did manage to oversee some beneficial reforms in fiscal, forest, postal, and police administration, while creaming off substantial revenues for himself. He was, however, unable to prevent the conscription of his subjects for Napoleon's armies (nearly a thousand were killed in Spain and Russia) or the ruin of Neuchâtel's industries by the Continental System.

Despite the deterioration in his relations with the emperor and Napoleon's ill-tempered outbursts during the Russian campaign, Berthier faithfully fulfilled his duties to the end. After the first abdication he led the marshals to meet Louis XVIII at Compiègne. Regarded with suspicion by both sides, he rejected Napoleon's appeal to join him during the Hundred Days. He was given protection by his father-in-law, the king of Bavaria, but died at Bamberg on 1 June 1815, following a fall from a window while watching a parade of troops.

Related entries: Army; Switzerland

Suggestions for further reading:
Connelly, Owen, ed. 1985. *Historical Dictionary of Napoleonic France, 1799–1815.* Westport, CT: Greenwood.
Raeuber, Charles. 1987. "Berthier," in David G. Chandler, ed., *Napoleon's Marshals.* New York: Macmillan.
Watson, Sidney John. 1957. *By Command of the Emperor: A Life of Marshal Berthier.* London: Bodley Head.

Biens Nationaux

Name given to properties confiscated from the crown, the Church, *émigrés,* and political suspects and subsequently offered for sale by Revolutionary government, starting in 1790. Speculation in *biens nationaux* reached extravagant proportions under the Directory, but the state never benefited from sales to the extent it should have done. Sales continued under the consulate and empire, but on a greatly reduced scale, while the Concordat of 1801 guaranteed the Revolution's confiscation of Church property. Buyers who defaulted on payments, as many had done under previous regimes, were now pursued with Napoleonic vigor. All sales of *biens nationaux* were maintained at the Restoration, confirming the economic gains of many bourgeois and peasants.

Related entries: Economy; Peasants

Suggestions for further reading:
Bergeron, Louis. 1981. *France under Napoleon.* Princeton: Princeton University. Press.
Sutherland, D. M. G. 1985. *France, 1789–1815: Revolution and Counter-Revolution.* London: Fontana.

Bignon, Louis Pierre Edouard (1771–1841)

Born at La Meilleraye, Bignon entered the diplomatic service in 1797, serving in minor posts until 1805, when Napoleon appointed him minister to Hesse-Cassel and then to Baden in 1808. He was made resident in Warsaw in 1810 and, though removed during Napoleon's Russian campaign, he returned after the disaster, remaining until the withdrawal of French troops was complete. Continuing in Napoleon's service, during the Hundred Days Bignon served as undersecretary for foreign affairs. After the Restoration Bignon was elected to the Chamber of Deputies, served as interim minister of foreign affairs after the Revolution of 1830, and was reelected in 1831 and 1834.

In his will Napoleon had commissioned Bignon to write "the history of French diplomacy from 1792 to 1815," a work which became the first extended history of the Napoleonic period, appearing as the *History of France since the 18 Brumaire* in a total of fourteen volumes, including four published posthumously, between 1828 and 1850. From 1829 onward Bignon was given access to the archives and to Napoleon's correspondence, thereby being able to combine personal recollection and pioneer research. He was not uncritical of Napoleon, especially over Spain and the creation of the Imperial nobility.

Related entries: Diplomatic Service

Suggestions for further reading:
Whitcomb, Edward A. 1979. *Napoleon's Diplomatic Service.* Durham, NC: Duke University Press.

Blücher, Gebhard Leberecht von (1742–1819)

Born near Rostock on the Baltic coast, Blücher enlisted in the Swedish army in 1756 at the age of fourteen and four years later transferred to the Prussian army of Frederick the Great. Frustrated at lack of promotion and with a reputation for insubordination he quit the service in 1773, causing King Frederick to remark: "Captain von Blücher may go to the devil as soon as he pleases" (Palmer 1984, p. 44). Reinstated in 1778, he fought against the French revolutionary armies in 1793–1794 and was promoted to brigadier general, a remarkable achievement for a nonnoble.

Irritated by the lack of military action after 1795 and convinced that a clash with Napoleon was inevitable, Blücher called for universal conscription in Prussia and became one of the leaders of the war party in 1805. At the disastrous battles of Jena-Auerstädt he retreated in good order and surrendered to Marshal Bernadotte at Ratkau, his exemplary conduct being one of the few bright spots in the Prussian performance. After the Treaty of Tilsit Blücher became military governor of Pomerania and a strong supporter of Prussian army reforms, but was afflicted by illness and depression until news of Napoleon's problems in Spain revived his spirits.

In 1813 Blücher, at the age of seventy, was placed in command of the Silesian army, the most active Prussian force in the field against Napoleon, fighting at Lützen and Bautzen. But his greatest triumph was at the Battle of Leipzig, after which he played a leading role in the invasion of France. After Napoleon's abdication he was given the title of prince of Wahlstadt and given a huge welcome and an honorary degree from the University of Oxford on a visit to England. During the Hundred Days Blücher was given command of Prussian forces in Belgium. Defeated by Napoleon at the Battle of Ligny, he nevertheless arrived in the nick of time at Waterloo, saving the day for the Allies. After 1815 he retired to his estates in Silesia.

Known to his men as "Marshal Forwards," Blücher was a popular and respected commander, sharing the hardships of his men as well as the glory. He was one of the few commanders who realized that bold tactics were necessary to defeat Napoleon and was consistently intransigent in seeing the necessity to oppose him by all possible means.

Related entries: Jena-Auerstädt, Battles of; Leipzig, Battle of; Ligny, Battle of; Prussia; Waterloo, Battle of

Suggestions for further reading:
Palmer, Alan. 1984. *An Encyclopaedia of Napoleon's Europe.* London: Weidenfeld and Nicolson.
Parkinson, Roger. 1975. *The Hussar General: The Life of Blücher, Man of Waterloo.* London: Peter Davies.

Bonaparte, Carlo (1746–1785)

Napoleon's father came from a line of Corsican gentry who traced their ancestry back to a Florentine noble of the twelfth century. He married Maria Letizia in 1764 and together they fought with the Corsican patriots of Pasquale Paoli against the Genoese and the French in 1768–1769. Napoleon was born months after their escape from the defeat of the nationalists. Carlo accepted an amnesty from the victorious French, became friendly with the royal governor, the comte de Marboeuf, and took the French title of comte himself, an essential move if his family was to prosper. He put his legal training to use as a prosecutor in the royal courts, was a member of the Corsican delegation at the coronation of Louis XVI, and was elected to the Corsican estates. Although comfortably off, Carlo was also somewhat extravagant, but even in straitened times he ensured the education of four of his children—Napoleon, Joseph, Lucien, and Elisa—in France. After seeing Napoleon successfully through the academy of Brienne, he died at Montpellier, probably of stomach cancer, at the premature age of thirty-nine.

Related entries: Bonaparte, Maria Letizia; Corsica

Suggestions for further reading:

Carrington, Dorothy. 1988. *Napoleon and his Parents: On the Threshold of History.* London: Viking.

Geer, Walter. 1928–1929. *Napoleon and his Family: The Story of a Corsican Clan.* 3 vols. London: George Allen and Unwin.

Markham, Felix. 1975. *The Bonapartes.* London: Weidenfeld and Nicolson.

Bonaparte, Caroline, Queen of Naples (1782–1839)

According to Hortense de Beauharnais, her schoolmate, Napoleon's youngest sister, originally known as Maria Annunziata, possessed "an art of attracting and charming, with a grace that had something of an Eastern slave girl's seduction in it" (Seward 1986, p. 92). Universally recognized as ambitious, amoral, and intelligent, she was also, says Hortense, "courageous, determined and emotional: the charm which made one long to serve her could not hide her lust for total domination and her envy of everyone else's success" (Seward 1986, p. 93). Among the many men she charmed in her youth was Joachim Murat, whom she married at Mortefontaine in 1800. From then on her ambition was tied to Murat and her plans for their four children.

When Murat was made king of Naples in 1808, Caroline ensured that Napoleon made her joint ruler, so that she could succeed to the throne if her husband was killed in battle. As queen she encouraged Murat to be independent and to try and exploit Italian nationalist feeling, while pretending to Napoleon that she was acting only in his interest. She was responsible for raising the social style of court life in Naples, presiding over the brilliant palaces of Portici, "the Neapolitan Fontainebleau," and Caserta, but her scheming continued, as she complained about Murat to Napoleon and vice versa. In the interests of her sons, in 1809 she tried unsuccessfully to have Murat named as Napoleon's successor should the emperor be killed fighting in Spain, and in 1810 opposed Napoleon's marriage to Marie-Louise, preferring that the emperor should have no direct legitimate heir. Sent to escort the future empress from Munich to Paris, Caroline made an immediate and lasting enemy of her.

In 1813–1814, as Napoleon's empire crumbled, Caroline encouraged Murat in his efforts to preserve his crown, giving him full support in his efforts to reach an accommodation with the Allies. She appears to have had fewer scruples about betraying Napoleon than did her husband. During the Hundred Days, however, Murat ignored her advice, attacked the Allies, calling upon the Italians to rise against Austrian rule, and thereby lost their kingdom. When he returned to Naples on 21 May 1815 he was faced by popular revolt, tried, and shot, while Caroline took refuge on a British warship before being taken to Vienna. Styling herself the Contessa di Lipona (an anagram of Napoli), she lived under surveillance in Austria until 1824, when she moved to Trieste. She may, much to Napoleon's disgust, have secretly married her new companion, General Francesco Macdonald, a soldier of Scottish origin formerly in Neapolitan service, who remained with her for the rest of her life. Caroline lived in Trieste until 1831, when she moved to Florence, living there in some style until her death in 1839. Of the children she had such great plans for, her two sons emigrated to the United States, and her daughters married into the Italian nobility.

Extravagant and ambitious, Caroline was undoubtedly also very charming, with a liking for music and a remarkable memory for names and faces. Metternich, who detested the upstart Bonapartes, nevertheless observed that she possessed "quite extraordinary social tact." On the other hand, her ambition was more personal than familial. Her mother, Maria Letizia, told her: "Only

Caroline, Queen of Naples, and her Children by *François Gérard. For all her ambition and political acumen, Caroline Bonaparte was a devoted mother, and during their residence in Naples she and her husband, Joachim Murat, spent as much time as possible with their children. (Giraudon/Art Resource)*

over your dead body should your husband have been allowed to strike at your brother, your benefactor and your master!" Talleyrand, possibly recognizing a kindred spirit, says that Caroline "had the mind of a Cromwell in the body of a pretty woman. Born with a forceful character, graceful, charming, inexpressibly attractive, she lacked only the gift of knowing how to conceal her love of power" (Seward 1986, p. 93).

Related entries: Murat, Joachim; Naples, Kingdom of

Suggestions for further reading:
Bear, Joan. 1972. *Caroline Murat: A Biography.* London: Collins.
Cole, Hubert. 1972. *The Betrayers: Joachim and Caroline Murat.* London: Eyre Methuen.
Seward, Desmond. 1986. *Napoleon's Family.* London: Weidenfeld and Nicolson.
Weiner, Margery. 1964. *The Parvenu Princesses: Elisa, Pauline and Caroline Bonaparte.* London: John Murray.

Bonaparte, Elisa, Grand Duchess of Tuscany (1777–1820)

Sometimes called the most Napoleonic of the Bonaparte sisters, Elisa (Maria Anna) was probably the most intelligent and capable of all Napoleon's siblings. The eldest surviving daughter of Carlo and Maria Letizia Bonaparte, she was sent to Saint-Cyr, the most exclusive girls' school of the ancien régime, at the age of seven, remaining out of touch with her family until she was fifteen. In May 1797, when Napoleon was no more than a rising general, she married her fellow Corsican, Felix Bacciochi, of whom Metternich remarked: "Napoleon would have preferred a brother-in-law not quite so destitute of intellect" (Seward 1986, p. 36). Lucien Bonaparte complained that Bacciochi did "nothing but scrape his violin" (Seward 1986, p. 36). Elisa's achievements were hers alone, owing nothing to her good-looking but vapid husband.

Napoleon created Elisa Princess of Piombino in 1805 and Duchess of Lucca in 1806. Lucca prospered under her rule. Silk production doubled in three years, marshes were drained, and the alum deposits of Piombino developed profitably. Her greatest achievement was in reviving the famous but moribund marble quarries of Carrara, which she financed through a special state bank. The artists and sculptors of Carrara supplied all official busts of dignitaries throughout the empire, including 500 of Napoleon in the single month of September 1808. Lucca also became a significant cultural center as Elisa established libraries, university chairs, a medical college, a Napoleonic Institute modeled on the Institut Français, and the Istituto Elisa, a school for girls of noble birth inspired by Saint-Cyr. Elisa governed her state like an eighteenth-century enlightened despot and established a court of which the principal adornment was the outstanding violinist and composer Niccolo Paganini.

Her success as a ruler led Napoleon to create her grand duchess of Tuscany in 1809, but since Tuscany was annexed directly to the French Empire she was effectively Napoleon's viceroy and enjoyed less freedom of action than at Lucca. Elisa held court at the Pitti Palace in Florence, which she restored and refurbished in competition with her sister Caroline's court in Naples. The intellectual elite of Italy gravitated toward Florence, and the Academy *La Crusca* produced a Tuscan dictionary that was widely used to standardize the Italian language.

In 1813–1814 as the empire fell, the turncoat Joachim Murat occupied Elisa's states, but he could not save her position. Assuming the title of countess of Compignano, she spent the last five years of her life near Trieste, obtaining an annual pension from the Austrians and continuing to patronize artists and the theater. She died of a fever nine months before Napoleon's death. Elisa's abilities, as well as her arrogant manner and sharp tongue, probably made her too much like Napoleon for his own comfort, and as brother and sister they were never close. He said of her that she "had the mind and strength of a man," which he may not have meant entirely as a compliment, and which probably indicates his own unease with her talents.

Related entries: Tuscany, Grand Duchy of

Suggestions for further reading:
Geer, Walter. 1928–1929. *Napoleon and his Family: The Story of a Corsican Clan*. 3 vols. London: George Allen and Unwin.
Markham, Felix. 1975. *The Bonapartes*. London: Weidenfeld and Nicolson.
Seward, Desmond. 1986. *Napoleon's Family*. London: Weidenfeld and Nicolson.
Weiner, Margery. 1964. *The Parvenu Princesses: Elisa, Pauline and Caroline Bonaparte*. London: John Murray.

Bonaparte, Jérôme, King of Westphalia (1784–1860)

Napoleon's youngest brother could never live down a reputation for irresponsibility and wild living, but redeemed himself in the last years of the empire and gained distinction in old age during the reign of his nephew, Napoleon III. Napoleon sent Jérôme to sea in 1800, intending him to become a naval commander, and he saw some action in the Caribbean before deciding that life before the mast was not for him. In July 1803, without leave, he visited the United States, and on Christmas Eve married Elizabeth Patterson, much-admired southern belle and daughter of a Baltimore millionaire. Their union caused consternation and anger among the Bonaparte family. Napoleon had the marriage annulled, and when the couple returned to Europe refused to allow "Miss Patterson" to enter territory under French control. Elizabeth found her way to London, where in May 1805 she gave birth to a son, Jerome Napoleon.

Jérôme reestablished himself in his brother's favor by commanding a Bavarian division in the Prussian campaign of 1806, and in 1807 Napoleon made him king of Westphalia and arranged his marriage to Princess Catherine of Württemberg, a first cousin of Alexander I. Despite his frivolous reputation and the notorious wild parties at his court, Jérôme proved a surprisingly able ruler of his kingdom between 1807 and 1813. Napoleon imposed a constitution and his handpicked officials on Jérôme and Catherine. German ministers, officials, and judges presided over the introduction of a version of the Civil Code, the abolition of feudalism and serfdom, reorganization of the administration, and beneficial reforms in education. The Westphalian Parliament played a real role in affairs until 1810, when resistance to Napoleon's ever growing financial demands robbed Jérôme of what popularity he had succeeded in gaining.

Jérôme remained unpredictable and all too conscious of his status. He took great pride in his army, which drew on Hessian military tradition, fought well, and helped break down provincialism and religious prejudices. Jérôme commanded the Tenth Corps in the Wagram campaign, and his dedication to Napoleon was never in doubt. In the Russian campaign of 1812, however, he was sent home by Napoleon after refusing to serve under Louis Nicolas Davout. Jérôme and Catherine were forced to abandon their kingdom in October 1813 and when the empire collapsed found refuge in Switzerland. Rallying to Napoleon during the Hundred Days, Jérôme distinguished himself at Waterloo, where, though wounded, he was one of the last to leave the field.

After the definitive end of the empire, Jérôme lived mostly in Italy, where Catherine bore him two sons and a daughter. After Catherine's death in 1835 he secretly married a Florentine widow, Giustina Pecori. He was allowed to return to Paris in 1847 and was appointed governor of the Invalides in 1849 and, under Napoleon III, a senator and marshal of France. He lived in the Palais Royal, where in 1855 he received Queen Victoria, who found him an "odd old man, rather tall and very civil." When he died in 1860 he was buried near Napoleon in Les Invalides.

Jérôme may have been the most frivolous of Napoleon's brothers, showing a flair for parading in extravagant uniforms remarkable even by the standards of the Bonaparte family, but he founded two distinguished lineages. Elizabeth Patterson Bonaparte's grandson, Charles Joseph Bonaparte, was secretary of the navy and attorney general under President Theodore Roosevelt between 1905 and 1909. Napoleon Joseph, Jérôme's second son by Catherine of Württemberg, became the Bonaparte pretender in 1879 on the death of the son of Napoleon III. Jérôme's great-grandson, Prince Napoleon, a successful international businessman, hero of the Resistance, and pretender to the throne, died in 1997.

Related entries: Danube Campaigns; Waterloo, Battle of; Westphalia, Kingdom of

Suggestions for further reading:
Connelly, Owen. 1965. *Napoleon's Satellite Kingdoms.* New York: Free Press.
Kircheisen, Friedrich Max. 1932. *Jovial King: Napoleon's Youngest Brother.* London: E. Mathews and Marrot.
Markham, Felix. 1975. *The Bonapartes.* London: Weidenfeld and Nicolson.

Bonaparte, Joseph, King of Naples, King of Spain (1768–1844)

Napoleon's elder brother possessed social charm and a fair degree of political skill, but failed as a military commander. Napoleon judged him "too good to be a king" (Connelly 1985, pp. 80–81). Originally intended for the priesthood, he became a lawyer instead and was a rising star in Corsican politics before the revolt of Pasquale Paoli in 1793 forced the Bonapartes to flee to France. In 1794 Joseph married Julie Clary, sister of Désirée, and adding to her considerable dowry by wise investments, built up a considerable fortune during the period of his brother's rise and ascendancy.

Between 1796 and 1799 under the Directory Joseph acted as a legislator, as a member of the Council of Five Hundred, and as a diplomat on missions to Parma and Rome. He put his reconciliatory talents to use during the coup of 18 Brumaire and under the consulate acted as Napoleon's personal envoy, deeply involved in the negotiations of the Treaties of Lunéville and

François Gérard's **Joseph Bonaparte** *portrays Joseph as king of Spain standing in front of his throne, bedecked in ermine and blue velvet robes. His left hand rests on the scepter while he holds his hat casually in his right hand. The whole portrait combines magnificence with a hopeful "popular" touch. (Lauros-Giraudon/Art Resource)*

Amiens and the Concordat of 1801. Joseph initially opposed the creation of the empire, but in 1806 Napoleon made him king of Naples. Here he promulgated a constitution, attempted to abolish feudalism and reform the administration, and managed to reconcile the Catholic Church by conscientious observance of his religious duties. This latter success probably induced Napoleon to persuade a reluctant Joseph that he would make an acceptable king of Spain, a delusion the failure of which cannot be blamed on Joseph.

As king of Spain between 1808 and 1813 Joseph tried to woo Spanish liberals, but faced massive popular rebellion, which forced him to abandon Madrid only eight days after arriving there. He attempted to rule according to the Constitution of Bayonne, but his efforts were impractical and led him to neglecting military affairs, much to Napoleon's annoyance. Never accepted as ruler by the Spanish people, Joseph wanted to be an enlightened monarch but was forced to be a soldier king, a role for which he was totally unsuited. When the duke of Wellington's decisive victory at Vitoria on 21 June 1813 brought an end to the Peninsular War, Joseph had to flee ignominiously back to his estate of Mortefontaine, near Paris. He formally abdicated on 11 December 1813. During the Allied invasion of France in 1814 Joseph was head of government in Paris while Napoleon headed the army. He escaped to Switzerland, returned to serve during the Hundred Days, and accompanied Napoleon to Rochefort after the defeat at Waterloo. While Napoleon was being sent into permanent exile, Joseph slipped onto an American ship and arrived in New York at the end of July 1815.

Joseph brought an estate at Bordentown, New Jersey, and between 1815 and 1832 he made friends in high places, was received by President Andrew Jackson, and was elected to the American Philosophical Society. In 1832 he left for Europe to support the cause of Napoleon II, but the prince died before he arrived. Banned from France, he first settled in England and then in 1841 joined his much neglected wife in Italy. He died in Florence on 28 July 1844, and Julie survived him for only eight months. In 1862 Napoleon III had Joseph's remains removed to the Invalides to rest near those of Napoleon. Characterized as "the gentle Bonaparte," Joseph's considerable talents were well employed in times of peace, but unsuited to the times of war his brother inflicted on Spain and Europe.

Related entries: Brumaire, Coup of Year VIII; Hundred Days; Naples, Kingdom of; Peninsular War; Spain

Suggestions for further reading:
Connelly, Owen. 1968. *The Gentle Bonaparte: A Biography of Joseph, Napoleon's Elder Brother.* New York: Macmillan.
Connelly, Owen, ed. 1985. *Historical Dictionary of Napoleonic France, 1799–1815.* Westport, CT: Greenwood.
Glover, Michael. 1971. *Legacy of Glory: The Bonaparte Kingdom of Spain, 1808–1813.* New York: Scribner.
Lovett, Gabriel H. 1965. *Napoleon and the Birth of Modern Spain.* 2 vols. New York: New York University Press.
Ross, Michael. 1976. *The Reluctant King: Joseph Bonaparte, King of the Two Sicilies and Spain.* London: Sidgwick and Jackson.

Bonaparte, Louis, King of Holland (1778–1846)

Napoleon's third brother, born at Ajaccio, Louis started his career as a soldier. Commissioned in the artillery in 1795, he served as Napoleon's aide-de-camp in the first Italian and Egyptian campaigns between 1796 and 1799. He transferred to the cavalry in 1799 but retired almost immediately through ill health. On 4 January 1802 Louis married Hortense de Beauharnais, with whom he had three sons, two of whom died in infancy, but the third, Charles Louis Napoleon Bonaparte, lived to become Napoleon III in 1850. Louis's poor relations with Hortense, however, were to become one cause of friction with his brother the emperor.

With the creation of the empire in 1804 Louis became grand constable, adding the title of commander of reserves in 1805, and briefly governor general of the departments beyond the Alps. In June 1806 Napoleon made Louis king of Holland, but during his reign as Lodewijk I he enraged Napoleon by his pro-Dutch and nationalist policies, refusing to accept that the only role for his kingdom was to be exploited for the greater glory of his brother. The historian Jean Tulard describes Louis as "an excellent sovereign" who "'took to heart the interests of his state,'" adding, "from thence onwards a conflict with his brother was inevitable." He learned Dutch, formed a Dutch ministry and governed with a Parliament, maintained traditional rights and religious freedom, and introduced educational reforms, a flood control program, and the foundations of a national health service. Even more serious from Napoleon's point of view, Louis refused to organize military conscription, rejected the Napoleonic law codes as "un-Dutch," and refused to enforce the Continental System, which he called "immoral" (Connelly 1985, pp. 80–81).

In 1810, therefore, Napoleon forced Louis to abdicate and annexed Holland to France. Louis took the title of Count of Saint-Leu and found asylum in Austria, settling at Graz before moving to Switzerland in 1813. In January 1814 he offered his services to Napoleon as "a Frenchman wishing to share the dangers of the moment," but was ignored. Taking refuge in Lausanne and then in Italy, Louis refused Napoleon's invitation to return during the Hundred Days, observing his brother's final downfall from a distance in Rome. Thereafter he spent most of his remaining years in Florence, moving to Livorno shortly before his death in July 1846.

Louis was the author of several books of poetry and history, a novel, *Marie ou les peines d'amour* (1812), and most notably three volumes of *Historical Documents and Reflections on the Government of Holland,* which when published in 1820 further enraged the exiled and dying Napoleon against his independent-minded brother. Although liable to fits of paranoia and a bad husband to a talented wife who deserved much better, Louis as king of Holland showed talent and a sympathy for his subjects that proved stronger than family feeling or the glories of the empire.

Related entries: Beauharnais, Eugénie-Hortense Cecile de; Continental System; Holland, Kingdom of; Netherlands

Suggestions for further reading:
Connelly, Owen. 1965. *Napoleon's Satellite Kingdoms.* New York: Free Press.
Connelly, Owen, ed. 1985. *Historical Dictionary of Napoleonic Frace, 1799–1815.* Westport, CT: Greenwood.
Markham, Felix. 1975. *The Bonapartes.* London: Weidenfeld and Nicolson.
Schama, Simon. 1977. *Patriots and Liberators: Revolution in the Netherlands, 1780–1813.* New York: Knopf.

Bonaparte, Lucien, Prince of Canino (1775–1840)

Napoleon owed much to his fiery younger brother but could never control him, and Lucien was the only member of the Bonaparte clan to receive no title under the empire. Born at Ajaccio, Lucien was educated in France at the Collège d'Autun, but returned to Corsica on the outbreak of the Revolution. He became a fervent Jacobin, and his denunciation of Pasquale Paoli in Jacobin clubs led to the Bonaparte family's flight from Corsica in 1793. In revolutionary Paris Lucien developed his skills as a politician and radical orator. An ardent supporter of Robespierre during the Terror, he was imprisoned briefly in 1794, but soon made a comeback under the Directory. Also in 1794 he defied his family and married Christine Boyer, an innkeeper's daughter. Elected to the Council of Five Hundred in 1798, Lucien was its president in 1799 when Napoleon returned from Egypt. In this capacity he became the hero of the coup of 18 Brumaire, rallying the troops to support Napoleon and propelling his brother to power. Lucien had acted to save the Republic, and the slow realization that he had helped to kill it troubled him for the rest of his life.

As minister of the interior in 1799 Lucien began the systematic collection of statistics and drew up the first list of prefects, but as ambassador to Spain in 1800 he clashed with the increasingly imperious Napoleon and left his brother's service. A widower since May 1800, in May 1803 he married Alexandrine Jouberthon, a stockbroker's widow of dubious reputation, once more defying the wishes of his family. Napoleon demanded he renounce his new wife, but instead Lucien went to Rome with Alexandrine, their child, and both their children by previous marriages. Here Pope Pius VII befriended the family. Napoleon offered Lucien the crown of Italy in 1805 and possibly that of Spain in 1807 if he would divorce Mme. Jouberthon, but he refused, choosing instead to live on an estate near Rome with the papal title of prince of Canino.

When Napoleon's troops entered Rome in 1808, Lucien found his brother's rule oppressive and planned to emigrate with his family to the United States. However, they were captured at sea by the Royal Navy and taken to England, where Lucien lived the life of a country gentleman, first at Ludlow Castle in Shropshire, then at Thorngrove in Worcestershire, until 1814. His years in England were undisturbed, but the suggestion in British propaganda that he was there voluntarily disturbed him, and

eventually the family returned to a Rome now free from Napoleonic rule.

Despite all their personal and political differences, Lucien rallied to Napoleon during the Hundred Days and attempted to revive his inspirational oratorical skills in his brother's service. He rushed to Paris and after Waterloo tried in vain to rally support in the Senate for Napoleon's son, the king of Rome. Saved from reprisals by Pius VII, Lucien spent the rest of his life with his second wife and their ten children in Italy, devoting himself to the study of the ancient Etruscans and the composition of many writings, including his unfinished *Memoirs* and a book on the Hundred Days. He died at Viterbo in 1840. Lucien's independence and uncommonly principled behavior, especially in the 1800s, caused Sir Walter Scott to comment: "A Frenchman refusing a crown and declining to part with his wife is indeed one of the most uncommon exhibitions in an age fertile in novelties."

Related entries: Brumaire, Coup of Year VIII; Corsica; Hundred Days; Pius VII, Pope; Prefects; Statistics

Suggestions for further reading:
Atteridge, Andrew Hilliard. 1909. *Napoleon's Brothers.* London: Methuen.
Goodspeed, Donald James. 1965. *Bayonets at St. Cloud: The Story of the 18th Brumaire.* London: Rupert Hart-Davis.
Markham, Felix. 1975. *The Bonapartes.* London: Weidenfeld and Nicolson.

Bonaparte, Maria Letizia (1750–1836)

Napoleon's mother was born Maria Letizia Ramolino at Ajaccio, married Carlo Bonaparte on 2 June 1764, and bore him twelve children, six sons and six daughters, of whom Napoleon was the second of the eight who survived infancy. She participated with her husband in Pasquale Paoli's revolt of 1768–1769, but her princi-

Even as the mother of the First Consul, Napoleon's mother continued to live in relative simplicity in her house in the Rue St. Dominique, Paris. (Alinari/Art Resource)

little interest in politics. According to Metternich Letizia cared only for money and nothing for social elevation: "She had an immense income but without her son's explicit instructions would have done nothing but invest it." In fact this focus on investment was very wise: her great wealth, acquired from jewelry and shrewd investment, allowed her to live comfortably for over twenty years after the fall of the empire. Otherwise in the years of dominance she tried to employ her resolve and common sense in the interests of her children, but was more often ignored than heeded.

In 1814 she joined Napoleon briefly on Elba and returned to Paris during the Hundred Days, finally saying farewell to her son at Malmaison on 29 June 1815. Leaving Paris with Fesch, she made her way through Switzerland to Rome, where she was to live quietly for the rest of her life, outliving Napoleon by fifteen years.

Related entries: Bonaparte, Carlo; Corsica; Fesch, Joseph

Suggestions for further reading:
Carrington, Dorothy. 1988. *Napoleon and his Parents: On the Threshold of History.* London: Viking.
Markham, Felix. 1975. *The Bonapartes.* London: Weidenfeld and Nicolson.
Martineau, Gilbert. 1978. *Madame Mère: Napoleon's Mother.* London: John Murray.
Stirling, Monica. 1961. *A Pride of Lions: A Portrait of Napoleon's Mother.* London: Collins.

pal concern as a young wife was to take care of Carlo's often disordered finances, a necessity that instilled the habits of frugality and basic common sense that she retained even at the height of her son's glory. Forced to flee Corsica in 1793, she moved the family home first to Toulon, then to Marseille, but spent most of the years of Napoleon's primacy in Paris, with the official title of "Madame, Mère de l'Empereur," generally known as "Madame Mère."

Under the empire Madame Mère retained her frugal habits, an intense religious devotion, and a down-to-earth sense of realism. Her laconic "If only it lasts . . ." became famous. She encouraged Napoleon to seek reconciliation with the Church—her half-brother Joseph Fesch became cardinal-archbishop of Lyon—but otherwise took

Bonaparte, Pauline, Duchess of Guastalla (1780–1825)

Napoleon's favorite and most beautiful sister seemed to revel in scandal. She never showed any of the political capabilities or ambitions of Elisa or Caroline, being content to outdo them in wit and extravagance, but she showed more in the

Antonio Canova's **Venus Reclining** *(1804–1808) plays upon Pauline Bonaparte's beauty and scandalous reputation. She is posing as Venus, the Goddess of Love, while her brother posed as Mars, the God of War. (Alinari/Art Resource)*

way of common humanity. Under the Directory Pauline attracted and encouraged the attentions of many of her brother's fellow officers, until in 1797 an embarrassed Napoleon forced her into marriage with General Charles Victor Leclerc. For the first year of the consulate she was queen of Parisian society, but in 1802 Napoleon insisted that she accompany Leclerc to Haiti, where he was in command of the expedition against the rising of Toussaint L'Ouverture. Leclerc contracted yellow fever, and Pauline returned to France a widow with a sickly four-year-old son.

Pauline lost no time in getting married again to an Italian nobleman, Prince Camillo Borghese, but conjugal life with a feeble husband among the aristocracy of Rome did not suit her. Her son died in 1804, a tragedy which seems to have had a traumatic effect on her nervous health. Pauline's extramarital affairs shocked Roman high society, but the single greatest scandal, which she seems to have enjoyed particularly, arose when she posed nude for Antonio Canova's sculpture, *Venus Reclining,* in 1808. In 1806 Napoleon granted her the tiny duchy of Guastalla in northern Italy, which she described as "a single miserable village with a few beastly pigs," and she did not live there until 1810, after she had clashed with the new empress, Marie-Louise. Unlike the other members of the family, Pauline had always enjoyed good relations with Joséphine.

Whatever the difficulties caused by her scandalous lifestyle, Pauline remained faithful to Napoleon. She was the only sister to visit him on Elba in 1814, enlivening four of his ten months there with balls and amateur theatricals. On Napoleon's fall, Pope Pius VII, with whom she got on surprisingly well, secured a settlement with her estranged husband, granting her a sizable share of the Borghese properties in Italy. She sold her principal home in the Rue

Saint-Honoré in Paris to the British government, and it remains the British embassy to this day. Pauline had amassed a huge personal fortune, but her precarious health deteriorated rapidly in 1823–1824. She died in Florence, probably, like Napoleon, from cancer of the stomach, on 9 June 1825. The warmhearted side of Pauline's character, inseparable from her wild and promiscuous side, was shown near the end when she persuaded her mother to receive her American nephew, Jerome Bonaparte, son of her brother Jérôme and Elizabeth Patterson.

Related entries: Elba; Empire Style; Leclerc, Charles Victor Emmanuel

Suggestions for further reading:
Dixon, Pierson. 1966. *Pauline: Napoleon's Favourite Sister.* New York: D. McKay.
Markham, Felix. 1975. *The Bonapartes.* London: Weidenfeld and Nicolson.
Ortzen, Len. 1974. *Imperial Venus: The Story of Pauline Bonaparte-Borghese.* New York: Stein and Day.
Weiner, Margery. 1964. *The Parvenu Princesses: Elisa, Pauline and Caroline Bonaparte.* London: John Murray.

Bonapartism

Napoleon's nephew Louis Napoleon, elected president of the Second Republic in 1849, declared that "the name of Napoleon is in itself a political programme." Yet Napoleon's legacy was so ambiguous and open to conflicting interpretations that Bonapartism as a political force could be left-wing or right-wing, authoritarian or democratic, or simply defined mostly by commitment to a strong state and national unity as against the divisiveness of party politics.

Louis Napoleon, who became the Emperor Napoleon III in 1851, defined Bonapartism as "internally: order, authority, religion and the well-being of the people; externally: national dignity." The legend of Napoleon as revolutionary emperor and savior of the nation was kept alive between 1815 and 1848 by opponents of, first, the restored Bourbons and then the Orleanist monarchy after 1830. Louis Napoleon's election by universal male suffrage in 1849 showed the strength of popular Bonapartism among the peasant masses, and as Napoleon III he never lost that support. However, defeat in the Franco-Prussian War of 1870 led to the accusation that the Bonapartes had led France to disaster twice, first at Waterloo, then at Sedan. Bonapartism continued for a while as a significant political force under the Third Republic, but it split into left-wing and right-wing factions and became merely one means among several of expressing dissatisfaction with the real and imagined shortcomings of the "regime of the parties."

The death of the dashing Prince Imperial fighting the Zulus in South Africa in 1879 marked the end of serious Bonapartist pretensions to a restored throne, and the family was banned from living on French soil in 1886. But the fear of a "plebiscitary" authoritarian form of democracy, bypassing parliamentary institutions, has continued to haunt French politics throughout the twentieth century. Both Marshal Pétain and General de Gaulle were accused by their enemies of Bonapartism, but such connections are vague at best and based on very simplistic readings of French history. The last Bonapartist pretender, Prince Napoleon, a successful international businessman and Resistance hero, died in 1997.

Related entries: Napoleonic Legend

Suggestions for further reading:
Alexander, R. S. 1991. *Bonapartism and the Revolutionary Tradition in France: The Fédérés of 1815.* Cambridge: Cambridge University Press.
Furet, François. 1992. *Revolutionary France, 1770–1880.* Oxford: Blackwell.
Gildea, Robert. 1994. *The Past in French History.* New Haven: Yale University Press.
Rothney, John. 1969. *Bonapartism after Sedan.* Ithaca, NY: Cornell University Press.

Tulard, Jean. 1985. *Napoleon: The Myth of the Saviour.* London: Methuen.

Borodino, Battle of (7 September 1812)

The climactic battle of Napoleon's Russian campaign took place at the village of Borodino, some seventy miles west of Moscow, when the Russian army under Mikhail Kutuzov halted in its retreat toward the ancient capital and turned to fight, taking up position along a line of high ground broken by ravines. Napoleon's forces had been worn down in the long pursuit of the Russians and now numbered some 130,000 men and 590 guns facing 120,000 Russians with 640 guns along a four-mile front. The Russian fortifications, designed by Prince Bagration, could withstand wave after wave of French attacks and allow an orderly retreat if necessary.

Napoleon's attack began with an artillery barrage at dawn, and Eugène de Beauharnais, commanding the French left, soon captured the village of Borodino. But the battle turned into a bludgeoning match, resulting in bloody stalemate. The French corps under Marshals Jozef Poniatowski, Michel Ney, and Louis Davout slowly pushed the Russians back, aided by Joachim Murat's cavalry, assaulting the Russian center and left again and again. By midafternoon the Russians had withdrawn, but only about a mile to another defensive position on another line of hills. They had only seriously wavered when Bagration was mortally wounded, and then only briefly. Napoleon, who was not in the best of health all day, ignored Murat's pleas to commit the Imperial Guard to the battle, decided not to gamble, and the battle died away inconclusively. The Prussian military theorist and reformer, Carl von Clausewitz, who was in Russian service at the time, wrote: "In the whole of the battle there was not a trace of superior skill or intelligence: it was simply a test of strength, and in this the two armies were almost equal. What ensued in the end was merely a slight tipping of the balance in favour of the side that was led with greater vigour and was more familiar with war."

During the night Kutuzov withdrew toward Moscow, allowing the French to claim a victory. But Napoleon had failed to destroy the Russian army as he had hoped, and French casualties were about 30,000, or one in four, including ten generals killed. Russian losses were also enormous, but Kutuzov had plenty of reserves to call upon and could afford not to care if Napoleon proclaimed himself victorious. He had stretched and depleted the French forces and preserved the Russian army. Napoleon called Borodino "the most terrible of all my battles. . . . The French showed themselves worthy of victory and the Russians of being invincible." The Russian retreat opened up the road to Moscow, Napoleon's principal objective, but as Clausewitz pointed out, "a total victory would have cost him more than he was able to pay." Russia could not be conquered like other countries by the decisive engagement Napoleon always sought.

Related entries: Bagration, Pyotr Ivanovich, Prince; Beauharnais, Eugène Rose de; Kutuzov, Mikhail Ilarionovich; Lannes, Jean; Ney, Michel; Poniatowski, Jozef, Prince; Russian Campaign

Suggestions for further reading:
Chandler, David G. 1974. *The Campaigns of Napoleon: The Mind and Method of History's Greatest Soldier.* New York: Macmillan.
———. 1994. "Borodino: 1812," in his *On the Napoleonic Wars: Collected Essays.* London: Greenhill.
Duffy, Christopher. 1972. *Borodino and the War of 1812.* London: Seeley.
Holmes, Edward Richard. 1971. *Borodino 1812.* London: Batsford.
Lee, Nigel de. 1987. "Poniatowski," in David G. Chandler, ed. *Napoleon's Marshals.* New York: Macmillan.

Bourrienne, Louis Antoine Fauvelet de (1769–1834)

Napoleon's first military secretary was born at Sens and studied with Napoleon at the academy of Brienne. He planned to become a diplomat, but left France during the Revolution, only returning in 1797 when he was appointed military secretary to Napoleon, serving him in Italy, Egypt, and Syria. Bourrienne was competent in his post, but also proved to be an embezzler on a grand scale. Napoleon sacked him in 1804 and sent him to Hamburg where he continued in his embezzling ways: he sold passports illicitly and profited from the black market in goods made scarce under the Continental System.

In 1810 a commission of inquiry found that Bourrienne had embezzled some 2 million *livres* while in Hamburg, and Napoleon ordered him to repay it. But he had still not complied in 1814. At the Restoration in 1815 Talleyrand secured his appointment as minister of posts, but his tenure of office was short-lived. To escape his creditors he settled near Charleroi in Belgium, where he dictated ten volumes of memoirs of dubious accuracy. Bourrienne's mind began to go in the 1820s, and he died in 1834 in an insane asylum near Caen.

Related entries: Army

Suggestions for further reading:
Bergeron, Louis. 1981. *France under Napoleon.* Princeton: Princeton University Press.

Brienne, Military Academy

The military school at Brienne Le Château was founded in 1777, one of twelve such academies established during the eighteenth century to augment the *École Militaire* in Paris. Pupils were educated for the army at the expense of the state, with the most gifted finishing their education at the prestigious Paris academy. Napoleon entered Brienne on 13 May 1779, at the age of nine, and remained until 30 October 1784, when he duly progressed to the *École Militaire.* The Brienne academy was closed in 1790.

Related entries: *École Militaire*

Suggestions for further reading:
Ratcliffe, Bertram. 1981. *Prelude to Fame: An Account of the Early Life of Napoleon up to the Battle of Montenotte.* London: Warne.

Brumaire, Coup of Year VIII

The almost bloodless coup which overthrew the Directory on 9–10 November 1799 (18–19 Brumaire, Year VIII in the Revolutionary calendar) allowed Napoleon to assume unchallengeable political control of France, making possible the four years of authoritarian rule under the consulate. The chief plotters, Paul Barras, Joseph Fouché, Charles-Maurice de Talleyrand, and especially Emmanuel Sieyès, were seeking to replace the Directory with a stronger executive and saw Napoleon as a "safe" general, free from royalist sympathies, who would allow them to carry through their plans.

The conspiracy involved calling an emergency meeting of the two legislative chambers of the Directory, the Council of Ancients and the Council of Five Hundred, under the pretext of a Jacobin plot. Napoleon was to be appointed commander of the troops in Paris, the two councils transferred out of Paris to Saint-Cloud, and the five Directors forced to resign, making way for three consuls. With the help of Lucien Bonaparte, who had been made president of the Council of Five Hundred, the relevant decrees were passed, while Napoleon addressed the Council of Ancients at the Tuileries. The three directors who were in the

F. Vieira's **The Sitting of the Council of Five Hundred at St. Cloud** *is a dramatic rendering of Napoleon's appearance to harangue the Council of Five Hundred. It shows an imaginary assassination attempt, which nevertheless became part of the Napoleonic legend. (Corbis/Gianni Dagli Orti))*

plot—Sieyès, Roger Ducos, and Barras— submitted their resignations, and the two others were held under guard in the Luxembourg palace.

The chambers met at Saint-Cloud surrounded by large bodies of troops assembled in the courtyard outside the palace. Napoleon addressed the Council of Ancients, but for once his eloquence deserted him. He declared that the Directory was in the pay of the British and that there was a plot against the Republic. But he met hostility from some members and had to be persuaded to leave. At the Council of Five Hundred he met violent opposition from Jacobin deputies and was dragged from the hall by his soldiers. Lucien adjourned the session, joined his brother, and Napoleon ordered grenadiers with fixed bayonets to clear the hall.

In the evening around sixty of the scattered Five Hundred were rounded up and voted to accept Napoleon, Sieyès, and Ducos as provisional consuls with authority to revise the constitution. After the Council of Ancients, still in session, had been forced to go along, the legislature was adjourned for six weeks and Jacobin members excluded. The new constitution was completed in six weeks, proclaimed on 25 December 1799, and accepted by plebiscite in February 1800.

The coup of Brumaire was a close-run thing, but it laid the basis for the consulate. Many of Sieyès's complex constitutional ideas survived alongside Napoleon's more direct and authoritarian approach. As first consul Napoleon was to have far greater powers than his colleagues, directly influencing appointments to the Senate and other legislative bodies, and directly choosing and removing all high officials. Skilful propaganda in newspapers, pamphlets, and posters justified the coup. But it was a myth that Napoleon was the sole victor, replacing the weak rule of the Directory with the strong government that France required. Nor was the Republic threatened with military disaster: other generals had already turned the tide. Many members of the chambers of the Directory continued to sit in the legislature of the consulate. But the coup did open the way for Napoleon's rule under the consulate and then the empire after 1804.

Related entries: Barras, Paul François Jean Nicolas, Vicomte de; Bonaparte, Lucien, Prince of Canino; Consulate; Directory; Ducos, Pierre Roger; Fouché, Joseph; Murat, Joachim; Sieyès, Emmanuel Joseph; Talleyrand-Périgord, Charles-Maurice de

Suggestions for further reading:
Arnold, Eric A., ed. 1994. *A Documentary Survey of Napoleonic France.* Lanham, MD: University Press of America, pp. 14–22.
Goodspeed, Donald James. 1965. *Bayonets at St. Cloud: The Story of the 18th Brumaire.* London: Rupert Hart-Davis.
Lefebvre, Georges. 1965. *The Directory.* London: Routledge and Kegan Paul.
Lyons, Martyn. 1975. *France under the Directory.* Cambridge: Cambridge University Press.
Morton, John B. 1948. *Brumaire: The Rise of Bonaparte.* London: T. Werner Levine.
Thompson, J. M. 1952. *Napoleon Bonaparte, His Rise and Fall.* Oxford: Basil Blackwell.

Brune, Guillaume Marie Anne (1763–1815)

Born at Brive-la-Gaillarde in central France, Brune moved to Paris as a printer's apprentice and after 1789 an enthusiastic revolutionary journalist and supporter of Georges Danton. He passed from service in the Parisian National Guard to enlistment in the army in 1792, and in 1793 fought against the Counter-Revolution in Normandy and at Bordeaux, where he distinguished himself by his ruthlessness. Returning to Paris in 1795 he first met Napoleon when taking part in the suppression of the rising of Vendémiaire.

In September 1796 Brune was surprisingly given a command under André Masséna in the Army of Italy. Here he showed his personal bravery, if not outstanding military expertise, and fought at the battles of Arcola and Rivoli, earning the rank of divisional general in 1797. The year 1798 saw Brune in Switzerland, charged with laying hands on the Swiss national treasury and crushing resistance to the French, both of which he did in his usual remorseless manner. He then performed a similar role in Holland as commander of all French troops in the Batavian Republic, repulsing the attempted Allied invasion of 1799.

Despite his valuable services Napoleon remained suspicious of the republican convictions of this revolutionary turned soldier. Brune briefly succeeded Masséna as commander in chief in Italy and was equally fleetingly president of the War Department of the Council of State before Napoleon dispatched him to Constantinople as ambassador to Turkey. Here he spent two frustrating years between 1802 and 1804, being outmaneuvered by the Russians on the diplomatic front. Brune was mollified with the title of marshal, but his appointment in 1805 as governor general of the Hanseatic towns was a form of exile. When he signed a treaty with Sweden in a "republican" form disapproved of by Napoleon, he was recalled in disgrace in October 1807 and remained unemployed for seven years. He rallied to the Bourbons in 1814, but during the Hundred Days transferred his allegiance back to Napoleon, who forgot former differences by making him governor of Provence. Forced to retreat, he made for Paris but was assassinated by royalist fanatics in Avignon on 2 August 1815 and his body thrown into the river Rhône.

Related entries: Batavian Republic; Italian Campaigns; Masséna, André; Ottoman Empire

Suggestions for further reading:
Shepperd, Alan. 1987. "Brune" in David G. Chandler, ed., *Napoleon's Marshals.* New York: Macmillan.

Bussaco, Battle of (27 September 1810)

The battle of Bussaco was fought during the Peninsular War between the French Army of Portugal commanded by André Masséna and Anglo-Portuguese forces under Arthur Wellesley, duke of Wellington. The fighting centered on the Sierra de Bussaco, north of Coimbra, where Wellington succeeded in turning Masséna's attack and diverting the French from Estremadura. In bitter hand-to-hand fighting the French suffered 4,480 casualties, while the Allies lost 626 men. Bussaco was not a decisive battle, and Wellington was forced to resume his retreat toward Lisbon, but it dealt a grave blow to French morale, at the same time demonstrating to the British the worth of the newly formed Portuguese army.

Related entries: Masséna, André; Peninsular War; Wellington, Duke of

Suggestions for further reading:
Chambers, George L. 1910. *Bussaco.* London: Sonnenschein.
Glover, Michael. 1963. *Wellington's Peninsular Victories: Busaco, Salamanca, Victoria, Nivelle.* London: Batsford.
Horward, Donald David. 1965. *The Battle of Bussaco: Massena vs Wellington.* Tallahassee: Florida State University.

C

Cadoudal, Georges (1771–1804)

A determined opponent of the Revolution since 1793, this Breton farmer's son was involved in the two most serious attempts to assassinate Napoleon. Cadoudal had joined the rebellion in the Vendée in 1793 and proved himself as a leader of *chouannerie,* one of the best-known leaders of the Counter-Revolution. In March 1800 Napoleon as first consul offered Cadoudal a general's commission or a generous annual income if he would abandon political activity, but Cadoudal refused and fled to England, setting up a training camp for anti-Bonapartist terrorists in Hampshire. Meanwhile, however, Napoleon's signing of the Concordat of 1801 put an end to serious guerrilla activity in France.

The first royalist attempt to kill Napoleon, the Opera Plot of December 1800, was found to be the work of two of Cadoudal's agents, though he himself always denied knowledge of it. In August 1803 Cadoudal returned secretly to Paris, and another conspiracy was hatched, this time involving Generals Jean-Charles Pichegru and Jean-Victor Moreau. The plan was to kidnap and kill Napoleon, open the frontiers to royalist and Allied invaders, and install Louis XVIII as king. But Joseph Fouché's police had infiltrated the royalist network, and the conspirators were easily apprehended. Cadoudal was arrested on 13 February 1804 and guillotined on 25 June. Napoleonic legend credited him with the famous last words: "I came to make a king and instead I have made an emperor."

Related entries: *Chouannerie;* Counter-Revolution; Imperial Police; Moreau, Jean-Victor; Opera Plot; Pichegru, Jean-Charles; Royalists; Vendée Revolt

Suggestions for further reading:
Godechot, Jacques. 1981. *The Counter-Revolution: Doctrine and Action, 1789–1804.* Princeton: Princeton University Press.

Calabria, Revolt in (1806–1811)

The province of Calabria, part of the Kingdom of Naples, was described by one French officer as "a paradise . . . inhabited by devils." Already the scene of an anti-French revolt in 1799, Calabria saw revolt break out again shortly after Joseph Bonaparte's entry into Naples in 1806. Peasant resistance, building on the brigandage inherent to the region, was sparked off by the requisitions of the French army, commanded by Jean Reynier, and spurred on by the British admiral, Sir Sidney Smith. In July 1806 British troops landed and defeated the French at Maida, thereby encouraging partisans to attack and wipe out the small French garrisons scattered through the countryside, and soon the French were just barely holding on in the towns. But the partisan leaders were individualists in the brigand tradition. The British commander in Sicily, Sir John Stuart, found them barbarous and, to Smith's fury, evacuated his fever-ridden troops.

The arrival of a relief army under André Masséna swung things in favor of the French. They now built roads and bridges to facilitate communications, used flying columns to pursue partisan bands, and recruited native Calabrian troops. But the French could never wipe out the partisans, who would reappear as soon as the French columns left any particular area. The introduction of conscription in 1809–1810 caused revolt to flare up again, more widespread than ever. Only the ruthless policy of the military governor, Jean-Baptiste Manhès, including the wholesale massacre of villages supporting the rebels and the starving out of the partisan bands, could put down the revolt. The last leader was captured and executed in November 1811.

The insurrection in Calabria cost the French 20,000 casualties and was marked by atrocities on both sides. It was essentially a peasant insurrection, directed against the pro-French townspeople as much as the invaders. It prefigured the guerrilla warfare of the Peninsular War and thus the partisan wars of the twentieth century.

Related entries: Guerrilla Warfare; Masséna, André; Naples, Kingdom of

Suggestions for further reading:
Davis, John A. 1990. "The Impact of French Rule on the Kingdom of Naples, 1806–1815," *Ricerche Storiche* 20, pp. 367–405.
Finley, Milton. 1989. "The Most Monstrous of Wars: Suppression of Calabrian Brigandage, 1806–1811," *Consortium on Revolutionary Europe: Proceedings* 18, pp. 251–266.
Grab, Alexander. 1995. "State Power, Brigandage and Rural Resistance in Napoleonic Italy," *European History Quarterly* 25, pp. 39–70.

Cambacérès, Jean-Jacques Régis de (1753–1824)

A survivor of revolutionary politics, Cambacérès became second consul during the consulate and arch-chancellor during the empire, typifying the analytical finesse and enormous capacity for work of the ideal Napoleonic administrator. Born into a family of lawyers at Montpellier, he too followed a legal career, and entered politics as a member of the Convention and deputy for the department of the Hérault. In 1793 during the Terror Cambacérès kept his head and worked on the first abortive attempt at a codification of French civil law, anticipating his work on Napoleon's Civil Code. Under the Directory he was elected to the Council of Ancients and served briefly as minister of justice. He owed his position as second consul after the coup of 18 Brumaire to his ability to advise the still inexperienced Napoleon on the intricacies of politics and the law.

Cambacérès was for practical purposes head of the administration of justice between 1799 and 1814, the titular ministers of justice being subordinated to his authority. The new court system was in his hands; he approved all judicial appointments; and he dealt with much of the ministry's business personally. In Napoleon's absence Cambacérès presided over the majority of meetings of the Council of State and also over the Senate, acquiring great influence and patronage. Napoleon while on campaign still ruled France, but his orders passed through Cambacérès, who kept the routine of administration working and informed the emperor about the state of public opinion. But his most lasting contribution was in the formal formulation of the Civil Code, and next to Napoleon himself he was chiefly responsible for its completion and implementation.

More than any other individual, Napoleon could rely on Cambacérès for prudent advice and intelligent execution of his orders. The arch-chancellor's natural caution caused him to oppose the abduction of the duke of Enghien, the establishment of the empire, the involvement in Spain, Napoleon's marriage to Marie-Louise, and the invasion of Russia. These stands took courage on his part, but he had always avoided clear-cut political decisions, and his prudence and efficiency were invaluable to Napoleon. Cambacérès applied the same care and consideration to his own financial affairs, amassing a substantial personal fortune by sound investments and the acquisition of considerable estates. Though exiled in Brussels from 1815 to 1818, he spent his last years in comfortable retirement on his lands.

Related entries: Civil Code; Consulate; Council of State; Directory; Senate

Suggestions for further reading:
Bergeron, Louis. 1981. *France under Napoleon.* Princeton: Princeton University Press.
Church, Clive H. 1981. *Revolution and Red Tape: The French Ministerial Bureaucracy 1770–1850.* Oxford: Clarendon Press.
Holtman, Robert B. 1967. *The Napoleonic Revolution.* Philadelphia: Lippincott.

Campo Formio, Treaty of (October 1797)

The Treaty of Campo Formio established the peace that ended Napoleon's Italian campaign. By the end of March 1797 Napoleon was at Klagenfurt, threatening Vienna, but far from his bases and with an unstable situation in Italy at his back. The Austrians sued for peace, but the preliminary agreement signed at Leoben on 18 April revealed the differences between Napoleon, who had committed himself to the pro-French parties in Italy, and the Directory, who wanted to secure Belgium and the Rhineland for France and were willing to give up Napoleon's Italian conquests in return. By the terms of Leoben Austria ceded Belgium to France and recognized the French satellite states in Italy. The Rhineland was not mentioned. The Directory was unhappy, but facing war-weariness and royalist agitation in France agreed to Napoleon's terms.

Napoleon now transformed Genoa into the Ligurian Republic and created the Cisalpine Republic in northern Italy. At the final peace concluded at Campo Formio Austria recognized the Cisalpine Republic and the French annexation of Belgium and promised to support French claims to the Rhineland at a future conference, which in the event was never held. In return Venice was divided between Austria, the Cisalpine Republic, and France. Austria gained most: the city of Venice itself, Dalmatia, Istria, and most of the mainland territories. The Cisalpine Republic gained a strip of the mainland, and France received the Ionian Islands, seen by Napoleon as vital for naval operations in the Mediterranean.

The treaty was accepted by the Directory and brought temporary peace between France and Austria. However, it was little more than an armed truce. Austria did not genuinely accept the French gains, and the resumption of hostilities only awaited a suitable occasion.

Related entries: Austria; Cisalpine Republic; Italian Campaigns

Suggestions for further reading:
Chandler, David G. 1974. *The Campaigns of Napoleon: The Mind and Method of History's Greatest Soldier.* New York: Macmillan.
Jackson, Sir William Godfrey Fothergill. 1953. *Attack in the West: Napoleon's First Campaign Re-read Today.* London: Eyre and Spottiswoode.

Canning, George (1770–1827)

The witty and resolutely Tory Canning was an ardent supporter of

William Pitt and influential in the formation of British policy against Napoleon. Having been secretary of the navy under Pitt in 1804, Canning was appointed foreign secretary by the duke of Portland in March 1807. He encouraged the expedition of September 1807 against Copenhagen, which resulted in the destruction of the Danish fleet, and urged vigorous support for the Spanish rebellion against Napoleonic rule. However, in this he clashed with his colleague Viscount Castlereagh, who would have preferred a more active British policy in the Low Countries. Their personal antagonism led to Canning's resignation in September 1809 and a duel on Putney Heath in which Canning was slightly injured. He now devoted his time to encouraging vigorous pursuance of the Peninsular War and served as ambassador to Lisbon between 1814 and 1816. Canning was to return to the Foreign Office after Castlereagh's suicide in 1822 and finally became prime minister just five months before his death.

Related entries: Castlereagh, Robert Stewart, Viscount; Great Britain

Suggestions for further reading:
Dixon, Peter. 1976. *Canning: Politician and Statesman.* London: Weidenfeld and Nicolson.
Hinde, Wendy. 1989. *George Canning.* Oxford: Basil Blackwell.
Rolo, Paul Jacques Victor. 1965. *George Canning: Three Biographical Studies.* London: Macmillan.

Carl August, Duke of Weimar (1757–1828)

The duke who had turned Weimar into the cultural center of Germany was a nominal ally of Napoleon between 1806 and 1813, but only through expediency. On taking control of his small principality from his widowed mother in 1775 Carl August brought such intellectual giants as Goethe, Herder, and Schiller into government and transformed the University of Jena into a leading cultural force. He had fought against France as a Prussian general in 1792–1793 and did the same in the war of 1806, which resulted in catastrophic defeat for Prussia. Napoleon was persuaded to let his state survive, but Carl August was compelled to join the Confederation of the Rhine and profess loyalty to the emperor. Nevertheless his liberalism made him a natural opponent of Napoleon, who called him Europe's "most troublesome prince." Carl August joined the Allies in 1813 and was rewarded at the Congress of Vienna with an expansion of his territory and the new title of grand duke of Saxe-Weimar-Eisenach. The constitution of his new state in 1816 was the first in Germany and granted complete freedom of the press.

Related entries: Confederation of the Rhine

Suggestions for further reading:
Sheehan, James J. 1989. *German History, 1770–1866.* Oxford: Clarendon Press.

Carnot, Lazare Nicolas (1753–1823)

Known as the "organizer of victory" in the revolutionary wars, Carnot gained equal distinction as a scientist, soldier, and politician, was important in promoting Napoleon's early career, and served him so far as was compatible with his strict republican principles. Born in Nolay in Burgundy and educated at the army engineering school at Mézières, before the Revolution Carnot had already acquired a reputation as a military engineer and with his studies on the operation of machines. He entered politics in 1791; as a member of the Convention voted for the death of Louis XVI; and was effectively minister of war in successive regimes between 1793 and 1797. As such he organized fourteen French armies to repel invading forces and then occupy Belgium, Switzerland, and the Rhineland.

Carnot's brilliant staff work involved the advancement of many young officers, and it was he who promoted Napoleon from captain to general after the siege of Toulon. And as part of Carnot's strategic plan for a three-pronged attack on Austria in 1796 he made Napoleon commander in chief of the Army of Italy. After the coup of 18 Brumaire Napoleon named Carnot as minister of war in April 1800, but he found that his authority was weakened by the independent actions of the generals and by all crucial matters being referred to Napoleon as first consul.

Carnot never made a secret of his republican beliefs, resigned as minister after the Marengo campaign, and opposed all the measures transforming the consulate into the empire. With the abolition of the Tribunate in 1807 he retired from politics. However, when France was in danger in 1814 Carnot was recalled, promoted to general, and appointed as governor of Antwerp, which he defended with skill against Bernadotte's Swedish forces, only surrendering after the armistice had been signed. In 1815, during the Hundred Days, he served as minister of the interior, and urged Napoleon not to abdicate after Waterloo. As a regicide and implacable opponent of the Bourbons, Carnot was exiled at the Restoration, first in Poland and from 1816 to his death in Magdeburg.

During his periods out of politics and in his exiled final years Carnot pursued his mathematical and scientific research. His work on machine motion had significant practical applications, and his works on defensive fortification drew on his distinguished contribution to the physics of work and energy in engineering mechanics. He also applied himself to related problems in geometry and to the foundations of calculus. Carnot's eldest son, Sadi, was to become famous in the field of thermodynamics, and a grandson, also called Sadi, was president of the French Republic from 1887 until his assassination in 1894.

Related entries: Hundred Days; Revolutionary Wars; Toulon, Siege of

Suggestions for further reading:
Gillispie, Charles C. 1971. "Carnot, Lazare-Nicolas-Marguerite," in Charles Coulston Gillispie, ed., *Dictionary of Scientific Biography*, vol. 3. New York: Charles Scribner's Sons.
Lyons, Martyn. 1975. *France under the Directory.* Cambridge: Cambridge University Press.
Watson, Sidney John. 1954. *Carnot.* London: Bodley Head.

Castiglione, Battle of (5 August 1796)

Although not a major Napoleonic victory, the battle of Castiglione was nevertheless significant in the success of Napoleon's first Italian campaign. In late July 1796, as two Austrian armies advanced on either side of Lake Garda, Napoleon was forced to break off the siege of Mantua and face the more serious threat of the army of Dagobert von Würmser, which was advancing across the rivers Adige and Mincio. In the action at Castiglione, Charles Augereau and André Masséna sought to lure Würmser forward so that the French cavalry could attack his flank. The maneuver failed, but the Austrians were forced back to Peschiera. A month later Napoleon gained a more decisive success in the battle of Bassano.

Related entries: Italian Campaigns

Suggestions for further reading:
Chandler, David G. 1974. *The Campaigns of Napoleon: The Mind and Method of History's Greatest Soldier.* New York: Macmillan.
Jackson, Sir William Godfrey Fothergill. 1953. *Attack in the West: Napoleon's First Campaign Re-read Today.* London: Eyre and Spottiswoode.

Castlereagh, Robert Stewart, Viscount (1769–1822)

As British foreign secretary after 1812, Castlereagh was the prime mover in the building of the final coalition against Napoleon. An Ulster Protestant, he had been chief secretary for Ireland from 1798 to 1801, working with William Pitt for the union with Great Britain while also favoring Catholic Emancipation. He became a cabinet minister in 1802 as president of the Board of Control, dealing with Indian affairs, and then in 1805–1806 as secretary for war and the colonies, when his plans for a British land force for use in Europe was abandoned for financial reasons. Castlereagh became war minister again between April 1807 and September 1809, a period that saw the beginning of the Peninsular War and the disaster of the Walcheren expedition. Criticism of Castlereagh's handling of the Walcheren affair by George Canning led to a duel between the two men in September 1809.

Castlereagh returned to office as foreign secretary in February 1812. During 1813 and 1814 he spent much time on the Continent (a new departure for a British foreign secretary), keeping the anti-Napoleon coalition together. He remained abroad after the signing of the Treaty of Paris in May 1814 and played a leading role in the Congress of Vienna, so becoming one of the principal architects of the post-Napoleonic settlement in Europe. With the duke of Wellington, he chose Saint Helena as a suitable place of exile for the fallen Napoleon.

After 1815 Castlereagh became identified in the public mind with the repressive domestic policies of Lord Liverpool's government. His austere manner and disdain for criticism made him unpopular. When he committed suicide in 1822 as a result of growing depression and unwitting involvement in a homosexual scandal he was widely hated. Crowds cheered as he was buried in Westminster Abbey. His friend Lord Cornwallis found him "so cold that nothing can warm him," while Louis de Caulaincourt thought him "just and passionless" (*Dictionary of National Biography* 1909, p. 1244). But for all that his had been one of the major contributions to the construction of a Europe after Napoleon.

Related entries: Canning, George; Great Britain; Vienna, Congress of; Walcheren Expedition

Suggestions for further reading:
Derry, John W. 1976. *Castlereagh*. London: Allen Lane.
Dictionary of National Biography. 1909. Vol. 18: 1233–1245.
Hinde, Wendy. 1981. *Castlereagh*. London: Collins.
Webster, Charles K. 1950. *The Foreign Policy of Castlereagh*. London: G. Bell.

Catholic Church

The religious question was one of the most serious facing Napoleon when he became first consul in 1799. During the Revolution the Catholic Church had lost its property (converted into *biens nationaux*), been subjected to the Civil Constitution of the Clergy, and faced official attempts to replace Catholicism with new "civic" religions, such as the Cult of the Supreme Being. But the major conflict arose from the division of the clergy into the constitutional, who accepted the Civil Constitution, and the refractory, who refused it and became effectively outlaws. This split was a major factor in the rising in the Vendée, which kept many French troops tied down in western France.

After his victory at Marengo in July 1800 Napoleon opened negotiations with Pope Pius VII. The result was the Concordat of 1801, which put an end to the schism in the clergy and brought religious peace to France. Napoleon could take credit for the reconciliation of church and state. Pius VII came to Paris, albeit under duress, for Napoleon's coronation in December 1804, but pope and emperor were bound to clash over Italian affairs. Politics threatened to disrupt the religious agreement. When Napoleon annexed the Papal States in 1808–1809 Pius excommunicated him. He had the pope seized and imprisoned at Fontainebleau. This humiliation of the pontiff served to revive religious passions at the time when the empire had to face its greatest and eventually fatal crisis and contributed strongly to opposition to Napoleon in France and among Catholics everywhere.

Napoleon had succeeded early in reconciling Catholics, especially the conservative French peasantry, to his rule, without antagonizing the influential anticlerical elements in France. But by an ironic turn of events his thirst for domination of Italy and Europe and harassment of the head of the Church contributed to his loss of popularity and his downfall.

Related entries: Concordat; Papacy; Pius VII, Pope

Suggestions for further reading:
Dansette, Adrien. 1961. *Religious History of Modern France*. 2 vols. London: Nelson.
Gibson, Ralph. 1989. *A Social History of French Catholicism 1789–1914*. London: Routledge.
Hales, Edward Elton Young. 1960. *Revolution and Papacy, 1769–1846*. London: Eyre and Spottiswoode.
———. 1962. *Napoleon and the Pope*. London: Eyre and Spottiswoode.
Hufton, Olwen. 1983. "The Reconstruction of a Church, 1796–1801," in Gwynne Lewis and Colin Lucas, eds., *Beyond the Terror: Essays in French Regional and Social History*. Cambridge: Cambridge University Press, pp. 21–52.
Jedin, Hubert, ed. 1981. *History of the Church, Vol. VII: The Church between Revolution and Restoration*. London: Burns and Oates.
MacManners, John. 1969. *The French Revolution and the Church*. London: Society for the Promotion of Christian Knowledge.

Caulaincourt, Armand Augustin Louis de, Marquis de (1773–1827)

Born into a noble family with a long military tradition, under Napoleon Caulaincourt became a skilful diplomat and was foreign minister at the time of the emperor's downfall. Despite his origins, he fought with distinction in the armies of the Republic in the Vendée and in Germany, and by 1799 had risen from trooper to colonel. Napoleon, probably on the advice of Charles-Maurice de Talleyrand, sent Caulaincourt on a diplomatic mission to Saint Petersburg in 1801 and appointed him an aide-de-camp in 1802. As such he was involved in the kidnapping of the duke of Enghien in 1803, while as grand master of the horse in 1804 he supervised the efficient movement of the emperor throughout his territories and was responsible for his personal security.

Caulaincourt became a general in 1805 and was with Napoleon at the Battles of Austerlitz, Jena, and Friedland. Between 1807 and 1811 he was ambassador to Russia, where he tried to promote moderation and peace and established cordial personal relations with Tsar Alexander I. Caulaincourt advised Napoleon against the invasion of Russia in 1812, but was in regular attendance throughout the campaign and after the retreat from Moscow accompanied Napoleon on his journey to Paris. Unlike the perpetually devious Talleyrand, Caulaincourt always spoke his mind directly to Napoleon and never intrigued behind his back.

In November 1813 Napoleon appointed Caulaincourt foreign minister in succession to Hugues Bernard Maret. Caulaincourt made use of his good relations with Alexander I to try to secure honorable peace terms for France, but Napoleon rejected all his efforts. Acting as intermediary with the tsar,

Caulaincourt settled the terms of Napoleon's first abdication. He again served as foreign minister during the Hundred Days, and after the Restoration was allowed to live in retirement on his estates. In 1822–1823 he compiled valuable memoirs using notes he had made during his career. The authentic version was eventually published in 1933, and two volumes appeared in English: *With Napoleon in Russia* (New York, 1935) and *No Peace with Napoleon* (1936).

Related entries: Abdication, First; Alexander I, Tsar of Russia; Diplomatic Service; Hundred Days

Suggestions for further reading:
Caulaincourt, Armand Augustin Louis de. 1930. *Memoirs of General de Caulaincourt, Duke of Vicenza,* ed. Jean Hanoteau. 3 vols. London: Cassell.
Caulaincourt, Armand Augustin Louis de. 1935. *With Napoleon in Russia,* ed. George Libaire. New York: William Morrow.
Whitcomb, Edward A. 1979. *Napoleon's Diplomatic Service.* Durham, NC: Duke University Press.

Censorship

Napoleon as first consul and emperor imposed ever increasing restrictions on freedom of expression in France, with provisions that were then extended throughout his conquered domains. Freedom of the press had been declared by the Revolution in 1789, but censorship of the stage was reimposed in 1794, and under the Directory agitation for the overthrow of the government was made a criminal offence. But censorship was made much more rigorous under the consulate. From September 1800 all new books were examined by the police before publication, while five dramatic censors reported on the moral and political content of new plays to the minister of the interior, whose authorization was necessary for their staging. Similarly sixty of the seventy-three newspapers published in Paris were banned, and the contents of the thirteen survivors strictly supervised by the Press Bureau. Outside Paris the only newspapers allowed were those authorized by the prefects.

Censorship became most stringent in 1810. The newly created imperial censor or *Directeur Général de l'imprimerie et de la librairie* supervised all newspapers, and in 1811 the number of Paris papers was reduced to four, while each department was to have only one. The censor also read all manuscripts before publication, with orders to reject all content deemed harmful to the dignity of the throne or the interests of the empire. At the same time the minister of police vetted all stage plays, and theaters could only be opened by order of Napoleon himself.

Despite all the restrictions critical authors such as Benjamin Constant, René de Chateaubriand, and Mme. de Staël did find ways of making their views known, and in the *Acte Additionnel* during the Hundred Days of 1815 freedom of publication was guaranteed for almost all publications. This belated liberalism on Napoleon's part, however, was to no avail. Not only in France but throughout his empire severe measures had been taken in a vain attempt to silence Napoleon's critics.

Related entries: Press

Suggestions for further reading:
Arnold, Eric A. 1979. *Fouché, Napoleon and the General Police.* Washington: University Press of America.
———. 1994. *A Documentary Survey of Napoleonic France.* Lanham, MD: University Press of America, pp. 37–38, 297–305.
———. 1996. *A Documentary Survey of Napoleonic France: A Supplement.* Lanham, MD: University Press of America, pp. 64–70.
Holtman, Robert B. 1950. *Napoleonic Propaganda.* Baton Rouge: Louisiana State University Press.

Centralization

Napoleon was the true heir of the Revolution in increasing the power of central government in France, imposing a uniformity of institutions throughout the country, and removing any intermediaries between the individual and the state. His reforms in local government, appointment of prefects, codification of law, education, the collection of statistics, and taxation all aimed at centralization and control. Delpierre, a member of the Tribunate under the consulate, expressed what became the Napoleonic ideal: "the chain of command descends without interruption from the minister to the citizen and transmits the law and the orders of the government into every corner of society with the speed of an electric current." Excessive centralization, usually identified with Jacobinism but more properly Napoleonic, was long seen as making French government too remote and bureaucratic, but the trend was only reversed with the decentralizing reforms of the 1980s.

Related entries: Education; Law, Codification of; Local Government; Prefects; Statistics; Taxation

Suggestions for further reading:
Bergeron, Louis. 1981. *France under Napoleon*. Princeton: Princeton University Press.
Church, Clive H. 1981. *Revolution and Red Tape: The French Ministerial Bureaucracy 1770–1850*. Oxford: Clarendon Press.

Champagny, Jean-Baptiste de Nompère de (1756–1834)

The son of a cavalry officer, Champagny became a hardworking and faithful diplomat and minister for Napoleon, but he lacked initiative and the flair of his more flamboyant cohorts. He had been active in political life in the early years of the Revolution, but was imprisoned during the Terror. His political career was revived by Napoleon after the coup of

18 Brumaire with his appointment to the Council of State, specializing in naval matters. Champagny served as ambassador to Vienna between 1801 and 1804, owing his advance to the patronage of Charles-Maurice de Talleyrand.

On his return to France he succeeded Jean-Antoine Chaptal as minister of the interior, where he showed himself to be a competent administrator but too docile even for Napoleon, who was dismissive about his lack of initiative. As minister of foreign affairs between August 1807 and April 1811, he consulted his predecessor, Talleyrand, rather more than Napoleon knew or would have appreciated. Champagny's relations with Klemens von Metternich, then Austrian ambassador, were especially cool. Metternich despised what he saw as Champagny's sycophancy toward Napoleon. However, the two men did collaborate in negotiating Napoleon's marriage to Marie-Louise.

Champagny's docility did have its limits. When he warned Napoleon against the invasion of Russia in 1811 he was demoted to the post of intendant of the Domains of the Crown and replaced by Hugues-Bernard Maret. During the Russian campaign Champagny was Marie-Louise's secretary of state and acted as the chief intermediary between the court in Paris and the army in the field. He rallied to Napoleon during the Hundred Days and was subsequently in disgrace after the Restoration. Throughout his career Champagny prided himself on making the bureaucratic machines under his control run more smoothly and efficiently. But this valuable if unspectacular work led to his being overshadowed by such outstanding figures as Chaptal and Talleyrand.

Related entries: Centralization

Suggestions for further reading:
Church, Clive H. 1981. *Revolution and Red Tape: The French Ministerial Bureaucracy 1770–1850*. Oxford: Clarendon Press.

Chaptal, Jean Antoine
(1756–1832)

One of the most remarkable figures of his age, Chaptal gained renown as industrial chemist, entrepreneur, and Napoleon's minister of the interior between 1800 and 1804. Born into a family of small landowners in the Cévennes, before the Revolution Chaptal had founded a chemical factory at Montpellier where he had applied the new theoretical chemistry of Antoine Lavoisier to industrial processes with great success. A supporter of the Revolution, he became active in politics, but fell foul of the Terror. Chaptal was saved from the guillotine by Lazare Carnot and placed in charge of the gunpowder factory at Grenelle, where he speeded up the manufacturing process, allowing the insatiable needs of the Revolutionary armies to be met successfully.

Under the consulate Napoleon appointed Chaptal to the Council of State, where he drafted the law of February 1800 which provided France with its enduring structure of prefects and local government. Promoted to minister of the interior in November 1800, Chaptal not only showed himself to be an extremely efficient administrator but also took far-reaching initiatives that proved of lasting significance. During Chaptal's tenure of office channels of command and communication with the prefects were improved; standards of cleanliness and care in hospitals and prisons in Paris were improved; and new construction of canals, roads, and public buildings was begun. Most originally, the *École des Mines* and *Conservatoire des Arts et Métiers* were established, providing technical education combining theory and practical application in the manner that Chaptal himself practiced in his own factories. With the help of a team of like-minded administrators he provided official encouragement for new industrial initiatives, but with mixed success.

Chaptal resigned as minister in July 1804, allegedly in a fit of pique when he thought (probably wrongly) that Napoleon was having an affair with his mistress, the actress Thérèse Bourgoin. He remained a member of the Senate, of which he became treasurer, but devoted most of his time to his chemical factories, especially a large plant at Neuilly, near Paris. He also turned his property at Chanteloup into a model farm, experimenting with the cultivation of sugar beets. His support for Napoleon during the Hundred Days lost him favor for a while, but from 1818 onward his advice was valued by governments concerned with France's expanding factory system and the wine industry. Chaptal wrote several books, including popularizing works on chemistry and a major study of French industry, published in 1819.

Related entries: Education; Industry; Local Government

Suggestions for further reading:
Bergeron, Louis. 1981. *France under Napoleon.* Princeton: Princeton University Press.
Church, Clive H. 1981. *Revolution and Red Tape: The French Ministerial Bureaucracy 1770–1850.* Oxford: Clarendon Press.
Crosland, Maurice Pierre. 1967. *The Society of Arcueil: A View of French Science at the Time of Napoleon.* London: Heinemann.
Lyons, Martyn. 1994. *Napoleon Bonaparte and the Legacy of the French Revolution.* London: Macmillan.

Charles, Archduke of Austria
(Karl von Habsburg)
(1771–1847)

The brother of Francis I and London's favorite Austrian general, Charles was one of Napoleon's most able military opponents, but constantly hampered by the inadequacies of the Austrian military machine. He had entered the army in 1790 and attained some famous successes during the revolutionary wars, notably in 1796 when his defeat of the armies of Jean Moreau and Jean-Baptiste Jourdan forced the French to abandon the right bank of the Rhine and earned Charles acclaim as the savior of Germany. But he was denied a political role by court intrigue, and by the time he was sent to Italy to revitalize the Austrian army against Napoleon it was too late. In 1799 Charles again inflicted defeats on the French in Germany before being forced to resign his command. However, renewed Austrian defeat in 1800 led to the downfall of his principal rival, Baron Franz von Thugut, and in 1801 Charles was named field marshal, president of the Imperial War Council, and minister of war.

An epileptic and of a sensitive nature, a combination that left him prone to debilitating crises of self-doubt, Charles now faced a long battle for military reform in a highly conservative society. He succeeded in streamlining the military administration and abolished lifelong service for conscripts. But his efforts were hampered by opposition from the nobility and financial constraints, and he was aware that Austria was in no condition to renew the fight against Napoleon. However, his advice was ignored, and he lost all his offices when Austria renewed the war in 1805. Sent to Italy, he achieved Austria's only real success of the war, defeating André Masséna at Caligiero. The disaster of Austerlitz proved that Charles had been right in his view of Austrian unpreparedness for war.

Recalled again after the defeat, Charles was named *Generalissimus,* with command of all forces in wartime and a supervisory role in peace. Resuming his attempts at reform, he created a military reserve and reorganized the general staff. But he still faced interference and criticism from enemies at court and was reduced to treating the symptoms of problems, not their causes, in an outdated, class-ridden system more suitable to the age of Frederick the Great than that of Napoleon. Reluctantly giving in to pressure for a new war in 1809, he was counting on a general uprising of the German people against Napoleon, which never came. While he checked Napoleon at Essling, his defeat at Wagram led to Napoleon's occupation of Vienna and Charles's final downfall. While still acting as adviser to his brother, he devoted the rest of his life essentially to his family and to writings on military affairs, of which the *Principles of Strategy* (1813) was widely acclaimed and translated into several languages.

Charles is remembered as a courageous soldier, but his weakness against Napoleon was that, aware of Austrian deficiencies, he was unwilling to risk his army to gain total victory. "The first lost battle," he wrote in 1809 before the Wagram campaign, "is the death sentence of the monarchy and the present dynasty" (Gates 1997, p. 121). This perception, combined with his sensitive character, meant that he would never be a renowned leader of men like Napoleon or Wellington.

Related entries: Austria; Danube Campaigns; Essling, Battle of; Francis I, Emperor of Austria; Wagram, Battle of

Suggestions for further reading:
Brauer, Kinley, and William E. Wright, eds. 1990. *Austria in the Age of the French Revolution, 1789–1815.* Minneapolis: Center for Austrian Studies, University of Minnesota.
Gates, David. 1997. *The Napoleonic Wars, 1803–15.* London: Edward Arnold.
Rodger, A. B. 1964. *The War of the Second Coalition, 1798–1801.* New York: Oxford University Press.
Rothenberg, Gunther E. 1982. *Napoleon's Great Adversaries: The Archduke Charles and the Austrian Army, 1792–1813.* London: Batsford.
———. 1982. "The Archduke Charles and the Question of Popular Participation in War," in *Consortium on Revolutionary Europe: Proceedings 1982,* pp. 214–224.

Charles IV, King of Spain
(1742–1819)

*O*f decidedly mediocre character and abilities, and unprepared for rule, Charles succeeded to the throne of Spain in 1788, but throughout his reign was dominated by his wife, Maria Luisa of Parma, and her lover, Manuel Godoy. Between 1801 and 1808 he supported Napoleon's political and economic policies, while Godoy became ever more unpopular. On 17 March 1808 a rising known as the Tumult of Aranjuez forced Charles to dismiss Godoy, and two days later he was forced to abdicate in favor of his son, Ferdinand VII. He appealed to Napoleon, hoping to be restored, but in the fateful meeting at Bayonne both he and Ferdinand were forced to renounce the throne in favor of Joseph Bonaparte. Charles spent his remaining years in exile, at first at Compiègne and Marseille, before in 1812 settling in Rome, where he died on 20 January 1819, just three weeks after his formidable wife.

Related entries: Ferdinand VII, King of Spain; Godoy, Manuel; Spain

Suggestions for further reading:
Hilt, Douglas. 1987. *The Troubled Trinity: Godoy and the Spanish Monarchs.* Tuscaloosa: University of Alabama Press.
Lovett, Gabriel H. 1965. *Napoleon and the Birth of Modern Spain.* 2 vols. New York: New York University Press.
Lynch, John. 1989. *Bourbon Spain, 1700–1808.* Oxford: Basil Blackwell.

Chateaubriand, François Auguste René, Vicomte de
(1768–1848)

*O*ne of the first great French Romantic writers, by 1800 Chateaubriand, the son of a minor Breton nobleman, had already traveled in the American wilderness, fought in the *émigré* armies against the Revolution, and almost starved to death in exile in London. But the publication of his *Atala* (1801) and especially *Le Génie du Christianisme* (*The Spirit of Christianity,* 1802) won him the approval of Napoleon at a time when the first consul was seeking reconciliation with Catholicism. Chateaubriand was appointed as secretary to the French embassy in Rome, but he resigned after the assassination of the duke of Enghien. Back in France in 1807, Chateaubriand's literary fame grew. Napoleon tried to win back his support by securing his election to the Académie Française in 1811, but secure in the protection of society hostesses such as Madame Récamier, Chateaubriand was never reconciled. After the Restoration he resumed his diplomatic career, but his relationship with all governments remained difficult. In his partly fictional autobiography, the *Mémoires d'outre-tombe,* Chateaubriand exaggerated his role in events. He said of Napoleon: "He threw himself on the universe and shook it" (Furet 1992, p. 222).

Related entries: Romanticism

Suggestions for further reading:
Chateaubriand, François Auguste René de. 1965. *The Memoirs of Chateaubriand,* ed. Robert Baldick. Harmondsworth, England: Penguin.
Furet, François. 1992. *Revolutionary France, 1770–1880.* Oxford: Basil Blackwell.
Sieburg, Friedrich. 1961. *Chateaubriand.* London: George Allen and Unwin.

Cherasco, Treaty of
(28 April 1796)

*T*he agreement that ended the opening phase of Napoleon's first Italian campaign compelled King Victor Amadeus of Piedmont to withdraw from the war. He granted the French free passage over the river Po and garrisons in the towns of Cuneo, Ceva, and Tortona. Of little significance in itself, Cherasco played an important part in building up Napoleon's military reputation and international fame.

Related entries: Italian Campaigns

Suggestions for further reading:
Chandler, David G. 1974. *The Campaigns of Napoleon: The Mind and Method of History's Greatest Soldier.* New York: Macmillan.
Jackson, Sir William Godfrey Fothergill. 1953. *Attack in the West: Napoleon's First Campaign Re-read Today.* London: Eyre and Spottiswoode.

Chouannerie

The violent opposition to the Republic in the inland rural areas of western France, which had started in 1792, continued to be a thorn in the side of Napoleonic government, especially in its early years. Conscription, royalist agitation, and British support led to a rising in Brittany, Anjou, Maine, and lower Normandy in the autumn of 1799 that briefly appeared threatening to the consulate. The British landed supplies in Brittany, and in October *chouans* (peasants), among whose leaders was Georges Cadoudal, momentarily seized the important towns of Le Mans, Nantes, and La Roche-Bernard. Napoleon employed a typical mixture of ruthlessness and conciliation in dealing with *chouannerie*. Military action and the murder of several *chouan* leaders in 1800 were followed by an amnesty, while the Concordat of 1801 helped calm Catholic opposition. But a form of politicized banditry persisted in the west, and there was always a chance that with good leadership and British support it could turn once again into insurrection. After 1805, however, with Cadoudal and the other principal leaders dead, the security forces were in control of all but the most isolated and impenetrable areas. But supporters of the regime still lived precarious lives, and in 1815 new leaders arose to call "Whites" to arms against Napoleon in a form akin to the White Terror. Royalist leaders, however, had never been enthusiastic about *chouannerie* and its chiefs, giving more support to the more organized and controllable resistance of the Vendée.

Related entries: Cadoudal, Georges; Conscription

Suggestions for further reading:
Godechot, Jacques. 1981. *The Counter-Revolution: Doctrine and Action, 1789–1804.* Princeton: Princeton University Press.
Hutt, Maurice. 1983. *Chouannerie and Counter-Revolution.* 2 vols. Cambridge: Cambridge University Press.
Sutherland, Donald. 1982. *The Chouans: the Social Origins of Popular Counter-Revolution in Upper Brittany, 1770–1796.* New York: Oxford University Press.
Tilly, Charles. 1976. *The Vendée.* Cambridge: Harvard University Press.

Cisalpine Republic

Created by Napoleon in 1797 with the support of Italian revolutionaries, the Cisalpine Republic was the principal "sister" republic in Italy during the period of French control. After defeating the Austrians during his first Italian campaign, Napoleon organized the Duchy of Milan and other conquered territories as the Lombard Republic, intending to use it as a personal political power base. The Directory had to accept Napoleon's policy, and he encouraged revolutionaries in the Duchy of Modena and the papal states of Ferrara and Bologna, south of the river Po, to proclaim the Cispadane Republic. In 1797 Napoleon joined the Cispadane with the Austrian possessions of Milan and Mantua, the Valtelline, and western Venetia to form the Cisalpine Republic, with Milan as its capital. Swept away by the armies of the Second Coalition in 1799, it was revived by the French in 1800, renamed the Republic of Italy in 1801, with Napoleon as president, before being transformed into the Kingdom of Italy in 1805, with Napoleon as king and Eugène de Beauharnais as viceroy.

The republic was independent in name only: the two constitutions imposed by Napoleon in 1797 and 1798 effectively restricted democratic participation, and a series of purges removed the radical revolutionaries from government. The Cisalpine had to maintain an army under French command, subsidize a French army on its soil, and exclude British imports. Nevertheless middle-class revolutionaries welcomed the partial export of the principles of the Revolution to Italy.

The country was divided into departments, allowing the uniform application of the law; a wide measure of press freedom was enjoyed; torture was abolished; and economic reforms stimulated the circulation of goods within the newly unified territory. Church lands were confiscated, religious orders suppressed, and civil marriage introduced; state-supported schools replaced church schools, and religious toleration was proclaimed. The ordinary people, suffering from land shortage, taxation, and conscription, gained little by these changes, but the memory of the Cisalpine Republic did serve to stimulate Italian nationalist ideas in the nineteenth century. Neither the Directory nor Napoleon was interested in the unification of the whole of Italy, but by joining together a series of states, partially overcoming the spirit of particularism, and forcing people from different regions to work together, the Cisalpine had helped to strengthen the belief that unity was more than an impractical dream.

Related entries: Italian Campaigns

Suggestions for further reading:
Hearder, Harry. 1983. *Italy in the Age of the Risorgimento, 1790–1870*. London and New York: Longman.
Woolf, Stuart J. 1991. *A History of Italy, 1700–1860: The Social Constraints on Political Change*. London: Routledge.

Ciudad Rodrigo, Siege of (January 1812)

*T*he taking of the fortress of Ciudad Rodrigo on the river Agueda by the duke of Wellington was crucial in destroying the French hold on northern Spain during the Peninsular War. Ciudad Rodrigo, commanding the Spanish side of the "northern corridor" between Spain and Portugal, had been blockaded and taken by Michel Ney and André Masséna in 1810. But Wellington ousted the French after heavy fighting in bitter weather during an eleven-day siege starting on 19 January 1812. This allowed the British commander to advance to the key city of Salamanca in June.

Related entries: Peninsular War; Wellington, Duke of

Suggestions for further reading:
Gates, David. 1986. *The Spanish Ulcer: A History of the Peninsular War*. London: Allen and Unwin.
Glover, Michael. 1974. *The Peninsular War, 1807–14*. Hampden, CT: Archon Books.

Civil Code

*T*oward the end of his life Napoleon declared that he had counted for his survival as much on his Civil Code of 1804 as on his military victories. The work of a commission on which Jean Portalis was the dominant figure, the Code Napoléon (as it came to be called) placed the new system of law created by the Revolution on a sound footing and fulfilled the unifying ambitions of different currents of eighteenth-century thought, including Enlightenment thinkers and reformist ministers of the ancien régime.

The preamble to the Code declared: "Roman laws, decrees, general or particular customs, statutes and regulations cease to have the force of general or special law in

The Napoleonic Code Crowned by Time *by Jean Baptiste Mauzaisse portrays the significance of the Napoleonic Code and its lasting influence in every part of Europe that came under Napoleon's control. In this extravagant portrayal, Time blesses Napoleon as he writes the inspired code. (Giraudon/Art Resource)*

matters which are the subject of the laws contained in the present Code." The privileges and inequalities embodied in the innumerable codes and customs of the ancien régime were definitively abolished. The ideas of personal liberty, freedom of conscience, and equality before the law were consecrated in the Code. But the aspects concerned with property were equally significant in reassuring property owners, above all the purchasers of *biens nationaux,* that their position was safe under Napoleonic rule. Property rights were made as absolute as possible, and while the Code urged makers of wills not to divide property overmuch, by granting provisions for divisions of estates it helped to consecrate small as well as large property.

The Code also introduced the notion of *bonnes moeurs,* bringing the law to bear against behavior seen as offensive to public morality, while the section on the family reinforced the patriarchal power of the husband as head of the household, relegating women to a position of inferiority. If peasants and bourgeois property owners gained most from the Code, women were the main losers. The equality of the sexes proclaimed by the Revolution was denied by Napoleon, the "Mediterranean" patriarch.

The Code was introduced in those regions of Napoleon's empire where the French succeeded in establishing stable rule, principally in western Germany, the Low Countries, and northern Italy. Here many of its provisions were retained by the restored regimes after 1815. It is still the basis of French law and that of more than twenty other countries worldwide today.

Related entries: Law, Codification of; Portalis, Jean Etienne Marie

Suggestions for further reading:
Arnold, Eric A., ed. 1994. *A Documentary Survey of Napoleonic France.* Lanham, MD: University Press of America, pp. 151–164.
Goy, Joseph. 1989. "Civil Code," in François Furet and Mona Ozouf, eds., *Critical Dictionary of the French Revolution.* Cambridge: Harvard University Press.
Holtman, Robert B. 1967. *The Napoleonic Revolution.* Philadelphia: Lippincott.
Schwarz, Bernard, ed. 1956. *The Code Napoleon and the Common Law World.* New York: New York University Press.

Clary, Bernadine Eugénie Désirée (1779–1860)

*D*ésirée, as she was known, daughter of a prosperous Marseille silk merchant, was reputedly the big love of the young Napoleon's life, but it is difficult to distinguish romantic legend from fact. The Clary and Bonaparte families first met in 1794 when Joseph Bonaparte as secretary of the Committee of Public Safety was apparently instrumental in obtaining the release of Désirée's brother, Etienne, from prison. Joseph married Désirée's sister, Julie Clary, on 1 August 1794. Napoleon became infatuated with the vivacious Désirée, but she was only fourteen years old, and after he returned to Paris she responded hardly at all to Napoleon's correspondence. In the meantime he fell in love with and married Joséphine de Beauharnais.

The desirable Désirée had several suitors and was set to marry General Leonard Duphot, but he was assassinated before they could tie the knot. She eventually married Jean-Baptiste Bernadotte on 17 August 1798. A son, Oscar, was born on 4 July 1799, and Napoleon became his godfather.

When Bernadotte was elected crown prince of Sweden in 1810 Désirée reputedly had to consult a map to find out where it was. After a brief visit to the Nordic kingdom she returned to live in Paris, ignoring Bernadotte's adherence to the coalition against Napoleon. Bernadotte became King Charles XIV of Sweden in 1818, but Désirée remained in Paris until 1823, when Oscar married Joséphine, daughter of Eugène de Beauharnais. As Queen Desideria she finally became well respected in Sweden, as consort to Bernadotte and after 1844 Queen Mother to Oscar. She died in Stockholm on 17 December 1860.

Related entries: Bernadotte, Jean-Baptiste Jules

Suggestions for further reading:
Palmer, Alan. 1990. *Bernadotte: Napoleon's Marshal, Sweden's King.* London: John Murray.
Ratcliffe, Bertram. 1981. *Prelude to Fame: An Account of the Early Life of Napoleon up to the Battle of Montenotte.* London: Warne.

Coalitions

*F*irst Coalition: formed in 1792 against Revolutionary France, by 1794 it comprised Prussia, Austria, most of the German states, Piedmont-Sardinia, Naples, other minor Italian states, Spain, Great Britain, and the United Provinces of the Netherlands. Prussia and Spain made peace with France in 1795. Napoleon's defeat of Austria in his first Italian campaign left only Britain still at war.

Second Coalition: formed in late 1798 following Napoleon's Egyptian campaign, it comprised Britain, the Ottoman Empire, Austria, Russia, and some minor European states. The coalition fell apart after Napoleon's second Italian campaign and French victories in Germany. Britain made peace by the Peace of Amiens.

Third Coalition: formed in 1805 after the establishment of the Kingdom of Italy and

Napoleon's annexation of Piedmont, Elba, and Genoa. The major participants were Austria, Russia, and Britain, but it was short-lived and disintegrated after Napoleon's victory at Austerlitz (2 December 1805).

Fourth Coalition: formed by Britain, Prussia, and Russia after Napoleon's creation of the Confederation of the Rhine and his bullying treatment of neutral Prussia. It dissolved after the battles of Jena-Auerstädt and Friedland. Britain, however, remained at war and would be so continuously until Napoleon's defeat.

Fifth Coalition: alliance in 1808–1809 between Austria and Britain, with support from rebellious Spain. The Austrians hoped for a national rising in Germany against Napoleon, but were defeated decisively at Wagram.

Sixth Coalition: alliance formed by Russia and Sweden after Tsar Alexander I withdrew from Napoleon's Continental System. It was followed by Napoleon's invasion of Russia and subsequent disastrous retreat.

Seventh Coalition: formed in 1813 by Russia, Sweden, and Prussia, with backing from Britain, it was joined by Austria and other German states as Napoleon's armies retreated across Germany. Naples under Joachim Murat joined in January 1814. This was the alliance which, by opening up a second front from Spain, finally defeated Napoleon and forced his first abdication in April 1814.

Eighth Coalition: formed to oppose Napoleon during the Hundred Days, it comprised the same countries as the Seventh Coalition, plus the new Kingdom of the Netherlands. This was the alliance that defeated Napoleon at Waterloo on 18 June 1815.

Suggestions for further reading:
Blanning, T. C. W. 1995. *The Napoleonic Wars 1803–1815.* London: Edward Arnold.
Craig, Gordon A. 1966. "Problems of Coalition Warfare: The Military Alliance against Napoleon," in his *War, Politics and Diplomacy.* London: Weidenfeld and Nicolson.

Deutsch, Harold C. 1938. *The Genesis of Napoleonic Imperialism.* Cambridge: Harvard University Press.
Esdaile, Charles J. 1995. *The Wars of Napoleon.* London and New York: Longman.
Muir, Rory. 1996. *Britain and the Defeat of Napoleon.* New Haven: Yale University Press.
Ross, Steven T. 1981. *European Diplomatic History, 1789–1815.* Malabar, FL: Krieger.
Schroeder, Paul. 1987. "The Collapse of the Second Coalition," *Journal of Modern History* 59, pp. 244–290.
Schroeder, Paul W. 1994. *The Transformation of European Politics 1763–1848.* New York: Oxford University Press.

Code of Criminal Procedure

Promulgated in 1808, this Code completed the organization of the justice system decreed by Napoleon as first consul by the Law of 27 Ventôse Year VIII (18 March 1800). This law had abolished the Revolutionary principle of the election of judges and allowed the first consul to appoint almost all legal officials, though judges were given tenure for life as a guarantee of their independence. The new Code authorized the appointment of judges by prefects and the quashing of a jury's verdict by the Senate if it was held to be against the interests of the state. The overall effect of the Code of Criminal Procedure was to favor the prosecution over the defendant and to strengthen Napoleon's authoritarian government.

Related entries: Law, Codification of

Suggestions for further reading:
Holtman, Robert B. 1967. *The Napoleonic Revolution.* Philadelphia: Lippincott.

Commercial Code

This Code of 1807 was intended to regularize conformity in business transactions, but it was the least comprehensive of the Napoleonic Codes and offered little that was new. It established principles for the responsibilities of shareholders in joint stock companies, but left many anomalies and took little account of the considerable development of commercial techniques during the eighteenth century. Thus, although it provided a blueprint for company law in the nineteenth century, it needed constant updating. The provisions of the Code reflect Napoleon's prejudices against the mortgaging of real property and against money lending at interest.

Related entries: Economy; Law, Codification of

Suggestions for further reading:
Holtman, Robert B. 1967. *The Napoleonic Revolution*. Philadelphia: Lippincott.

Concordat

Napoleon as first consul in 1800 sought reconciliation with the Catholic Church for several reasons: to help end the rebellion in the Vendée; to improve the international standing of the consulate; and to make use of the clergy as representatives of the established political order in the dioceses and villages of France and in conquered Catholic territories. Following his victory at Marengo Napoleon could negotiate with the new pope, Pius VII, from a position of strength. Long, tortuous, and secret negotiations with the papal representatives culminated in the journey to Paris of the papal secretary of state, Cardinal Ercole Consalvi. The finished document was signed by the pope in July 1801 but not published until Easter 1802.

The Concordat overturned the Revolutionary principle of the separation of church and state and restored Catholicism to a privileged position as the "religion of the majority of the French people." It provided for the establishment of a new episcopate with bishops nominated by the state

and consecrated by the pope. The bishops chose their own lower clergy, and all clerical salaries were paid by the state. Church property sold as *biens nationaux* remained in the hands of its purchasers. The Organic Articles, added unilaterally by Napoleon, were never accepted by the pope. Freedom of religion was later guaranteed by Napoleon's Civil Code. Sources of conflict remained over investiture and marriage laws, especially divorce, but Napoleon's attempt in 1813 to impose a second "Concordat of Fontainebleau'" giving greater powers to French bishops at Rome's expense, was repudiated by Pius VII and never became operative.

Napoleon achieved his political aim of reuniting the French clergy and rejected criticism from anticlerical ex-revolutionaries in the government and the professions. "They will say I am a papist," he said, "but I am nothing at all. In Egypt I was a Muhammedan; here I will be a Catholic, for the good of the people." In 1817 Pius VII, despite all the personal indignities he had suffered at Napoleon's hands, called the Concordat "the saving act of a Christian and a hero," because it had restored Catholicism in France. It remained in operation until the separation of church and state in 1905.

Related entries: Bernier, Abbé Etienne; Catholic Church; Organic Articles; Pius VII, Pope

Suggestions for further reading:
Arnold, Eric A., ed. 1994. *A Documentary Survey of Napoleonic France*. Lanham, MD: University Press of America, pp. 114–120.
Dansette, Adrien. 1961. *Religious History of Modern France*. 2 vols. London: Nelson.
Hales, Edward Elton Young. 1962. *Napoleon and the Pope*. London: Eyre and Spottiswoode.
Jedin, Hubert, ed. 1981. *History of the Church, Vol. 7: The Church between Revolution and Restoration*. London: Burns and Oates.
Kafker, Frank A., and Laux, James M., eds. 1989. *Napoleon and His Times: Selected Interpretations*. Malibar, FL: Krieger.
Walsh, Henry Horace. 1933. *The Concordat of 1801: A Study of the Problems of Church and State*. New York: Columbia University Press.

Confederation of the Rhine

*F*ollowing his victory at Austerlitz Napoleon was able, on 12 July 1806, to establish the Confederation of the Rhine or *Rheinbund* as a league of sixteen German states, linked into close alliance with France and intended as a buffer between himself and his potential enemies to the east. After the defeat of Prussia in 1806 and Russia in 1807 twenty-three other states joined the Confederation, which eventually encompassed the whole of the old German Reich apart from Austria, Prussia, and lands belonging to Denmark and Sweden. As a result the Holy Roman Empire was abolished, and in return for loyalty and military assistance to France the medium-sized and relatively well-integrated states of the Confederation retained full sovereignty over their territories.

Napoleon and his chief supporter in Germany, Karl von Dalberg, Archbishop of Regensburg-Aschaffenburg, who was named Prince Primate of the Confederation, tried to promote the creation of a central government with a representative Diet, but were fatally hampered by the determination of the states to retain their sovereignty. Collective institutions were never formed, and after his intervention in Spain in 1808 Napoleon was content with mobilizing the resources of the Confederation to feed the French war machine. In 1813 the Confederation fell apart, as its members scrambled to join the Allies. Nevertheless, the events of 1806 and the establishment of the *Rheinbund* represent a historic turning point in German history: the traditional political order was permanently overturned and the foundations were laid for reform of state and society in those western and southern German states, including Bavaria and the Kingdom of Westphalia, where territorial transformations profoundly changed the political landscape.

Related entries: Bavaria, Kingdom of; Berg, Grand Duchy of; Carl August, Duke of Weimar; Frankfurt, Grand Duchy of; Saxony; Westphalia, Kingdom of

Suggestions for further reading:
Schmitt, H. A. 1983. "Germany without Prussia: A Closer Look at the Confederation of the Rhine," *German Studies Review* 6, pp. 9–39.
Shanahan, William O. 1981. "A Neglected Source of German Nationalism: The Confederation of the Rhine, 1806–13," in Michael Palumbo and William O. Shanahan, eds., *Nationalism: Essays in Honor of Louis L. Snyder.* Westport, CT.: Greenwood Press. pp. 106–132.
Sheehan, James J. 1989. *German History, 1770–1866.* Oxford: Clarendon Press.

Conscription

*T*he draft system, first introduced by the Jourdan Law of September 1798 and widened in 1799, 1800, 1802, and 1806, successfully ensured adequate manpower for Napoleon's armies, but evasion and desertion created a serious and growing police problem for his regime. The law, under which all single men who reached the age of twenty in a given year formed the class of that year and were liable to call-up until age twenty-five, fell most heavily on the poorer classes, as wealthier men were allowed to send substitutes in their place. Estimates of the total number mobilized by conscription vary from 1.6 million to 3.6 million, but possibly up to half a million either evaded the draft entirely or deserted and returned to their villages, often at harvest time. Many joined bands of brigands or royalists. The worst crisis arose in 1812–1813, when entire companies of the retreating French armies melted away as they reached the frontiers.

For the peasantry, conscription was seen as a kind of tax that took people rather than money or goods. To remove men from the land was to condemn the land to death. The historian Alan Forrest states: "Over conscription, as over no other single issue, the interests of the state and the local community were seen to come into open conflict, and the state had no other recourse but to repression" (Forrest 1989, p. viii). When draft time approached young men got married in suspiciously large numbers, records of birth dates vanished, and, especially in remote or mountainous regions, men simply disappeared. A sizable number even resorted to self-mutilation so as to be unfit for service.

Pursuit of refractory conscripts by the *gendarmerie* brought country people face to face with the law as never before, tied up police manpower, and became the main point of friction between the village and the state. Nevertheless, by the end of the Napoleonic period the idea of national military service had come to be seen as a normal, if unpopular and resented, feature of life for young French males, whatever the regime in power.

Related entries: Army; *Chouannerie;*
Gendarmerie; Jourdan, Jean–Baptiste

Suggestions for further reading:
Arnold, Eric A. 1966. "Some Observations on the French Opposition to Napoleonic Conscription, 1804–1806," *French Historical Studies* 4, pp. 452–462.
———, ed. 1994. *A Documentary Survey of Napoleonic France.* Lanham, MD: University Press of America. pp. 3–14.
Forrest, Alan. 1989. *Conscripts and Deserters: The Army and French Society during the Revolution and Empire.* New York: Oxford University Press.
Rogers, H. C. B. 1974. *Napoleon's Army.* London: Allen.
Woloch, Isser. 1986. "Napoleonic Conscription: State Power and Civil Society," *Past & Present,* no. 111 (May 1986), pp. 101–129.

Constant, Benjamin (1767–1830)

*T*he Swiss-born writer gained his greatest literary and political fame after 1815, but his relationship with Napoleon illustrates the ambivalent attitudes of many liberals. Constant was appointed to the Tribunate in 1799 thanks to the influence of his mistress, Mme. de Staël, with whom he enjoyed a stormy relationship between 1794 and 1811. But he strongly advocated giving the Tribunate real power and as a consequence was purged in 1802. Constant went into exile and in 1814 supported Jean-Baptiste Bernadotte for the French throne. When Napoleon landed in France at the beginning of the Hundred Days, Constant wrote a violent newspaper diatribe against the modern "Attila" and "Genghis Khan." But within three weeks he joined the Council of State and was primarily responsible for drawing up the *Acte Additionnel,* known as *la benjamine* by contemporaries, which created, very briefly, a liberal empire. In his political writings Constant showed himself equally opposed to despotism and to democracy, which he identified with the tyranny of the majority.

Related entries: *Acte Additionnel;* Staël, Germaine de

Suggestions for further reading:
Constant, Benjamin. 1988. *Political Writings,* trans. and ed. Biancamaria Fontana. Cambridge: Cambridge University Press.
Wood, Dennis. 1993. *Benjamin Constant.* London and New York: Routledge.

Constitutions

*F*rance under Napoleon had four constitutions: that of the Year VIII (13 December 1799), which created the consulate; that of the Year X (2–4 August 1802), which created the Consulate for Life; that of the Year XII (18 May 1804), which created the empire; and finally the *Acte Additionnel* of 22 April 1815 during the Hundred Days.

The Constitution of the Year VIII was the work of Emmanuel Joseph Sieyès, revised by Napoleon. It was, in accordance with Sieyès's principles, "short and obscure." The first consul, chief of state, was named for ten years and the post given to Napoleon by name. The two other consuls had only a consultative role. In a complicated electoral system citizens elected communal notables, who in turn elected departmental notables, who in turn chose national notables. The Senate, composed of eighty members named for life, in theory chose the consuls and the members of the legislative bodies, the Legislative Body *(corps législatif)* and Tribunate. The latter was to discuss laws; the former, an "assembly of mutes," merely to vote on them. A Council of State, named by the first consul, was to draft new laws and judge administrative disputes. The Senate had the responsibility of safeguarding the constitution, but could modify it by a *senatus consultum* as proposed by the consuls. The main effect of the Constitution of the Year VIII was to provide Napoleon with quasi-dictatorial powers.

The Constitution of the Year X, promulgated through *senatus consulta,* further strengthened the Napoleonic dictatorship. Napoleon's appointment as consul for life was approved by plebiscite. The first consul was provided with a Privy Council, and Sieyès's complex and impractical electoral system replaced. Electoral colleges in each department, elected by universal manhood suffrage from among its richest notables, nominated two persons for each opening in the Tribunate or Legislative Body. At the same time, the Tribunate, which had shown some mild opposition to Napoleon, was reduced from one hundred to fifty members.

The creation of the empire by the Constitution of the Year XII transformed the life consulship into a hereditary monarchy. The Constitution regulated succession to the throne, provided the emperor with a salary or "civil list" (equal to that of Louis XVI in 1790), and systematized the formation of a court. The Tribunate was retained, but would be abolished in 1807. Two senatorial commissions were established to safeguard individual liberty and freedom of the press, but were ineffectual.

The final constitution, the *Acte Additionnel,* drafted by Benjamin Constant during the Hundred Days, attempted to reestablish the empire on more liberal lines. It was confirmed by a referendum, which was ignored by the vast majority of the population, and only operated for two months until the defeat at Waterloo on 18 June 1815.

Related entries: *Acte Additionnel;* Consulate; Council of State; Empire; Legislative Body; Plebiscites; Senate; Sieyès, Emmanuel Joseph; Tribunate

Suggestions for further reading:
Arnold, Eric A., ed. 1994. *A Documentary Survey of Napoleonic France.* Lanham, MD: University Press of America, pp. 22–35, 180–204, 348–56.
Bergeron, Louis. 1981. *France under Napoleon.* Princeton: Princeton University Press.
Collins, Irene. 1979. *Napoleon and his Parliaments.* London: Edward Arnold.
Holtman, Robert B. 1967. *The Napoleonic Revolution.* Philadelphia: Lippincott.

Consulate

The consulate, the regime established after the coup of 18 Brumaire, was consolidated by the Constitution of the Year VIII and modified in 1802 by the Constitution of the Year X. The idea of consulship was inspired, as were many of the institutions and symbols of the Revolution, by the Roman Republic and fitted in with the prevalent neoclassicism. Napoleon was first consul, but the original second and third consuls, Emmanuel Joseph Sieyès and Roger Ducos, were soon replaced by Jean-Jacques de Cambacérès and Charles François Lebrun, who were more inclined to accept Napoleon's thinly veiled dictatorship. Napoleon was made consul for life, with power to nominate his successor, by the new Constitution of 1802. The consulate ended with the *senatus consultum* of 18 May 1804, which created the empire

The characteristic pose and stance affected by Napoleon are already apparent in this portrait of the first consul wearing the uniform of the Chasseurs of the Guard. (Giraudon/Art Resource)

and proclaimed Napoleon emperor of the French.

Related entries: Brumaire, Coup of Year VIII; Cambacérès, Jean-Jacques Régis de; Constitutions; Ducos, Roger; Lebrun, Charles François; Sieyès, Emmanuel Joseph

Suggestions for further reading:
Arnold, Eric A., ed. 1994. *A Documentary Survey of Napoleonic France.* Lanham, MD: University Press of America. pp. 16–19, 22–35, 135–138.
Sydenham, M. J. 1974. *The First French Republic, 1792–1804.* London: Batsford.

Continental System

Napoleon by the end of 1806 had defeated Austria, Prussia, and Russia, but could not defeat Great Britain as long as it controlled the seas. The Continental System, closing continental Europe to British goods, was his attempt "to vanquish the sea by the power of the land." The Berlin Decrees of 21 November 1806, declaring Britain to be in a state of blockade, were complemented by the Milan Decrees of 23 November and 17 December. Napoleon believed that through this economic warfare the British economy would be disrupted, causing social and political instability, which would force Britain to give up the fight against him.

The system was imposed on Napoleon's subject states in Europe during 1807 and adopted by Russia after the Treaties of Tilsit in July 1807. The occupation or annexation of Spain and Portugal in 1807–1808, the Papal States in 1809, Holland in 1810, and the Hanseatic towns and Duchy of Oldenburg in 1810–1811 all in theory extended the system. Measures loosening it somewhat through licenses for trade were reversed by the Fontainebleau decree of 18 October 1810. Maintaining the blockade with any effectiveness was obviously dependent on French military dominance, and as this collapsed in 1813–1814, so did the Continental System.

Historians are divided about the efficacy of the Continental System, but it manifestly failed to force Britain to sue for peace. Britain's command of the seas allowed it to trade with the New World, and only when its relations with the United States were bad between 1810 and 1812 was severe disruption caused to British commerce. Smuggling was ignored or even encouraged by governments reluctantly forced into applying the blockade, and this in turn tempted customs officers into corruption. The maritime ports of continental Europe, including the Atlantic seaboard of France, suffered greatly, and this suffering indirectly served to confirm British naval and commercial power. And although Britain was hit by social unrest during the economic crisis of 1810–1811, the political system was not seriously threatened, government credit remained good, and industrial production continued to expand. The progress of the industrial revolution was barely hindered, if at all.

Some areas of the continental interior did benefit from the lack of competition from Britain. In Belgium and the Rhineland trade was reoriented toward continental markets, boosting manufacture of textiles, metals, and wine, especially between 1807 and 1810. The cotton and chemical industries in France itself received a similar fillip. As a result the blockade speeded up the shift of focus of the French economy away from the Atlantic coast toward the interior. However, the mainly agricultural regions of Napoleon's empire suffered, increasing the unpopularity of French rule.

Given French naval weakness and an economy geared to war, the Continental System seemed a logical way of striking at Britain. But it is clear that Napoleon never understood the strength of the British economy, especially the system of government finance. His intervention in Spain in 1808 and the subsequent popular uprising blew an enormous hole in the blockade, which merchants and smugglers everywhere in Europe were eager to exploit. It has been argued that had Napoleon not invaded Russia in 1812 the pressure on Britain could have been maintained. It is difficult to deny, however, that Spain and Russia fatally weakened the Continental System for almost the whole of its period of operation, and that in 1815 Britain's economic advance over its continental rivals was much greater than it would otherwise have been.

Related entries: Berlin Decrees; Economy; Fontainebleau Decree; Great Britain; Milan Decrees

Suggestions for further reading:
Connelly, Owen. 1965. *Napoleon's Satellite Kingdoms.* New York: Free Press.
Crouzet, François. 1964. "Wars, Blockades and Economic Change in Europe, 1792–1815," *Journal of Economic History* 24, pp. 567–588.
Crouzet, François. 1989. "A Serious Cause of Social and Economic Dislocation," in Frank A. Kafker and James L. Laux, eds., *Napoleon and his Times: Selected Interpretations.* Malibar, FL: Krieger, pp. 179–191.
Ellis, Geoffrey. 1981. *Napoleon's Continental Blockade: The Case of Alsace.* Oxford: Clarendon Press.
Hecksher, E. F. 1922. *The Continental System: An Economic Interpretation.* Oxford: Publications of the Carnegie Endowment for International Peace.

Copenhagen, Battle of (2 April 1801)

This action by the British fleet under Admiral Sir Hyde Parker was, together with the death of Tsar Paul I, instrumental in destroying the armed neutrality of the North. Twenty-six British ships of the line, backed by thirty support vessels, bombarded the Danish fleet and the shore batteries of Copenhagen intermittently for five and a half hours, with heavy casualties on both sides. It was on this occasion that Vice-Admiral Horatio Nelson, commanding the British vanguard, famously put his telescope to his blind eye so as not to see Hyde Parker's signals ordering him to stop the engagement with the shore batteries. The action at Copenhagen helped secure British control of the seas and boosted Nelson's reputation as a naval hero.

Related entries: Armed Neutrality; Denmark; Nelson, Horatio, Lord

Coronation

By crowning himself emperor on 2 December 1804 Napoleon, in the words of the historian François Furet, "distanced himself from the Revolution without drawing any nearer to the kings" (Furet 1992, p. 239) of Europe. Using insignia rep-

Coronation of Napoleon I *(1806–1807) by Jacques–Louis David. A gorgeous if inaccurate portrayal of Napoleon's coronation, David's work contains nearly a hundred portraits, including members of the imperial family, the dignitaries of the Empire, Pope Pius VII, and David himself. (Giraudon/Art Resource)*

resenting the "honors of Charlemagne," thereby eliminating the whole Capetian line of kings of France and claiming direct political descent from the great Emperor of the West, Napoleon crowned himself and Joséphine during a three-hour ceremony in the cathedral of Notre Dame in Paris.

The "Carolingian kitsch" ceremonial was conducted on a grand scale, designed to impress the people with the majesty of the new empire, and consecrated by the presence of Pope Pius VII. The pope enthroned Napoleon at the cathedral entrance, thereby adding his blessing to the emperor's elevation. The Bonaparte family and the new grand dignitaries of the empire attended in all their glory, creating petty disputes over precedence worthy of the court of Louis XIV. Carefully orchestrated acclamations and artillery salvoes accompanied the processions of emperor and pope through the streets of Paris.

Napoleon by his oath swore to uphold the principles of the Revolution and "to govern with the sole aim of the interests,

happiness and glory of the French people." But the coronation was also a spectacular confirmation that the Revolution was now over. Napoleon was no longer leader of the French Republic, but hereditary absolute sovereign, surrounded by a court and soon by a new aristocracy. Among the crowd, the six-year-old Jules Michelet, writing fifty years later, recalled only "a mournful and dismal silence" (Furet 1992, p. 248).

Related entries: Beauharnais, Marie Rose Joséphine de; David, Jacques-Louis; Empire; Pius VII, Pope

Suggestions for further reading:
Furet, François. 1992. *Revolutionary France, 1770–1880.* Oxford: Basil Blackwell.
Holtman, Robert B. 1950. *Napoleonic Propaganda.* Baton Rouge: Louisiana State University Press.

Corsica

Napoleon's native island lies about a hundred miles southeast of the

Napleon's birthplace, the Casa Buonaparte in Ajaccio, in a nineteenth-century print. Today it houses a museum dedicated to him. (Alinari/Art Resource).

Mediterranean coast of France. It belonged to the Republic of Genoa until 1768, when it was ceded to France, but between 1729 and 1768 the island had been in a state of revolt for independence under the leadership of Pasquale Paoli, and the struggle had aroused widespread interest and sympathy in Europe. Napoleon was born in the capital, Ajaccio, on 15 August 1769, and he and his brothers remained embroiled in Corsican politics until 1793. Thereafter he only visited it briefly for three days in 1799. Corsica was occupied by the British from February 1794 to November 1796, but from then on remained in French hands, despite ambitious schemes by Britain and Russia to use it as a naval base.

Related entries: Paoli, Pasquale

Suggestions for further reading:
Carrington, Dorothy. 1971. *Granite Island: A Portrait of Corsica*. London: Longman.

Corunna, Battle of (16 January 1809)

La Coruña, the provincial capital of Galicia in northwestern Spain, was first used as a British base during the Peninsular War in 1808. When the British commander, Sir John Moore, then in Salamanca, heard that the main French force under Napoleon and Nicolas Jean Soult was at Leon, he decided to fall back on Corunna. The retreat over the Cantabrian Mountains cost the British some 5,000 men, but 28,000 arrived safely, and on 14 January 1809 a British convoy appeared to evacuate them. Soult's pursuing force approached the town as cavalry and guns were being loaded. On the afternoon of 16 January Soult attacked the British lines, seeking to cut off the harbor, but faced fierce resistance. After three hours of violent combat in rocky terrain Soult gave up the attack. Moore had been fatally wounded and was buried the following morning as the embarkation resumed. Some 27,000 men eventually reached England safely.

Related entries: Moore, Sir John; Peninsular War; Soult, Nicolas Jean de Dieu

Suggestions for further reading:
Hibbert, Christopher. 1961. *Corunna*. London: Batsford.

Council of State

Established in December 1799, the Council of State was Napoleon's principal advisory body under both consulate and empire. It was meant to be a body of experts, chosen entirely by Napoleon, with purely consultative functions and therefore allowed greater freedom for dissent than the Senate, Tribunate, or Legislative Body. Of the twenty-nine first members, ten were lawyers, nine were educational or scientific specialists, and four were military men. The majority of Council members held office for more than five years, providing valuable continuity in the administration. They were paid a stipend of 25,000 francs a year, but slackness could lead to instant dismissal.

The Council was initially divided into five sections—War, Navy, Finance, Law, and Internal Affairs—soon joined by another on foreign relations, and it only met occasionally as a general meeting, normally under Napoleon's presidency. The councillors are known to have discussed over 60,000 questions, including such important matters as the codification of law and the Concordat. The Council was assisted by a special secretariat, while high-flying young civil servants could be attached to sections of the Council as supplementary advisers or *auditeurs*. The Council of State has survived to this day in France in the form of a supreme judicial advisory body and guardian of the constitution.

Related entries: Constitutions

Suggestions for further reading:
Arnold, Eric A., ed. 1996. *A Documentary Survey of Napoleonic France: A Supplement*. Lanham, MD: University Press of America. pp. 18–22.
Church, Clive H. 1981. *Revolution and Red Tape: The French Ministerial Bureaucracy 1770–1850*. Oxford: Clarendon Press.
Freedeman, Charles E. 1961. *The Conseil d'Etat in Modern France*. New York: Columbia University Press.

Counter-Revolution

Opposition to the Revolution was as old as the Revolution itself, but had never constituted a united movement. The term "Counter-Revolution," therefore, can be extended to include the very different political theories of Edmund Burke and Joseph de Maistre, military forces led from abroad by *émigrés,* the rising in the Vendée, and the federalist revolt of 1793 against the overriding authority of Paris. The young Napoleon's actions during the siege of Toulon in December 1793 helped put an end to the greatest threat to the Revolution since 1789. His popularity and heroic image, however, were probably enhanced by the fact that, unlike other generals, his military reputation was made abroad rather than in killing French people at home. The coup of 18 Brumaire, followed by Napoleon's victories in Italy in 1800 and the advent of peace, helped to extinguish serious counterrevolutionary activity. Under Napoleonic rule active royalism took the form of plots to kill him, disguised and secret organizations, and the active *chouannerie,* often indistinguishable from mere banditry.

Related entries: Cadoudal, Georges; *Chouannerie; Émigrés;* Royalists;Vendée Revolt

Suggestions for further reading:

Godechot, Jacques. 1981. *The Counter-Revolution: Doctrine and Action, 1789–1804.* Princeton: Princeton University Press.

Lewis, Gwynne. 1978. *The Second Vendée: the Continuity of Counter-Revolution in the Department of the Gard, 1789–1815.* New York: Oxford University Press.

Sutherland, D. M. G. 1985. *France, 1789–1815: Revolution and Counter-Revolution.* London: Fontana.

Danube Campaigns

*T*he campaign of 1805, which became known as the Austerlitz campaign, the Jena-Auerstädt-Friedland campaign of 1806–1807, and the Wagram campaign of 1809 all show Napoleon at the height of his military powers and provide the best illustrations of his methods of waging war. Between August and December 1805 he won swift and decisive victories over the Austrian and Russian armies, and between September 1806 and June 1807 struck north from the Danube to defeat Prussia and inflict a second defeat on the Russians.

When the Third Coalition went to war in 1805 it hoped that Italy would be the main theater of operations, but Napoleon, transforming his Army of England into the first *Grande Armée,* marched seven corps from the Channel coast to the upper Danube in less than six weeks. The French had reached the Danube between Ulm and Regensberg by 7 October, outmaneuvering the Austrian general Karl Mack, who was trapped in Ulm. The battle of Ulm (15–20 October 1805) marked the end of Austrian resistance and opened up the road to Vienna. The Austro-Russian forces commanded by Mikhail Kutuzov proved more difficult to corner. Ignoring Austrian demands to fall back on Vienna, the wily Russian veteran crossed the Danube to its north bank on 8–9 November, attacked and

nearly defeated the corps of Marshal Joseph Mortier, and linked up with further Austrian forces to form an army of 86,000 men. Napoleon, however, faced with Allied forces converging from the west and south, lured the main Russian force, now commanded by Tsar Alexander I, into attacking him at Austerlitz (2 December 1805). This crushing defeat forced the Austrians to sue for peace and ended the Third Coalition.

After the Treaty of Pressburg (26 December 1805) Napoleon kept six corps stationed in the Danube valley. And when war threatened with Prussia in September 1806 he was able to move them northward, cut the advancing Prussian lines of communication, and force them into the decisive battles of Jena-Auerstädt on 14 October. The remainder of the campaign, culminating in the battle of Friedland (14 June 1807), was therefore fought on Prussian soil.

By the time of the Wagram campaign in 1809 the Austrian army had been reorganized by the Archduke Charles, many of Napoleon's best troops were pinned down in Spain, and the French forces were divided and spread over a line seventy-five miles long. Napoleon arrived to take command at Donauwörth on 17 April 1809. He immediately showed his ability to maneuver individual corps swiftly, and between 19 and 23 April inflicted five defeats on the comparatively cumbersome Austrians at Tengen,

Abensberg, Landshut, Eckmühl, and Regensberg. While Charles, bloodied but not destroyed, withdrew in orderly fashion along the north of the Danube, Napoleon moved along the southern bank to Vienna, which surrendered on 13 May. Napoleon tried to move his army across the Danube below Vienna, but was checked at the battle of Essling (21–22 May 1809). Within six weeks, however, he had succeeded in transferring his army to the north bank and defeated Charles at the battle of Wagram (5–6 July). The archduke sued for an armistice, which was signed on 12 July.

Related entries: Austerlitz, Battle of; Eckmühl, Battle of; Essling, Battle of; Friedland, Battle of; Jena-Auerstädt, Battles of; Ulm, Battle of; Wagram, Battle of

Suggestions for further reading:
Arnold, James R. 1991. *Crisis on the Danube: Napoleon's Austrian Campaign of 1809.* London: Arms and Armour.
Chandler, David G. 1974. *The Campaigns of Napoleon: The Mind and Method of History's Greatest Soldier.* New York: Macmillan.
Rothenberg, Gunther E. 1982. *Napoleon's Great Adversaries: The Archduke Charles and the Austrian Army, 1792–1814.* London: Batsford.

Danubian Principalities

The Ottoman provinces of Moldavia and Wallachia, populated mostly by Romanians with a Greek ruling class, served Napoleon's purpose in embroiling Turkey in war with Russia in 1806. His special ambassador in Constantinople, General Horace Sébastiani, warned Sultan Selim II about Russian interference in the principalities and promised French support. The alliance amounted to a declaration of war and Russia invaded. However, although the Romanians may have placed their hopes in Russia to gain independence, the principalities remained under Ottoman rule in 1815.

Related entries: Ottoman Empire

Suggestions for further reading:
Jewsbury, George F. 1976. *The Russian Annexation of Bessarabia, 1774–1828: A Study of Imperial Expansion.* Boulder, CO: East European Quarterly.
———. 1979. "Nationalism in the Danubian Principalities, 1800–1825: A Reconsideration," *East European Quarterly* 13, pp. 287–296.

Daru, Pierre Antoine Noël Bruno (1767–1829)

Napoleon's invaluable intendant general, who kept his armies fed, clothed, paid, and otherwise supplied, was also a historian and translator of Latin poetry. Born in Montpellier, Daru first joined the quartermaster corps in 1784, rose through the ranks rapidly during the revolutionary wars, and in 1799 became chief quartermaster of the Army of Switzerland under André Masséna. But he really prospered under the consulate and empire, became secretary general of the Ministry of War, and was appointed to the Tribunate in 1802 and as intendant of the imperial household in 1805.

Although Daru retained liberal sympathies, he clearly did not express them too loudly, and in any case during the wars of 1805–1807 became indispensable to the military administration. He was named intendant general of the *Grande Armée* in August 1805 and also served as commissioner charged with the execution of the Treaty of Pressburg in 1806 and that of Tilsit in 1807. He was responsible for the food, clothing, transport, and medical services of the army, while as intendant of the conquered territories he levied the contributions that paid for the army's supplies and returned a surplus to Napoleon's treasury. When war with Austria resumed in 1809 Daru took up his post once again. His voluminous reports of his receipts and expenses show a thoroughness and attention to detail that enabled him to keep the army supplied largely on contributions levied in the occupied territories. In April 1811 he succeeded Hugues Maret as secretary of state. In this capacity he accompanied Napoleon on the Russian campaign of 1812–1813 and aided the new intendant general of the *Grande Armée,* Mathieu Dumas. Daru held the post of minister of the administration of war in 1813 and again during the Hundred Days. Despite this fidelity to Napoleon he was allowed to devote himself to historical research after the Restoration and was given the title of count by Louis XVIII in 1819.

Daru could be outspoken. He opposed Napoleon's marriage to Marie-Louise, preferring that he should marry a Frenchwoman, warned against the invasion of Russia, and favored acceptance of the Austrian peace terms in 1813. But he carried out the emperor's orders impeccably: Napoleon found him the ablest of all his administrators, with "judgement, spirit, a great capacity for work, and a soul and body of iron" (Connelly 1985, p. 143).

As a scholar, Daru's massive eight-volume *History of the Venetian Republic* showed a mastery of vast amounts of documentation and a critical spirit, similar qualities to those he showed as an administrator, coupled with a dry, matter-of-fact irony. It is not surprising that such virtues would be more appreciated by Napoleon than by Daru's young cousin, Stendhal, who was for a while in love with his wife and found him dogged but unimaginative and passionless.

Related entries: Army; *Grande Armée*

Suggestions for further reading:
Chandler, David G. 1974. *The Campaigns of Napoleon: The Mind and Method of History's Greatest Soldier.* New York: Macmillan.
Church, Clive H. 1981. *Revolution and Red Tape: The French Ministerial Bureaucracy 1770–1850.* Oxford: Clarendon Press.
Connelly, Owen, ed. 1985. *Historical Dictionary of Napoleonic France, 1799–1815.* Westport, CT: Greenwood.
Rogers, H. C. B. 1974. *Napoleon's Army.* London: Allen.

Daunou, Pierre Claude François (1761–1840)

Born in Boulogne, Daunou, a leading legislator and historian, had been an Oratorian priest before being defrocked during the Terror. His troubled political career during the Revolution, which included a spell of imprisonment, peaked under the Directory when as a prominent member of the Council of Five Hundred he was involved in educational reform and acted as commissioner for organizing the Roman Republic. Daunou disapproved of the coup of 18 Brumaire and refused to become a councillor of state, but he did take the position of president of the Tribunate between 1800 and 1802, when he was purged along with nineteen other *idéologues.* Napoleon, however, had come to appreciate Daunou's integrity and in 1804 appointed him director of the National Archives, which he reorganized thoroughly. He was also useful to Napoleon in 1809 when at the emperor's request he wrote his *Historical Essay on the Temporal Power of the Papacy,* which aided Napoleon in his conflict with Pius VII. Daunou was to remain an outspoken liberal for the rest of his life; he served as a deputy, edited the influential *Journal des Savants,* and wrote or edited scores of books and hundreds of articles on history, literature, and politics.

Related entries: *Idéologues;* Tribunate

Suggestions for further reading:
Collins, Irene. 1979. *Napoleon and his Parliaments.* London: Edward Arnold.

David, Jacques-Louis (1748–1825)

Under the Revolution and the empire David came to embody the artist as a public figure and made a great

Napoleon Crossing the Great St. Bernard *(1801–1802) by Jacques-Louis David. David abandons the austere classicism of his Revolutionary paintings for a romantic fantasy of Napoleon on a rearing white charger pointing the way to conquest and glory in Italy. In reality Napoleon, who was an indifferent horseman, crossed the Alps on a mule. (Giraudon/Art Resource)*

contribution to the glorification of Napoleon through portraits of the emperor and monumental paintings glamorizing his achievements and the imperial figure.

As a young artist David won the prestigious Prix de Rome in 1775 and studied in the papal capital for six years, adopting the style of neoclassicism. His *Oath of the Ho-*

ratii, painted in 1784, came to embody the stoic virtues and classical values adopted by the revolutionaries, and David followed it with other paintings in the same simple, severe, and uncompromising style. Under the Revolution David became a fervent Jacobin and a deputy to the National Assembly, where he voted for the death of Louis XVI. He became for a while the virtual "dictator of the arts" for the Jacobin regime, organizing festivities such as the "Feast of Reason," and helping to found a new Institute to replace the old Royal Academy of the Arts. David also painted memorials to the fallen heroes of the Revolution, most famously the celebrated *Death of Marat,* which has remained one of his most renowned works and which still retained the neoclassical style. He was imprisoned after the fall of Robespierre, but released through the efforts of his wife and pupils; in 1798 he met Napoleon and immediately became a devout Bonapartist, dedicated henceforth to the cult of the consul and emperor.

Napoleon realized the value of David as a painter of propaganda pictures and gave him the title of "first painter of the empire" and the most important official commissions. He produced *Napoleon Crossing the Alps* in 1801, using the new Romantic idiom, and worked for over two years on the massive *Coronation of the Emperor Napoleon,* which included over a hundred portraits and showed Napoleon (unhistorically) placing the crown on his own head. This was followed in 1810 by *The Emperor Distributing Eagles,* which consolidated the dual image of Napoleon as emperor and soldier.

After Napoleon's defeat David rejected any compromise with the restored Bourbons and fled into exile, first to Switzerland and then to Brussels, where he died. He continued painting up to the end, but with a notable falling off of the powers that had been best shown in exalting the values of the Revolution and in helping to create the immortal image of Napoleon as glori-

ous soldier and hardworking emperor. David declared of Napoleon, "there is a man to whom altars would have been raised in ancient times" (Lyons 1994, p. 191), and his paintings can be seen as celebrating a quasi-religious cult around the emperor. He also painted many portraits, including a refined classical Mme. Récamier and an acute portrayal of Pius VII, which deserves to be ranked among the masterpieces of portraiture.

Related entries: Empire Style; Propaganda

Suggestions for further reading:
Brookner, Anita. 1980. *Jacques-Louis David.* London: Chatto and Windus.
Friedlaender, Walter. 1952. *David to Delacroix.* Cambridge: Harvard University Press.
Lyons, Martyn. 1994. *Napoleon Bonaparte and the Legacy of the French Revolution.* London: Macmillan.
Nanteuil, Luc de. 1990. *Jacques-Louis David.* London: Thames and Hudson.
Roberts, Warren. 1989. *Jacques-Louis David: Revolutionary Artist.* Chapel Hill: University of North Carolina Press.

Davout, Louis Nicolas (1770–1823)

*D*avout, who eventually became duke of Auerstädt, prince of Eckmühl, and marshal of the empire, was born in Annoux, Burgundy, of an old noble family. He was educated at the military school of Auxerre and the *École Militaire,* Paris, commissioned into the Royal Champagne Cavalry in 1788, and served in the royal army until 1791, when he was dismissed for revolutionary activities. Volunteering for the revolutionary army, he reached the rank of brigadier general, serving in the armies of northern France and the Rhine until 1797. He met General Bonaparte in 1798, served with distinction in the Egyptian campaign, and was promoted to general of division in 1800. Davout's nomination among the first marshals of the empire in 1804 caused surprise and some criticism, but as commander of the Third Corps of the *Grande Armée* he contributed to the victory of Austerlitz in 1805 and in 1806 won a brilliant victory over the Prussians at Auerstädt, in recognition of which he was created duke of Auerstädt in 1808.

Davout commanded the Third Corps and was wounded at Eylau in 1807, and in the same year he was appointed governor general of the Duchy of Warsaw; then in 1809 he led the same corps at Eckmühl and Wagram and was created prince of Eckmühl. He commanded the First Corps during the invasion of Russia in 1812, was seriously wounded at the battle of Borodino, and commanded the rear guard during the retreat from Moscow. In 1813 he held Dresden and the lower Elbe, but after the defeat of Leipzig he was given command of the Hamburg region, where he was besieged for seven months. Following Napoleon's first abdication, Davout evacuated Hamburg in May 1814 on the orders of Louis XVIII and was exiled by the restored Bourbon to his estate at Savigny-sur-Orge.

Following Napoleon's return during the Hundred Days, the emperor appointed Davout minister of war on 20 March 1815, a post he held until 8 July. But as military governor of Paris he remained in the capital during the Waterloo campaign before briefly assuming command of the Army of the Loire as the allies entered Paris. He resubmitted to Louis XVIII on 14 July and was exiled once more to his estates. Davout's stand in defense of Marshal Michel Ney kept him out of favor at the court until 1817, when he was restored to the dignity of marshal before being readmitted to the peerage in 1819. He subsequently spent most of his time at Savigny-sur-Orge and died of consumption in Paris in 1823.

Widely regarded as one of Napoleon's most effective commanders, Davout was known as the "iron marshal." Severe, ambitious, and a strict disciplinarian, Davout was also incorruptible and universally respected even when not liked. Unlike most of the other marshals, he made no personal profits from plundering occupied territories and restrained the predatory instincts of his troops. His relations with other marshals, especially Joachim Murat and Jean-Baptiste Bernadotte, were frequently hostile, leading on occasions to violent arguments. But none of the other marshals showed his concern for the well-being of the rank-and-file troops, making him a popular commander despite his strict disciplinary code. Napoleon in exile on Saint Helena described Davout as "one of the purest glories of France" (Chandler 1987, p. 110).

Related entries: Austerlitz, Battle of; Borodino, Battle of; Eckmühl, Battle of; Eylau, Battle of; Hundred Days; Jena-Auerstädt, Battles of; Wagram, Battle of; Warsaw, Duchy of

Suggestions for further reading:
Chandler, David G. 1987. "Davout," in David G. Chandler, ed., *Napoleon's Marshals.* New York: Macmillan.
Gallagher, John G. 1976. *The Iron Marshal: A Biography of Louis N. Davout.* Carbondale: Southern Illinois University Press.

Decrès, Denis (1761–1820)

As Napoleon's minister of the navy between 1801 and 1814, Decrès made strenuous efforts to improve the French navy, but was hindered by lack of money, the inferior design of French ships, and the lack of an experienced officer corps. Decrès had a distinguished record in naval warfare, from the American Revolution to Napoleon's Egyptian campaign, and as a minister drove himself and his subordinates hard, showing himself to be a competent but unpopular administrator. He managed to accomplish Napoleon's strategy of rebuilding the fleet after the defeat of Trafalgar in 1805, but his efforts came too late. After serving in his old post briefly during the Hundred Days, Decrès retired from public life after 1815.

Related entries: Navy, French

Suggestions for further reading:
Glover, Richard. 1967. "The French Fleet, 1807–1814: Britain's Problem and Madison's Opportunity," *Journal of Modern History* 39, pp. 233–252.

Denmark

The Kingdom of Denmark, under the regency of Frederick VI, joined the League of Armed Neutrality in 1800, as a result of which the Danish fleet was destroyed by the British at the battle of Copenhagen. After the assassination of Tsar Paul I in 1801 put an end to the League of Armed Neutrality, Frederick allied himself briefly with Britain. With the proclamation of Napoleon's Continental System in 1807, however, the British feared that Denmark would close the Baltic and again bombarded Copenhagen. In reaction Frederick signed an alliance with Napoleon in October 1807, but proved himself a largely inactive ally, useful mainly in not opposing the emperor. Despite his virtual neutrality, after Napoleon's defeat in 1814 Frederick was forced to cede Norway to Sweden.

Related entries: Armed Neutrality; Copenhagen, Battle of

Suggestions for further reading:
Oakey, Stewart P. 1972. *A Short History of Denmark.* New York: Praeger.
Ruppenthal, Roland. 1943. "Denmark and the Continental System," *Journal of Modern History* 15, pp. 7–23.

Denon, Dominique Vivant (1747–1825)

Napoleon's director-general of museums between 1802 and 1815, Denon has been described as the most powerful museum curator there has ever been. He already had a long career as diplomat, artist, and traveler behind him when, at the age of fifty-one, he joined Napoleon's Egyptian campaign, during which, even in the midst of battle, he surveyed and made drawings of the pyramids and other Egyptian monuments. The results of his labors not only laid the basis for the science of Egyptology but also served to popularize the Egyptian style in France.

Art treasures looted from conquered lands were stored in the Louvre in Paris, and Denon suggested that the new art gallery be called the *Musée Napoléon*. He was named as director-general of museums in November 1802, charged with overseeing the Louvre, minting medals, hiring painters, erecting monuments, and administering ceramic and tapestry works. Thus, though no great artist himself, Denon could be said to be one of the main creators of the Empire style. He personally supervised the looting of artworks, following the victorious French armies to Italy, Germany, and Austria. His final and most successful mission, however, in Italy in 1811–1812, was undertaken in a time of peace, when Denon used his diplomatic skills to acquire an array of Renaissance masterpieces, which went on display in the Louvre in July 1814. Denon's collection was admired even by visiting British artists and connoisseurs, but he could not prevent its dismantling in 1815, when the victorious allies demanded the restitution of their property. Having presided with dignity over the ending of his work for Napoleon, Denon spent his last decade in retirement, arranging his private collection and preparing publications.

Related entries: *Description de l'Égypte; Empire Style; Musée Napoléon*

Suggestions for further reading:
Gould, Cecil H. M. 1965. *Trophy of Conquest: The Musée Napoléon and the Creation of the Louvre.* London: Faber & Faber.

Description de l'Égypte

After capturing Cairo in July 1798 during his Egyptian campaign, Napoleon set his scientists to work in the Institute of Egypt, modeled on the *Institut National*. Field teams were assigned to surveying the Isthmus of Suez, compiling detailed maps of Egypt, and exploring its ruins and antiquities. The monumental compilation of their findings, the *Description de l'Égypte,* was published in ten volumes of text and fourteen sumptuous volumes of plates between 1809 and 1828. The unreliable accounts of previous travelers were replaced by detailed archaeological descriptions, and Napoleon's imperialist venture had provided the impetus for the creation of the new science of Egyptology.

Related entries: Denon, Dominique Vivant; Egyptian Campaign

Suggestions for further reading:
Herold, J. Christopher. 1962. *Bonaparte in Egypt.* New York: Harper and Row.

Diplomatic Service

Napoleon never underestimated the importance of the diplomatic service in the conduct of international relations, maintaining an average of 130 diplomats in the field, with a further 250 in the consular service, not only in Europe, but in the Levant, the United States, and farther afield. Representation fluctuated according to the state of peace and the extension of the empire, but the traditional pattern was maintained. For example, ten embassies were preserved in Germany and a further eleven accredited to the Confederation of the Rhine.

Appointments were strongly influenced by family patronage and recommendation. There was no bureaucratic development of professionalism: Napoleon preferred to rely on experience and local knowledge. But his choices were not always suitable, as the nomination of François René de Chateaubriand to be secretary of the legation at Rome showed. He often chose men without any previous diplomatic experience, especially in his early years in power, when his preference went to the military. During the brief spell of peace in 1801–1802 almost all the ambassadors and plenipotentiaries were generals. Military diplomats were used to impress the courts to which they were sent, and although they were well qualified to report on potential enemy forces, were mostly unsuitable in other respects. With the return of *émigré* families, especially after 1810, aristocrats resumed their traditional role in diplomacy. By 1812–1813, 60 percent of heads of missions were nobles.

Diplomatic reports were Napoleon's main and most regular source of information about foreign countries. The highest priority was given to military information, but representatives were told that they should "neglect no detail, however small, if it can shed light on the state of the country, the spirit of the court, the character and attitudes of influential persons" (Woolf 1991, p. 67). They were also to act as instruments of propaganda, receiving regular circulars stressing military victories, the solidity of the regime, Napoleon's personal popularity, and the "lies" of Allied propaganda. In Allied and satellite states they played a leading role in internal affairs, taking or sharing responsibility for the raising of troops, enforcement of the economic blockade, and the payment of subsidies. Given Napoleon's personal direction of foreign affairs, diplomats enjoyed virtually no autonomy: they were pawns in the game of war and peace and in the occupied territories above all tools of conquest.

Related entries: Nobility

Suggestions for further reading:
Mowat, R. B. 1924. *The Diplomacy of Napoleon.* London: Edward Arnold.

Ross, Steven T. 1981. *European Diplomatic History, 1789–1815*. Malabar, FL: Krieger.

Whitcomb, Edward A. 1979. *Napoleon's Diplomatic Service*. Durham, NC: Duke University Press.

Woolf, Stuart. 1991. *Napoloeon's Integration of Europe*. London and New York: Routledge.

Directory

The regime that ruled France between 1795 and 1799 was systematically denigrated by official propaganda under Napoleon, being presented as a weak government, under which anarchy reigned and the Republic yearned for a savior. Named after its five-man executive known as Directors, it established a liberal economic policy and a theoretically liberal political system, but used illiberal measures to ensure majorities in elections and against coup attempts. But the Directory never succeeded in creating a "center" party between the extremes of Jacobinism and royalism and by 1799 was facing mass political apathy.

However, the Directory's fiscal and administrative reforms laid the basis for the work of the consulate. The tax system was simplified, the financial chaos of the Jacobin era ended by a return to metallic currency, and the Counter-Revolution combated effectively. But the Directors lost control over their generals: Napoleon in Italy ignored orders from Paris and followed a personal policy. The regime's popularity was at a low ebb in 1799, with rampant inflation caused by the abandonment of Jacobin controls, as well as widespread apathy, and discontent caused by the Directory's scant respect for political freedom. But Napoleon's dictatorship, established by the coup of 18 Brumaire, was not the inevitable outcome: he needed the support of disgruntled military men and constitutional revisionists to establish the consulate.

Related entries: Barras, Paul François Jean Nicolas, Vicomte de; Bonaparte, Lucien, Prince of Canino; Brumaire, Coup of Year VIII; Egyptian Campaign; Italian Campaigns; Jacobinism; Propaganda; Revolutionary Wars; Sieyès, Emmanuel Joseph; Talleyrand-Périgord, Charles-Maurice de

Suggestions for further reading:

Church, Clive H. 1973. "In Search of the Directory," in J. F. Bosher, ed., *French Government and Society, 1500–1850: Essays in Memory of Alfred Cobban*. London: Athlone Press.

Hunt, Lynn, et al. 1979. "The Failure of the Liberal Republic in France, 1795–1799: The Road to Brumaire," *Journal of Modern History* 51, pp. 734–759.

Lefebvre, Georges. 1965. *The Directory*. London: Routledge and Kegan Paul.

Lyons, Martyn. 1975. *France under the Directory*. Cambridge: Cambridge University Press.

Sydenham, M. J. 1974. *The First French Republic, 1792–1804*. London: Batsford.

Woronoff, Denis. 1984. *The Thermidorian Regime and the Directory, 1794–1799*. Cambridge: Cambridge University Press.

Dresden

The capital of Saxony, situated strategically on the river Elbe, became in 1813 the site of Napoleon's last victory of any consequence. He had already stayed there in 1807 after signing the Treaty of Tilsit and in May 1812 on the eve of the Russian campaign, when he had staged spectacular ceremonies to impress the rulers of Austria, Prussia, and most other German states. However, on 27 March 1813 the Army of Silesia under Gebhard von Blücher occupied Dresden. It was recovered by Napoleon after the battle of Lützen (2 May) and he made the city his advanced headquarters, even if he was rarely there himself. He did, however, receive Klemens von Metternich for two important conversations on 26 June and 30 June.

When hostilities renewed on 17 August 1813 Napoleon was absent from Dresden, and the Austro-Russian Army of Bohemia, commanded by Karl, Prince von Schwarzenberg, advanced on the city. This brought Napoleon hurrying back. On 26 August

Tsar Alexander I, against Austrian advice, insisted that Schwarzenberg should make a frontal assault on Dresden, but Napoleon counterattacked and recovered almost all the lost ground. On the following morning Napoleon took the initiative, coordinating attacks led by Joseph Mortier on the Allied left and Joachim Murat on their right. These attacks forced Schwarzenberg to retire hurriedly across the Austrian border to within a few miles of the Austro-Russian headquarters at Teplitz. Marshal Laurent Gouvion Saint-Cyr was left in command of Dresden while Napoleon rode to defeat at the battle of Leipzig. Saint-Cyr held out for three weeks against a Russian siege before surrendering on 31 October.

Related entries: Germany, Campaigns in; Gouvion Saint-Cyr, Laurent; Saxony

Suggestions for further reading:
Chandler, David G. 1974. *The Campaigns of Napoleon: The Mind and Method of History's Greatest Soldier.* New York: Macmillan.
Sheehan, James J. 1989. *German History, 1770–1866.* Oxford: Clarendon Press.

Ducos, Pierre Roger (1747–1816)

*T*hough generally considered a second-rank politician, always trailing in the wake of stronger-minded personalities, Ducos did play an important role in bringing Napoleon to power in 1799. A lawyer before the Revolution, Ducos represented his native department of the Landes in the Convention, where he voted for the death of Louis XVI. He gained a reputation as a staunch antiroyalist under the Directory, and joined his friend Paul Barras as a Director in June 1799. Switching his support to Emmanuel Sieyès, Ducos joined in the conspiracy to overthrow the Directory in the coup of 18 Brumaire and helped Sieyès draw up the plans for the consulate.

He was named third consul, but quickly realized that Napoleon was now the real master and only remained in office for a month. Ducos later served discreetly as vice-president of the Senate and was rewarded for his past services with the title of count of the empire and the Legion of Honour. At the Restoration he was first made a peer of France, until it was remembered that he was a regicide and he was expelled from the country. Ducos was killed in a carriage accident near Ulm in March 1816.

Related entries: Brumaire, Coup of Year VIII; Consulate; Directory

Suggestions for further reading:
Morton, John B. 1948. *Brumaire: The Rise of Bonaparte.* London: T. Werner Levine.

Duroc, Géraud Christophe Michel (1772–1813)

*N*apoleon's grand marshal of the palace was one of his most loyal servants and could even be described as a close friend. Born into a poor aristocratic family in Lorraine, Duroc joined the army of the Revolution in 1792. As an artillery lieutenant he served at the siege of Toulon in 1793, where he first met Napoleon. The newly famous General Bonaparte appointed Duroc one of his aides-de-camp in the Italian and Egyptian campaigns, after which Duroc returned to Paris with Napoleon and took part in the coup of 18 Brumaire. He was promoted to general of brigade in 1800 and general of division in 1803.

Appointed grand marshal of the palace in 1804, Duroc carried out his functions efficiently and economically and was in daily contact with Napoleon. He also acted as the emperor's personal envoy on diplomatic missions to Berlin, Vienna, St. Petersburg, and Copenhagen. Marriage to the daughter of a Spanish banker allowed him to amass a considerable personal fortune. His diplomatic finesse was often valuable in offsetting Napoleon's fits of temper, and in recognition of his tactful handling of Charles IV of Spain in 1808 he was created Duke of Frioul. Duroc was present at most of Napoleon's battles, and, although like most of the emperor's advisers he warned against the invasion of Russia in 1812, he always obeyed loyally. He was wounded while escorting Napoleon on the day after the battle of Bautzen, 22 May 1813, and died the next morning. Napoleon was for once genuinely moved by the death of one of his most valued confidants and friends.

Related entries: Bautzen, Battle of; Egyptian Campaign; Generals; Grand Dignitaries of the Empire; Italian Campaigns; Toulon, Siege of

Suggestions for further reading:

Mansel, Philip. 1987. *The Eagle in Splendour: Napoleon I and His Court.* London: George Philip.
Whitcomb, Edward A. 1979. *Napoleon's Diplomatic Service.* Durham, NC: Duke University Press.

E

Eblé, Jean-Baptiste (1758–1812)

The hero of Napoleon's crossing of the Berezina River during the retreat from Moscow in November 1812, Eblé was the son of an artillery sergeant and had risen to the rank of major general in the armies of the Revolution. He came to Napoleon's notice as artillery commander of the First Corps of the *Grande Armée* during the Austerlitz campaign, and between 1808 and 1811 served as minister of war in Jérôme Bonaparte's kingdom of Westphalia. He also served with distinction in the Peninsular War in 1811–1812. Eblé's engineers in the *Grande Armée* during the Russian campaign allowed Napoleon to advance swiftly across the rivers Niemen and Dnieper, and his bridging of the Berezina on 24–25 November 1812 facilitated the survival and escape of most of the remnants of the invading forces. Eblé collapsed and died in Königsberg as a result of debilitation from cold and exposure on New Year's Eve.

Related entries: Russian Campaign; Westphalia, Kingdom of

Suggestions for further reading:
Chandler, David G. 1994. "Retreat from Moscow," in his *On the Napoleonic Wars: Collected Essays.* London: Greenhill.

Eckmühl, Battle of (22 April 1809)

One of a series of victories over the Austrians during the early days of the Wagram campaign, Eckmühl inflicted a heavy though far from mortal blow on the army of the Archduke Charles. An Austrian attack on the French Third Corps under Louis Davout at the village of Eckmühl, some eleven miles south of Regensberg, was countered by an enveloping movement by Napoleon, employing Bavarian and Würtemberger troops commanded by Dominique Vandamme. Charles lost about a third of his men, killed, wounded, or captured, and was forced to abandon the town of Regensberg itself. But the bulk of Napoleon's forces was too tired by six days of fighting and marching to pursue the Austrian forces farther.

Related entries: Charles, Archduke of Austria; Danube Campaigns; Davout, Louis Nicolas

Suggestions for further reading:
Chandler, David G. 1974. *The Campaigns of Napoleon: The Mind and Method of History's Greatest Soldier.* New York: Macmillan.
Rothenberg, Gunther E. 1982. *Napoleon's Great Adversaries: The Archduke Charles and the Austrian Army, 1792–1814.* London: Batsford.

École Militaire

Napoleon graduated from the central military school of the ancien régime in 1785 at the age of sixteen. It had been founded in 1751 in Paris, where its buildings may still be seen on the Left Bank of the Seine. It was replaced by Napoleon's new military school at St. Cyr in 1802.

Suggestions for further reading:
Ratcliffe, Bertram. 1981. *Prelude to Fame: An Account of the Early Life of Napoleon up to the Battle of Montenotte.* London: Warne.

École Normale

Napoleon's law of 17 May 1808 creating regional normal schools (*écoles normales*), attached to *lycées,* for the training of teachers was never implemented, and the whole subject was curiously neglected. The first French normal school, based on the German model, was established in Strasbourg in 1810 on local initiative, but its success did not spread the idea elsewhere in France. Most educators, including the Christian brothers, who returned to France under Napoleon, preferred training through apprenticeship. However, Napoleon's foundation of the *École Normale Supérieure* in Paris in 1810 had momentous consequences, as it has gone on to produce many members of the French political and intellectual elite up to the present day.

Related entries: Education; *Lycées*

Suggestions for further reading:
Holtman, Robert B. 1967. *The Napoleonic Revolution.* Philadelphia: Lippincott.

École Polytechnique

The central institution in the new system of French higher education was founded in 1794 under the leadership of Lazare Carnot and Gaspard Monge; Napoleon changed it from a scientific establishment into a military school. Originally the "Central School of Public Works," in 1802 it absorbed the state artillery school, and in 1811 it was decided that its best students should henceforth become military engineers. Between 1811 and 1813 over 200 *Polytechnique* graduates were channeled into the artillery.

Related entries: Artillery; Education; Monge, Gaspard

Suggestions for further reading:
Williams, L. Pearce. 1956. "Science, Education and Napoleon I," *Isis* 47, pp. 369–382.

Écoles Centrales

Created in 1795 as supersecondary schools, one for every 300,000 inhabitants, between ninety and one hundred *écoles centrales* were founded in succeeding years. However, they did not suit Napoleon's educational plans, as courses lacked the kind of national uniformity he wanted to impose. Students effectively chose their own courses, too many of which were only vaguely defined. Napoleon abolished the *écoles centrales* in 1802, replacing them with *lycées* and the less elitist *écoles secondaires.*

Related entries: Education; *Lycées*

Suggestions for further reading:
Holtman, Robert B. 1967. *The Napoleonic Revolution.* Philadelphia: Lippincott.

Economy

The development of the French economy under Napoleon was dominated by the almost continuous military and economic warfare. The Commercial

Code helped to create modern forms of business organization, while the *École Polytechnique* and other technical schools helped prepare the way for French predominance in engineering. But this was for the future. Under Napoleonic rule the economic war with Britain and an exaggerated protectionism inflicted great damage on some sectors of the economy, while limiting progress in others.

A lack of radical innovation dominates the economic history of the period. The system of landholding had been profoundly changed by the Revolution, but agrarian France was still not on the move in any noticeable fashion. And the economic war exacerbated the effects of bad harvests and subsistence crises between 1798 and 1801 and again in 1803, 1805–1807, and 1811–1812. The imperial economy never recovered from the combined industrial and agricultural crises of 1810–1812. Equally seriously, the loss of overseas territories, the British blockade, and the Continental System ruined the hitherto flourishing commerce of the ports of France's Atlantic coast, most notably Bordeaux and Nantes. This loss was only partly offset by the opening up of vast continental markets to French goods, since the French market was itself open to goods from the economically advanced areas of Belgium and the Rhineland.

A shift in the economic geography is discernible under Napoleon, with eastern regions such as Alsace and Marseille on the Mediterranean coast as the principal beneficiaries. Progress in the cotton industry was also localized, but it did provide domestic piecework for peasants in Alsace, Picardy, Flanders, Normandy, and the Paris region, where agriculture did not guarantee adequate work or income. Overall, however, while French industrial output grew moderately, Britain widened its lead over the continent in both quantitative and qualitative terms. A certain optimism and belief in economic progress may be seen in France

in 1815, and the path to the future lay in industrial revolution. But France under Napoleon had done little to gain back the lead established by the British in most areas of the economy.

Related entries: Bank of France; Berlin Decrees; *Biens Nationaux;* Chaptal, Jean Antoine; Commercial Code; Continental System; Finance; Industry; Milan Decrees; Ouvrard, Gabriel Julien; Peasants; Population; Rural Code; Statistics; Taxation

Suggestions for further reading:
Bergeron, Louis. 1981. *France under Napoleon.* Princeton: Princeton University Press.
Forrest, Alan, and Peter Jones, eds. 1991. *Reshaping France: Town, Country and Region during the French Revolution.* Manchester: Manchester University Press.
Sutherland, D. M. G. 1985. *France, 1789–1815: Revolution and Counter-Revolution.* London: Fontana.

Education

Napoleon gave a considerable amount of personal attention to educational matters, and his reforms were to have lasting and profound effects in France. His purpose, however, was to create future leaders and administrators, and his approach was eminently political. "There will be no settled political state," he declared in 1805, "so long as there is not a teaching body with settled principles. So long as one does not learn from childhood whether to be republican or monarchist, Catholic or non-religious, etc., the State will not form a nation" (Bergeron 1981, pp. 32–33). The Napoleonic system, centralized through the Imperial University, was to teach pupils what to think more than how to think, but practice was not as simple or efficient as theory.

The creation of *lycées* was to be of lasting significance, but primary education was curiously neglected, and Napoleon's conservative view of the position of women meant that any progress in female education had to happen despite him, not because of him. In the memorandum he prepared for the model girls' school at Ecouen he opined that "the best education is that which a mother can give her daughters." Although he wished to see girls educated in regular establishments, the stress would be on religion and the practical activities of a dutiful wife. Primary education was the responsibility of the communes. Napoleon's reconciliation with the Catholic Church allowed church schools to be reestablished, and the communes were forced to rely heavily on the Brethren of the Christian Schools. Although Napoleon prevented the Church from regaining its pre-Revolutionary dominant position in French education, the rivalry between state and religious schools was to create incessant and bitter conflicts during the nineteenth century.

Related entries: Centralization; *École Normale; École Polytechnique; Écoles Centrales;* Imperial University; Local Government; *Lycées*

Suggestions for further reading:
Arnold, Eric A., ed. 1994. *A Documentary Survey of Napoleonic France.* Lanham, MD: University Press of America, pp. 120–129.
Barnard, Howard C. 1969. *Education and the French Revolution.* Cambridge: Cambridge University Press.
Bergeron, Louis. 1981. *France under Napoleon.* Princeton: Princeton University Press.
Holtman, Robert B. 1967. *The Napoleonic Revolution.* Philadelphia: Lippincott.
Palmer, R. R. 1985. *The Improvement of Humanity: Education and the French Revolution.* Princeton: Princeton University Press.

Egyptian Campaign

The French expedition of conquest in Egypt and Syria between 1798 and 1801 was meant to challenge British naval supremacy in the Mediterranean and to secure Egypt for further operations against the British in India. The British secretary of state for war, Henry Dundas, called the occupation of Egypt "the master key to all the commerce of the world" (Ehrman 1996, p. 142), an unusually farsighted view with which Napoleon would have been one of the few to agree. His political masters in the Directory were probably more interested in removing the dangerous general far from Paris.

The expedition under Napoleon's command sailed from Toulon on 19 May 1798, carrying in all 35,000 officers and men and 167 scholars. It captured Malta on 11–12 June, intending to use it as a naval base in the central Mediterranean, then sailed to the east, arriving off Alexandria on 30 June. Having encountered little resistance in taking the city, Napoleon moved south, defeated the army of the Mameluke rulers of Egypt in the battle of the Pyramids, and entered Cairo on 22 July. Napoleon was now in control of the lower Nile, and a French army pursued the fleeing Mamelukes to the south. Although the whole of Egypt was declared to be under French control, in Upper Egypt they only effectively controlled the major towns along the Nile.

Napoleon set about reordering the conquered country. Taxes were levied to support the new government, a mint was established to coin money, a postal service was created along with a health department, and the first printing presses in Egypt were put into operation. The Egyptian Institute was set up to research the country and introduce the ideas of the Enlightenment. These were the first Europeans to study the wonders of ancient Egypt, laying the foundations of modern Egyptology. The results were eventually published in the massive *Description de l'Égypte.*

The French position suffered a major blow on 1–2 August when the British under Horatio Nelson destroyed the entire French fleet in the battle of the Nile. This confirmed British control of the Mediterranean and made communication with France extremely difficult. Then the formation of the Second Coalition brought Austria and Russia back into the war on the

British side and persuaded the Ottoman Empire, nominal ruler of Egypt, to declare war on France. On 10 February 1799, with affairs in good order in Egypt, Napoleon marched from Cairo with 10,000 men to defeat the Turkish army in Syria. After a long march through the desert he reached Acre on 20 March and laid siege to the city. However, despite Napoleon's victory over the Turks at Mount Tabor on 16 April, Acre with British help held out for two months. Lack of siege equipment, illness in the French army, plague in Acre, and news of allied victories in Europe, all decided Napoleon to return to Egypt. Almost half the men who took part in the Syrian expedition did not return.

On his return to Cairo, Napoleon learned that a Turkish army of some 15,000 men had landed at Aboukir. With a force of 10,000, he rushed to the coast and defeated the Turks, thereby securing the French military position for the moment. On 23 August Napoleon turned over command in Egypt to General Jean-Baptiste Kléber and returned to France. Kléber immediately opened negotiations with the Turks and British to secure a French evacuation of Egypt, which he had long favored. Agreement was reached in January 1800, but Kléber was assassinated on 14 June before the terms of the evacuation could be carried out, and command of the French forces passed to Jean-François Menou. 1801 saw the end of the Egyptian expedition, as British and Turkish armies landed and besieged Cairo and Alexandria. Menou held out in Alexandria until September, when the final French troops were evacuated home aboard British ships.

Related entries: Coalitions; *Description de l'Égypte;* Directory; Kléber, Jean-Baptiste; Malta; Nelson, Horatio, Lord; Nile, Battle of the; Ottoman Empire; Pyramids, Battle of the

Suggestions for further reading:
Barthorp, Michael. 1978. *Napoleon's Egyptian Campaigns, 1798–1801.* London: Osprey.
Chandler, David G. 1974. *The Campaigns of Napoleon: The Mind and Method of History's Greatest Soldier.* New York: Macmillan.
Charles-Roux, François. 1937. *Bonaparte: Governor of Egypt.* London: Methuen.
Ehrman, John. 1996. *The Younger Pitt: The Consuming Struggle.* London: Constable.
Herold, J. Christopher. 1962. *Bonaparte in Egypt.* New York: Harper and Row.

Elba

Napoleon's first place of exile in 1814–1815 is a Mediterranean island situated between the west coast of Italy and Corsica, approximately 86 square miles in area and in 1814 with a population of about 12,000. It had been annexed to France in 1802 and in 1814 made a principality with the exiled Napoleon as its sovereign.

The emperor set about governing his tiny domain with enthusiasm. Mule tracks were turned into a road system, wells and drains dug, and Napoleon encouraged the growing of vegetables and planted vines, chestnut and olive trees from Corsica, and mulberry trees from Tuscany. Money was poured into improving mining and fishing. As a result, the initially hostile population was won over, comforted by the new prosperity and the spending of curious foreign visitors.

Napoleon chose the Villa dei Mulini as his palace, and the Villa San Martino as summer residence, with a court, an army of 1,600, and a navy of five small ships. His sister Pauline acted as hostess on formal occasions, but the Allies prevented the Empress Marie-Louise and his son from joining him. His anger and frustration were increased when the two million francs per year supposed to be sent him by Louis XVIII refused to materialize, forcing him to water down some of his schemes. This, plus the news of Louis's unpopularity in France, decided Napoleon to plot his escape. On 25 February 1815, while his English watch-

A stirring engraving by Gaitte depicts Napoleon returning from his exile in Elba to be enthusiastically greeted by the men who will soon die for him in the Hundred Days War. (Mary Evans Picture Library)

dog, Sir Neil Campbell, was away in Florence, Pauline announced that she was planning a grand ball, and the next day Napoleon, along with 500 men, secretly fled the island on board the brig *Inconstant,* disguised as a British warship. The famous "flight of the eagle" on 1 March led to the Hundred Days and the Waterloo campaign.

Related entries: Bonaparte, Pauline, Duchess of Guastalla; Hundred Days

Suggestions for further reading:
Hamilton-Williams, David. 1994. *The Fall of Napoleon: The Final Betrayal.* London: John Wiley.
Mackenzie, Norman. 1982. *The Escape from Elba: The Fall and Flight of Napoleon, 1814–1815.* New York: Oxford University Press.

Elections

Universal male suffrage existed theoretically in Napoleonic France, but was never practiced in any form recognizable to modern democracy. When Napoleon wished to lay claim to a popular mandate he did it by plebiscite. Under the Constitution of the Year VIII, citizens elected communal notables, who in turn chose departmental notables, who in turn chose national notables. The Senate then chose the members of the Legislative Body and Tribunate from the national lists. This cumbersome system was replaced in the Constitution of the Year X (1802) by electoral colleges in each district and department, elected by universal manhood suffrage from among the richest citizens, which nominated two persons for each opening in the Legislature or Tribunate. Electoral colleges were formed for life and received no new members until a third of the places were vacant. There was in fact only one renewal. The membership of the departmental colleges, chosen from among the 600 largest taxpayers in the Department, made up the notables who Napoleon saw as "the true people of France."

Related entries: Constitutions; Consulate; Legislative Body; Local Government; Notables; Plebiscites; Senate; Tribunate

Suggestions for further reading:
Bergeron, Louis. 1981. *France under Napoleon.* Princeton: Princeton University Press.
Collins, Irene. 1979. *Napoleon and his Parliaments.* London: Edward Arnold.

Émigrés

The precise number of people who emigrated from France to flee the Revolution is impossible to calculate, but was probably around 100,000, of whom a quarter were clergy and about 17 percent nobles. The various Revolutionary regimes had passed harsh laws against *émigrés,* although some had returned under the Directory after being struck from the notoriously inaccurate official lists. Napoleon as first consul declared that he wished to "reconcile all the French," but the Constitution of the Year VIII maintained the exclusion of all *émigrés* not included on a list of exceptions.

Napoleon clearly wanted *émigrés* to return, and decrees of 2 March 1800 and 26 April 1802 turned the policy around, declaring an amnesty for all those not on a proscribed list. Those still banned included chiefly those who had commanded armies against the Republic or held commissions in enemy armies and archbishops and bishops who refused to accept the Concordat of 1801 with the pope. The new policy provoked a rush to return. Between 40,000 and 50,000 *émigrés* returned in all, many to live quietly on what remained of their estates, but others to serve the new regime as diplomats or in the Senate, Council of State, or at court. A small number of the returnees left France again, but the remaining *émigrés* were mostly those excluded from the amnesty, joined by a small band of dissidents such as Mme. de Staël. The truly irreconcilable among the old *émigrés* remained in British service and returned with Wellington's army in 1814.

Related entries: Catholic Church; Counter-Revolution; Nobility; Royalists

Suggestions for further reading:
Arnold, Eric A., ed. 1996. *A Documentary Survey of Napoleonic France: A Supplement.* Lanham, MD: University Press of America, pp. 34–41, 48–51.
Godechot, Jacques. 1981. *The Counter-Revolution: Doctrine and Action, 1789–1804.* Princeton: Princeton University Press.
Greer, Donald M. 1951. *The Incidence of Emigration during the French Revolution.* Cambridge: Harvard University Press.
Weiner, Margery. 1960. *The French Exiles, 1789–1815.* London: John Murray.

Empire

The *senatus consultum* of 18 May 1804 that created the empire decreed that "the government of the Republic be entrusted to an Emperor," that Napoleon Bonaparte was henceforth "Emperor of the French," and that the imperial dignity was to be hereditary. Napoleon was declared emperor "by the grace of God and the constitution of the Republic." His coronation on 2 December 1804 consecrated the new regime on classical and Carolingian precedents, implying sovereignty over lands greater in extent than the traditional boundaries of the kingdom of France.

At its height in 1812 the Empire of the French comprised 130 departments as opposed to the 83 originally created in 1789. It included Belgian, Swiss, German, Piedmontese, and Italian departments annexed in 1809 or before, as well as the Hanseatic cities of Bremen, Hamburg, and Lübeck and the territories of the Kingdom of Holland, all annexed in 1810. The provinces of Illyria, the Duchy of Warsaw, and the Grand Duchies of Berg, Frankfurt, and Tuscany, although technically part of France, were ruled separately.

Related entries: Belgium; Berg, Grand Duchy of; Coronation; Frankfurt, Grand Duchy of; Grand Dignitaries of the Empire; Holland, Kingdom of; Illyria; Netherlands; Poland; Switzerland; Tuscany, Grand Duchy of; Warsaw, Duchy of

Suggestions for further reading:
Arnold, Eric A., ed. 1994. *A Documentary Survey of Napoleonic France.* Lanham, MD: University Press of America, pp. 180–204.
Furet, François. 1992. *Revolutionary France, 1770–1880.* Oxford: Basil Blackwell.

Empire Style

Despite the often ostentatious vulgarity of Napoleonic ceremonial and the throne rooms and royal suites designed for it, the prevailing style in art, architecture, decoration, and costume under Napoleon was a monumental neoclassicism meant to express the grandeur of the empire. Only the restless stirrings of Romanticism, through which artists could portray the heroic actions of the young Bonaparte, saved it from mere authoritarian sterility. The war between reason and passion produced the best art of the period, as exemplified in the work of Jacques-Louis David and his pupils, including the "romantic classicist" Antoine Jean Gros. The other partial counterweight to strict classicism was provided by the increase in knowledge of Egyptian art brought back from Napoleon's Egyptian campaign. A cult of Egyptomania was grafted onto classical models.

Napoleon as the central figure in the culture of the period believed that "what is big is always beautiful" (Tulard 1985, p. 224). The pure Empire style as an expression of power is therefore best seen in architecture, where Napoleon's activity was concentrated almost entirely in Paris. He wanted to make the French capital "not only the most beautiful city that has ever existed, but the most beautiful city imaginable" (Connelly 1985, p. 19). Paris would express Napoleon's revival of the Roman Empire and the ideals of antiquity. It would be studded with such monuments "as there used to be in Athens." The results are still there for all to see: the Arc de Triomphe, the Rue de Rivoli, the Vendôme column, the Bourse, the Madeleine (originally built as the Temple de la Gloire), the Arc du Carrousel, and various public buildings and fountains.

The Empire style is shown in more modest mode in sculpture and the decorative arts. Napoleon's favorite sculptor, Antonio Canova, gained Europe-wide fame with his busts and statues of the Bonaparte family. Probably his best known work, his semi-nude portrayal of Pauline Bonaparte as Venus, completed in 1808, exemplifies Canova's brand of sensuous classicism. Neoclassical sculpture in general seems to symbolize Napoleonic taste, despite Napoleon's personal aversion for public sculptures of himself. The same classical lines may be seen in Empire furniture, albeit partly hidden by carvings of imperial motifs and ornate drapery, in silverware, and even in carpets.

Although male fashion followed British models, settling into an ensemble style that would become the modern suit, the Empire style for women followed discreet classical lines. Female fashion under the Directory and Consulate, although supposedly inspired by antiquity, had reached semiclad extremes out of keeping with Napoleon's puritanical sobriety in such matters. Under the Empire waistlines were high and dresses and tunics straight: the female form was outlined but not emphasized. Sleeves were short and puffed. Mme. Récamier, the reigning beauty of the early empire, made white the fashionable color in the highest circles. Hair, cut short in "antique" style, was adorned with jewels and ribbons, and hairstyles became more complicated in the later days of the regime. Turbans, another Egyptian inspiration, were also in vogue. The Empire style of fashion, confined to a

François Gérard's portrait **Joséphine (1801)** *is more direct and intimate than later official portraits. She is shown relaxing at Malmaison, dressed in what became the Empire style. (Giraudon/Art Resource)*

small group of style-setting women, including Mme. Récamier and Pauline Bonaparte, complemented the pseudo-antique grandeur of its surroundings and of the grandiose public world Napoleon was trying to create. "The *style empire,*" writes the historian Timothy Wilson-Smith, "was not invented by Napoleon . . . but it looked as if it had been invented for Napoleon" (Wilson-Smith 1996, p. xxix).

Related entries: David, Jacques-Louis; Denon, Dominique Vivant; Gros, Antoine Jean; Récamier, Jeanne Françoise Julie Adélaïde; Romanticism; Vernet, Émile Jean Horace

Suggestions for further reading:
Boime, Albert. 1990. *Art in an Age of Bonapartism, 1800–15*. Chicago: University of Chicago Press.
Connelly, Owen, ed. 1985. *Historical Dictionary of Napoleonic France, 1799–1815*. Westport, CT: Greenwood.
Gonzalez-Palacios, Alvar. 1970. *The French Empire Style*. London: Hamlyn.
Honour, Hugh. 1968. *Neo-Classicism*. Harmondsworth, England: Penguin.
Tulard, Jean. 1985. *Napoleon: The Myth of the Saviour*. London: Methuen.

Wilson-Smith, Timothy. 1996. *Napoleon and His Artists.* London: Constable.

Enghien, Louis Antoine Henri de Condé, Duc d' (1772–1804)

The kidnapping and execution, amounting to judicial murder, of the duke of Enghien, last of the Condé Princes of the Blood, in 1804 put an end to royalist conspiracies against Napoleon at the cost of enraging the crowned heads of Europe. The seizure of Enghien, totally illegally, in neutral Baden, indicated Napoleon's meddling in the affairs of Germany and his desire to send a warning to Louis XVIII and the *émigrés* at his court. The duke was taken to Vincennes, tried for treason by a military court, and executed by firing squad on 20 March 1804. He was to be remembered as young and handsome and the last of a distinguished military line stretching back many generations. Tsar Alexander I, who had been deeply implicated in the murder of his own father, was especially outraged, broke off diplomatic relations with France, and began to make overtures to London and Vienna for a new alliance. Joseph Fouché's comment that the execution of Enghien "was worse than a crime, it was a mistake" has become proverbial.

Related entries: Royalism

Suggestions for further reading:
Arnold, Eric A. 1979. *Fouché, Napoleon and the General Police.* Washington: University Press of America.

Enlightenment

The question of Napoleon's relationship to the eighteenth-century movement of rational thought about society and politics permits of no easy answer. Those who see Napoleon as the heir to the Enlightenment can point to his attempted rationalization of government and administration, the codification of law, the preservation of civic equality and religious freedom. In this perspective Napoleon has been described as the last of the enlightened despots, the heir to such rulers as Frederick the Great of Prussia or Catherine the Great of Russia. For others, however, Napoleon's despotic government, with all power concentrated in the hands of the emperor, is a betrayal of both Enlightened thought and the best ideals of the Revolution. In the age of the American Revolution and in light of British constitutionalism, Napoleon's authoritarianism seems little different from absolute monarchy.

If Napoleon was in any way a product of the Enlightenment, it was through his belief in the triumph of merit, in careers open to the talented, and in the superiority of the present over the monarchic past. The young Napoleon was a great reader of Jean-Jacques Rousseau, and later of Voltaire and Montesquieu. Their influence certainly helps to explain his early commitment to Jacobinism. But once in power he distanced himself from the boldest thought of the eighteenth century and his own youthful idealism. Napoleon as emperor was above all a pragmatist, even in his preservation of many of the positive gains of the Revolution. The only knowledge he valued was practical knowledge. His attitude toward "nonuseful" knowledge is summed up in his words to Alexander von Humboldt in 1805: "You are interested in botany? So is my wife."

Related entries: Centralization; Education; *Idéologues;* Jacobinism; Law, Codification of

Suggestions for further reading:
Cobban, Alfred. 1960. *In Search of Humanity: The Role of the Enlightenment in Modern History.* New York: G. Braziller.
Hampson, Norman. 1968. *The Enlightenment.* Harmondsworth, England: Penguin.

Erfurt, Congress of (27 September– 14 October 1808)

The meeting between Napoleon and Alexander I at the small Thuringian town of Erfurt, sixty-five miles southwest of Leipzig, was a spectacular if ultimately empty dramatization of Napoleon's power. The congress was meant to strengthen the Franco-Russian alliance concluded by the Treaty of Tilsit in 1807, provide for cooperation against Austria, strengthen the Continental System, and not least impress the tsar and the princes of Germany. Erfurt therefore played host to two emperors and a horde of kings, princes, and dukes representing the whole of Germany except Prussia and Austria. The *Comédie Française* with Joseph Talma in the lead performed nine plays before a "pit full of kings," who then adjourned to a series of balls and banquets. But the diplomatic results were negligible: the alliance between France and Russia was confirmed, but Alexander avoided any further commitment against Austria. The tsar was in a stronger position than a year earlier, and rifts between him and Napoleon would not be long delayed.

Related entries: Alexander I, Tsar of Russia; Russia

Suggestions for further reading:
Niven, Alexander C. 1978. *Napoleon and Alexander I.* Washington: University Press of America.
Ragsdale, Hugh. 1980. *Détente in the Napoleonic Era: Bonaparte and the Russians.* Lawrence, KS: Regents Press.
Ross, Steven T. 1981. *European Diplomatic History, 1789–1815.* Malabar, FL: Krieger.

Essling, Battle of (21–22 May 1809)

Also known as the Battle of Aspern or Aspern-Essling, this engagement on the banks of the Danube was the only reverse suffered by Napoleon during the Wagram campaign of 1809. Having captured Vienna, Napoleon needed a decisive victory against the main Austrian army to force the Austrian monarchy to the negotiating table. Having successfully bridged the Danube at Lobau Island Napoleon aimed to establish his troops on the north bank at the villages of Aspern and Essling, but now faced a series of attacks by the Archduke Charles, the Austrian commander in chief. Although the villages were defensible, the destruction of the Lobau pontoon bridge meant that Napoleon could not bring up sufficient reinforcements to continue the fighting. Under continuous artillery barrage and infantry assaults the French fell back to the bridgehead. Among the 20,000 to 25,000 men killed or wounded on each side was Marshal Jean Lannes. Although the battle fizzled out and despite the fact that the French had been rebuffed rather than routed, the news of a defeat for Napoleon spread across Europe, giving his enemies hopes, which would, however, be shattered by the battle of Wagram seven weeks later.

Related entries: Charles, Archduke of Austria; Danube Campaigns; Wagram, Battle of

Suggestions for further reading:
Gates, David. 1997. *The Napoleonic Wars, 1803–15.* London: Edward Arnold.
Horward, Donald D. 1987. "Lannes," in David G. Chandler, ed., *Napoleon's Marshals.* New York: Macmillan.
Parker, Harold T. 1983. *Three Napoleonic Battles.* Durham, NC: Duke University Press.
Rothenberg, Gunther E. 1982. *Napoleon's Great Adversaries: The Archduke Charles and the Austrian Army, 1792–1814.* London: Batsford.

Eylau, Battle of (7–8 February 1807)

This indecisive battle in Napoleon's Polish campaign has been described by the historian David Gates as "one of the

Jean-Antoine Gros's **Napoleon at the Battle of Eylau** *(1808) is a subtle piece of propaganda showing Napoleon and his marshals surveying the horrors of the field of Eylau the day after battle. Grateful Poles and Lithuanians kneel before their savior while a dying common soldier lifts his arms to salute the Christ-like emperor. (Scala/Art Resource)*

most gory and confused engagements in military history" (Gates 1997, p. 71). The main French army, under nagging attacks from Prince Bagration's Russian rearguard, occupied the town of Preussisch-Eylau, just inside the East Prussian border, on 7 February 1807, but the main Russian force under Count Levin Bennigsen was in position in the plains to the north of Eylau.

On the morning of 8 February the rolling terrain was buried under a meter of snow, and a raging blizzard obscured the movements of both armies. In the ensuing confusion, the Russians laid an artillery barrage on Eylau, and Napoleon, who had probably not originally intended any major initiative, found his initial moves repulsed. The Russians penetrated Eylau and almost captured his headquarters. His position was saved, however, by a remarkable charge against the Russian batteries by the cavalry

of Joachim Murat and by the reinforcement of his center by the arrival of the corps commanded by Michel Ney and Louis Davout. In the ensuing appalling hand-to-hand mêlée the Russians, despite the arrival of Prussian reinforcements, were gradually driven back. Bennigsen's forces withdrew during the night, having lost some 25,000 casualties, with the exhausted French only able to mount a desultory pursuit.

French losses were on a similar horrific scale to those of the Allies, and Napoleon's cavalry, despite their outstanding bravery against the Russian guns, had been shattered. Napoleon had lost many experienced troops, and he immediately set about rebuilding the morale of his army. Ney, viewing the carnage in the cold light of dawn, observed: "What a massacre! And with no result!" Even Napoleon in the official bulletin of the battle declared: "Such a sight as this should inspire rulers with love of peace and hatred of war" (Gates 1997, pp. 73–75). The town of Eylau was renamed Bagrationovsk when the Red Army occupied the region in 1945.

Related entries: Bagration, Pyotr Ivanovich, Prince; Murat, Joachim; Ney, Michel

Suggestions for further reading:
Gates, David. 1997. *The Napoleonic Wars, 1803–15*. London: Edward Arnold.

Federalism

The federalist revolt against the Jacobin government in 1793 engulfed
large areas of France and major cities including Lyon, Bordeaux, Marseille, and
Toulon. This major crisis of the Revolution
did, however, provide opportunities for ambitious soldiers. Napoleon first gained fame
as artillery commander in the siege of
Toulon against the federalists and their
British reinforcements between September
and December 1793.

Related entries: Toulon, Siege of

Suggestions for further reading:
Sutherland, D. M. G. 1985. *France, 1789–1815:
Revolution and Counter-Revolution*. London:
Fontana.
Sydenham, M. J. 1981. "The Republican Revolt
of 1793," *French Historical Studies* 12, pp.
120–138.

Fédéré Movement

The latent support for Napoleon during the Hundred Days was shown in
the spontaneous formation in May 1815 of
units of *fédérés* who sought to infiltrate the
National Guard and swore fidelity to the
emperor and the empire. Dedicated to preventing a second Bourbon Restoration, the
fédérés wanted Napoleon to become a revolutionary emperor, fulfilling and consolidating the work of the Revolution. In some
parts of France the *fédérés* were predominantly middle class, but the 14,000 *fédérés
travailleurs* of Paris were drawn from the
popular classes. Fearful of revolutionary violence, Napoleon refused to arm the
Parisian *fédérés,* his most fervent supporters,
or use them for a coup against the assemblies, and abdicated instead. For all the emperor's distrust of them, the *fédérés* showed
the existence of a popular Bonapartism that
was to persist throughout the nineteenth
century.

Related entries: Bonapartism; Hundred Days

Suggestions for further reading:
Alexander, R. S. 1991. *Bonapartism and the
Revolutionary Tradition in France: The Fédérés of
1815.* Cambridge: Cambridge University
Press.

Ferdinand VII, King of Spain (1784–1833)

As prince of Asturias and heir to the
Spanish throne Ferdinand continu-
ally plotted against his father, Charles IV, his
mother, Queen Maria Luisa, and their first
minister, Manuel Godoy. His opposition to
the universally unpopular Godoy gained
Ferdinand a thoroughly undeserved popu-

larity, even among Spanish liberals. In 1808, as the French army approached Madrid, Ferdinand overthrew his father and proclaimed himself king, but Napoleon forced both claimants to abdicate. Ferdinand spent the next five years in comfortable exile in the château of Valençay, refusing British offers to help him to escape, while the Spanish people rose and sacrificed themselves on his behalf in the uprising against the French. He returned to Spain after Napoleon's first abdication in 1814, immediately renounced the liberal Cadiz Constitution of 1812, and persecuted his liberal opponents. Ferdinand's bad faith plunged Spain backwards, dashing the hopes of many who had supported him when he was in gilded exile, and his tyrannical rule led to a new revolt in 1820.

Related entries: Charles IV, King of Spain; Godoy, Manuel; Peninsular War; Spain

Suggestions for further reading:
Carr, Raymond. 1982. *Spain: 1808–1975*. 2nd ed. Oxford: Clarendon Press.
Lovett, Gabriel H. 1965. *Napoleon and the Birth of Modern Spain*. 2 vols. New York: New York University Press.
Lynch, John. 1989. *Bourbon Spain, 1700–1808*. Oxford: Basil Blackwell.

Fesch, Joseph (1763–1839)

Napoleon's "Uncle Fesch," a halfbrother of Maria Letizia Bonaparte, was ordained as a priest in 1785, but abandoned his clerical state to work for his nephew's war commissariat in 1796. This brought him considerable financial rewards, but in 1800 Napoleon as first consul recalled him to the Church. In 1802 he was named archbishop of Lyon, the highest position in the Gallican Church, and was made a cardinal in January 1803. Sent as ambassador to the Vatican in 1804, he transmitted the demand that Pius VII attend at Napoleon's coronation, but the demand was rejected by the pope, forcing Napoleon

to write personally and more politely to induce Pius to travel to Paris for the great occasion. Fesch himself also attended and was afterward named grand almoner of the imperial household and accumulated various other titles and incomes.

As churchman and imperial official Fesch acted first and foremost in his nephew's interests. In particular, he played an important role in securing the annulment of Napoleon's marriage to Joséphine de Beauharnais, at which he had officiated, opening the way for the new marriage to Marie-Louise. But he also used his position to restore the training of the priesthood in the empire. Klemens von Metternich described him as "a strange compound of bigotry and ambition," adding: "although sincerely devout, he was not far from believing Napoleon to be the instrument of Heaven and an all but supernatural being" (Seward 1986, p. 122).

Fesch had always adopted a somewhat bullying attitude toward Pius VII, especially when the pope was under French constraint between 1809 and 1813. On Napoleon's first abdication Fesch escorted his sister, "Madame Mère," to Rome. After returning to Lyon during the Hundred Days, he hurriedly regained safety in Italy after the second abdication. The pope did not allow him to return to Lyon, and he spent the rest of his life amassing a fabulous art collection, which on his death was bequeathed to Lyon and his birthplace of Ajaccio.

Related entries: Catholic Church; Papacy; Pius VII, Pope

Suggestions for further reading:
Hales, Edward Elton Young. 1962. *Napoleon and the Pope*. London: Eyre and Spottiswoode.
Seward, Desmond. 1986. *Napoleon's Family*. London: Weidenfeld and Nicolson.

Finance

Napoleon needed ever increasing amounts of money to finance his government, his armed forces, and his empire. Though no expert in financial matters, his reorganization of the collection of taxation put him on the way to a tight financial administration. Expenses were rigorously monitored and a sinking fund established, chiefly to intervene on the stock market and keep the price of government bonds high. In the rare years of peace the budget was balanced, and in war years nearly kept in balance by quartering troops abroad and levying contributions on allies and defeated enemies. But the principle that "war should pay for war" depended on victory, and the defeats of 1812–1813 hit the budget hard.

Napoleon consistently refused to resort to loans or to paper money, and on problems of credit his ideas have been described as primitive. The only alternative in the final years of crisis was an enormous increase in direct taxes, a significant element in his rising unpopularity. Although his ideas on public credit put Napoleon at a considerable disadvantage compared with Great Britain, he kept his regime going to the end and founded structures in budgetary control and banking that would endure.

Related entries: Bank of France; *Biens Nationaux;* Centralization; Economy; Industry; Taxation

Suggestions for further reading:
Bergeron, Louis. 1981. *France under Napoleon.* Princeton: Princeton University Press.
Clough, Shepherd B. 1939. *France: A History of National Economics, 1789–1939.* New York: Charles Scribner's Sons.
Holtman, Robert B. 1967. *The Napoleonic Revolution.* Philadelphia: Lippincott.

Five Days, Battles of

*T*his series of brilliant actions against the invading Allied armies in February 1814 constituted the high point of Napoleon's inspired but doomed defense of France and restored his own and the French army's martial reputation. Leading paltry forces of veterans and green conscripts, many of doubtful commitment, and amid general popular indifference, Napoleon personally led his ragtag army to four victories in five days, at Champaubert (10 February), Montmirail (11 February), Château-Thierry (12 February), and Vauchamps (14 February).

The immense difficulties he faced seemed to reinvigorate Napoleon. While the main Allied force under Prince Karl zu Schwarzenberg advanced toward Paris along the Seine valley, the Army of Silesia under Gebhard von Blücher progressed along the Marne. Blücher, overanxious to get to Paris and assuming that Napoleon would be held in the valley of the Seine by Schwarzenberg's vastly superior forces, badly overextended his forces, allowing Napoleon to take him by surprise. Striking north then west Napoleon overwhelmed a Russian corps at Champaubert, then a combined Russo-Prussian force at Montmirail, and on 12 February he drove his opponents across the Marne at Château-Thierry, capturing prisoners, guns, and baggage. Learning the next day that a Prussian force commanded by Blücher himself was moving westward toward Montmirail, Napoleon led his weary troops to meet it at Vauchamps on 14 February, forcing Blücher to withdraw toward Châlons.

Despite being "one of the most brilliant campaigns in military annals "(Gates 1997, p. 256), the Five Days battles could only slow down the inexorable Allied advance toward Paris. Paradoxically, the ultimate result of Napoleon's startling victories was to jolt his squabbling enemies back into cooperation. With stiffened resolve on 9 March they signed the Treaties of Chaumont, which committed them not only to continuing the war but to maintaining their collaboration for twenty years after any peace settlement.

Related entries: Blücher, Gebhard Leberecht von; Coalitions

Suggestions for further reading:

Chandler, David G. 1974. *The Campaigns of Napoleon: The Mind and Method of History's Greatest Soldier.* New York: Macmillan.

Gates, David. 1997. *The Napoleonic Wars, 1803–15.* London: Edward Arnold.

Hamilton-Williams, David. 1994. *The Fall of Napoleon: The Final Betrayal.* London: John Wiley.

Lawford, James P. 1977. *Napoleon: The Last Campaigns.* New York: Crown.

Fontainebleau Decree (18 October 1810)

*T*his final attempt to make Napoleon's Continental System effective was made after other measures that had weakened it by widening the range of licenses for trade. The new decree ordered the confiscation and sale by the state of intercepted unlicensed colonial goods, the destruction of prohibited manufactured goods, and stiffer penalties for smuggling. Its chief value was in increasing revenue through its first provision, and it remained in operation for the next two years.

Related entries: Continental System

Suggestions for further reading:

Hecksher, E. F. 1922. *The Continental System: An Economic Interpretation.* Oxford: Publications of the Carnegie Endowment for International Peace.

Fouché, Joseph (1760–1820)

*N*apoleon's feared but untrustworthy Minister of Police was one of the great political survivors, usually to be relied upon to be playing both ends against the middle. Born at Nantes, the son of a merchant sea captain, Fouché received a full education, intending to be a teacher, but was soon caught up in Revolutionary politics. A zealous Jacobin, he was nevertheless close to Paul Barras, and became Minister of General Police for the Directory shortly before the coup of 18 Brumaire, which he supported by neglecting to inform the Directors of the plot against them. Retained in his post by the consulate, in May 1802 Fouché was diplomatically absent from the meeting of the Council of State which created Napoleon consul for life, and four months later was dismissed.

Reappointed as minister of police in July 1804 with greater powers than previously, Fouché held the post until May 1810, when he was dismissed for making contacts with the British. Using every available technique bequeathed by the ancien régime and the Revolution, Fouché put in place a network of informers to create the first modern political police. As the most feared and probably the best-informed member of the government he was in a position both to feather his nest and send his own agents to London. But his intriguing reached its height in 1814–1815. After Napoleon's first abdication, Fouché warned the restored Bourbons that the exiled emperor might land in southern France, while at the same time plotting with Bonapartist officers to proclaim a regency in the name of Napoleon II. During the Hundred Days he was again minister of police, but after Waterloo took the lead in making contact with Louis XVIII and securing Napoleon's second abdication.

Despite his regicide past, Fouché served the restored monarchy briefly as minister of police between July and September 1815. During this time he drew up a list of those who had served Napoleon on his return, causing Charles-Maurice de Talleyrand, himself no mean intriguer, to comment sardonically: "One must do M. Fouché the justice to recognize that he has left out none of his friends" (Horne 1996, p. 383). Though exiled as a regicide, he served as a diplomatic envoy in Saxony for a year before retiring to Trieste to enjoy the fruits of a lifetime of wheeler-dealing in peace.

Related entries: Abdication, First; Abdication; Second; Barras, Paul François Jean Nicolas, Vicomte de; Brumaire, Coup of Year VIII; Censorship; Constitutions; Hundred Days; Imperial Police; Malet Conspiracy; Opera Plot; Opposition Movements

Suggestions for further reading:
Arnold, Eric A. 1979. *Fouché, Napoleon and the General Police.* Washington: University Press of America.
Cole, Hubert. 1971. *Fouché: The Unprincipled Patriot.* London: Eyre and Spottiswoode.
Cubberley, R. E. 1969. *The Role of Fouché during the Hundred Days.* Madison: Wisconsin University Press.
Horne, Alistair. 1996 *How Far from Austerlitz? Napoleon 1805–1815.* London: Macmillan.

Francis I, Emperor of Austria (1768–1835) (Holy Roman Emperor as Francis II, 1792–1806; Emperor of Austria as Francis I, 1806–1835)

Almost immediately on his succession to the throne of the Holy Roman Empire in 1792 Francis II was at war with France. Thereafter he was a party in all the successive coalitions against Revolutionary and Napoleonic France, while blocking reforms within Austria as leading onto the slippery slope toward revolution. As a succession of treaties imposed by Napoleon from Campo Formio in 1797 to Schönbrunn in 1809 reduced the Habsburg domains to Austria, Hungary, Bohemia, and Styria, Francis was forced to dissolve the Holy Roman Empire in 1806, while consistently opposing the radical reform of the army proposed by the Archduke Charles and any kind of internal political change.

Conscientious but ineffective and totally lacking in imagination, Francis was fortu-nate in being served by the equally reactionary but skillful and realistic Klemens von Metternich, who was appointed foreign minister in 1809. It was Metternich rather than his master who managed to steer a diplomatic course between France and Russia and accept the marriage between Napoleon and Marie-Louise, Francis's eldest surviving daughter. Francis saw the defeat of Napoleon as a victory over the Revolution and revolutionary ideas, never making any distinction between French radicalism and Napoleon's armies. For the rest of his reign after 1815 he left it largely to Metternich to preserve the status quo in Austria and Europe.

Related entries: Austria; Charles, Archduke of Austria; Coalitions; Marie-Louise von Habsburg, Empress; Metternich, Klemens Wenceslas Lothar, Fürst von

Suggestions for further reading:
Bérenger, Jean. 1994. *A History of the Habsburg Empire.* London and New York: Longman.
Langsam, Walter C. 1930. *The Napoleonic Wars and German Nationalism in Austria.* New York: Columbia University Press.
————. 1949. *Francis the Good: The Education of an Emperor, 1768–1792.* New York: Macmillan.

Frankfurt, Grand Duchy of

Napoleon reorganized the territory around Frankfurt-am-Main as the Grand Duchy of Frankfurt in 1810, essentially for the benefit of Eugène de Beauharnais, who was due eventually to lose the income from the Kingdom of Italy to the benefit of Napoleon's son or sons. The first grand duke was Karl Theodor von Dalberg, prince primate of the Confederation of the Rhine, who was to be succeeded by Eugène.

The grand duchy, with its approximately 300,000 inhabitants, was divided into four departments—Frankfurt, Hanau, Aschaffen-burg, and Fulda—administered by prefects assisted by appointed councils. The grand duke ruled with a state council and estates elected by departmental colleges. Local administration was based on the French model, with departments divided into districts and municipalities governed by mayors with elected municipal councils. The Napoleonic legal codes were introduced in 1811, serfdom abolished, and Jews emancipated. The emancipation edicts, however, were tied to high redemption payments, as Napoleon's financial requirements limited the effectiveness of reforms. But the middle and lower levels of the administration witnessed a minor social revolution, as nobles were replaced with bourgeois officials.

The grand duchy was dissolved after the battle of Leipzig in October 1813, and Emperor Francis I made a ceremonial entry into Frankfurt on 6 November. At the Congress of Vienna Frankfurt regained its former status as a free city, which it remained until absorbed by Prussia in 1866.

Related entries: Confederation of the Rhine

Suggestions for further reading:
Sheehan, James J. 1989. *German History, 1770–1866*. Oxford: Clarendon Press.

Frederick William III, King of Prussia (1770–1840; reigned 1797–1840)

Frederick William, great-nephew of Frederick the Great, presided over the near-liquidation of Prussia by Napoleon and then over its reconstruction. During his early years on the throne he was sympathetic to reform, accomplishing the liberation of peasants on crown lands, but backed down in the face of the great landowners and remained suspicious about any form of representative government. Until 1805 Frederick William's foreign policy consisted of neutrality coupled with slow

reaction to external events. When he finally entered the war against Napoleon in 1806 the result was the disastrous defeat of Jaen-Auerstädt. The survival of the Prussian monarchy owed more to the decisiveness of Frederick William's wife, Louise of Mecklenburg, and to the diplomacy of Alexander I than it did to the king himself.

Although in effect a client king of Napoleon until 1813, unable even to reside in Berlin between October 1806 and Christmas 1809, Frederick William did at last give support to the civil and military reforms necessary for Prussian revival. When he joined the fight against Napoleon in 1813 Frederick William issued emotional appeals to the German people to rise against the foreign invader, but any hopes for radical political reform would be dashed after 1815. The king was present at the battles of Bautzen, Dresden, and Leipzig and entered Paris behind Alexander I in 1814. At the Congress of Vienna he managed to cooperate with Russia and compromise with Austria. After 1815 he maintained the essential reforms of the Napoleonic period and pursued progressive economic and religious policies, so that, despite the persecution of political dissidents, his fellow autocrats considered him less repressive than was desirable.

Related entries: Louise of Mecklenburg, Queen of Prussia; Prussia

Suggestions for further reading:
Haffner, Sebastian. 1980. *The Rise and Fall of Prussia*. London: Weidenfeld and Nicolson.
Ross, Steven T. 1981. *European Diplomatic History, 1789–1815*. Malabar, FL: Krieger.

Freemasonry

The Masonic lodges of France had been persecuted during the Terror but reemerged under the Directory. Napoleon realized that freemasonry could be useful to his regime as part of the establishment and reorganized it into a single rite, the Grand Orient, deist and rationalist in ideology. Headed by Napoleon's brothers, leading ministers like Jean-Jacques de Cambacérès, generals, prefects, administrators, and local notables, the Grand Orient expanded rapidly and by 1814 controlled 886 lodges and 337 chapters in France. The most rapid spread of masonry was in the army, which in 1805 had 132 lodges. A quarter of all infantry officers were masons.

Freemasonry followed Napoleon's armies into Europe, contacting and absorbing indigenous lodges and creating new ones. In all some 400 lodges were set up by army officers in conquered Europe. They were seen as a way of winning over local elites, with most success in Germany, Italy, and Switzerland. In the Rhineland, for example, there were seventeen lodges, with 170 French and 345 local members. But French-dominated masonry was weak in Holland and in the Duchy of Warsaw, where it was identified entirely with Napoleonic rule, sporting arms bearing the Napoleonic "N," but opposed by the powerful Catholic clergy. It failed totally in Spain and Portugal, where local elites refused completely to join lodges dominated by French army officers.

Suggestions for further reading:
Roberts, J. M. 1972. *The Mythology of the Secret Societies*. London: Secker and Warburg.
Woolf, Stuart. 1991. *Napoleon's Integration of Europe*. London and New York: Routledge.

Friedland, Battle of (14 June 1807)

This decisive victory for Napoleon in the spring campaign of 1807 effectively forced Tsar Alexander I to negotiate the Treaty of Tilsit in July of that year. Some 50,000 Russians under Levin von Bennigsen faced 80,000 of the *Grande Armée,* which had been wintering in Poland after defeating the Prussians in the campaigns of 1806. Friedland shows to the full Napoleon's ability to size up a situation, suck an enemy into a major battle, and tailor his tactics to take maximum advantage of the ground and the enemy's dispositions.

Napoleon had sent his five army corps northwards along the left bank of the River Alle in East Prussia, hoping to reach the Russian base of Königsberg before the Russians. On 13 June a detachment of cavalry from the French advance guard under Jean Lannes encountered Russian cavalry near Friedland, a small town on the left bank of the Alle some thirty-five kilometers from Königsberg. During the night, Bennigsen moved his forces across the river to the Friedland side, believing Napoleon and his main force to be much farther away than they actually were. Lannes swiftly brought up the rest of his corps, but when fighting began in the early hours of 14 June the Russians enjoyed overwhelming numerical advantage. Despite a series of vigorous cavalry charges led by Emmanuel de Grouchy, Lannes sent desperately for help from Napoleon, who was still at Eylau, twenty kilometers to the southwest.

Napoleon acted decisively, reminding the messenger, Captain Marbot, that 14 June was the anniversary of the battle of Marengo. While Lannes's corps continued to resist the Russians, Napoleon stationed himself on elevated land and saw that Bennigsen, counting neither on Lannes's resistance nor Napoleon's swift arrival, had put himself in a dangerous position, with a river to his rear and with every likelihood of being outnumbered. The arrival of the Imperial Guard, the corps commanded by Michel Ney and Joseph Mortier, and heavy cavalry gave the French the numerical advantage when the battle proper began in the late afternoon, after Napoleon had given his men time for rest. The plan was simple and worked perfectly.

Mortier and Lannes kept the Russian center and right occupied, while Ney's corps, supported by cavalry charges and an artillery barrage the likes of which the Russian troops had never seen before, hit the Russian left wing from the front and flank, driving it back into Friedland and destroying the bridges constructed by the Russians in crossing the Alle, which were their only avenue of retreat. Mortier and Lannes then advanced against the Russian center and right, starting a slaughter that lasted until nightfall. Russian casualties were estimated at between 18,000 and 20,000 dead or wounded, the French between 7,000 and 8,000.

Related entries: Germany, Campaigns in

Suggestions for further reading:

Lunt, James D. 1987. "Grouchy," in David G. Chandler, ed., *Napoleon's Marshals.* New York: Macmillan.

Parker, Harold T. 1983. *Three Napoleonic Battles.* Durham, NC: Duke University Press.

G

Gaudin, Martin Michel Charles (1756–1844)

Napoleon's minister of finance between 1799 and 1814 and again during the Hundred Days in 1815 was an experienced financial official who had entered the tax-collecting service of the monarchy in 1779 and continued to serve the various regimes of the Revolution. Under Napoleon Gaudin was responsible for the collection of taxes, a task he performed with honesty and method. He recruited a hierarchy of tax collectors and prepared the national *cadastre,* the survey of land that served as the basis for local tax assessment. Gaudin taught Napoleon much about the basics of sound financial administration, and the emperor appreciated his "clear ideas and severe probity" (Connelly, 1985, p. 203), giving him the title of duke of Gaeta. After the Restoration Gaudin served in the Chamber of Deputies and was governor of the Bank of France from 1820 to 1834.

Related entries: Finance; Statistics; Taxation

Suggestions for further reading:
Bergeron, Louis. 1981. *France under Napoleon.* Princeton: Princeton University Press.
Connelly, Owen, ed. *Historical Dictionary of Napoleonic France, 1799–1815.* Westport, CT: Greenwood.

Gendarmerie

The mounted *gendarmerie* was the one police force Napoleon kept out of the hands of the untrustworthy Joseph Fouché, entrusting its command instead to Marshal Adrien de Moncey. A traditional force, primarily concerned with imposing order in the countryside, under Napoleon the *gendarmerie* in many areas expended much effort on attempts to round up refractory conscripts and deserters. This helped to make *gendarmes* as unpopular as they were too few in number, underfinanced, and corruptible.

Related entries: Conscription; Imperial Police

Suggestions for further reading:
Arnold, Eric A. 1979. *Fouché, Napoleon and the General Police.* Washington: University Press of America.

Generals

Promotion in the Napoleonic armies was still based on the Revolutionary principles of merit, talent, and elections, but Napoleon gradually suppressed the remaining elective element, and from 1805 onward personally nominated all his generals. Himself sometimes called "the most civilian of generals," Napoleon robbed his generals of the powers of patronage and independence that had played such a role in his own rise to prominence, powers that had led to several prominent generals changing sides during the revolutionary wars. Though the idea that each Napoleonic general "carried a marshal's baton in his knapsack" was a myth, Napoleon wanted and got generals who were both educated in the theory of warfare and experienced on the battlefield. As part of the new elite of notables it was in the generals' interest to serve Napoleon well, but he allowed them little initiative on campaign or in battle. Napoleon was the only master in his army. Generals were honored and an integral part of the ruling elite, but the Napoleonic regime cannot be called a military dictatorship in the modern sense of the word.

Related entries: Army

Suggestions for further reading:
Bertaud, Jean-Paul. 1986. "Napoleon's Officers," *Past & Present,* no. 112 (August 1986), pp. 91–111.
Rogers, H. C. B. 1974. *Napoleon's Army.* London: Allen.

Genoa

The principal seaport in the western Mediterranean had been one of the great Italian republics and ruler of Corsica until 1768. Jacobin feeling had developed strongly in Genoa during the early 1790s, and when the city was captured during Napoleon's first Italian campaign in 1796 the Ligurian Republic was established as a satellite "sister republic" of France. André Masséna was besieged there between April and June 1800, causing great suffering to the people. The republic lasted until 1805, when Genoa was absorbed into France. Napoleon made a ceremonial entry on 30 June 1805. After Napoleon's defeat in 1814–1815 Genoa was incorporated into the Kingdom of Sardinia-Piedmont, a move which led to vigorous debate and condemnation in the British parliament.

Related entries: Italian Campaigns; Ligurian Republic

Suggestions for further reading:
Chandler, David G. 1974. *The Campaigns of Napoleon: The Mind and Method of History's Greatest Soldier.* New York: Macmillan.

Germany, Campaigns in

The Jena-Auerstädt-Friedland campaign in 1806–1807 assured Napoleon's control of east-central Europe and forced Russia to sue for peace, and illustrates his way of fighting a devastating war of maneuver. The campaign of 1813, however, known in German history as the War of Liberation, showed that following the disaster in Russia he could no longer withstand the Seventh Coalition, as the German states backed by Russia finally united against him.

In 1806 he faced the still unreformed and poorly led Prussian army, of which Carl von Clausewitz remarked that "behind the fine facade, all was mildewed" (Gates 1997, p. 52). While the Prussians advanced into the Erfurt-Weimar region of central Germany, Napoleon performed one of his surprising *manoeuvres sur les derrières,* moving six corps and the Imperial Guard through the rocky and twisting roads of mountainous Thuringia, thereby penetrating into the Prussians' rear and cutting their communications with Dresden, Leipzig, and Berlin. Throwing his net around the retreating Prussians, he defeated them decisively at the battle of Jena-Auerstädt (14 October 1806) and entered Berlin on 25 October.

The Prussians, however, despite the almost complete collapse of the monarchy, could still fight on with Russian support.

Napoleon's army spent the winter in Prussian Poland, confronting the Russians in the bloody and pointless battle of Eylau (7–8 February 1807). In the spring Napoleon moved back onto the offensive, again using his cavalry to operate in the enemy's rear. At the Battle of Friedland on 14 June 1807 he inflicted such a severe defeat on them that Alexander I was forced to negotiate the Treaty of Tilsit.

In 1813 Napoleon was fighting with forces very different from the disciplined and battle-hardened *Grande Armée* of 1806–1807. The remnants of this force who had survived the Russian campaign, commanded by Eugène de Beauharnais, were concentrated in Saxony, while Napoleon, heading an army made up largely of inexperienced conscripts, crossed into Germany in April 1813. He defeated the Russo-Prussian forces at the battles of Lützen (2 May) and Bautzen (20 May), forcing them to retire beyond the river Oder, but these were costly victories and Napoleon accepted an armistice, which lasted from 4 June to 10 August, so as to gain time to rebuild his army. When the armistice ended he faced a coalition of Austria, Great Britain, Spain, Russia, Prussia, and Sweden.

Eugène in Saxony faced an impossible situation, with Austrian, Prussian, and Swedish armies converging on him from all directions. The Allies for once adopted the sensible strategy of only attacking isolated French corps, inflicting a series of defeats on those commanded by Nicolas Oudinot at Gross-Beeren (23 August), Jacques Macdonald on the Katzbach (26 August), Dominique Vandamme at Kulm (29–30 August), and Michel Ney at Dennewitz (16 September). Bavaria, France's traditional ally in Germany, defected to the Allies on 8 October. The three allied armies finally converged on Napoleon in the battle of Leipzig (16–19 October), the defeat that forced him to retire beyond the Rhine, leaving only a few besieged French garrisons to hold out briefly in Germany. The character of the war as a German national uprising against Napoleon has been exaggerated by nationalist historians, but it was decisive in his collapse, creating negative effects in Holland, Spain, and Italy.

Related entries: Austria; Bautzen, Battle of; Bavaria, Kingdom of; Coalitions; Confederation of the Rhine; Dresden; Eylau, Battle of; Jena-Auerstädt, Battles of; Leipzig, Battle of; Lützen, Battle of; Prussia; Saxony

Suggestions for further reading:
Chandler, David G. 1974. *The Campaigns of Napoleon: The Mind and Method of History's Greatest Soldier.* New York: Macmillan.
Connelly, Owen. 1987. *Blundering to Glory: Napoleon's Military Campaigns.* Wilmington, DE: Scholarly Resources.
Esposito, Vincent J., and John R. Elting. 1964. *A Military History and Atlas of the Napoleonic Wars.* New York: Praeger.
Gates, David. 1997. *The Napoleonic Wars, 1803–15.* London: Edward Arnold.
Gill, John H. 1992. *With Eagles to Glory: Napoleon and His German Allies in the 1809 Campaign.* Novato, CA: Presidio Press.
Petre, F. Loraine. 1972. *Napoleon's Conquest of Prussia, 1806.* London: Arms and Armour.
———. 1974. *Napoleon's Last Campaign in Germany, 1813.* London: Arms and Armour.

Gneisenau, August Wilhelm Anton Meithardt von (1760–1831)

One of the leading figures in the drive to modernize the Prussian army after the defeat of Jena in 1806, Gneisenau had been commissioned into the infantry in 1786, fought at Jena as a major, and became celebrated for his defense of the Baltic port of Kolberg in 1807. As a member of the Military Reorganization Commission he assisted Gerhard von Scharnhorst in a reform of the army based on the experience of facing Napoleon, seeking to open up recruitment and the appointment of officers to men of merit regardless of social origins. He was among the most radical of the reformers, viewed in reactionary circles as a dangerous revolutionary.

Gneisenau resigned his commission in 1808, but was used in secret missions to Britain, Austria, Russia, and Sweden in 1809 and 1810. Along with Gebhard von Blücher he believed that peace could only be secured by the total defeat of Napoleon, and he argued in vain for war in 1811. Between 1813 and 1815 he was Blücher's chief of staff, but his desire for an independent command was frustrated by court intrigue. Gneisenau made a notable contribution to the plan of operations in the battle of Leipzig, and during the Hundred Days after the defeat at Ligny he was responsible for the decision to move in the direction of Waterloo, thereby ensuring Napoleon's defeat. Gneisenau retired in 1816 and was made a field marshal in 1825 on the tenth anniversary of Waterloo, a belated recognition of the part his drive and initiative had played in making the Prussian army a fit adversary for Napoleon.

Related entries: Prussia; Scharnhorst, Gerhard Johann David von

Suggestions for further reading:
Shanahan, William O. 1945. *Prussian Military Reforms, 1786–1813*. New York: Columbia University Press.

Godoy, Manuel (1767–1851)

The dominant figure in Spanish politics during the reign of Charles IV, Godoy served at various times as first minister, commandant of the army, grand admiral of the navy, and (reputedly) lover of Queen Maria Luisa. He was responsible for the alliance between Spain and France in 1795, earning himself the purely honorific title of "Prince of Peace." When Napoleon became emperor in 1804 Godoy collaborated with France in every way possible,

thereby causing economic difficulties in many regions of Spain. The Treaty of Fontainebleau in October 1807 allowed French troops to cross Spain to invade Portugal, in effect an invasion of Spain itself. Godoy's pro-French policies, his anticlericalism, and his personal flamboyance made him unpopular with the Spanish aristocracy and common people alike, and he had made a particular enemy of the heir to the throne, the future Ferdinand VII. Napoleon for his part despised Godoy. When Ferdinand overthrew his father in 1808 Godoy barely escaped with his life, but he was present at the meeting at Bayonne when both Charles and Ferdinand were deposed. He spent the rest of his life in exile, first with Charles and Maria Luisa in Rome, later in Paris. His memoirs, published in 1836, have been described as a masterpiece of complacency.

Related entries: Charles IV, King of Spain; Ferdinand VII, King of Spain; Spain

Suggestions for further reading:
Chastenet, Jacques. 1953. *Godoy: Master of Spain.* London: Batchworth Press.
Hilt, Douglas. 1987. *The Troubled Trinity: Godoy and the Spanish Monarchs.* Tuscaloosa: University of Alabama Press.

Gouvion Saint-Cyr, Laurent (1764–1830)

Born in Toul, the son of a tanner, Gouvion left home and traveled to Italy and Paris as an artist. Abandoned by his mother, he nevertheless took her name of Saint-Cyr, preferring her memory to that of his abusive father. In 1792 he volunteered for the army, using the name Gouvion Saint-Cyr, and through the 1790s served in the Rhineland and his beloved Italy. Named commander of the Army of Rome in March 1798, he refused to serve under André Masséna, whom he despised for his greed and corruption, and was removed in July. As corps commander of the Army of the Rhine, he received his saber of honor from Consul Bonaparte and won the second battle of Biberach, his greatest personal success, on 9 May 1800.

Napoleon was always suspicious of Saint-Cyr's attitude but valued his abilities highly enough to send him to Spain as ambassador to Madrid, where he was reasonably successful and negotiated the sale of Louisiana to the United States. Back in Italy as head of the observation corps of the Kingdom of Naples, he clashed violently with Joachim Murat, his complete opposite in temperament and outlook. Saint-Cyr's reluctance to administer the oath of allegiance to the empire, on the grounds that the army should be above politics, caused his recall to France, where he was effectively inactive between 1804 and 1808, being recompensed somewhat with a string of titles, including that of count of the empire in 1808.

Recalled as commander of the Army of Catalonia in September 1808, Saint-Cyr was soon in trouble with Napoleon again, and he was suspended from active service in November 1809 on unjust charges of deserting his command. This injustice allowed his successor, Charles Augereau, who had delayed his arrival in Catalonia, to claim the credit for military successes prepared by Saint-Cyr. The suspension lasted three years, until Napoleon's Russian campaign of 1812, in which Saint-Cyr commanded the Bavarian corps, one of the most active and heroic sections of the *Grande Armée*. Under Saint-Cyr the Bavarians secured a famous victory in the battle of Polotsk on 18 August 1812, and further distinguished themselves in the defense of Dresden in the autumn of 1813. These were the years of Saint-Cyr's reconciliation and good relations with Napoleon, and he was created a marshal of the empire on 27 August 1812. Taken prisoner after the fall of Dresden, Saint-Cyr was only a distant spectator of Napoleon's fall.

During the Hundred Days Saint-Cyr tried to return to action, hoping to serve France rather than either side, but retired to his estate near Boulogne in disgust. Although he was distrusted by the extreme royalists or *Ultras,* Louis XVIII appointed him minister of war in July 1815, but his plans for reorganizing the French army were opposed by *Ultras* who wished to restore the order of the ancien régime, and he resigned in September. He became known as a left-wing liberal in the House of Peers and as minister of war again in 1819 succeeded in implementing major army reforms, including the reintegration of many Napoleonic veterans.

Stoic and restrained in character, in sharp contrast to most of the other Napoleonic marshals, Saint-Cyr was also scrupulously honest and maintained an exalted moral view of the role of the army. This attitude caused his problems with Napoleon's demands for personal loyalty to himself. But the emperor could not ignore Saint-Cyr's capacities, especially as a defensive commander and in mapping terrain, where his talents as an artist proved invaluable, first to the Revolutionary then the Napoleonic armies.

Related entries: Dresden; Naples, Kingdom of; Peninsular War; Russian Campaign

Suggestions for further reading:
Coates-Wright, Philip. 1987. "Gouvion Saint-Cyr," in David G. Chandler, ed., *Napoleon's Marshals.* New York: Macmillan.

Goya y Lucientes, Francisco de (1746–1828)

One of the greatest painters in European history, Goya left an astonishing record of the brutalities of the struggle of the Spanish people against Napoleonic occupation as well as penetrating portraits of some of the leading figures of the age. He had become official court painter to Charles IV in 1799, but his liberal sympathies were made obvious in his viciously satirical portrayals of the backwardness of Spanish society. In his two great paintings, the *Dos de Mayo* and *Tres de Mayo*, Goya showed the fury of the uprising against the French in Madrid on 2–3 May 1808, but these paintings were not seen until after Napoleon's fall.

Goya accepted the patronage of Joseph Bonaparte when Napoleon's brother became king of Spain, but his courtly work decreased as he was torn between his liberalism and his patriotic abhorrence of foreign rule. The collection of engravings, *The Disasters of War*, published in 1814, records the vicious cruelties of guerilla warfare with unforgettable vividness. When asked why he depicted Spanish as well as French barbarism, Goya replied: "To tell men forever that they should not be barbarians" (Herold 1983, p. 205). The restored king Ferdinand VII pardoned Goya for his collaboration with Joseph, but the painter was disgusted by the reactionary nature of Ferdinand's regime and spent his final years in France. Throughout his work one may see a commitment to the Enlightenment values rejected by the Spanish and betrayed by the French.

Related entries: Peninsular War; Spain

Suggestions for further reading:
Gassier, Pierre. 1985. *Goya: A Witness of his Times.* New York: Alpine Fine Arts Collection.
Herold, J. Christopher. 1983. *The Horizon Book of the Age of Napoleon.* New York: American Heritage Publishing Co./Bonanza Books.
Myers, Bernard S. 1964. *Goya.* London: Spring Books.
Williams, Gwyn A. 1976. *Goya and the Impossible Revolution.* London: Allen Lane.

Grand Dignitaries of the Empire

On the creation of the empire in 1804 Napoleon named a series of grand dignitaries, designed to give his new imperial court a status equal to those of the old monarchies of Europe. The six appointments were meant to reward public service, while also doubtless flattering the vanity of the recipients. Six grand dignitaries were appointed: Jean-Jacques Cambacérès became arch-chancellor; Charles Lebrun, arch-treasurer; Joseph Bonaparte, grand elector; Louis Bonaparte, high constable; Eugène de Beauharnais, arch-chancellor of state, and Joachim Murat, grand admiral. The appointments indicate Napoleon's desire to appeal to tradition and legitimacy while showing that his new nobility was not dependent on "feudal" origins. It is notable, however, that four of the six appointees were members of or allied by marriage to the Bonaparte family.

Related entries: Empire; Nobility

Grande Armée

The name *Grande Armée* was first used in 1805, but the force had its origins in the Army of England, the troops concentrated along the Channel and North Sea coasts for the invasion of Great Britain. Numbering some 350,000 men at its inception, the *Grande Armée* designated the principal body of French and allied forces operating under Napoleon's personal command. Having received intensive training and practiced new tactics, it allowed Napoleon to boast that "surely there is no finer army in Europe than mine today" (Kafker and Laux 1989, p. 232). The concentration of the bulk of his troops in his own hands gave Napoleon the advantage when it came to striking the decisive blow against his opponents. The army did, however, rely on Napoleon being in personal command, so that when he was absent, as in Spain in 1808–1809, the consequences could be disastrous.

The *Grande Armée*'s order of battle comprised seven corps, with additional allied corps, backed up by cavalry and artillery reserves and by the Imperial Guard. Command and control was exercised by Napoleon at Imperial Headquarters, which by 1812 had come to look like a small army in itself, but in battle he usually surrounded himself with a small escort of trusted subordinates. Napoleon made his own decisions, and the General Staff, presided over by Louis Berthier, existed solely to carry out his orders. This refusal to allow his corps commanders to act independently was initially one of Napoleon's great strengths, but by 1813 had become a liability. The military historian J. F. C. Fuller commented on the 1813 campaign: "Wherever Napoleon was, success was assured; wherever he was not, it was disaster" (Kafker and Laux, p. 234).

The army of 1805 was the first *Grande Armée* and fought at Ulm, Austerlitz, Jena, and Friedland. A considerable part of its forces were switched to Spain in 1808, but it was speedily reunited in 1809 and fought at Essling and Wagram. The *Grande Armée* assembled its greatest strength for the Russian campaign of 1812, leading to its destruction. A new *Grande Armée* was assembled for the war of 1813–1814, but when Napoleon fought his last campaign in 1815 the title was no longer used, and his forces were known as the Army of the North.

Related entries: Army; Berthier, Louis Alexandre; Danube Campaigns; Germany, Campaigns in; Russian Campaign

Suggestions for further reading:
Bowden, Scott. 1990. *Napoleon's Grande Armée of 1813*. Chicago: The Emperor's Press.
Elting, John R. 1988. *Swords around a Throne: Napoleon's Grande Armée.* New York: Free Press.
Kafker, Frank A., and James M. Laux, eds. 1989. *Napoleon and His Times: Selected Interpretations.* Malibar, FL: Krieger.
Pivka, Otto von. 1977. *Armies of 1812.* Cambridge, England: Stephens.
Rogers, H. C. B. 1974. *Napoleon's Army.* London: Allen.
Woloch, Isser. 1979. *The French Veteran from the Revolution to the Restoration.* Chapel Hill: University of North Carolina Press.

Great Britain

By the late eighteenth century Britain was the predominant commercial and naval power in the world, and it became the most implacable enemy of Revolutionary and Napoleonic France, at war between 1793 and 1802 and again from 1803 to 1814. The small British army played little role until 1808, British strategy being based on naval power, with occasional attacks on the periphery of Napoleon's empire. The British navy, having recovered from the bungling which had led to serious mutinies in 1797, scored an unprecedented series of naval victories culminating at Trafalgar in 1805, assured British control of the Channel and the Mediterranean, and helped to extend Britain's commercial empire in the West Indies, the Indian Ocean, and the South Atlantic at the expense of France and its allies, especially the Dutch.

On the other hand, the British landings in Calabria and Walcheren were at best ineffective, at worst disastrous. Britain's reluctance to commit large numbers of troops to continental warfare only ended with the Peninsular War from 1808 onward. British troops now played a major role in Spain, in the invasion of France in 1814, and at Waterloo in 1815. But standing armies were traditionally unpopular in Britain, and, although threats of French invasion led to the enthusiastic formation of local militias and volunteer forces in 1797, 1801, and 1803–1805, the main British contribution to land warfare against Napoleon lay in subsidies to Austria, Prussia, and Russia. Britain's main strength, apart from the navy, lay in its financial institutions. London was the center of the European money market, and reforms in state finances overseen by William Pitt in the 1790s, especially the establishment of a sinking fund for government debts, helped British diplomacy in cobbling together coalitions against Napoleon.

Napoleon's Continental System, therefore, while it did considerable damage to British trade on the continent, could not fulfil its purpose of starving the country into submission. Only in 1811 did Britain face major financial and social crisis. The working classes suffered economic distress due to attempts to protect agriculture and to unemployment caused by the introduction of new machinery in the textile industry, leading to the Luddite disturbances in the North and Midlands. The Napoleonic wars and accompanying patriotic enthusiasm also meant the postponement of much needed political reforms, stoking up problems for the years after 1815. Unrest in Ireland, revolving around the terms of the Union with Britain in 1800 and the question of Catholic Emancipation, led to the resignation of Pitt in 1801 and continued to be a major headache for British governments.

But if on the domestic front all was far from well in 1815, diplomatically and commercially Britain emerged from the Napoleonic wars in a position of renewed strength. The Prussian general August von Gneisenau commented: "Great Britain has no greater obligation to any mortal on earth than to this ruffian Napoleon. For through the events which he has brought about, England's greatness, prosperity, and wealth have risen high. She is the mistress of the sea and neither in this dominion nor in world trade has she now a single rival to fear."

Related entries: Castlereagh, Robert Stewart, Viscount; Coalitions; Continental System; Liverpool, Robert Banks Jenkinson, Earl of; Navy, British; Nelson, Horatio, Lord; Peninsular War; Pitt, William the Younger; Trafalgar, Battle of; Walcheren Expedition; Wellington, Duke of

Suggestions for further reading:
Christie, Ian R. 1982. *Wars and Revolutions: Britain, 1760–1815*. London: Edward Arnold.
Cookson, J. E. 1997. *The British Armed Nation 1793–1815*. Oxford: Clarendon Press.
Emsley, Clive. 1979. *British Society and the French Wars*. New York: Macmillan.
Glover, Richard. 1973. *Britain at Bay: Defence Against Bonaparte, 1803–14*. New York: Barnes and Noble.
Guy, Alan J., ed. 1990. *The Road to Waterloo: The British Army and the Struggle against Revolutionary and Napoleonic France*. London: National Army Museum.
Hall, Christopher D. 1992. *British Strategy in the Napoleonic Wars*. Manchester: Manchester University Press.
Muir, Rory. 1996. *Britain and the Defeat of Napoleon*. New Haven: Yale University Press.
Sherwig, John M. 1969. *Guineas and Gunpowder: British Foreign Aid in the War with France*. Cambridge: Harvard University Press.

Gros, Antoine Jean (1771–1835)

*T*he favorite pupil of Jacques-Louis David, Gros also became a valued propagandist of Napoleon through painting, but portrayed the emperor's heroic deeds in a more human and individual and less monumental fashion. He first encountered Napoleon during the Italian campaign in 1796. Visiting Genoa for the purpose of studying the paintings of Rubens, Gros was presented to Joséphine and accompanied her to Milan, where she introduced him to her husband. His painting of Napoleon, flag in hand and inspiring his troops at the battle of Arcola, so flattered its subject that Gros was given the post of inspector of revenues, following the campaign, observing military events at first hand, and selecting art objects for transportation to France.

As a member of Napoleon's entourage Gros had the opportunity to develop his talents, especially in portraiture, and in 1801 Napoleon expressed his wish that Gros should paint for him exclusively. His *Bona-*

In all his depictions of Napoleon, Jean Antoine Gros detected a saintlike quality that escaped other observers. Bonaparte Visiting the Plague Victims at Jaffa (1804) is Gros's version of an episode from Napoleon's Egyptian campaign. Bonaparte touches a plague victim and becomes a royal, even superhuman, figure bringing comfort and relief by his presence. (Alinari / Art Resource)

parte Visiting the Plague Victims at Jaffa (1804), an unhistorical representation of an episode of the Egyptian campaign, portrayed Napoleon as a kind of saint, bringing comfort to plague-stricken soldiers by his presence and his "royal" touch. Conceived on a massive scale, it combined the influence of Italian baroque painting with an incipient Romanticism and helped to create the myth of Napoleon as a great leader, but also an ordinary soldier, the "little corporal," imbued with a superhuman capacity for sympathy with the humble soldiers under his command. This image reached its peak with his portrayal of Napoleon after the battle of Eylau, where the emperor as magnanimous victor, tired and pensive, seems to bless the dead on all sides and big-heartedly accepts the submission of a Lithuanian hussar and other Russian soldiers, one of whom seems to be praying to him. The weary Napoleon, saddened by the spectacle of slaughter, grants absolution to his enemies.

In addition to the monumental paintings glorifying Napoleon, Gros also executed many portraits, his subjects including Jérôme Bonaparte and Christine Boyer, the long-dead first wife of Lucien Bonaparte. In 1812 he was commissioned to decorate the dome of the Pantheon, which he completed in 1824, with Napoleon excluded from the ranks of the great Frenchmen commemorated within.

Gros adapted easily to the Restoration; his style, blending the classicism of David with the new Romanticism, continued to be popular for many years, and in 1824 he was made a baron by King Charles X. But he fell out of favor with both the public and the monarchy in the 1830s, and in

1835, after his painting of *Hercules and Diomedes* had been ridiculed, he committed suicide by drowning himself in four feet of water in the forest of Meudon.

Related entries: Napoleonic Legend; Personality, Cult of; Propaganda

Suggestions for further reading:
Wilson-Smith, Timothy. 1996. *Napoleon and His Artists.* London: Constable.

Grouchy, Emmanuel, Marquis de (1766–1847)

A hereditary noble, cavalryman, and the last to be given his baton, Grouchy was in several ways the odd man out among Napoleon's marshals. He was also blamed, not least by Napoleon himself, for the defeat at Waterloo, but few historians today would go along entirely with this scapegoating.

Intended for the military from birth, Grouchy entered the royal army at the age of fourteen. Invalided out in 1787, he subsequently supported the Revolution and returned to the colors in 1791, fighting against the royalist rebels of the Vendée and in Brittany. In 1798 he served under Jean Moreau in Italy and was wounded and captured at the battle of Lodi. He commanded an infantry division at Hohenlinden (3 December 1800) and served Napoleon with great distinction in the German campaigns of 1806–1807. He commanded the Second Dragoon Division in the pursuit of the Prussians after the battles of Jena-Auerstädt, which has been described as "the greatest sustained pursuit in history" (Lunt 1987, p. 142); commanded the dragoons at Eylau (8 February 1807), where he was wounded; and was a cavalry commander at Friedland (14 June 1807), the battle that ended the Fourth Coalition.

As governor of Madrid in 1808, Grouchy was responsible for suppressing the rising of 2 May, then back in Germany served with Louis Davout's corps at Wagram (6 July 1809) and so impressed Napoleon that he made him colonel-general of *chasseurs* and thus a grand officer of the empire. Grouchy was on the semiactive list between 1809 and 1811, returning for the Russian campaign of 1812. He commanded Eugène de Beauharnais's cavalry at Borodino and performed sterling service during Napoleon's retreat from Moscow. After retiring briefly as physically unfit in 1813 he returned again as a cavalry commander during the Allied invasion of France in 1814, fighting in all the major engagements of the campaign.

When he rallied to Napoleon during the Hundred Days, Grouchy became the twenty-sixth and last marshal of the empire. He put down the royalist rising led by the Duke of Angoulême in the south of France and commanded Napoleon's right wing at Ligny, defeating the Prussians under Blücher. Grouchy was sent in pursuit of the Prussian army, while Napoleon and Michel Ney pursued Wellington's Anglo-Dutch army toward Brussels. Grouchy lost contact with Blücher on 17 June 1815. The next day his advance guard encountered a Prussian force at Wavre, unaware that Blücher had reorganized and was marching for Waterloo, nine miles away, where Napoleon had engaged Wellington. Having no specific orders to reinforce Napoleon, whose commands to him were at best ambiguous, Grouchy and his 33,000 troops heard the guns of Waterloo, but his essentially cautious nature prevented his moving. Had he marched to Waterloo, his presence would have evened the odds, which were swung against Napoleon by the arrival of Blücher. By not moving, however, he allowed Napoleon to pin the blame on him for the defeat.

Grouchy's retreat after Waterloo was masterly, but it did him no good. After Napoleon's second abdication he turned his troops over to Davout and, proscribed by the new Bourbon regime, emigrated to the United States. Amnestied in 1819, he returned to France in 1821, was placed on the retired list, and restored to the rank of marshal of France in 1831. For the rest of his life after 1815, however, his main concern was the battle of print to clear his name over the defeat of Waterloo. He exchanged violent pamphlets and articles with General Etienne Gérard, who had served under him in the campaign and claimed to have begged him to "march to the guns." Grouchy's memoirs, published by his son in 1873–1874, were also directed at clearing his name, unsuccessfully at the time. Historians today are inclined to be more generous, acknowledging that Grouchy may have been slow off the mark but considering that, in sticking too closely to Napoleon's orders, he was more sinned against than sinning.

Related entries: Danube Campaigns; Germany, Campaigns in; Italian Campaigns; Waterloo, Battle of

Suggestions for further reading:
Hamilton-Williams, David. 1993. *Waterloo: New Perspectives: The Great Battle Reappraised.* London: Arms and Armour.
Hibbert, Christopher. 1998. *Waterloo.* London: Wordsworth Military Library.
Lunt, James D. 1987. "Grouchy," in David G. Chandler, ed., *Napoleon's Marshals.* New York: Macmillan.
Parker, Harold T. 1983. *Three Napoleonic Battles.* Durham, NC: Duke University Press.

Guerrilla Warfare

The *guerrilla* or "little war" had its origins in the eighteenth century, when it meant actions by small bodies of mobile troops detached from the main armies and operating on the wings or in the enemy's rear. But it was as a demonstration of popular resistance to Napoleonic occupation that it acquired its modern connotations as a war of liberation. In areas of preexisting social and economic tensions and with a popular tradition of paramilitary activity or brigandage, guerrilla insurrections could harass or tie down large numbers of Napoleon's occupying troops. The distinction became blurred between brigandage and national resistance. Thus guerrillas played an essential role in the revolt in Calabria and the revolt in the Tyrol, and in 1810 Illyria saw guerrilla outbreaks among the Serbs and Croats of the old military frontier between the Austrian and Ottoman Empires. But it was in Spain during the Peninsular War that the most celebrated guerrilla bands and leaders acquired the image of popular heroes.

In Spain the "little war" was little in name only. Guerrilla bands made up mostly of armed peasants were either molded into more conventional units by professional soldiers or practised indiscriminate banditry against the French and their Spanish supporters. Spanish governments tried to impose their authority on the guerrillas, but while Napoleon's troops occupied most of the country this proved impossible. Their continual shadowy presence caused French commanders to overestimate their effectiveness, but they did provide intelligence for Allied commanders, force the French to

Goya's **Disasters of War** *dramatically conveys the brutality of the Spanish guerrilla struggle against Napoleon's forces. (The Trustees of the British Museum, London)*

maintain garrisons to protect convoys, and even occasionally cooperate effectively with Allied forces. Their most forceful contribution in purely military terms came when they reinforced the forces of the duke of Wellington in his campaign of 1812.

By 1812 between 35,000 and 50,000 guerrillas were at large, often proving as bothersome for their allies as they were for the French. Large areas of the countryside were in a state of virtual anarchy. By itself guerrilla warfare could not defeat Napoleon, and the existence of the partisan bands hampered attempts to create an effective regular Spanish army. But they had been left to carry the fight alone for long periods in 1809 and 1810, and guerrillas successful in harrying the French gained a reputation, however undeserved, as national heroes. Their example was to serve as an inspiration to Italian and Polish nationalists in the nineteenth century.

Related entries: Calabria, Revolt in; Peninsular War; Tyrol, Revolts in

Suggestions for further reading:

Chandler, David G. 1994. "Wellington and the Guerrillas," in his *On the Napoleonic Wars: Collected Essays.* London: Greenhill.

Esdaile, Charles J. 1988. "Heroes or Villains? The Spanish Guerrillas and the Peninsular War," *History Today* 38 (April 1988), pp. 29–35.

———. 1991. "The Problem of the Spanish Guerrillas," in Alice D. Berkeley, ed. *New Lights on the Peninsular War.* Lisbon: British Historical Society of Portugal.

Eyck, F. Gunther. 1986. *Loyal Rebels: Andreas Hofer and the Tyrolean Uprising of 1809.* Lanham, MD: University Press of America.

Finley, Milton. 1991. "Patriots or Brigands? The Calabrian Partisans, 1806–1812," *Consortium on Revolutionary Europe, Proceedings 1991*, pp. 161–170.

H

Haiti

The French colony of Saint-Domingue, making up the western third of the island of Hispaniola, had seen the black slave rebellion led by Toussaint-L'Ouverture successfully defy both French and British attempts to secure control since 1797. In December 1801, however, Napoleon dispatched a French force commanded by his brother-in-law, General Charles Leclerc, to reimpose French rule and restore slavery. The French force landed in February 1802, and in May Toussaint surrendered after receiving guarantees of continued freedom for blacks. Leclerc, however, following Napoleon's instructions, began a pacification program designed to restore slavery and the plantation system.

In August 1802, with resistance increasing, an epidemic of yellow fever killed thousands of French soldiers. Insurrection spread throughout the colony, and by late October only the main towns remained under French control. Leclerc succumbed to the fever in early November, and his successor, General J. B. de Rochambeau, launched a counteroffensive. But with the renewal of war with Britain in May 1803 the French suffered increasingly from lack of supplies and reinforcements, and Rochambeau surrendered to the blockading British navy on 30 November.

On 1 January 1804 the independence of the Republic of Haiti was proclaimed, and in October Jean-Jacques Dessalines, the most successful Haitian general, followed Napoleonic precedent by proclaiming himself emperor. Dessalines was assassinated in 1806, and after a power struggle the mulatto leader, Alexandre Pétion, became the first president of independent Haiti.

Related entries: Leclerc, Charles Victor Emmanuel; Toussaint-L'Ouverture, François Dominique

Suggestions for further reading:
Bryan, Patrick E. 1984. *The Haitian Revolution and its Effects.* London: Heinemann.
James, C. L. R. 1938. *The Black Jacobins: Toussaint L'Ouverture and the San Domingo Revolution.* London: Secker and Warburg.

Helvetic Republic

The French satellite republic in Switzerland under the Directory and consulate lasted with great difficulty from 1798 to 1803, but not even Napoleon could overcome the centuries-long traditions of autonomy within the Swiss Confederation and impose a French-inspired unity. With Napoleon's victories in Italy in 1796, the shortest route from Paris to Milan ran through a Switzerland that had to be "democratized." The French in collusion with Swiss patriots declared that the confederation should be transformed into a French-style "Republic, one and indivisible"; Geneva and Mulhouse were to be annexed to France; and the complex political system simplified into a structure of free and equal cantons.

The Swiss, however, did not readily accept the changes. The cantons that rejected the new arrangement and the rebellious peasants of the Valais were defeated in May 1798 and the new constitution put into effect on the back of French arms. Switzerland was divided into nineteen cantons, roughly equal in area, and the republic headed by a directory of five members, aided by a legislative body and a senate elected by universal male suffrage. Each canton was administered by a prefect; feudalism was abolished, and numerous reforms introduced. The regime only functioned with difficulty, and two directors believed hostile to France were forced to resign in June 1798.

With the renewal of war in 1799 Switzerland became a major theatre of operations, and when over half the territory of the Helvetic Republic was occupied by Austrian and Russian forces, opposition to the centralist constitution of 1798 was reinforced. Napoleon, in power in France, was forced constantly to mediate between centralists and federalists, eventually giving way to federalism. By an act of 19 February 1803 the autonomy of the cantons was recognized in a new Helvetic Confederation, from which the Valais was excluded, becoming an independent republic tightly controlled by France. The attempt to centralize Switzerland on the model of the French Republic had failed completely.

Related entries: Switzerland

Suggestions for further reading:
Oechsli, Wilhelm. 1922. *History of Switzerland.* Cambridge: Cambridge University Press.

Hofer, Andreas (1767–1810)

An innkeeper's son from an Alpine valley near Innsbruck, Hofer attained legendary status as the leader of the Tyrolean revolt against Napoleon. In 1796 and 1805 he fought as a sharpshooter against the French in the Tyrol, rising to the rank of captain in the Austrian army. In 1805 the Tyrol was granted to Bavaria, Napoleon's ally, and in the spring of 1809 Hofer led the Tyrolean militia to success, driving the Bavarians out of Innsbruck. But the Treaty of Schönbrunn (14 October 1809) returned the Tyrol to Bavaria, and Hofer led guerrilla action against the French army of Marshal François Lefebvre. Hofer was encouraged by false hopes of Austrian help, but his hiding place was betrayed to the French, and he was captured on 27 January 1810. Taken in chains to Mantua, Hofer was court-martialed, and when the court could not reach a decision Napoleon personally ordered him to be executed before the Austrians could present any pleas for clemency. Hofer was executed on 18 February 1810, soon becoming the hero of Tyrolean songs, plays, and novels.

Related entries: Guerrilla Warfare; Tyrol, Revolts in

Suggestions for further reading:
Eyck, F. Gunther. 1986. *Loyal Rebels: Andreas Hofer and the Tyrolean Uprising of 1809.* Lanham, MD: University Press of America.

Hohenlinden, Battle of (3 December 1800)

The victory of General Jean Moreau over the young Austrian archduke John at the Bavarian village of Hohenlinden, some thirty miles east of Munich, finally decided the Austrians to make peace and break up the Second Coalition. Much to Napoleon's annoyance Moreau's triumph was greeted in Paris as the equal of his own defeat of the Austrians at Marengo six months previously. It was thus Moreau rather than Bonaparte who finally forced Austria to seek an armistice, resulting in the Treaty of Lunéville of 9 February 1801.

Related entries: Coalitions; Moreau, Jean-Victor

Related entries: Batavian Republic; Bonaparte, Louis; Netherlands

Suggestions for further reading:
Connelly, Owen. 1965. *Napoleon's Satellite Kingdoms.* New York: Free Press.
Ellis, Geoffrey. 1991. *The Napoleonic Empire.* Atlantic Highlands, NJ: Humanities Press International.
Schama, Simon. 1977. *Patriots and Liberators: Revolution in the Netherlands, 1780–1813.* New York: Knopf.

Holland, Kingdom of

When Napoleon transformed the Batavian Republic into the Kingdom of Holland in May 1806, with his brother Louis as king, he hoped thereby to see Holland governed in the interests of France and the Bonaparte dynasty, but he was to be severely disappointed. Louis not only implemented and continued the reforms in taxation and education introduced by the Republic, but proved to be his own master, trying to protect the Dutch people from his brother's excessive and constant demands.

During Louis's short reign a new criminal code was introduced, measures taken to encourage agriculture, and the Royal Academy of Sciences and the Royal Library established; Louis resisted Napoleon's demand for troops and was at best half-hearted in his support for the Continental System. Despite his often erratic and extravagant behavior, Louis's policies made him popular with the people, and he managed to deflect Napoleon's complaints until 1810.

In November 1809 Louis was summoned to Paris, where he was forced to agree to cede territory to France and enforce the Continental System. When he returned to Holland in April 1810 he found that his power had been usurped by French officials. Louis abdicated on 1 July 1810, and the Kingdom of Holland was annexed to France.

Hundred Days

The phase "hundred days" was first used by the comte de Chabrol, prefect of the Seine, to describe the period from Napoleon's return to Paris on 20 March 1815 to his second abdication on 22 June. The attempted reestablishment of the empire was Napoleon's most extraordinary venture, but it was doomed to failure because of the international context. Escaping from Elba, Napoleon landed on French soil with a small band of loyal followers, and by 6 March had secured control of Grenoble, the capital of Dauphiné. Contrary to Bonapartist legend, the emperor's return was not greeted with overwhelming enthusiasm, but it was accepted. The rule of the restored Bourbons was widely unpopular; Napoleon on his march to Paris avoided royalist strongholds; and most importantly the army, reduced in numbers and neglected by the Bourbons, was easily won over. Louis XVIII and his court fled ignominiously, finally on 30 March arriving in Ghent in the Low Countries.

Napoleon formed a government that included Louis Davout (war), Joseph Fouché (police), Lazare Carnot (interior), and Louis Caulaincourt (foreign affairs). In an attempt to rally liberal support he granted liberty of the press, and had Benjamin Constant draw up the *Acte Additionnel* establishing a parliamentary regime. However, the victorious Allies put aside their differences, dashing Napoleon's hopes that either Austria or Russia might declare themselves neutral, and war became his only hope for survival. By May he had assembled an army of 300,000, but most of his marshals had not returned. Only a rapid movement into the Low Countries against the armies of Wellington and Blücher could produce victory.

The defeat at Waterloo on 18 June doomed Napoleon's new empire, bringing to an end a period that had always had an air of unreality about it. On his return to Paris on 21 June he found Fouché the master of the situation and a legislative assembly demanding his abdication. Fouché and Davout signed an armistice with Wellington and Blücher, sent Napoleon's army away to the south, and arranged Napoleon's departure for Rochefort and thence into exile on Saint Helena. Louis XVIII returned to Saint-Denis on 3 July and received Fouché, presented to him by Talleyrand: "Vice leaning on the arm of crime," commented René de Chateaubriand (Tulard 1985, p.

340). The old regicide and former minister of police had smoothed the way for a second restoration of the Bourbons.

Related entries: Abdication, Second; *Acte Additionnel;* Blücher, Gebhard Leberecht von; Coalitions; Constant, Benjamin; Davout, Louis Nicolas; Elba; *Fédéré* Movement; Fouché, Joseph; Ligny, Battle of; Louis XVIII; Talleyrand-Périgord, Charles-Maurice de; Waterloo, Battle of; Wellington, Duke of

Suggestions for further reading:
Alexander, R. S. 1991. *Bonapartism and the Revolutionary Tradition in France: The Fédérés of 1815.* Cambridge: Cambridge University Press.
Brett James, Antony. 1964. *The Hundred Days: Napoleon's Last Campaign from Eyewitness Accounts.* New York: Macmillan.
Cubberley, R. E. 1969. *The Role of Fouché during the Hundred Days.* Madison: Wisconsin University Press.
Hamilton-Williams, David. 1994. *The Fall of Napoleon: The Final Betrayal.* London: John Wiley.
Schom, Alan. 1992. *One Hundred Days: Napoleon's Road to Waterloo.* New York: Oxford University Press.
Tulard, Jean. 1985. *Napoleon: The Myth of the Saviour.* London: Methuen.

Idéologues

The term *idéologue* was coined by Napoleon in 1800 as a term of disparagement for those republican intellectuals who turned against his regime. But, although he applied it very broadly, it is better applied to the small group of thinkers who had supported the coup of 18 Brumaire in the hope that basic liberties would be maintained, but later became critical outsiders in Napoleon's dictatorial regime. The *idéologues* shared a belief in human perfectibility derived from the ideas of Etienne de Condillac, the eighteenth-century philosopher and one of the founders of modern psychology, and the mathematician Antoine Nicolas Condorcet. Their views were best expressed by comte Antoine Destutt de Tracy, who had invented the word *idéologie,* meaning the "science of ideas," in 1796 in his *Éléménts d'Idéologie* (1801–1815), the fourth and final volume of which he held back until after Napoleon's fall. As a member of the Senate Tracy proposed the deposition of Napoleon on 2 April 1814.

Idéologues, including Benjamin Constant and Pierre Daunou, formed an opposition to Napoleon within the Tribunate, until twenty of them were purged in 1802. They then largely retired from active politics, accepting appointments from Napoleon while maintaining a kind of muffled opposition. Mme. de Staël was close to the *idéologues* without ever being one; Emmanuel Sieyès was a close associate; but Pierre Louis Roederer was the only true *idéologue* to fill significant office under Napoleon. Other prominent *idéologues* included the liberal economist Jean-Baptiste Say, the physiologists Georges Cabanis and François Bichat, and the psychologist Philippe Pinel, one of the first physicians to treat the mentally ill as medical cases. Despite sticking admirably to their principles, the *idéologues* never constituted a political party and were unable or unwilling to appeal to a broader public opinion. Napoleon's attitude was summed up by a statement he reputedly made to Karl von Dalberg in 1806: "All you *idéologues* act according to ready-made theories; I am a practical man, I make the best of what opportunity offers."

Related entries: Constant, Benjamin; Daunou, Pierre Claude François; Roederer, Pierre Louis; Staël, Germaine de; Tribunate

Suggestions for further reading:
Head, Brian. 1985. *Ideology and Social Science: Destutt de Tracy and French Liberalism.* Dordrecht, Netherlands: Nijhoff.
Kaiser, Thomas E. 1980. "Politics and Political Economy in the Thought of the Ideologues," *History of Political Economy* 12 pp. 141–160.
Kennedy, Emmet. 1978. *A Philosophe in the Age of Revolution: Destutt de Tracy and the Origins of Ideology.* Philadelphia: American Philosophical Society.

Staum, Martin S. 1980. *Cabanis: Enlightenment and Medical Philosophy in the French Revolution.* Princeton: Princeton University Press.

Illyria

*I*n 1805 by the Treaty of Pressburg Napoleon took control of the formerly Austrian and Venetian lands on the Adriatic coast, to which Ragusa (Dubrovnik) was added in 1808. Between 1806 and 1809 these areas of present-day Slovenia, Croatia and Bosnia, nominally part of the Kingdom of Italy, were governed by Marshal Auguste Marmont, with civil administration under Vincenzo Dandolo. In 1809 further territories ceded by Austria by the Treaty of Schönbrunn were added to create the Illyrian Provinces, which now stretched from Trieste to Dubrovnik and included the cities of Fiume (Rijeka) and Ljubljana. The military district of Croatia was granted a special regime, which preserved its traditional social order, but elsewhere the years of French rule introduced radical changes.

Under Marmont's governorship education and communications were improved in Dalmatia. The Civil Code was introduced in family law, succession, and inheritance. Convents were suppressed, church property confiscated, and the ecclesiastical tithe abolished. Legal possession of peasant land was transferred from the state to the peasants themselves, a land tax replaced the former state tithe, and the alienation of peasant ownership made almost impossible.

Ljubljana became the capital of the Illyrian Provinces, and by a decree of 25 December 1809 Marmont centralized the government and effected uniformity in administrative and legislative practice in the ten intendancies (reduced to six in 1811) of the new Illyria. In 1812, first under General Henri Bernard and then under Jean Andoche Junot, the Civil Code was adopted in its entirety, and French taxes were imposed. Conscription had been introduced in 1810.

The official abolition of feudalism in 1811 made the regime popular for a while with the peasants, but turned the nobles toward support for Austria. The regime was supported by radical intellectuals, but it gradually alienated other classes. Peasant discontent was aroused by the abolition of customary rights, while the urban middle classes, especially in Trieste, were hit hard by the economic effects of war and the Continental System. And while the parish clergy remained neutral, the Catholic religious orders, especially the Franciscans, fiercely opposed French rule and whipped up popular unrest.

The Congress of Vienna returned the Illyrian Provinces to Austria, but the impression left by Napoleonic rule in popular tradition was not as negative as in many areas of Europe. The French years had seen the beginnings of a cultural awakening among the south Slavs, especially in Slovenia and Croatia. The area had experienced its first modern state administration and the first stirrings of national awareness. Even the emperor of Austria was forced to admit that the episode had not been totally negative, remarking to Metternich: "It is a great pity that marshal Marmont was not two or three years longer in Dalmatia" (Chandler 1987, p. 259).

Related entries: Austria; Junot, Andoche; Marmont, Auguste Frédéric Louis Viesse de

Suggestions for further reading:
Bjelovuc, Harriet. 1970. *The Ragusan Republic: Victim of Napoleon and its own Conservatism.* Leiden: E. J. Brill.
Carter, Francis W. 1972. *Dubrovnik (Ragusa): A Classic City-State.* London: Seminar Press.
Chandler, David G. 1987. *Napoleon's Marshals.* New York: Macmillan.
Ellis, Geoffrey. 1991. *The Napoleonic Empire.* Atlantic Highlands, NJ: Humanities Press International.
Woolf, Stuart. 1991. *Napoleon's Integration of Europe.* London and New York: Routledge.

Imperial Catechism

The new catechism devised by Napoleon and abbé Etienne Bernier in 1806 shows the extent to which spiritual authority of the Catholic Church following the Concordat of 1801 was to be subservient to the will of the emperor. Children were taught loyalty to Napoleon and the Bonaparte dynasty and deference to those in government over them. "Napoleon I, our Emperor" had restored religious worship, preserved public order "by his profound and active wisdom," and now defends the state with the strength of his arm. Napoleon's young subjects owed him "love, respect, obedience, loyalty, military service and the taxes ordered for the preservation and defence of the Empire and his throne" (Arnold 1994, p. 222). Pope Pius VII refused to recognize the imperial catechism, but the pliant French clergy accepted it. Along with the introduction of the Festival of Saint Napoléon on 15 August, the papacy found it one of the most discomfiting of Napoleon's innovations.

Related entries: Catholic Church; Concordat; Pius VII, Pope

Suggestions for further reading:
Arnold, Eric A., ed. 1994. *A Documentary Survey of Napoleonic France.* Lanham, MD: University Press of America, pp. 221–224.
Hales, Edward Elton Young. 1962. *Napoleon and the Pope.* London: Eyre and Spottiswoode.

Imperial Guard

Not, as its name implies, a personal bodyguard for Napoleon, the Imperial Guard was in fact a military elite with its own infantry, cavalry, artillery, and services. It was Napoleon's ultimate reserve, made up of veterans and almost never committed to battle. The Guard was multinational, with Egyptian, Italian, Polish, German, Swiss, and other units as well as French. The Old Guard was formed between 1800 and 1806, the Middle Guard between 1806 and 1809, and the Young Guard thereafter, the whole growing in numbers from 8,000 in 1805 to 80,000 in 1812. From the Guard, 60,000 marched into Russia in 1812, and the Old Guard battalions were the last to be committed into battle at Waterloo. When they were thrown back it was a sign that Napoleon had lost the battle. In later years the Imperial Guard became the focus of heroic stories and legends and was revered alike by old soldiers and Bonapartists.

Related entries: Army; Waterloo, Battle of

Suggestions for further reading:
Lachouque, Henry. 1997. *The Anatomy of Glory: Napoleon and His Guard.* London: Greenhill.

Imperial Police

Centralized in the Ministry of General Police under Joseph Fouché and then Anne Jean Savary, Napoleon's police force played a vital part in maintaining the authority of the imperial regime in France and may be seen as Europe's first modern political police. A law of 10 July 1804 established four regional councillors of state for police affairs and a sophisticated system, by the standards of the time, for obtaining, storing, and retrieving information. Under Savary after 1810 the police system became more heavy-handed and arbitrary than under Fouché, whom Napoleon had (rightly) never completely trusted.

Related entries: Fouché, Joseph; Savary, Anne Jean Marie René

Suggestions for further reading:
Arnold, Eric A. 1979. *Fouché, Napoleon and the General Police.* Washington: University Press of America.

Imperial University

Not a university in the usual sense of the word, Napoleon's Imperial University, set up in 1808, was the tip of the pyramid of the new centralized education system and constituted a teaching corporation, theoretically made up of all those involved in the education of males in France. At its head stood a grand master, chosen by Napoleon, aided by a Council of Thirty. Napoleon's choice for the top post, Louis de Fontanes, used his position to favor Catholics within the education system, but his conservative ideas on education were probably not far removed from the emperor's own.

The university was an active body, with a chancellor, a treasurer, and up to thirty inspectors general reporting to the council. Schools at all levels reported to one of twenty-seven regional academies, headed by rectors appointed by the grand master, and the grand master himself was rector of Paris. In its six years of existence under Napoleon the university, though not securing the desired monopoly of teaching, enabled the government to establish strict control over schooling. The historian Geoffrey Best notes its essential nature: "Its perfectly hierarchical organization was in essence military, with the First Consul Emperor as commander-in-chief" (Best 1982, p. 118). Much of its organization and even more of its spirit is still evident in French education today.

Related entries: Education; *Lycées*

Suggestions for further reading:
Arnold, Eric A., ed. 1994. *A Documentary Survey of Napoleonic France.* Lanham, MD: University Press of America, pp. 259–280.
Best, Geoffrey. 1982. *War and Society in Revolutionary Europe, 1770–1870.* London: Fontana.
Holtman, Robert B. 1967. *The Napoleonic Revolution.* Philadelphia: Lippincott.

Industry

France under Napoleon experienced no industrial takeoff, but under the shelter of Napoleon's protectionist policies, did make progress in some key areas. The effects of economic blockade and warfare held back progress in the iron industry, where manufacturers remained content with traditional preindustrial methods, and the technological gap between France and Britain widened. Iron production remained largely limited to areas rich in both iron ore and forests to provide wood, and innovations were small-scale and local. The development of heavy industry based on coal and iron still lay in the future.

The most important industrial sector remained textiles. While older branches of the textile industry continued to decline or stagnate, cotton, the new industry of the eighteenth century, took large steps along the road of mechanization under Napoleonic rule, at least until 1810. Mules, spinning jennies, and waterframes rapidly replaced hand spinning, and the expanding cotton industry established itself not only in Paris, but also in the cities and environs of Rouen, Lille, and Mulhouse, the new industrial centers of Normandy, northern France, and Alsace. In the absence of British and Indian cloths, excluded by the Continental System, a somewhat artificial cotton boom lasted until shortages of raw material caused bankruptcies after 1810. The return of peace and British competition in 1815 placed the cotton industry in a precarious position, but it was still in a reasonable state to face the future.

The other sector where progress continued was the chemical industry, where innovation depended as much on science as on entrepreneurial initiative. Enterprises headed by chemists joined by personal links developed the industry around its main centers in Paris and Marseille. The most celebrated chemist and industrialist, Jean Antoine

Chaptal, was also one of Napoleon's most effective ministers; other examples included the Darcet family, engaged in the refining of metal and the production of artificial soda, and Auguste Jacquemart, brother of a prominent banker and himself a manufacturer of soap.

Related entries: Chaptal, Jean Antoine; Continental System; Economy

Suggestions for further reading:
Arnold, Eric A., ed. 1994. *A Documentary Survey of Napoleonic France.* Lanham, MD: University Press of America. pp. 169–173.
Bergeron, Louis. 1981. *France under Napoleon.* Princeton: Princeton University Press.
Crouzet, François. 1964. "Wars, Blockade and Economic Change in Europe, 1792–1815," *Journal of Economic History* 24, pp. 567–588.
Ellis, Geoffrey. 1981. *Napoleon's Continental Blockade: The Case of Alsace.* Oxford: Clarendon Press.
Forrest, Alan, and Peter Jones, eds. 1991. *Reshaping France: Town, Country and Region during the French Revolution.* Manchester: Manchester University Press.

Institut National

*T*he *Institut National des Sciences et des Arts* was established in 1795 to replace the various scientific and cultural academies of the ancien régime. As a reward for his victories in the first Italian campaign, Napoleon was elected to the First Class of the Institute, that of Physical and Mathematical Sciences, on 25 December 1797. He initially took his membership of this predominant section very seriously and took scholars from the Institute to Egypt, where he created the Institute of Egypt in Cairo.

As first consul Napoleon continued to favor the scientific activities of the institute but came to resent criticism of his authoritarianism from *idéologues* in the Class of Moral and Political Sciences. The politically inspired reorganization of 1803, therefore, divided this section into harmless new classes covering French Language and Literature and History and Ancient Literature, with the sciences retaining their privileged position.

The government of the empire retained its interest in the institute, now renamed the *Institut de France.* Members were classified as public servants and given generous stipends, and members of the First Class were consulted by ministerial departments and the army on aspects of public utility. But any idea of collective scientific research soon disappeared, and the Institute's chief function came to be the diffusion of private research. Official consultations became restricted to minor technical matters. Despite his growing mistrust, Napoleon kept the institute alive, and it survives to this day, still housed under the imposing Collège Mazarin on the Left Bank of the Seine opposite the Louvre.

Related entries: *Description de l'Égypte; Idéologues*

Suggestions for further reading:
Hahn, Roger. 1971. *The Anatomy of a Scientific Institution: the Paris Academy of Sciences, 1666–1803.* Berkeley: University of California Press.
Williams, L. Pearce. 1956. "Science, Education and Napoleon I," *Isis* 47, pp. 369–382.

Italian Campaigns

*N*apoleon's first Italian campaign, 1796–1797, made him the most famous and successful general of the French Republic, while his second campaign of 1800 was vital in securing the rule of the consulate on firm foundations. On both occasions his prestige and power were enhanced enormously.

Napoleon took command of the Army of Italy in March 1796 at the age of twenty-six, with orders to prevent the Aus-

David's sketch shows General Bonaparte at the time of his first Italian campaign in 1796–1797. (Library of Congress)

tiglione, he drove the remnants of Dagobert von Wurmser's forces into Mantua. Further victories at Arcola in November 1796 and Rivoli in January 1797 forced the Mantua garrison to surrender and freed Napoleon to mount an offensive over the Alps towards Vienna. Already carefully cultivating his heroic image, Napoleon dominated the armistice negotiations at Leoben leading to the Treaty of Campo Formio. He was now the greatest military hero of the Republic, and the stage was set for his future ambitions.

If the campaign of 1796–1797 made Napoleon famous in France and Europe, that of 1800 ensured his political survival after the coup of 18 Brumaire. The warweary French public demanded a speedy conclusion to the war against the Second Coalition. In fact only Austria was still actively engaged in the fighting, and Napoleon's aim, as the leading figure in the new consulate regime, was to defeat them without allowing any other general to gain the credit and popular acclaim. He decided to launch the campaign in Italy, downgrading the German theater to a secondary role.

Napoleon placed André Masséna in command of the garrison at Genoa, hoping to attract the main body of the Austrian forces in Italy toward the Ligurian port, while he himself led an army of 60,000 men across the Alps into Lombardy, scene of his earlier triumphs. By 1 June 1800 he was again in Milan. But while Napoleon busied himself against the scattered Austrian forces in Piedmont, the main Austrian force under General Michael Melas had taken Genoa. Napoleon thought that the Austrians were preparing to retreat rather than fight, and he detached units to block potential escape routes. He therefore faced the Austrians at Marengo on 14 June with unnecessarily depleted forces. The closely contested battle was presented by Napoleon as a major victory. His popularity in France received another boost, but the war

trians and their allies from reinforcing Habsburg forces in Germany. The campaign was meant to be a secondary action, but Napoleon's outstanding victories allowed him effectively to impose his own policy on the Directory in Paris. With only a small, ill-equipped army at his disposal, Napoleon waged a war of movement, striking shrewd and stinging blows against isolated elements of the numerically superior Austrian and Piedmontese armies. In the summer of 1796, after defeating the Piedmontese at the battle of Mondovi he forced them out of the war, and turning on the Austrians he overcame them at Lodi and seized Milan. Moving east he surrounded a large Austrian force at Mantua.

The Austrian attempts to relieve Mantua were poorly coordinated, allowing Napoleon to concentrate his forces and turn on their forces separately. In August 1796, following the battles of Lonato and Cas-

dragged on in Germany until December 1800, when the French under Jean Moreau won a decisive victory at Hohenlinden. Napoleon finally achieved his aim of peace with Austria in 1801.

Related entries: Arcola, Battle of; Austria; Bassano, Battle of; Bussaco, Battle of; Campo Formio, Treaty of; Castiglione, Battle of; Coalitions; Consulate; Directory; Genoa; Mantua; Marengo, Battle of; Masséna, André; Mondovi, Battle of; Napoleonic Legend; Papal States; Personality, Cult of; Propaganda; Revolutionary Wars; Rivoli, Battle of; Venice

Suggestions for further reading:
Burton, Reginald George. 1912. *Napoleon's Campaigns in Italy, 1796–97 and 1800.* London and New York: G. Allen.
Chandler, David G. 1974. *The Campaigns of Napoleon: The Mind and Method of History's Greatest Soldier.* New York: Macmillan.
Jackson, Sir William Godfrey Fothergill. 1953. *Attack in the West: Napoleon's First Campaign Re-read Today.* London: Eyre and Spottiswoode.
Phipps, Ramsay Weston. 1926–1939. *The Armies of the First French Republic and the Rise of the Marshals of Napoleon I.* 5 vols. London: Humphrey Milford.

Italy, Kingdom of

The Kingdom of Italy was formed in 1805 from the former Cisalpine Republic, with Napoleon as king and Eugène de Beauharnais as viceroy. It incorporated the northern and eastern plains of Italy. Venice was added to the original Cisalpine territories in 1806, followed by the Papal States of Urbino, Macerata, Ancona, and Camerino in 1807, and the southern Tyrol in 1809. In all some 7 million subjects lived in Eugène's kingdom, supporting an army of 100,000 men.

Eugène was allowed little political initiative, but succeeded in creating a surprisingly broad basis of support among his people for several years. The administration of the kingdom was reorganized on French lines, with twenty-four departments under prefects appointed by the viceroy, who also nominated a senate for the passage of legislation. The Napoleonic Codes became the basis of law administered through courts on the French model. In the army and administration careers were open to the talented, with new nobles and educated commoners employed in high office alongside members of the old nobility. The whole was overseen by a ministry formed entirely of Italians, dominated by Francesco Melzi d'Eril as grand chancellor. The minister of finance, Giuseppe Prina, miraculously kept the budget in balance, despite Napoleon's demands for taxation, until 1813. Schools and universities were brought under central control, and grants were provided for scholars and scientists and the arts encouraged through a royal academy, a conservatory of music, and an academy of fine arts.

The economy, however, presents a more equivocal impression. Eugène protested against Napoleon's exorbitant demands for money, and Prina succeeded in keeping taxes lower than in France. But the Continental System subordinated the needs of Italian producers to a damaging tariff system. Enterprising farmers and manufacturers converted to the export of raw silk and food, and even began growing cotton, so that the System could be circumvented.

The Italian troops in Napoleon's armies continued to fight well, with 20,000 lost in Russia in 1812. But by 1814 Eugène's attempts to hold on to his kingdom by reaching agreement with the Allies were doomed to failure. Prina was killed by a mob in Milan, and other representatives of the Napoleonic order were threatened. The Austrians moved back into control of northern Italy. Within a few years, however, Italian patriots came to look back on the Kingdom of Italy, with all its faults, as the precursor of national unity. Its tricolor flag of red, white, and green was adopted as the banner of united Italy.

Related entries: Beauharnais, Eugène Rose de; Continental System; Melzi d'Eril, Francesco; Papal States

Suggestions for further reading:

Connelly, Owen. 1965. *Napoleon's Satellite Kingdoms.* New York: Free Press.

Grab, Alexander. 1988. "The Kingdom of Italy and Napoleon's Continental Blockade," *Consortium on Revolutionary Europe, Proceedings, 1988,* pp. 587–604.

Hearder, Harry. 1983. *Italy in the Age of the Risorgimento, 1790–1870.* London and New York: Longman.

Oman, Carola. 1966. *Napoleon's Viceroy: Eugène de Beauharnais.* London: Collins.

Rath, Reuben J. 1941. *The Fall of the Napoleonic Kingdom of Italy, 1814.* New York: Columbia University Press.

Woolf, Stuart. 1991. *Napoleon's Integration of Europe.* London and New York: Routledge.

Jacobinism

The term Jacobin, first used in 1790 to describe members of the revolutionary club, the Society of Friends of the Constitution, which met at the former Dominican (Jacobin) convent in Paris, became associated with the Montagnard government of 1793–1794 led by Maximilien Robespierre. Napoleon and his brothers were Jacobin supporters in the early 1790s, helping to organize clubs in Corsica, and Napoleon's pamphlet *Le Souper de Beaucaire* can be read as pro-Jacobin. He owed his command of the artillery during the siege of Toulon to the Corsican Jacobin, Antonio Cristoforo Saliceti, and Robespierre's sister, who knew him in 1794, described him as a convinced Montagnard. The sincerity of Napoleon's Jacobinism is, however, open to doubt in view of his overriding ambition. He later explained: "I was then very young and my opinions were not yet settled."

By the time of the Directory Jacobinism was associated with the radical democratic opposition, and Napoleon was definitely anti-Jacobin. The myth of a "Jacobin conspiracy" was used to justify the coup of 18 Brumaire, and during the consulate Napoleon continued to play on moderate fears of a Jacobin coup. The Opera Plot to assassinate Napoleon on 24 December 1800 was blamed on "Jacobins." Some 130 were arrested and deported to the Seychelles or Guiana, where half were to die in exile, and none were pardoned even when it had been established that the plot was the work of royalists. Throughout Napoleon's rule the police kept a watchful eye on all suspected "Jacobins" and "anarchists," and displays of overt republicanism were limited to the words or actions of reckless individuals.

Italian Jacobinism was somewhat different from the French original. *Giacobini,* drawn mostly from the ranks of the professional middle classes, wanted an independent, unified, and secular Italian republic. Many Italian exiles had played a role in the Revolution, and the *Giacobini* placed their faith in French invasion leading to mass insurrection against the Italian princes and the papacy. But the *Giacobini* lacked popular support, and Napoleon colluded with more moderate Italian republicans in the formation of so-called "sister republics" under French control. With the passage of time the *Giacobini* came to be seen as the forerunners of Italian unification, but during the Napoleonic era in Italy they were distrusted by the French, and rejected by Italians as being too closely associated with the invader.

Related entries: Corsica; Directory; Opera Plot; Opposition Movements; Saliceti, Antonio Cristoforo; *Souper de Beaucaire, Le*

Suggestions for further reading:
Brinton, Crane. 1930. *The Jacobins.* New York: Macmillan.

Lefebvre, Georges. 1967. *The French Revolution from 1793 to 1799.* London: Routledge and Kegan Paul.

Woloch, Isser. 1970. *Jacobin Legacy: The Democratic Movement under the Directory.* Princeton: Princeton University Press.

Jena-Auerstädt, Battles of (14 October 1806)

The double victory of Napoleon and Louis Davout over the Prussians exposed the incompetent leadership of the Prussian army and led to the collapse of the state. Although neither side was ever fully aware of what the other was doing, Napoleon's more decisive way of waging war proved superior to the hidebound Prussian approach. When war between France and Prussia threatened in September 1806 the Prussian army of 171,000 troops moved into the Weimar region of central Germany, but Napoleon moved his 180,000 men in three columns to the Prussian rear, cutting off their lines of communication toward Dresden, Leipzig, and Berlin. He was thus able to throw a net around the retreating Prussians and engage them between Jena and Auerstädt to the east of Weimar.

The Prussian forces were divided into three armies. The main force under the duke of Brunswick, accompanied by King Frederick William III, marched to the northeast, while the other two armies, one under Prince von Hohenlohe and a smaller force under Ernst von Rüchel, guarded the flank and rear around Jena. On the morning of 14 October Napoleon's main force of 96,000 men (only 54,000 of which he had to use) engaged Hohenlohe's 53,000 on the plains north of Jena. After fierce fighting, by midafternoon the Prussians were in full retreat.

At the same time Davout's Third Corps had engaged Brunswick's superior forces at Auerstädt, eleven miles to the north. Napo-

leon had to acknowledge that the Third Corps performed wonders. For two hours the leading division, commanded by General Charles Gudin, fought off two Prussian divisions, plus the cavalry under Gebhard von Blücher. When the other French divisions arrived to support the vanguard, Brunswick was mortally wounded and the king took command, but was incapable of making his numerical advantage count. The Prussians were driven off in all directions, and a pursuit led by Joachim Murat's cavalry destroyed all semblance of Prussian discipline and morale. While thousands of mutinous and starving Prussian troops were rounded up, Frederick William fled to Königsberg. Berlin, the Prussian capital, was left to its fate.

The Prussian soldiers had fought with considerable courage, but their commanders had displayed not only tactical inflexibility but sheer incompetence. Napoleon's victory was complete. Hermann von Boyen, a young Prussian officer badly wounded in the battle, wrote: "The carefully assembled and apparently unshakable military structure of Prussia was suddenly shattered to its very foundations" (Sheehan 1989, p. 234). Napoleon had suffered fewer than 7,000 casualties, while around 11,000 Prussians were killed or injured and 15,000 captured. Carl von Clausewitz observed: "It was not just a case of a style which had outlived its usefulness but the most extreme poverty of imagination to which routine has ever led" (Gates 1997, p. 64).

Related entries: Davout, Louis Nicolas; Germany, Campaigns in; Prussia

Suggestions for further reading:
Chandler, David G. 1974. *The Campaigns of Napoleon: The Mind and Method of History's Greatest Soldier.* New York: Macmillan.
———. 1987. "Davout," in David G. Chandler, ed. *Napoleon's Marshals.* New York: Macmillan.
Gates, David. 1997. *The Napoleonic Wars, 1803–15.* London: Edward Arnold.
Sheehan, James J. 1989. *German History 1770–1866.* Oxford: Clarendon Press.

Jews

Napoleon's personal attitude toward the Jewish people is difficult to determine, with both friendly and hostile statements being more or less reliably recorded. He certainly showed no more respect for Judaism as a religion than he did for Christianity or Islam. Yet his memory was long revered by Jews in Germany, as his armies continued the work of the revolutionary armies in imposing civil equality for Jews in conquered territories. "Wherever his victorious legions came," writes the American Jewish historian Abram Leon Sacher, "the walls of the ghetto fell and the Jews walked forth free and unafraid" (Sacher 1989, p. 296). Even the beginnings of Jewish emancipation in Prussia after the defeats of 1806–1807 may be attributed indirectly to Napoleon, as Prussian reformists perceived emancipation as economically and politically beneficial. The story that in 1799 he appealed to the Jews of Asia and Africa for support, promising them a homeland in Palestine, is however a legend.

Napoleon sought to follow the tradition of the Revolution in pursuing the economic, social, and political assimilation of French Jewry. He demanded their obedience through a religious settlement parallel to that imposed on Catholics and Protestants. In 1806 he convened an Assembly of Jewish Notables from France, Italy, and Germany to redefine traditional Judaism in accordance with Napoleonic ideas of patriotism and social morality. This assembly was followed in 1807 by the Grand Sanhedrin of European rabbis, supposed to adapt the laws of Moses "to the customs and usages of the present." Adding his own brand of pragmatism to revolutionary ideals, Napoleon wanted above all to obtain Jewish consent to civil marriage, taxation, conscription, and whatever changes he may have wished to make to commercial practices.

By an Imperial Edict of 18 March 1808 Jewish worship in France and its annexed territories was organized through a central consistory in Paris, with an approved synagogue in each department with a Jewish community. Napoleon's wishes with regard to the Jews were largely met within France, where he could be assured that they regarded themselves as French citizens on a par with all others, and in areas under direct French rule. But he made no attempt to appeal to Jewish sentiment in enemy countries. Jews in Russia and Prussia supported their own rulers against him, and the Rothschilds, the biggest banking house in Europe, proved of considerable help to the British and Austrians in providing funds for troops and negotiating loans and subsidies to anti-French rulers.

Suggestions for further reading:
Arnold, Eric A., ed. 1994. *A Documentary Survey of Napoleonic France.* Lanham, MD: University Press of America, pp. 224–226, 280–287.
Hyman, Paula E. 1991. *The Emancipation of the Jews of Alsace.* New Haven: Yale University Press.
Malino, Frances. 1978. *The Sephardic Jews of Bordeaux: Assimilation and Emancipation in Revolutionary and Napoleonic France.* University, Alabama: University of Alabama Press.
Sacher, Abram Leon. 1989. "Napoleon and the Jews," in Frank A. Kafker and James M. Laux, eds., *Napoleon and His Times: Selected Interpretations.* Malibar, FL: Krieger. pp. 296–300.
Schwarzfuchs, Simon. 1979. *Napoleon, the Jews and the Sanhedrin.* London: Routledge and Kegan Paul.
Sorkin, David Jan. 1987. *The Transformation of German Jewry, 1780–1840.* New York: Oxford University Press.

Jourdan, Jean-Baptiste (1762–1833)

The son of a surgeon of Limoges, Jourdan first saw military action between 1779 and 1781, serving in the American War of Independence and the West Indies before being discharged in 1784. Elected as captain of the National Guard of

Limoges in 1789, he restarted a military career that saw him emerge as a hero of the Revolution. As commander of the Army of the Moselle, responsible for holding the frontier with Luxemburg and southern Belgium, Jourdan led the French to victory over the Austrians at Fleurus (26 June 1794), a triumph which assured French control over Belgium for the next twenty years. Jourdan resigned his command in 1795, but became active in politics. As president of the Council of Five Hundred under the Directory he was responsible for the so-called Jourdan Law, which created the system of military conscription used by Napoleon. Rejoining the army in 1798 he performed feebly in the fighting against the Second Coalition in 1799.

True to his republican principles and despite his disillusionment with the Directory, Jourdan opposed the coup of 18 Brumaire and was briefly imprisoned. Napoleon, however, wanting republican heroes to legitimize his power, freed him in 1800, made him inspector general of the infantry and the cavalry, and in 1804 created him a marshal of the empire. But he was never given positions in accord with his rank. Jourdan replaced the rapacious André Masséna as chief of staff to King Joseph Bonaparte in Naples in 1806 and, forming a lasting friendship with Napoleon's elder brother, followed him to Spain in 1808. As chief of staff of the Army of Spain in 1808–1809 and again in 1812–1813 Jourdan faced an impossible task trying to coordinate the efforts of marshals who acted as laws unto themselves, but he was nevertheless forced to accept ultimate responsibility. He thus became the scapegoat for the defeats at Talavera (1809) and at the decisive battle of Vitoria (1813), which brought a final end to the Napoleonic kingdom of Spain.

Jourdan rallied to Napoleon during the Hundred Days in 1815, but played little active part, and Louis XVIII restored his rank as marshal and created him a peer of France

in 1817. He was still serving in 1830, when he was made governor of Les Invalides, a position he held until his death at the age of seventy-one. Jourdan was a capable soldier rather than a great one, but Napoleon, looking back during his time on Saint Helena, realized that he had behaved badly toward him. "Jourdan is a true patriot," he said, "and that is the answer to many things that have been said about him" (Glover 1987, p. 168).

Related entries: Conscription; Peninsular War.

Suggestions for further reading:
Glover, Michael. 1987. "Jourdan," in David G. Chandler, ed. *Napoleon's Marshals.* New York: Macmillan.

Junot, Andoche (1771–1813)

A former law student and volunteer in the revolutionary armies, Junot was a sergeant at the siege of Toulon in 1793. Napoleon, appreciating his coolness under fire, made Junot his secretary and secured him rapid promotion. He served his patron in Italy and Egypt, where he was wounded in a duel with an officer who had criticized Napoleon. After a brief spell as ambassador to Portugal Junot fought at Austerlitz and, in 1807, commanded the almost bloodless conquest of Portugal, being rewarded with the title of duke of Abrantès. However, Napoleon never forgave him for being driven out of Portugal by the duke of Wellington in the following year, and he never received the marshal's baton for which he seemed destined.

Junot fought in the Wagram campaign of 1809 and again in Spain in 1810. But when he commanded the Eighth Corps in the Russian campaign of 1812 his health was failing, and he returned a broken man. Napoleon made Junot governor of the Illyrian Provinces in 1813, but by now it was clear that he was going insane. Shipped back to his father's home near Dijon, he jumped from a window to his death in July 1813.

Junot's wife, Laure Permon, better known as the duchess of Abrantès, wrote gossipy memoirs of the Napoleonic era as well as harrowing accounts of the horrors of the Peninsular War, which she had witnessed at first hand traveling with her husband's troops.

Related entries: Illyria; Portugal

Suggestions for further reading:
Gates, David. 1986. *The Spanish Ulcer: A History of the Peninsular War.* London: Allen and Unwin.
Oman, Charles W. C. 1902–1930. *A History of the Peninsular War.* 7 vols. Oxford: Clarendon Press.

K

Kalisch, Treaty of (28 February 1813)

The alliance between Prussia and Russia following Napoleon's defeat in the Russian campaign of 1812 committed Russia to assist Prussia to regain the territory lost by the Treaty of Tilsit in 1806. An accompanying proclamation by Frederick William III and Alexander I calling on the German princes to rise against Napoleon met with little response among rulers and people anxious at seeing the Russians and Prussians advancing from the east.

Related entries: Coalitions; Prussia; Russia

Suggestions for further reading:
Ross, Steven T. 1981. *European Diplomatic History, 1789–1815.* Malabar, FL: Krieger.

Kellermann, François Christophe (1735–1820)

Already an experienced soldier with the rank of major general in 1789, Kellermann became one of the heroes of the Revolution by playing a crucial role in the battle of Valmy (20 September 1792), which saved France from Prussian invasion. He was commander of the Army of Italy in 1796, replaced by Napoleon, and in September 1797 retired from active duty. Although Kellermann did not support the coup of 18 Brumaire, Napoleon was anxious to secure the support of this republican hero. Kellermann was made a senator in 1799 and later president of the Senate, while in 1804 he became the oldest of the marshals of France. During Napoleon's great military campaigns Kellermann commanded reserve troops, putting his organizational abilities to good use, but he never took the field. He refused to rally to Napoleon during the Hundred Days, and as an octogenarian participated in the reorganization of the army under the Restoration.

Related entries: Revolutionary Wars; Senate

Suggestions for further reading:
Hofschröer, Peter. 1987. "Kellermann," in David G. Chandler, ed., *Napoleon's Marshals.* New York: Macmillan.

Kléber, Jean-Baptiste (1753–1800)

One of the most competent generals of the Republic, Kléber played a distinguished part in Napoleon's Egyptian campaign. Before 1798 he had already served in the Vendée (in 1793) and in Germany (between 1794 and 1796) and had shown himself a first-rate tactician and commander. However, disagreements with his superiors led to his resignation in February 1797. Assigned to the Army of Egypt under Napoleon, he was wounded in the attack on Alexandria on 2 July 1798, but still served in all the principal battles in Syria. When Napoleon returned to France in August 1799 Kléber was named commander in chief in Syria and Egypt. He negotiated a treaty for the evacuation of the French with the British admiral Sir Sydney Smith, only to have it rejected by the government of William Pitt. Kléber crushed the Turkish army at Heliopolis on 23 March 1800 and put down the revolt in Cairo in April. But he was assassinated by a young Muslim fanatic, Suleiman el Halepi, on 14 June 1800.

Related entries: Egyptian Campaign

Suggestions for further reading:
Barthorp, Michael. 1978. *Napoleon's Egyptian Campaigns, 1798–1801.* London: Osprey.
Chandler, David G. 1974. *The Campaigns of Napoleon: The Mind and Method of History's Greatest Soldier.* New York: Macmillan.
Herold, J. Christopher. 1962. *Bonaparte in Egypt.* New York: Harper and Row.

Kutuzov, Mikhail Ilarionovich (1745–1813)

*T*he wily old fox of the North, as Napoleon called him, is remembered as the chief instrument of the emperor's downfall in Russia. Kutuzov was an immensely experienced soldier and diplomat who had lost his right eye in 1773 during the Russian war of 1770–1774 against the Turks. As well as distinguishing himself in the armies of Count Rumyantsev and Alexander Suvorov, Kutuzov learned in the Turkish wars the valuable lesson, also applied by Napoleon, that the object of warfare was not the occupation of territory but the destruction of enemy forces. But, unlike Napoleon, he saw that this destruction was not necessarily always best achieved in one decisive battle.

In 1801 Kutuzov distanced himself from the plot against Tsar Paul I, thereby earning the mistrust of Alexander I, who sent him into virtual exile. With the formation of the Third Coalition in 1805, however, Alexander was compelled to recall one of his most resourceful and intelligent commanders. Forced to act jointly with the Austrians, Kutuzov managed to preserve the Russian army intact after Napoleon's victory in the battle of Ulm. He proposed withdrawal to Russia but was overruled by Alexander, who took personal command and insisted on forcing Napoleon into a decisive engagement. The result was the disaster of Austerlitz, after which Kutuzov withdrew the remnants of the Russian army in good order to Poland. Alexander, peevishly and unjustly, blamed Kutuzov for Austerlitz. For the next six years he again occupied minor posts, until he was recalled in 1811 to prosecute the simmering war against Turkey in Moldavia. Within a few months he had forced the Turks to sign the Treaty of Bucharest, thereby freeing Russia from the Turkish entanglement as war threatened with Napoleon.

When Napoleon's *Grande Armée* invaded Russia in June 1812, the Russians retreated, and in August after the loss of Smolensk Alexander was compelled, with great reluctance, to replace Barclay de Tolly with Kutuzov as commander in chief. After the battle of Borodino on 7 September, Kutuzov decided to continue the retreat beyond Moscow. "Napoleon," he said, "is a torrent which as yet we are unable to stem; Moscow will be the sponge to suck him dry" (Palmer 1984, p. 170). He summarily rejected all armistice proposals from Napoleon and waited for the French to retreat. Only then did he harry the retreating *Grande Armée* all the way to the river Berezina, disrupting the orderly progress of the retreat and inflicting heavy casualties.

When in the spring of 1813 the Allies began their advance into Germany, Kutuzov commanded the main Russian army. But his health, which had long been uncertain, gave way, and he died at Bunzlau in Silesia on 28 April 1813. Kutuzov does not deserve the sole credit for Napoleon's defeat in Russia; the strategy of retreat had already been pursued by Barclay de Tolly. On the other hand, it is equally wrong to criticize him for being lethargic and unwilling to give battle. His previous career proved that he could act swiftly and decisively when occasion demanded. The Russians probably had no option but to adopt delaying tactics against the invasion. Kutuzov carried them out with outstanding success.

Related entries: Austerlitz, Battle of; Borodino, Battle of; Danube Campaigns; Russian Campaign; Ulm, Battle of

Suggestions for further reading:
Duffy, Christopher. 1972. *Borodino and the War of 1812*. London: Seeley.
Palmer, Alan. 1984. *An Encyclopaedia of Napoleon's Europe*. London: Weidenfeld and Nicolson.
Parkinson, Roger. 1976. *The Fox of the North: The Life of Kutuzov, General of War and Peace*. London: Peter Davies.
Riehn, Richard K. 1991. *1812: Napoleon's Russian Campaign*. New York: John Wiley.
Tarle, E. 1942. *Napoleon's Invasion of Russia, 1812*. London: Allen and Unwin.

L

La Plaigne, Léon Charles de (1806–1881)

One of the two illegitimate sons acknowledged by Napoleon, the other being the child of Marie Walewska, "le comte Léon's" contribution to history lay in his existence, proof that Napoleon could father children. Napoleon's affair with Léon's mother, Eléonore Deruelle de La Plaigne, was brief and meaningless, but he showered income and gifts upon the child who made his divorce from Joséphine more feasible. Any hopes Napoleon may have had for Léon were unfulfilled. An inveterate gambler, he spent most of his life sponging off his Bonaparte relatives and died in poverty.

Suggestions for further reading:
Aronson, Theo. 1965. *The Golden Bees: The Story of the Bonapartes.* London: Oldbourne.

Lacuée, Jean Gérard (1752–1841)

Napoleon called Lacuée, minister of war administration between 1810 and 1813, his most able administrator after Pierre Daru. Lacuée had been influential in the reorganization of the army during the Revolution, and Napoleon called on his experience in drafting legislation about con-

scription. Between 1806 and 1810 as director general of the combined bureau dealing with conscription and payrolls Lacuée had direct access to Napoleon. Appointed minister of war administration on 3 January 1810, Lacuée oversaw the enormous task of organizing the supply of both the *Grande Armée* for the invasion of Russia and the new forces raised for the campaign of 1813. Lacuée's correspondence showed that he stood up to Napoleon over details of the enforcement of conscription and opposed the marriage to Marie-Louise and the Russian adventure. He resigned his office in November 1813 when he could no longer support Napoleon's continuation of the war.

Related entries: Conscription; *Grande Armée*

Suggestions for further reading:
Church, Clive H. 1981. *Revolution and Red Tape: The French Ministerial Bureaucracy 1770–1850.* Oxford: Clarendon Press.
Rogers, H. C. B. 1974. *Napoleon's Army.* London: Allen.

Lafayette, Marie Paul Joseph Roch Gilbert du Motier, Marquis de (1757–1832)

The hero of the American Revolution and creator of the Paris National Guard had been a prisoner of the Prussians and then the Austrians since 1792 when a special provision of the Treaty of Campo Formio, negotiated by Napoleon, secured his release in September 1797. He took up residence first in Holstein then in Holland, but on hearing of the coup of 18 Brumaire hurried to Paris under an assumed name. Lafayette's name was stricken from the list of *émigrés* in May 1800, but he rejected offers of a seat in the Senate and the ambassadorship to the United States and in March 1802 requested his retirement from the army. He did not reenter politics until after Napoleon's fall, when he became a leader of the liberal opposition under the Restoration.

Suggestions for further reading:
Gottschalk, Louis R., and Margaret Maddox. 1969–1973. *Lafayette in the French Revolution.* 2 vols. Chicago: University of Chicago Press.

Lannes, Jean (1769–1809)

Volatile, courageous, impetuous, and tenacious, Lannes came to typify the dash and bravery of the Napoleonic army, while also showing a personal attachment to Napoleon not always shown by his other commanders. A Gascon farmer's son who first saw action in the Pyrenees in 1792, he fought with distinction in almost all the significant campaigns of the revolutionary and Napoleonic wars until he became the first of Napoleon's marshals to die in battle.

Lannes first served under Napoleon in Italy in 1796–1797, distinguishing himself in the battles of Bassano, Arcola (where he was wounded three times), Lodi, and Rivoli. During the Egyptian campaign of 1798–1799 he was wounded again at the siege of Acre and at Aboukir. Returning to France with Napoleon, he supported but played no active role in the coup of 18 Brumaire. In 1800, confirmed as a divisional general, he won Montebello, the preliminary action to Marengo, and fought with

conspicuous bravery in the main battle, checking the Austrian attacks at the height of the fighting. A diplomatic mission to Portugal in 1801 was less suited to his talents, and he spent 1804 at Ambleteuse in preparation for the abandoned invasion of England. Napoleon, who regarded Lannes as a personal friend, made him a marshal in 1804.

In 1805 Lannes fought at Ulm and Austerlitz, where his infantry halted Prince Bagration's cavalry; he commanded the center of Napoleon's army and launched the first attack at Jena (10 October 1806); he was wounded seriously again when defeating a Russian force at Pultulsk (26 December 1806); and in June 1807 he set the stage for Napoleon's climactic victory at Friedland. Dispatched to Spain in 1808, Lannes commanded at the siege of Saragossa, negotiating the city's surrender in February 1809. Back in Germany in April, he fought a string of battles, culminating at Essling, where on the second day of this exceptionally bloody battle he was mortally wounded by a chance shot, dying nine days later on 31 May 1809.

Napoleon mourned Lannes's death deeply. Lannes had served courageously and with a deep sense of loyalty since their days together in Italy. As a leader Lannes was always in the thick of the action, as shown by his numerous wounds: a ball in the neck suffered at the siege of Acre nearly cost him his life and left him with difficulties in speaking and his head inclined permanently to one side. This impetuosity could cause problems with other commanders—his relations with the equally hotheaded Joachim Murat were strained if not hostile—but also made him the epitome of the elan and panache of the Napoleonic soldier.

Related entries: Arcola, Battle of; Austerlitz, Battle of; Bassano, Battle of; Danube Campaigns; Essling, Battle of; Italian Campaigns; Jena-Auerstädt, Battles of; Lodi, Battle of; Marengo, Battle of; Peninsular War; Rivoli, Battle of; Ulm, Battle of

Suggestions for further reading:
Horward, Donald D. 1987. "Lannes," in David G. Chandler, ed., *Napoleon's Marshals.* New York: Macmillan.
Parker, Harold T. 1983. *Three Napoleonic Battles.* Durham, NC: Duke University Press.

Larrey, Dominique Jean (1766–1842)

Although the medical care of soldiers in battle remained appallingly primitive during the Napoleonic wars, Larrey's work in ameliorating the suffering of the wounded and his skill at performing amputations make him one of the greatest figures in the history of military medicine. Larrey became famous during the revolutionary wars when as a surgeon in the Army of the Rhine he organized a system of mobile field hospitals, allowing surgeons to follow armies and avoid delays in treating the wounded. Napoleon called upon him to organize the ambulances in his first Italian campaign and again in the Egyptian campaign, where his personal bravery and devotion, helping to move the wounded to hospitals in the thick of battle, were outstanding. From then on Larrey was present in all Napoleon's major military campaigns.

In addition to receiving numerous honors and posts, Larrey served as surgeon in chief of the Imperial Guard. He distinguished himself in particular at the dreadful Battle of Eylau (18 February 1807), moving the wounded in extremely cold weather, at Wagram (5–6 July 1809), and during the Russian campaign of 1812 as chief surgeon of the *Grande Armée.* His observations on the effects of cold on the wounded gave rise to further research and writings. Larrey was also present at Waterloo, where he was wounded and taken prisoner. After the Restoration he pursued a distinguished career in medicine, receiving the highest honors and publishing numerous works of lasting value in his field.

Related entries: Army

Suggestions for further reading:
Dible, James H. 1970. *Napoleon's Surgeon.* London: William Heinemann.
Richardson, Robert G. 1974. *Larrey: Surgeon to Napoleon's Imperial Guard.* London: John Murray.
Vess, David M. 1975. *Medical Revolution in France, 1789–1796.* Gainesville: University Presses of Florida.

Las Cases, Emmanuel Augustin, Comte de (1766–1842)

The man who wrote the *Mémorial de Sainte-Hélène* and thereby became a prime mover in the creation of the Napoleonic legend was, ironically, a nobleman who emigrated from France at the time of the Revolution and fought in the *émigré* army of the Prince de Condé. He returned to France in 1802, eventually rising at Napoleon's court to become chamberlain in 1810. After seeing Napoleon again during the Hundred Days, he volunteered to accompany him in exile to Saint Helena. Las Cases's motives for creating the *Mémorial,* published in 1823, are obscure: either he acted out of personal devotion to Napoleon or he saw the chance to write a best-seller. He stayed on Saint Helena for eighteen months before being expelled by the governor, Sir Hudson Lowe, possibly as a result of a deliberate maneuver by Napoleon. Las Cases used considerable journalistic skill in presenting Napoleon as a martyr for democracy, liberty, and peace. Later in life he sat in the Chamber of Deputies between 1830 and 1842 and accompanied Napoleon's remains on their return from Saint Helena to Paris in 1840.

Related entries: *Mémorial de Sainte-Hélène;* Napoleonic Legend

Suggestions for further reading:
Harvey, A. D. 1998. "Napoleon—the Myth," *History Today* 48 (January 1998), pp. 27–32.

Korngold, Ralph. 1960. *The Last Years of Napoleon: His Captivity at St. Helena.* Princeton: Van Nostrand.

Law, Codification of

The various law codes promulgated by Napoleon between 1804 and 1810 may properly be considered his most lasting achievement, and the Civil Code has been called one of the few books that have influenced the whole world. The Revolution had made various attempts to replace the approximately 400 codes used in France under the ancien régime, but had made little progress until Napoleon took matters in hand. The Civil Code of 1804 was followed by the Code of Civil Procedure (1806), the Commercial Code (1807), the Criminal Code and Code of Criminal Procedure (1808), and the Penal Code (1810). The Rural Code was never put into effect. Despite all their defects and authoritarian tendencies, taken together the Napoleonic Codes embodied for the first time in modern history a system of unified law applicable without distinction to all classes of citizens. As such they made permanent the essential achievements of the Revolution: national unity and civic equality.

Related entries: Civil Code; Code of Criminal Procedure; Commercial Code, Penal Code; Rural Code

Suggestions for further reading:
Holtman, Robert B. 1967. *The Napoleonic Revolution.* Philadelphia: Lippincott.
Lyons, Martyn. 1994. *Napoleon Bonaparte and the Legacy of the French Revolution.* London: Macmillan.

Lebrun, Charles François (1739–1824)

Essentially a competent administrator, Lebrun attained brief political prominence as third consul after the coup of 18 Brumaire. He had held various administrative posts under the monarchy, been imprisoned during the Terror, and been a member of the Council of Ancients under the Directory. As consul until 1802 Lebrun contributed to the reorganization of justice and finance. In 1804 Napoleon appointed him arch treasurer of the empire and, after forcing Louis Bonaparte to abdicate as king of Holland in 1810, sent Lebrun to prepare for its integration with France. After the Restoration Lebrun lived out his final years in obscurity, but his exercise of patronage under Napoleon, especially in the appointment of prefects, had brought him considerable wealth and influence.

Related entries: Consulate; Netherlands

Suggestions for further reading:
Church, Clive H. 1981. *Revolution and Red Tape: The French Ministerial Bureaucracy 1770–1850.* Oxford: Clarendon Press.
Holtman, Robert B. 1967. *The Napoleonic Revolution.* Philadelphia: Lippincott.
Morton, John B. 1948. *Brumaire: The Rise of Bonaparte.* London: T. Werner Levine.

Leclerc, Charles Victor Emmanuel (1772–1802)

The son of a wealthy mill-owner from Pontoise, Leclerc had joined the army as a volunteer in 1791 and first encountered Napoleon at the siege of Toulon. His rise through the ranks continued in Italy in 1796, when Napoleon recommended his promotion to general of brigade, and he sealed his connection with the Bonaparte family by marrying Pauline Bonaparte in 1797. A general of division in 1799, he took part in the coup of 18 Brumaire and served in the Army of the Rhine under Jean Moreau. However, Leclerc's promising military career was destined for an ignominious end when in October 1801

Napoleon appointed him commander of the expedition to regain control of Haiti. After initial success, Leclerc was faced by general insurrection by September 1802, and he succumbed to the yellow fever that had decimated his forces.

Related entries: Bonaparte, Pauline, Duchess of Guastalla; Haiti

Suggestions for further reading:
James, C. L. R. 1938. *The Black Jacobins: Toussaint L'Ouverture and the San Domingo Revolution.* London: Secker and Warburg.
Ortzen, Len. 1974. *Imperial Venus: The Story of Pauline Bonaparte-Borghese.* New York: Stein and Day.

Lefebvre, François Joseph (1755–1820)

Eventually to become duke of Danzig and marshal of France, Lefebvre was the son of a former trooper turned miller from Rouffach in Alsace. He was the most proletarian of Napoleon's marshals and has been dismissed by some historians as "the complete sergeant major." He enlisted in the army in 1773 and under the Revolution gained rapid promotion, becoming a major general in 1794. Between 1794 and 1799 Lefebvre served in the Rhineland and Germany and therefore never with or under Napoleon. Scrupulously honest himself, he had developed a dislike for the venal politicians of the Directory and, when consulted by Napoleon about the coup of 18 Brumaire, replied: "Yes, let us throw the lawyers into the river!" (Rothenberg 1987, p. 222). Lefebvre played no active part in the coup; he was one of the impeccably republican generals whom Napoleon wanted to win over. He was made a senator in 1800 and a marshal in 1804.

Lefebvre's talents were as a loyal and steady troop commander: he had no capacity for independent command and his few personal initiatives, notably in Spain in 1808–1809, usually turned out badly. Whenever called upon, however, he fought bravely, as at Jena (1806), at the siege of Danzig (1807), and in Spain. He commanded the infantry of the Old Guard in the Russian campaign of 1812, taking part in all the horrors of the retreat from Moscow. In 1814, at the age of sixty, he fought valiantly during the Allied invasion of France, but in April reluctantly joined the group of marshals urging Napoleon to abdicate. Lefebvre was credited with persuading the victorious Alexander I that Alsace, his homeland, should remain French. His support for Napoleon during the Hundred Days led to temporary disgrace, but he was restored to his rank and honors in 1819, a year before his death.

Bluff and unsophisticated, Lefebvre and his wife, Catherine Hübscher, a former washerwoman who passed into legend as "Madame Sans-Gêne," caused consternation at the imperial court by their lack of pretensions and tendency to preface their remarks with "when I was a sergeant" or "when I did the washing." Only two of their fourteen children survived infancy, and their only surviving son was killed in the Russian campaign. Honesty and truthfulness distinguished both Lefebvres, who spent much of their fortune helping friends and supporting charities. Lefebvre himself never took part in the squabbling that marked relations between some of the other, more flamboyant marshals. His straightforward bluntness may be summed up by his famous address to the people of a newly "liberated" town in Franconia: "We have come to bring you Liberty and Equality, but don't lose your heads about it; the first one of you who moves without my permission will be shot" (Rothenberg 1987, p. 226).

Related entries: Abdication, First; Jena-Auerstädt, Battles of; Peninsular War; Russian Campaign

Suggestions for further reading:
Rothenberg, Gunther E. 1987. "Lefebvre," in David G. Chandler, ed. *Napoleon's Marshals.* New York: Macmillan.

Legion of Honor

The *Légion d'honneur* was instituted as a reward for loyal service to the nation under the consulate in 1802, but the first crosses were not handed out until July 1804. Originally the Legion was to have comprised fifteen cohorts each with 250 members, civilian and military, sworn to devote themselves to the service of the Republic, oppose the restoration of feudalism, and maintain liberty and equality. Legionnaires were to be graded into five classes, be guaranteed special privileges, and receive stipends, though under the empire these were replaced by decorations attached to a red ribbon. Old republicans were unhappy with the introduction of the Legion, and indeed it did become associated with Napoleon's new nobility. By 1814 there were some 32,000 members of the Legion, of whom over 30,000 were military men. As a symbol of meritocracy, however, the Legion survived Napoleon's fall and is today one of the greatest honors the French Republic can bestow.

Related entries: Nobility; Notables

Suggestions for further reading:
Arnold, Eric A., ed. 1994. *A Documentary Survey of Napoleonic France.* Lanham, MD: University Press of America, pp. 129–132.
Bergeron, Louis. 1981. *France under Napoleon.* Princeton: Princeton University Press.

Legislative Body

The *Corps Législatif,* established by the Constitution of the Year VIII (1799) and little changed by the constitutions of 1802 and 1804, voted on laws but was meant to represent the regime to the people rather than the other way around. The 300 members of the legislature were selected by the Senate from a national list drawn up by a complex process of indirect election and scrutinized by Napoleon. In all slightly more than 700 men served between 1800 and 1814. Every department had to have at least one representative in the assembly, which normally met for four months each year.

The Legislative Body had little power. Members listened to speeches by members of the Council of State or the Tribunate and then voted for or against measures without debating them. Unsurprisingly, negative votes were seldom recorded. The legislators were selected to represent Napoleon's ideal elite of mature males with a record of service to the state and strong ties to the land. Over three-quarters held office under the empire, one-third held the Legion of Honor, and one-third became imperial nobles. Over time survivors of the revolutionary assemblies became rare. In Napoleon's eyes the notables were the true representatives of France.

Related entries: Constitutions; Nobility; Notables

Suggestions for further reading:
Beck, Thomas D. 1974. *French Legislators, 1800–1834.* Berkeley: University of California Press.
Collins, Irene. 1979. *Napoleon and his Parliaments.* London: Edward Arnold.

Leipzig, Battle of (16–19 October 1813)

The "Battle of the Nations," fought around the city in Saxony where the river Elster converges with several tributaries, lost Napoleon control of Germany during that country's "war of liberation." Napoleon's 442,000 troops were brought to bay around Leipzig and the small town of Lindenau by superior Austrian, Russian, Prussian, and Swedish forces. On 16 October 1813 Napoleon launched an offensive against the Army of Bohemia, commanded

Pigeot's **The Retreat of the French** *portrays a disastrous defeat for Napoleon at the hands of the Austrian, Russian, Prussian, and Swedish forces when he attempted to take Leipzig in 1813. This defeat cost Napoleon his dreams for Germany. (Mary Evans Picture Library)*

by Karl zu Schwarzenberg, which was converging on Leipzig from the south, but the offensive soon ran out of steam, and to the north of the city the Army of Silesia, under Gebhard von Blücher, pinned down the French corps commanded by Marshal Louis Marmont, depriving Napoleon of the opportunity to unite his forces and win a decisive victory.

With the arrival the following day of the Army of the North, Swedes and Prussians commanded by Jean-Baptiste Bernadotte, the initiative passed to the Allies. Now arrayed in a huge semicircle to the north, south and east of Leipzig, on 18 October the Allied forces began a concerted assault, making their superior numbers tell and slowly pushing Napoleon's forces back through the Leipzig suburbs. Seeing his position to be untenable Napoleon ordered a phased retreat across the Elster to Lindenau. All proceeded according to plan until a

panic-stricken sapper corporal prematurely blew up the bridge across which the troops were to pass. The French rearguard, some 30,000 men, were cut off and forced to surrender. Others, including Marshal Josef Poniatowski, were drowned trying to swim the Elster.

The Battle of the Nations was a costly victory for the Allies. They lost at least 54,000 killed or wounded, and the French probably 38,000. Some 5,000 Saxon troops had gone over to the Allies, the first of Napoleon's German troops to defect as the Allies advanced. Several thousand sick were left behind in the city's overcrowded hospitals, churches, and schools. Disease, the handmaiden of war, killed most of them, and typhus soon spread through the congested streets of Leipzig. Among the many civilian victims was Friedrich Wagner, a city policeman, who left a wife and a six-year-old son named Richard.

Related entries: Germany, Campaigns in; Poniatowski, Josef, Prince

Suggestions for further reading:
Chandler, David G. 1974. *The Campaigns of Napoleon: The Mind and Method of History's Greatest Soldier.* New York: Macmillan.
Gates, David. 1997. *The Napoleonic Wars, 1803–15.* London: Edward Arnold.
Petre, F. Loraine. 1974. *Napoleon's Last Campaign in Germany, 1813.* London: Arms and Armour.

Ligny, Battle of (16 June 1815)

This preliminary action two days before the battle of Waterloo may be considered as Napoleon's last victory, if not a very significant one. Three Prussian corps under Gebhard von Blücher were concentrated in the village of Ligny, and when Napoleon's forces, with the Imperial Guard in the van, fell upon them they scattered, and Blücher was nearly killed when he was thrown from his horse. Napoleon, however, had also suffered heavy casualties and did not have the resources to follow up the victory, allowing August von Gneisenau to restore order in the Prussian ranks.

Related entries: Blücher, Gebhard Leberecht von; Gneisenau, August Wilhelm Anton Neidhardt von; Hundred Days; Waterloo, Battle of

Suggestions for further reading:
Chandler, David G. 1980. *Waterloo: The Hundred Days.* London: Osprey.

Ligurian Republic

This "sister" republic created out of the former republic of Genoa lasted from 1797 to 1805. Genoese territory had been violated by both the French and the Austrians in 1796, and following Napoleon's victories in his first Italian campaign pro-French Genoese patriots demanded a republic on the lines of the Cisalpine Republic, which had been established in April 1797. Following fighting in Genoa between pro- and anti-French factions, the Ligurian Republic was proclaimed on 6 June 1797, and a constitution, drawn up by a commission under Napoleon's supervision, was proclaimed on 11 November and approved by plebiscite on 2 December.

Legislative councils were chosen by a system of indirect election and in turn appointed a Directory. The feudal regime, which was of little importance in Genoa, was abolished; Catholicism was recognized as the state religion; provision was made for public assistance and education; and a permanent alliance with the French Republic was declared. In August 1798 the councils were purged by the French and the Genoese Jacobins, and the archbishop of Genoa, who was hostile to the French, was exiled to Novi.

When the French were forced to retreat from Italy in the spring of 1799, the Ligurian Republic alone escaped invasion by Austro-Russian forces. French troops commanded by André Masséna shut themselves up in Genoa, but, after running out of provisions and munitions, capitulated on 4 June 1800, ten days after Napoleon's victory at Marengo. The Ligurian Republic was reconstituted in 1802 with a new constitution drawn up by Antonio Cristoforo Saliceti. After the annexation of Piedmont to France on 11 September 1802, however, it was evident that Genoa, which was sure to be a major naval base in future fighting in the Mediterranean, would not remain independent for long. The Ligurian Republic was annexed to the French Empire on 30 June 1805.

Related entries: Genoa; Italian Campaigns; Masséna, André; Saliceti, Antonio Cristoforo

Liverpool, Robert Banks Jenkinson, Earl of (1770–1828)

Though outshone in British politics by stronger personalities such as George Canning and Viscount Castlereagh, Lord Liverpool, who became prime minister in May 1812, held together a government containing those conflicting characters and steered Britain through the final years of the struggle against Napoleon. Holding government office almost continuously from 1793 to 1827, Liverpool became foreign secretary in February 1801 and conducted the negotiations leading to the Peace of Amiens in 1802. The assassination of Spencer Percival led to his succeeding to the highest office in the land, and he was to head the British government for almost fifteen years.

Related entries: Amiens, Peace of; Great Britain

Suggestions for further reading:
Gash, Norman. 1984. *Lord Liverpool: The Life and Political Career of Robert Banks Jenkinson, Second Earl of Liverpool, 1770–1828.* London: Weidenfeld and Nicolson.

Local Government

The Constituent Assembly of 1789–1791 had completely reorganized local government in France, creating a uniform and rational division of the country into department, districts, cantons, and communes under elective local officials. Napoleon accepted the principle of the new arrangement but appointed his own officials to impose the will of central government: prefects for departments, subprefects for enlarged districts called *arrondissements,* and mayors for communes. Advisory councils for these officials were appointed and served for information and consulta-tion. Napoleon thus established a structure of French local government capable of future democratization, which has endured to the present day, the only radical modification being the creation of the regions in the 1980s. Local officials communicated along well-defined channels with ministers in Paris, who in turn reported to Napoleon. Although Napoleon himself was incapable of delegating authority, he nevertheless provided stability and opportunities for prefects and others to create networks of patronage around themselves.

Related entries: Prefects

Suggestions for further reading:
Arnold, Eric A., ed. 1994. *A Documentary Survey of Napoleonic France.* Lanham, MD: University Press of America, pp. 45–51.
Bergeron, Louis. 1981. *France under Napoleon.* Princeton: Princeton University Press.
Ellis, Geoffrey. 1983. "Rhine and Loire: Napoleonic Elites and Social Order," in Gwynne Lewis and Colin Lucas, eds., *Beyond the Terror: Essays in French Regional and Social History, 1794–1815.* Cambridge: Cambridge University Press.
Holtman, Robert B. 1967. *The Napoleonic Revolution.* Philadelphia: Lippincott.
Whitcomb, Edward A. 1974. "Napoleon's Prefects," *American Historical Review* 79, pp. 1089–1118.

Lodi, Battle of (10 May 1796)

This action of Napoleon's first Italian campaign, securing the crossing of the river Adda at Lodi, eighteen miles southeast of Milan, allowed the French to occupy western Lombardy and Milan itself. An Austrian rearguard of 8,500 men and 14 cannon defended the bridge at Lodi against attacks led by André Masséna and Louis Alexandre Berthier. The Austrians lost 2,000 men and their artillery, while the French lost 1,000. The Directory in Paris publicized Lodi as a great victory and in so doing helped to create the Bonaparte legend. The image of Napoleon as standard-bearer leading his men across the bridge is purely imaginary, although he had shown personal bravery and gained the respect of his men by reconnoitering and personally directing the battle.

Related entries: Italian Campaigns; Napoleonic Legend

Suggestions for further reading:
Jackson, Sir William Godfrey Fothergill. 1953. *Attack in the West: Napoleon's First Campaign Re-read Today*. London: Eyre and Spottiswoode.

Louis XVIII, King of France (1755–1824; reigned 1814–1824)

The pretender to the throne of France between 1795 and 1814 with the title of count of Provence, Louis was the eldest surviving brother of Louis XVI, executed in 1793. He had fled France in 1791, and was proclaimed king in June 1795 following the death in captivity of the ten-year-old dauphin, known as Louis XVII. In exile Louis busied himself with conspiracies and proclamations for the restoration of the monarchy and turned down various overtures from Napoleon, who, in 1800 and again in 1803, promised indemnities and other rewards if he would renounce his claims. On the creation of the empire in 1804 he denounced Napoleon's "usurpation."

In 1807 Louis went to England, where he was to spend the rest of his exile. However, British plans for a future after Napoleon did not necessarily mean restoration of the Bourbons, and they vetoed Louis's plans to act as regent for the captive Bourbon king of Spain. Louis had to act carefully, at the risk of alienating his more extreme supporters. In January 1814 he issued a proclamation, which became the Charter of 1814, recognizing many of the changes and institutions resulting from the Revolution, and then negotiated the terms of his return with Charles-Maurice de Talleyrand. Aloof, unknown to his people, and grotesquely fat, Louis quickly lost much goodwill and fled to Ghent during the Hundred Days. As king, however, he tried to follow a moderate policy, curbing the vengeful instincts of the ultraroyalists gathered around his brother, the count of Artois, the future Charles X, who was to lose the legitimate Bourbon line to the throne for good.

Related entries: Abdication, First; *Émigrés;* Hundred Days; Royalists

Suggestions for further reading:
Mansel, Philip. 1981. *Louis XVIII.* London: Blond and Briggs.

Louise of Mecklenburg, Queen of Prussia (1776–1810)

Napoleon paid the wife of Frederick William III the backhanded compliment of calling her "the only real man in Prussia." Louise was indeed his most resolute opponent at the Prussian court, calling him "this devilish being, sprung from the mire." Favoring close ties with Russia, the queen, as resolute as she was attractive, became the center of the war party in the events leading up to Prussia's declaration of war on Napoleon in September 1806. And in the subsequent campaign she accompanied the troops, only returning to Berlin just before the battles of Jena-Auerstädt.

After these defeats Louise tried to counter the defeatism of the court, asserting her influence over her less able husband and gathering the reformers who would resurrect Prussia around her. She reluctantly attended the negotiations leading to the Treaty of Tilsit in 1807, where she tried to influence both Napoleon and her great admirer, Tsar Alexander I. Louise must take much of the credit for Prussia's survival as an independent kingdom. Her health began to fail shortly after Tilsit, but she survived long enough to lose her illusions about Alexander during a visit to Saint Petersburg in 1809. Louise collapsed and died on 19 July 1810. Although an autopsy revealed lung and heart problems, it was popularly said that Napoleon and Alexander had made her die of sorrow. Her tomb at Charlottenburg became a place of pilgrimage for German nationalists, and in 1871 her second son, Wilhelm, became the first emperor of a Prussian-dominated Germany.

Related entries: Frederick William III, King of Prussia; Prussia

Suggestions for further reading:
Aretz, Gertrude. 1929. *Queen Louise of Prussia.* New York: G. P. Putnam's Sons.
Sheehan, James J. 1989. *German History, 1770–1866.* Oxford: Clarendon Press.

Lowe, Sir Hudson (1769–1844)

Appointed governor of Saint Helena in April 1816 with orders to enforce new restrictions on the exiled Napoleon, Lowe's career and character ensured that only very bad relations could result. Born in Galway, the son of an army surgeon, the then Captain Hudson Lowe had been involved in the siege of Corsica in 1793 and remained there on garrison duty for two years. In 1799 he organized the Corsican Rangers, made up mostly of royalist *émigrés,* and fought with them against the French in Egypt in 1800–1801. The reorganized and renamed Royal Corsican Ranger Battalion under Lowe garrisoned the island of Capri between 1803 and 1808 before being ejected by the superior forces of Joachim Murat. In 1813–1814 Lowe was attached to Gebhard von Blücher's Prussian army as a senior liaison officer and participated in

thirteen major battles. As a result he was knighted, promoted to major general, and decorated by Prussia and Russia.

The antipathy between Lowe and Napoleon was mutual, immediate, and permanent. Lowe had only five meetings with "General Bonaparte," as he was ordered to call him, before Napoleon refused to see him again. Napoleon became a recluse, waging a petty campaign against his "jailer," in which he was aided and abetted by his companions, including his personal physician, Dr. Barry O'Meara. Stories of Lowe's supposed pettiness reached England, leading to a relaxation of some of the restrictions on Napoleon, but Lowe, fearing an attempt to escape, would not ease security.

Throughout his period as Napoleon's "jailer" Lowe showed himself to be unimaginative and pedantic in carrying out his orders to the letter, but he was far from the monster of cruelty depicted in O'Meara's *Napoleon in Exile: A Voice from Saint Helena,* published in 1823. Public opinion turned against Lowe, who did not help his cause by threatening to sue O'Meara, then backing down. After six years in the colonial service in Ceylon between 1825 and 1831, Lowe returned to England and spent his last years trying to justify his actions on Saint Helena. He died in poverty in London in January 1844.

Related entries: Saint Helena

Suggestions for further reading:
Korngold, Ralph. 1960. *The Last Years of Napoleon: His Captivity at St. Helena.* London: Victor Gollancz.
Martineau, Gilbert. 1968. *Napoleon's St. Helena.* London: John Murray.

Lunéville, Treaty of (9 February 1801)

Negotiated largely by Joseph Bonaparte, this peace between Austria and

France effectively ended the Second Coalition and drove the Habsburgs out of all Italy except Venice; Austria reaffirmed all the concessions made by the Treaty of Campo Formio and ceded the Grand Duchy of Tuscany to the duke of Parma, whose lands now formed part of the Cisalpine Republic. The left bank of the Rhine was incorporated into France, with its dispossessed rulers to be compensated elsewhere in Germany.

Related entries: Austria; Coalitions

Suggestions for further reading:
Arnold, Eric A., ed. 1994. *A Documentary Survey of Napoleonic France.* Lanham, MD: University Press of America. pp. 83–89.
Deutsch, Harold C. 1938. *The Genesis of Napoleonic Imperialism.* Cambridge: Harvard University Press.
Ragsdale, Hugh. 1968. "Russian Influence at Lunéville," *French Historical Studies* 5, pp. 274–284.
Ross, Steven T. 1981. *European Diplomatic History, 1789–1815.* Malabar, FL: Krieger.

Lützen, Battle of (2 May 1813)

The first major engagement of Napoleon's 1813 campaign in Germany was fought around a group of five villages twelve miles southwest of Leipzig and four miles south of the small town of Lützen. Having concentrated a force of 69,000 men, the Russians and Prussians under Prince Wittgenstein attacked what they thought was merely the flank guard of Michel Ney's Third Corps. However, Ney's entire corps was digging in, and although taken by surprise and outnumbered the new conscripts fought back vigorously. As the rest of the French army rushed to Ney's support, Napoleon himself galloped over from Leipzig and plunged into the fray, as a ferocious struggle developed during which the villages of Klein Görschen and Rahna changed hands several times. Among the wounded was Gerhard von Scharnhorst, who died of his wounds several weeks later.

As dusk fell and 140,000 of Napoleon's troops converged on the battlefield the Russo-Prussian army was forced onto the defensive. The Eleventh Corps under Jacques Macdonald and the Sixth Corps under Louis Marmont severely mauled the Russian reinforcements, which had been slow in arriving. The Allies abandoned the field, but most escaped in the darkness. Napoleon's shortage of cavalry prevented him from mounting an effective pursuit, and though he had won a victory his losses were probably greater than those of the Allies, with at least 18,000 killed, wounded, or captured.

The battle of Lützen enabled Napoleon to occupy Dresden five days later, but for his exhausted troops it was a Pyrrhic victory. Nevertheless it was one of those battles in which Napoleon's swift thinking and personal engagement had played a decisive role. "Of all his career," recalled Marmont, "this is probably the day on which Napoleon incurred the most personal danger on the battlefield. He exposed himself constantly, leading back to the charge the defeated troops of the Third Corps" (Gates 1997, p. 236). For the first time, however, a weakness in his army, the shortage of cavalry horses, prevented him from turning a victory into a decisive rout.

Related entries: Germany, Campaigns in

Suggestions for further reading:
Chandler, David G. 1974. *The Campaigns of Napoleon: The Mind and Method of History's Greatest Soldier.* New York: Macmillan.
Gates, David. 1997. *The Napoleonic Wars, 1803–15.* London: Edward Arnold.
Petre, F. Loraine. 1974. *Napoleon's Last Campaign in Germany, 1813.* London: Arms and Armour.

Lycées

New secondary schools providing a thorough education (especially for the sons of officers), the *lycées,* created in

1802, were meant to be the cornerstone of the new French educational system. Each court of appeal area was to have at least one *lycée,* while the principle of equality of opportunity was honored by the provision of scholarships. A common curriculum was imposed in 1809, together with the baccalaureate examination that is still a prerequisite for entry into higher education in France today. Under Napoleon the *lycées* were not as successful as was hoped. The strict discipline and centralized regulations were unpopular, and the relatively few pupils drawn almost entirely from the middle and upper classes. The emphasis was on teaching the humanities, with the sciences relegated to a limited number of classes, generally poorly attended. Nevertheless, the first foundations had been laid for a system of elite secondary schools, essentially to provide future state functionaries.

Related entries: Education; Imperial University

Suggestions for further reading:
Bergeron, Louis. 1981. *France under Napoleon.* Princeton: Princeton University Press.
Holtman, Robert B. 1967. *The Napoleonic Revolution.* Philadelphia: Lippincott.

Macdonald, Jacques Étienne Joseph Alexandre (1765–1840)

Duke of Taranto, marshal of France, Macdonald was born at Sedan to a Jacobite father distantly related to the romantic Flora Macdonald. He was a solid professional soldier with no interest in political intrigue who served the Bourbons, the Republic, Napoleon, and the Bourbons again, with the same steady resolve. He had gained rapid promotion during the revolutionary wars without coming into sustained contact with Napoleon, being more friendly with Jean-Victor Moreau, whose military capacities he much admired. His lack of contact with Napoleon was unfortunate for Macdonald because it meant that Napoleon never entirely trusted him, only recognizing his qualities late in the day.

Although he supported the coup of 18 Brumaire, Macdonald's friendship with Moreau made Napoleon suspicious of him, and in 1804, after Macdonald had publicly defended Moreau against charges of treason, he was exiled to his estate near Bourges. The recall to arms came in March 1809, as a result of Napoleon's serious shortage of experienced commanders. Sent to the Army of Italy, Macdonald supported and became friends with Eugène de Beauharnais, and then won back the emperor's favor by leading the vital charge on the second day of the Battle of Wagram, where he became the only Napoleonic marshal to be awarded his baton in the field. After a short period of unhappy and reluctant service in Spain, Macdonald spent the Russian campaign of 1812 mostly in the Baltic provinces. He fought in all the battles of Napoleon's German campaign of 1813, showing great courage at Leipzig, where he only escaped by swimming the river Elster.

In March 1814 Macdonald joined Michel Ney and other marshals in demanding Napoleon's first abdication. His palpable honesty impressed Tsar Alexander I during the negotiation of the abdication terms, and Napoleon now acknowledged that "only during these recent circumstances have I brought myself to appreciate the full nobility of his character." Macdonald refused to support Napoleon during the Hundred Days, and under the Restoration retained his rank, served as minister of state, and became grand chancellor of the Legion of Honor. His open disapproval of many of the actions of the restored monarchy earned him the nickname "His Outspokenness," of which he was very proud, but he continued to fulfil his duties until the end of his life.

Macdonald's *Recollections,* belatedly published in 1892, reveal a serious, conscientious, and considerate man, with little subtlety or sense of humor. But his claim that his guides in life were honor, fidelity, and impartiality was no sham. A professional soldier, as he saw it his first duty was to France, his second to whoever happened to be ruling France. More subtle minds like Napoleon's were bound to be suspicious. He was however the subject of a rare Napoleonic joke: noting that Macdonald had never fought the British, Napoleon declared that he dared not let him within the sound of the bagpipes.

Related entries: Abdication, First; Germany, Campaigns in; Wagram, Battle of

Suggestions for further reading:
Hankinson, Alan. 1987. "Macdonald," in David G. Chandler, ed., *Napoleon's Marshals.* New York: Macmillan.
Macdonald, Jacques. 1893. *Recollections of Marshal Macdonald,* ed. Camille Rousset, trans. S. L. Simeon. 2 vols. London: Bentley and Sons.

Malet, Claude François de (1754–1812)

The leading figure in the Malet conspiracy of 1812 was described by the writer Charles Nodier, who knew him personally, as formed by nature "to keep tyrants from sleeping soundly," but a less charitable view would portray him as bizarre if not completely mad. Though of minor noble origin, Malet was undoubtedly a firm and consistent republican, who by 1799 had risen to the rank of brigadier general in the army of the Revolution. As commanding officer in the Charente department he loudly opposed Napoleon's elevation to the life consulate and later the creation of the empire. Malet's visceral aversion to Napoleon got him cashiered in 1807. He immediately tried to organize a plot against Napoleon, was imprisoned, and in 1810 was transferred to a mental institution just outside Paris. It was from here that he emerged in October 1812 to announce that Napoleon was dead in Russia and launch his conspiracy. Malet was executed along with his principal accomplices on 29 October 1812.

Related entries: Malet Conspiracy

Suggestions for further reading:
Artom, Guido. 1970. *Napoleon is Dead in Russia: The Extraordinary Story of One of History's Strangest Conspiracies.* London: Allen and Unwin.

Malet Conspiracy

The strange conspiracy staged by Claude de Malet was the reason for Napoleon's return to Paris, leaving his retreating army, in December 1812. When Malet escaped from the asylum where he was detained on 23 October there had been no news from Napoleon for several weeks. Malet and his fellow plotters, including a royalist priest and two generals, produced forged documents, convincing the prefect of the Seine department that Napoleon had been killed in Russia and that a new republican government had been formed. The conspirators persuaded most of the garrison commanders in Paris that their story was true, and even held Anne Jean Marie René Savary, the minister of police, in custody. However, Malet's behavior became ever more bizarre, and when he shot dead a general who asked for his credentials, troops were marched into Paris from Saint-Cloud, Savary released, Malet and his followers captured, and order restored by General Laborde and Jean-Jacques Régis de Cambacérès. Malet and fifteen accomplices were tried during the night and shot the next day.

The affair convinced Napoleon that if an apparent lunatic could succeed as well as Malet had, then seasoned and devious politicians like Joseph Fouché or Charles-Maurice de Talleyrand could easily seize the reins of government in his absence. "My presence in Paris is essential for France," he declared, and he was back in his capital on 19 December 1812. Malet may not have been so mad when, asked by the presiding judge at his trial to name his accomplices, he replied: "All of France and even you if I had succeeded."

Related entries: Malet, Claude François de

Suggestions for further reading:
Arnold, Eric A., ed. 1996. *A Documentary Survey of Napoleonic France: A Supplement.* Lanham, MD: University Press of America.
Artom, Guido. 1970. *Napoleon is Dead in Russia: The Extraordinary Story of One of History's Strangest Conspiracies.* London: Allen and Unwin.

Malta

Napoleon seized the island of Malta from the Knights of St. John in June 1798 while en route for Egypt. Two months later Horatio Nelson commenced a naval blockade, but the French garrison commanded by General Vaubois held out until September 1800. The British now took control of Malta. Meanwhile, Tsar Paul I, who had been offered the Grand Mastership of the Knights, made the proposed capture of Malta one of his reasons for joining the Second Coalition. Paul and his successor Alexander I continued to support the claims of the Knights against both France and Britain. The British undertook to restore Malta to the Knights in the Peace of Amiens, but it was too valuable to them as a base in the Mediterranean. The first Treaty of Paris in 1814 recognized the annexation of Malta by Britain.

Related entries: Egyptian Campaign; Nelson, Horatio, Lord

Suggestions for further reading:
Gregory, Desmond. 1996. *Malta, Britain and the European Powers, 1793–1815.* Madison, NJ: Fairleigh Dickinson University Press.

Saul, Norman E. 1970. *Russian and the Mediterranean, 1797–1807.* Chicago: University of Chicago Press.

Mantua

The possession of this key fortress in Lombardy, set among the lakes and marshes of the river Mincio, was of crucial importance in Napoleon's first Italian campaign. Between June 1796 and February 1797 an Austrian garrison held out against a French blockade. But their position meant that they were unable to take advantage of any movement by Napoleon's forces. Some 14,000 Austrians perished from disease during the siege, although 16,000 survived. The fall of Mantua allowed Napoleon to concentrate his forces against those of the Archduke Charles.

Related entries: Italian Campaigns

Suggestions for further reading:
Chandler, David G. 1974. *The Campaigns of Napoleon: The Mind and Method of History's Greatest Soldier.* New York: Macmillan.
Jackson, Sir William Godfrey Fothergill. 1953. *Attack in the West: Napoleon's First Campaign Re-read Today.* London: Eyre and Spottiswoode.

Marengo, Battle of (14 June 1800)

The royalist agent Jean Guillaume Hyde de Neuville dubbed this victory in the second Italian campaign the "baptism of Napoleon's personal power." The Austrian commander, Friedrich von Melas, supposedly marching to the defense of Turin but in fact unfindable, was encamped in Alessandria, while Napoleon uncharacteristically divided his forces in the search for him. On the morning of 14 June 1800 Melas's troops pounced on the French forces commanded by Claude Victor and forced them back to the village of Marengo. At the same time an Austrian enveloping movement threatened Napoleon's own position, and by three o'clock in the afternoon a French defeat seemed certain. Napoleon was saved by the arrival of the corps commanded by General Louis Desaix, who had been alerted by the sound of gunfire during his own search for Melas. "The battle has been lost," remarked Desaix, "there is time to win another."

Desaix, leading fresh troops and supported by the cavalry of François Kellermann, personally led the attack, while the entire French artillery opened up on the unsuspecting Austrians. Before sunset the Austrians were routed, but Desaix had been killed by a bullet through the heart. Melas pulled back to Alessandria and the following day agreed to an armistice. Napoleon's victory bulletins turned a narrow escape into a predetermined victory, all part of the first consul's brilliant strategy. He wrote to Emperor Francis I "from the battlefield of Marengo, in the midst of suffering and surrounded by fifteen thousand corpses" (Herold 1983, pp. 114–115), imploring him to make peace, but the Austrians did not see Marengo as a crushing defeat. It was only after further French success in Italy and Germany, especially Jean Moreau's victory at Hohenlinden, that they were forced to accept Napoleon's terms for peace in the Treaty of Lunéville, signed on 9 February 1801.

Related entries: Italian Campaigns; Propaganda

Suggestions for further reading:
Arnold, Eric A., ed. 1994. *A Documentary Survey of Napoleonic France.* Lanham, MD: University Press of America. pp. 63–66.
Arnold, James R. 1987. "Victor," in David G. Chandler, ed. *Napoleon's Marshals.* New York: Macmillan.
Chandler, David G. 1994. "Adjusting the Record: Napoleon and Marengo," in his *On the Napoleonic Wars: Collected Essays.* London: Greenhill.

Herold, J. Christopher. 1983. *The Horizon Book of the Age of Napoleon.* New York: American Heritage Publishing Co./Bonanza Books.

Maret, Hugues Bernard (1763–1839)

A lawyer turned diplomat during the Revolution, Maret had been imprisoned by the Austrians in Milan when he was freed by Napoleon's army in May 1796, and he became one of his rescuer's most diligent and discreet servants. As secretary-general under the consulate and secretary of state under the empire, he was the essential middleman between Napoleon and his ministers, using his position to influence appointments and moderate the tone of Napoleon's decisions. Only Charles-Maurice de Talleyrand insisted on circumventing him by conferring with Napoleon directly. From 1800 onward Maret selected the stories to be published in the *Moniteur,* the official government newspaper.

Maret replaced Champagny as foreign minister in April 1811, largely because Napoleon could rely on him to develop the new policy leading to the invasion of Russia. But he returned to the secretariat in November 1813, when Napoleon wanted to pursue a peace policy. Maret remained in his old post during the last months of the regime, kept Napoleon informed about public opinion during the exile on Elba, and served again in the state secretariat during the Hundred Days. He went into exile for five years after the Restoration before retiring to his native Burgundy.

Related entries: Press

Suggestions for further reading:
Church, Clive H. 1981. *Revolution and Red Tape: The French Ministerial Bureaucracy, 1770–1850.* Oxford: Clarendon Press.

Marie-Louise von Habsburg, Empress (1791–1847)

Napoleon's second empress never attained the popularity of Joséphine de Beauharnais, but criticism of her ignores the fact that in her world women were trained to obey their husbands and fathers. The marriage of Napoleon and Marie-Louise in 1810 was the result of Napoleon's desire for a son and heir and for a dynastic marriage that would confirm the place of the Bonaparte dynasty in Europe. After being rebuffed by Russia, he turned to Austria, where Klemens von Metternich negotiated the union with the eighteen-year-old Marie-Louise, eldest surviving daughter of Francis I. The fact that she was the niece of Marie-Antoinette allowed Napoleon to refer casually to "my uncle, Louis XVI." For their part, Francis and Metternich hoped that the marriage would provide security for Austria through an alliance with a Napoleon at the height of his power.

Marie-Louise married Napoleon by proxy in Vienna on 11 March 1810; the couple first met at Courcelles, east of Soissons, on 27 March; and the religious marriage took place in the Louvre on 2 April. The new empress adapted quickly to Napoleonic court life, was treated with lavish affection by Napoleon, and on 20 March 1811 gave birth to a son, the future Napoleon II. After Napoleon embarked on his Russian adventure in 1812, Marie-Louise saw little of her husband, but remained loyal to him until the first abdication. When Napoleon was sent into exile on Elba Marie-Louise was taken into her father's protection and prevented from communicating with her husband. During the Hundred Days she remained in Austria and showed no desire to return to Napoleon or to see him succeed.

Marie-Louise survived Napoleon and their son, having two more marriages and four more children. When she died Metternich, who had shaped her adult life, was still Austrian foreign minister. Some fanciful older historians attributed Napoleon's downfall to his second marriage, and Marie-Louise has been seen as the avenger of Marie-Antoinette and a traitor who abandoned her husband and son for her own security. But this verdict is grossly unfair. Forced into an arranged diplomatic marriage, she nevertheless tried to do Napoleon's bidding as far as possible. But events were always far beyond her control, and her father won the battle for control of mother and son.

Related entries: Austria; Francis I, Emperor of Austria; Metternich, Klemens Wenceslas Lothar, Fürst von; Napoleon II, King of Rome

Suggestions for further reading:

Mansel, Philip. 1987. *The Eagle in Splendour: Napoleon I and His Court.* London: George Philip.

Oddie, E. M. 1931. *Marie Louise, Empress of France, Duchess of Parma.* London: E. Mathews and Marrot.

Stoeckl, Agnes de. 1962. *Four Years an Empress: Marie Louise, Second Wife of Napoleon.* London: John Murray.

Turnbull, Patrick. 1971. *Napoleon's Second Empress.* London: Joseph.

Marmont, Auguste Frédéric Louis Viesse de (1774–1852)

Marmont was a resourceful soldier in his younger days, and he became a remarkable administrator of Illyria, but his name will nevertheless always be associated with defeat and betrayal of Napoleon. Born into a family of minor nobility at Châtillon-sur-Seine in Burgundy, Marmont joined the army at the age of sixteen and was first noticed by Napoleon at the siege of Toulon in November 1793. He became Napoleon's aide-de-camp in 1796 and fought in all the major encounters of the Italian campaign of 1796–1797. Now a member of Napoleon's inner circle, Mar-

François Gérard's **The Empress Marie-Louise and the King of Rome** *portrays Napoleon's second empress and their son, who represents the future of the dynasty. (Alinari/Art Resource)*

160

mont fought as a general in the Egyptian campaign of 1798–1799, participated in the coup of 18 Brumaire, and showed particular resourcefulness as commander of the artillery at Marengo (14 June 1800). This specialty led to his appointment as commandant in chief of the artillery in 1803, charged with modernizing French gunnery.

Marmont was bitterly disappointed at not being named among the first of the Napoleonic marshals in 1804, but continued to serve in the *Grande Armée* and the Army of Italy, before being surprisingly named as governor-general of Dalmatia, later Illyria, in 1806. After seizing Ragusa from the Russians in 1807, Marmont proved himself a remarkable governor. It has been said that he built the only decent roads around Dubrovnik between the Romans and Tito. Marmont finally received his marshal's baton in 1809 after the Wagram campaign and in March 1811 succeeded André Masséna as commander of the Army of Portugal.

It was in Iberia that Marmont's problems with Napoleon began. Defeated by the duke of Wellington and badly wounded at the Battle of Salamanca (22 July 1812), despite having initially outmaneuvered the British commander, he took a year to recover, returning to fight in Germany in 1813 and in the defense of France in February and March 1814. On 5 April he surrendered his corps, prematurely in Napoleon's opinion, to the Allies, and this "treason" was to haunt him for the rest of his life. "That Marmont should do such a thing," Napoleon is said to have exclaimed, "a man with whom I have shared my bread." Marmont was struck from the list of marshals, refused to support Napoleon during the Hundred Days, and sat as one of the judges who condemned Marshal Michel Ney to death.

Covered with honors by the restored Bourbons, Marmont was vilified by Bonapartist writers and never again commanded troops in the field. In 1830 as governor of the first military district of Paris he failed to put down the revolutionaries seeking to overthrow King Charles X and was forced into exile, never to set foot in France again. His posthumously published *Memoirs* (1856–1857) devoted much space to defending his actions in 1814, but his death in Venice on 3 March 1852 went unmourned in Napoleon III's France.

Related entries: Artillery; Illyria; Marengo, Battle of; Ney, Michel; Peninsular War; Salamanca, Battle of

Suggestions for further reading:
Marmont, Louis Viesse de. 1974. *The Spirit of Military Institutions.* Westport, CT: Greenhill.
Pimlott, John L. 1987. "Marmont," in David G. Chandler, ed., *Napoleon's Marshals.* New York: Macmillan.

Marshals

Napoleon revived the ancien régime dignity of marshal as the highest position in the army in 1804, creating eighteen marshals of the empire. This first promotion was made up of heroes of the republic and officers who had served Napoleon, comprising, in order of precedence, Louis Berthier, Joachim Murat, Bon Adrien Jeannot de Moncey, Jean-Baptiste Jourdan, André Masséna, Charles Augereau, Jean-Baptiste Bernadotte, Nicolas Soult, Guillaume Brune, Jean Lannes, Joseph Mortier, Michel Ney, Louis Davout, Jean-Baptiste Bessières, François Kellermann, François Lefebvre, Dominique-Catherine Pérignon, and Philibert Sérurier.

Later promotions were Claude Victor in 1807, and Alexandre Macdonald, the hero of Wagram, Auguste Marmont, and Nicolas Oudinot in 1808. Louis Suchet was elevated in 1811 for services in Spain, and Laurent Gouvion Saint-Cyr during the Russian campaign of 1812. Jozef Poniatowski became the only non-Frenchman among the marshals in 1813, and Emmanuel Grouchy was promoted during the Hundred Days in 1815.

The marshals came from all social backgrounds and were greatly varied in their temperaments, characters, and ultimately in their attitudes toward Napoleon. As a group they were all personally courageous commanders, but prone to feuding among themselves, sometimes going as far as insubordination. They brought a great variety of military and civil experience to the leadership of the army and socially formed an important part of the hierarchy around the imperial throne.

Related entries: Augereau, Pierre François Charles; Bernadotte, Jean-Baptiste Jules; Berthier, Louis Alexandre; Brune, Guillaume Marie Anne; Davout, Louis Nicolas; Gouvion Saint-Cyr, Laurent; Grouchy, Emmanuel; Jourdan, Jean-Baptiste; Kellermann, François Christophe; Lannes, Jean; Lefebvre, François Joseph; Macdonald, Jacques Étienne Joseph Alexandre; Marmont, Auguste Frédéric Louis Viesse de; Masséna, André; Moncey, Bon Adrien Jeannot de; Murat, Joachim; Ney, Michel; Oudinot, Nicolas Charles; Poniatowski, Jozef; Soult, Nicolas Jean de Dieu; Victor, Claude

Suggestions for further reading:
Chandler, David G., ed. 1987. *Napoleon's Marshals.* New York: Macmillan.
———. 1994. "The Napoleonic Marshalate," in *On the Napoleonic Wars: Collected Essays.* London: Greenhill.
Macdonell, A. G. 1934. *Napoleon and His Marshals.* London: Macmillan.
Phipps, Ramsay Weston. 1926–1939. *The Armies of the First French Republic and the Rise of the Marshals of Napoleon I.* 5 vols. London: Humphrey Milford.

Masséna, André (1758–1817)

Duke of Rivoli, prince of Essling, marshal of France, Masséna was a natural fighter, unsophisticated and unrefined. He won victories in Italy and Switzerland that have earned him a place among the great soldiers of France, but his troubled career after 1800 shows a decline in his capacities. Born near Nice of plebeian origins, he owed his military career to the Revolution, progressing rapidly through the ranks to general of brigade in 1793. On assuming command of the Army of Italy in 1796, Napoleon appointed Masséna, who had already fought in Italy, commander of the advance guard. His valiant role in the first Italian campaign caused Napoleon to dub him the "dearest child of victory." But the most important assignment of his career was to take command of the Army of Switzerland in December 1798, when France faced imminent invasion from Austrian and Russian forces. In a brilliant maneuver Masséna destroyed the Austro-Russian forces at the battle of Zurich (25–28 September 1799) then turned on and defeated a Russian relief army. His victories in Switzerland saved France from invasion and had a decisive impact on the disintegration of the Second Coalition.

Following the coup of 18 Brumaire, in which he played no part, Masséna returned to Italy to command the French forces blockaded in Genoa. He held the city for almost three months under conditions dreadful for both the population and the occupying forces, evacuating with the honors of war only when his army was starving. His resistance allowed Napoleon time to cross the Alps and win the decisive victory of Marengo (14 June 1800). But Masséna's health was permanently damaged, and he was inactive for five years, returning to the colors in Italy and Poland between 1805 and 1807. In 1809 he fought at the battles of Essling and Wagram, but was wounded, further impairing his health and apparently also his spirit.

In April 1810 Napoleon appointed Masséna commander of the Army of Portugal, with orders to drive the forces of the duke of Wellington into the sea. Though defeated by Wellington at the battle of Bussaco (27 September 1810), he continued the invasion of Portugal, only retreating when forced to by lack of reinforcements and supplies. After an unsuccessful attack against Fuentes de Onoro in May 1811, Masséna was relieved of his command and returned to France in disgrace. Officers who had known him in Switzerland and met him again in Spain found him a different man, weary and broken in health. And the presence of his mistress, Henriette Leberton, disguised as a dragoon, as aide-de-camp caused dissension among his subordinates, especially Michel Ney and Andoche Junot. Blamed by Napoleon for defeat, Masséna was now a broken man and never again commanded an army in the field.

Made a peer by Louis XVIII at the Restoration, Masséna nevertheless somewhat wearily acknowledged Napoleon's government during the Hundred Days. This act of loyalty caused his final disgrace, and he retired to Nice, where he died on 4 April 1817.

Related entries: Bussaco, Battle of; Genoa; Italian Campaigns; Peninsular War; Switzerland

Suggestions for further reading:
Howard, Donald D. 1965. *The Battle of Bussaco: Masséna vs Wellington.* Tallahassee: Florida State University.
Marshall-Cornwall, Sir James. 1965. *Marshal Massena.* New York: Oxford University Press.
———. 1987. "Massena," in David G. Chandler, ed., *Napoleon's Marshals.* New York: Macmillan.

Melzi d'Eril, Francesco (1753–1816)

A minor Milanese nobleman by birth, Melzi played a leading role in the creation of the Cisalpine Republic in 1797, and became vice-president of the Italian Republic, effectively the head of state, on its creation in 1802. Very soon, however, Napoleon came to suspect that Melzi was seeking independence and recognition from Austria. When he created the King-

dom of Italy in 1804, therefore, Napoleon ignored Melzi's constitutional proposals and appointed Eugène de Beauharnais as viceroy. As grand chancellor of the kingdom Melzi deputized for Eugène during his absence at the wars in 1809 and 1812–13, but in 1814 as Napoleon's power crumbled he behaved deviously, contracting diplomatic illnesses, and he did not long survive the restoration of Austrian rule.

Related entries: Cisalpine Republic; Italy, Kingdom of

Suggestions for further reading:
Connelly, Owen. 1965. *Napoleon's Satellite Kingdoms.* New York: Free Press.

Mémorial de Sainte-Hélène

By means of the memoirs of Saint Helena," writes the historian Annie Jourdan, "the Emperor engaged his final battle and set about his final conquest, that of history itself." The *Mémorial de Sainte-Hélène,* written by the comte de Las Cases and published in 1823, became a prime source of the Napoleonic legend. Las Cases recounts Napoleon's "martyrdom" on Saint Helena, interspersed with lengthy quotes and paraphrases of Napoleon's conversations in which he seeks to justify his life and actions. Napoleon had, according to himself, imposed order on anarchy, "cleansed the Revolution, ennobled the common people, and restored the authority of kings." Dictatorship and restrictions on freedom were necessary to combat disorder; his wars had all been waged for defensive reasons; and the universal monarchy was "the fortuitous result of circumstances. . . . I was led to it step by step by our enemies themselves." His only sin, apparently, was ambition: "a great deal of it—but the grandest and noblest, perhaps, that ever was: the ambition of establishing and consecrating at last the kingdom of reason and the full exercise, the

This illustration from the **Mémorial de Sainte-Hélène** *shows Napoleon's indulgence in gardening. An image like this was especially suited to appeal to the peasantry, who could see Napoleon as a simple man of the people who would look after their interests. (Mary Evans Picture Library, London)*

complete enjoyment, of all human capabilities!" (Herold 1983, p. 397).

The publication of the *Mémorial* not only stirred the souls of his old soldiers and officers retired on half pay but appealed to peasants alarmed by the return of the old aristocracy. The image of the soulful martyr on his rock appealed also to the Romantic sensibility, previously more inclined toward anti-Enlightenment soul-searching and political royalism. Victor Hugo and Alexandre Dumas remembered that they were the sons of Napoleonic generals; Stendhal began his own tales of youth inspired by the Napoleonic epic; and Honoré de Balzac declared: "What Napoleon began with the sword, I finish with the pen."

Related entries: Las Cases, Emmanuel-Augustin, Comte de; Napoleonic Legend

Suggestions for further reading:
De Chair, Somerset, ed. 1992. *Napoleon on Napoleon.* London: Cassell.
Harvey, A. D. 1998. "Napoleon—the Myth," *History Today* 48 (January 1998), pp. 27–32.
Herold, J. Christopher. 1983. *The Horizon Book of the Age of Napoleon.* New York: American Heritage Publishing Co./Bonanza Books.
Jones, R. Ben. 1977. *Napoleon, Man and Myth.* London: Hodder and Stoughton.

Metternich, Klemens Wenceslas Lothar, Fürst von (1773–1859)

Although in his later years as Austrian foreign minister Metternich described himself as a "rock of order" in European politics, during the Napoleonic period, which he saw as the climax of his life, he pursued a pragmatic policy that included a period of alliance with Napoleon. Born in Koblenz into a family of high nobility, he witnessed the early violence of the Revolution as a student in Strasbourg, and in 1794 the Metternich family were driven from their estates by invading French armies. This instilled in the young Metternich a lifelong belief in political order and stability that became a determined opposition to liberalism and a commitment to the preservation of Austrian predominance in central Europe.

Metternich joined the Austrian diplomatic service in 1801, holding posts in Dresden and Berlin before becoming ambassador to Paris in 1806. Here he established close relations with Charles-Maurice de Talleyrand and could observe Napoleon at close quarters, admiring the efficiency of his administration but urging Vienna to adopt an aggressive response to his expansionism. The resulting war of 1809 was a disaster for Austria, but secured Metternich's appointment to the Foreign Ministry (where he was to remain until 1848), after he had negotiated the Treaty of Schönbrunn (14 October 1809).

In his new position of power Metternich pursued a realistic if unheroic policy toward Napoleon, which might be described as "alliance but with minimal support." He personally negotiated the marriage between Napoleon and Marie-Louise and showed great ingenuity in extricating Austria from any commitment to support Napoleon's Russian campaign of 1812. For Metternich at this time, Austria's interest lay in preserving Napoleonic France and its German allies as a counterweight to Prussia and Russia, especially the latter. As a result his relations with Alexander I were often strained, but he found a more congenial partner in Lord Castlereagh. His views prevailed in the Treaties of Paris of 1814 and 1815, where he managed to limit Prussian ambitions in Germany and preserve a reasonably strong France, without Napoleon but with many Napoleonic institutions intact.

The Congress of Vienna and peace settlement of 1815 saw Metternich at the height of his powers. The rift between Austria and Russia, especially over Poland and Saxony, was obvious, but Metternich and Talleyrand succeeded in restoring France as an essential component of the new conservative order in Europe. Metternich also reestablished Habsburg power and influence in Italy and in the new German Confederation. Austria emerged stronger and more influential than ever before. Metternich became the symbol of the system established in 1815, and like his system he lasted in office until finally driven out by the revolutions of 1848.

Related entries: Alexander I, Tsar of Russia; Austria; Coalitions; Danube Campaigns; Francis I, Emperor of Austria; Marie-Louise von Habsburg, Empress; Nationalism; Paris, Treaties of; Schönbrunn, Treaty of; Talleyrand-Périgord, Charles-Maurice de; Vienna, Congress of

Suggestions for further reading:
Kraehe, Enno Edward. 1963. *Metternich's German Policy, Vol. 1: The Contest with Napoleon, 1799–1814.* Princeton: Princeton University Press.
Palmer, Alan. 1972. *Metternich.* London: Weidenfeld and Nicolson.
Stearns, Josephine B. 1948. *The Role of Metternich in Undermining Napoleon.* Urbana: University of Illinois Press.

Milan Decrees

Together with the earlier Berlin Decrees, the Milan Decrees of November and December 1807 formed the basis of Napoleon's Continental System. Responding to the British Orders in Council of January and November 1807, which forced neutral ships to get British permission to trade with enemy ports, these new measures extended the ban on the import of British goods to the Continent to British goods carried by neutrals. The Berlin and Milan Decrees laid down the form of the Continental System between 1807 and 1810.

Related entries: Berlin Decrees; Continental System

Suggestions for further reading:
Arnold, Eric A., ed. 1994. *A Documentary Survey of Napoleonic France*. Lanham, MD: University Press of America. pp. 252–254.
Heckscher, E. F. 1922. *The Continental System: An Economic Interpretation*. Oxford: Publications of the Carnegie Endowment for International Peace.

Mollien, François Nicolas (1758–1850)

As minister of the treasury between 1806 and 1814 and again during the Hundred Days, Mollien, like Martin Gaudin, helped provide financial stability for Napoleon's regime on time-honored principles. Already an experienced financial administrator under the ancien régime, Mollien was appointed director of the Sinking Fund by Napoleon in 1800, where he introduced the double-entry bookkeeping he later extended throughout the treasury. Mollien's cautious approach could be taken too far, as when he opposed Napoleon's plans to establish branches of the Bank of France in all major cities, but he often recalled Napoleon to financial rectitude, for example over the prompt payment of army and navy contractors. After Napoleon's downfall Mollien turned down opportunities to serve other French governments as minister of finance, but as a member of the Chamber of Peers he offered sound advice to the governments of the Restoration and the July Monarchy.

Related entries: Finance

Suggestions for further reading:
Church, Clive H. 1981. *Revolution and Red Tape: The French Ministerial Bureaucracy 1770–1850*. Oxford: Clarendon Press.
Clough, Shepherd B. 1939. *France: A History of National Economics, 1789–1939*. New York: Charles Scribner's Sons.

Moncey, Bon Adrien Jeannot de (1754–1842)

Eventually to become duke of Conegliano and marshal of France, Moncey was born at Palise near Besançon, the son of a lawyer; he left school to join the army at the age of fifteen but enjoyed a checkered career until the Revolution, when he rose rapidly to the rank of major general by 1794. Between 1793 and 1795, the most successful period of his military career, Moncey distinguished himself in fighting in the Pyrenees. However, his association with known royalists and his open opposition to the war in the Vendée seemed to have brought his active career to an end by 1797.

Napoleon recalled Moncey to the colors in 1800, giving him commands in Switzerland and Italy. Even so, his nomination among the first marshals of the empire in 1804 was considered a surprise, being probably due to Napoleon's desire to associate old republican generals with his imperial regime. Moncey was back in Spain in 1808–1809, but with less success than in the 1790s, and for the rest of Napoleon's reign he only had command of reserve troops. In 1814, as commander of the Parisian National Guard, Moncey acquitted himself valiantly in the defense of the Clichy gate against the Allies, and he was one of the marshals who forced Napoleon's first abdication.

Moncey supported Napoleon during the Hundred Days, but played no active role in the emperor's last campaign. With the Bourbons restored, Moncey refused to head the court-martial of Michel Ney, declaring that he could not condemn a man who had served France and saved countless lives during the Russian campaign of 1812, an adventure Moncey himself had opposed. His honesty earned Moncey a brief term of imprisonment, but he returned to serve his country into extreme old age. As governor of the Invalides he received Napoleon's remains when they were brought back from Saint Helena in December 1840.

Moncey was not a great general, but a sensitive man of decency and honor who refused to wage war as ruthlessly as most of his contemporaries. His character earned him the respect even of France's most determined enemies in Spain. Napoleon considered his behavior frank and correct, calling him simply an honest man. In refusing to condemn Ney, Moncey wrote to Louis XVIII: "No Sire, if I am not allowed to save my country, nor my own life, then at least I will save my honour" (Beckett 1987, p. 306). His honorable nature and honesty undoubtedly hindered his career, though his longevity in service shows that both Napoleon and the Bourbons were capable of appreciating his qualities.

Related entries: Abdication, First; Ney, Michel; Peninsular War; Revolutionary Wars

Suggestions for further reading:
Beckett, Ian F. W. 1987. "Moncey," in David G. Chandler, ed., *Napoleon's Marshals.* New York: Macmillan.

Mondovi, Battle of (21 April 1796)

*T*his victory in Napoleon's first Italian campaign forced Piedmont-Sardinia to withdraw from the war, leaving the Austrians to face the French without significant Italian allies. Having fought a series of engagements against separate allied armies, Napoleon finally turned his full force against the Piedmontese under General Michael von Colli and crushed them at Mondovi. A week later Piedmont withdrew from the war by the Treaty of Cherasco.

Related entries: Italian Campaigns

Suggestions for further reading:
Rooney, David D. 1987. "Sérurier," in David G. Chandler, ed., *Napoleon's Marshals.* New York: Macmillan.

Monge, Gaspard (1746–1818)

*T*he leading French scientist of the age both benefited greatly and ultimately suffered from close association with Napoleon. Already before the Revolution Monge's work on problems of mathematical theory and the application of geometry to military questions had earned him the title of Royal Professor of mathematics and physics; he also conducted experiments in chemistry and between 1784 and 1792 was examiner of naval cadets, entailing tours of inspection of naval schools. After the fall of the monarchy Monge was unexpectedly named minister of the navy, and in 1792–1793 worked hard to reorganize the French fleet and expand arms and munitions production. After resigning in April 1793, Monge threw himself into the revolutionary war effort, improving manufacture of steel and gunpowder. He was involved in the new Central School for Public Works, predecessor of the École Polytechnique, and in the foundation of the *Institut National* in 1795–1796.

Monge became friendly with Napoleon in 1796, when he was sent to Italy to inspect and preserve the artistic and scientific objects captured by the French army and was charged with transmitting the terms of the Treaty of Campo Formio to the Directory. In 1797 he returned to France as director of the *École Polytechnique,* but after only three months was sent as political commissioner to Rome, where he helped to establish the "sister" Roman Republic. Approached by Napoleon in Italy, he now helped to organize the Egyptian campaign by selecting maps and other necessary information, and eventually gave in to Napoleon's request to take part. He participated in the taking of Alexandria in July 1798; after the capture of Cairo Napoleon charged him with the establishment of a printing press in the Egyptian capital, the creation of the Institute of Egypt, the administrative reorganization of the country, and tracing the course of the ancient Roman canal between the Nile and the Red Sea. Despite suffering severely from dysentery, he accompanied Napoleon to Palestine and Syria between February and June 1799.

Returning to France with Napoleon, Monge was relieved to be back in Paris, resuming the directorship of the *École Polytechnique.* After the coup of 18 Brumaire Napoleon rewarded Monge with a place in the Senate. Now a confirmed Bonaparte loyalist, he was elevated to the Legion of Honor in 1804, became president of the Senate in 1806, and was created count of Pélouse in 1808. All this time he continued his scientific work, publishing various treatises on mathematics.

In declining health during the last years of the empire, Monge did not suffer politically after the first abdication, continuing his work at the *Institut National,* but he made the mistake of renewing his friendship with Napoleon during the Hundred Days, when he accepted a peerage from the restored emperor. Fearing reprisals after Napoleon's defeat, the by now elderly Monge fled to the Netherlands in October 1815. Returning to Paris after five months he was expelled from both the *Institut* and the *École Polytechnique.* He died, exhausted and disillusioned, in October 1818.

Related entries: *École Polytechnique;* Egyptian Campaign; Industry; *Institut National*

Suggestions for further reading:
Taton, René. 1974. "Monge, Gaspard," in Charles Coulston Gillispie, ed., *Dictionary of Scientific Biography,* vol. 9. New York: Charles Scribner's Sons.

Montalivet, Jean-Pierre Bachasson, Comte de (1766–1823)

As minister of the interior between 1809 and 1814, Montalivet competently enforced Napoleon's policy of centralization. He had first encountered Napoleon as early as 1789, when he had been mayor of Valence, and under the consulate he was made prefect, first of the Manche, then of Seine-et-Oise, before advancing further under the empire as director of bridges and highways. At the Ministry of the Interior Montalivet endeavored to improve the quality of prefects and supervised the public works program, which included the building of canals, roads and bridges, the redevelopment of the ports of Cherbourg, Antwerp, and Ostend, and the construction of monuments and public buildings in Paris. He also made a valiant effort to organize relief during the economic depression of 1810–1811. Most important, though, Montalivet used his voluminous correspondence with prefects and their subordinates to present comprehensive reports on the state of the empire in 1809 and 1813.

Related entries: Centralization; Local Government; Prefects

Suggestions for further reading:
Bergeron, Louis. 1981. *France under Napoleon.* Princeton: Princeton University Press.
Perrot, Jean-Claude, and Stuart Woolf. 1984. *State and Statistics in France, 1789–1815.* London: Harwood Academic.

Moore, Sir John (1761–1809)

Born in Glasgow, Moore nearly crossed Napoleon's path when he served as a colonel attached to Pasquale Paoli in Corsica in 1794–1795, and again in

1801 when he commanded the landing of the British forces at Aboukir in Egypt, a campaign in which he was wounded. In 1808 Moore was sent to Portugal with 30,000 men to help Spanish resistance to Napoleon's invasion. By the middle of December he was at Salamanca, threatening the French communications between Bayonne and Madrid, but on hearing that Napoleon was turning to deal with the threat Moore led a brilliant retreat through the mountains to Corunna. Here he defied the efforts of the French under Nicolas Soult to prevent the British evacuation, but was mortally wounded in the fighting. Buried at Corunna, Moore was, in the words of Charles Wolfe, "left alone in his glory" (Horne 1996, p. 255), but his heroic death did not prevent him being blamed for the failure of the campaign.

Related entries: Corsica; Corunna, Battle of; Egyptian Campaign; Peninsular War; Soult, Nicolas Jean de Dieu

Suggestions for further reading:
Davies, David William. 1974. *Sir John Moore's Peninsular Campaign, 1808–1809*. The Hague: Nijhoff.
Horne, Alistair. 1996. *How Far from Austerlitz? Napoleon 1805–1815*. London: Macmillan.
Oman, Carola. 1953. *Sir John Moore*. London: Hodder and Stoughton.
Parkinson, Roger. 1976. *Moore of Corunna*. London: Hart-Davis, MacGibbon.

Moreau, Jean-Victor (1763–1813)

Moreau was one of the most brilliant generals of the revolutionary armies, being largely responsible for the conquest of Holland in 1795 and commander of the Army of the North and then the Army of the Rhine and Moselle in 1796. But he was never an ardent republican—his father had been guillotined during the Terror—and in 1797 he was placed on the inactive list, before being recalled in 1798 and fighting in Italy. He met Napoleon on the latter's return from Egypt and joined in the coup of 18 Brumaire, leading to a new rise in his fortunes.

Moreau assumed command of the Army of the Rhine in November 1799 and during the victorious campaigns in Germany in 1800 defeated the Austrians at the Battle of Hohenlinden. He retired from active duty in September 1801, but his persistent royalist sympathies caused him to join Charles Pichegru's conspiracy against Napoleon. He was arrested, imprisoned, and removed from the army. Moreau spent the years 1804–1813 in voluntary exile in the United States, but was summoned by Alexander I as an adviser to the Allies against Napoleon. In this capacity he was fatally wounded by French fire at Dresden in August 1813.

Related entries: Dresden; Hohenlinden, Battle of; Pichegru, Jean-Charles; Revolutionary Wars

Suggestions for further reading:
Bertaud, Jean-Paul. 1988. *The Army of the French Revolution*. Princeton: Princeton University Press.
Phipps, Ramsay Weston. 1926–1939. *The Armies of the First French Republic and the Rise of the Marshals of Napoleon I*. 5 vols. London: Humphrey Milford.

Mortier, Edouard Adolphe Casimir Joseph (1768–1835)

Duke of Treviso, marshal of France, Mortier was the most loyal of Napoleon's marshals (he even named his eldest son Napoleon), and he was also the best liked, the most modest, and the only one who spoke English. Born at Câteau-Cambrésis in northwestern France, the son of a wealthy cloth merchant and his English wife, Mortier entered the army through the National Guard of Dunkirk in 1798 and distinguished himself in some of the major campaigns and battles of the revolutionary wars, but never served under Napoleon. He supported the coup of 18 Brumaire, was promoted to divisional general during the Swiss campaign on 1799, and was appointed to command the military division of Paris in April 1800.

In 1803 Napoleon selected Mortier to lead the conquest and occupation of Hanover, Britain's only possession in continental Europe, and created him one of his original marshals of the empire in 1804. In subsequent campaigns in Germany between 1805 and 1807, Spain in 1810, and Russia in 1812, Mortier was seldom given independent command, but he always achieved results with small forces and successfully administered conquered territories. His calm under pressure at the battle of Friedland (1807) won Napoleon's particular admiration, and he was unique among French commanders in Spain in suffering no major setbacks or defeats. During the Russian campaign he commanded the Young Guard at the battle of Borodino and was made governor of Moscow, only partially carrying out Napoleon's order to destroy the city. Mortier was in every major battle in 1813–1814, commanding the Young Guard in Germany and the Old Guard during the campaign of France. He supported Napoleon during the Hundred Days, but was prevented by illness from joining the emperor at Waterloo.

Mortier continued to serve his country in various political and military appointments until 1835. He had known King Louis Philippe, brought to power by the Revolution of 1830, since the campaigns of 1792–1793, and served him as ambassador to Russia and briefly as minister of war in 1834–1835. But peaceful retirement in 1835 at the age of sixty-seven with a growing number of grandchildren was not to be his. On 28 July during a National Guard parade he was one of those killed by an "infernal machine" meant for Louis Philippe. Although not the most flamboyant of Napoleon's marshals, nor the greatest soldier, Mortier was ahead of his time as a trainer of the Young Guard and particularly in the care of army horses. The historian Randal Gray says that "as an honest and modest human being" Mortier surpassed all his colleagues (Gray 1987).

Related entries: Borodino, Battle of; Friedland, Battle of; Imperial Guard; Moscow

Suggestions for further reading:
Gray, Randal. 1987. "Mortier," in David G. Chandler, ed., *Napoleon's Marshals.* New York: Macmillan.

Moscow

*B*arbarous peoples are superstitious and have simple ideas," said Napoleon on the eve of his Russian campaign of 1812. "A terrible blow against the heart of the Empire, on Moscow the Great, Moscow the Holy, will deliver this blind and spiritless mass to me with one blow" (Tulard 1985, p. 61). Moscow had been capital of Russia until 1703 and was still the spiritual center of Orthodox Christianity. Taking the city, Napoleon was convinced, would force Tsar Alexander I to sue for peace.

The decision not to defend Moscow was taken by Mikhail Kutuzov, who believed that the occupation of the city would overstrain Napoleon's resources. The governor of Moscow, Count Fedor Rostopchin, although he disagreed with Kutuzov, ordered the evacuation of the city. Napoleon took up residence in the Kremlin on 15 September 1812, but was soon forced to take refuge in the Petrovsky Palace. Fires, the origin of which remains obscure, raged through Moscow. In four days three-quarters of the old, wood-built city was destroyed, while carousing and looting by Napoleon's drunken troops added to the destruction wrought by the fires.

Disappointed in his hope that the capture of the ancient capital would bring peace, Napoleon evacuated Moscow on 19 October. Joseph Mortier was left behind with orders to destroy what remained of the city, but ignored Napoleon's commands and withdrew his forces four days later. The terrible retreat from Moscow had begun. As the inhabitants returned to their homes during the following three months, infectious diseases ran rampant, decimating the population. But rebuilding began soon afterward and by 1816 had advanced sufficiently for the tsar to be received in state in the Kremlin.

Related entries: Kutuzov, Mikhail Ilarionovich; Mortier, Joseph; Russian Campaign

Suggestions for further reading:
Brett James, Antony. 1966. *1812: Eyewitness Accounts of Napoleon's Invasion of Russia.* New York: Macmillan.
Cate, Curtis. 1985. *The War of the Two Emperors: The Duel between Napoleon and Alexander, Russia, 1812.* New York: Random House.
Chandler, David G. 1994. "Retreat from Moscow," in his *On the Napoleonic Wars: Collected Essays.* London: Greenhill.
Riehn, Richard K. 1991. *1812: Napoleon's Russian Campaign.* New York: John Wiley.
Tarle, E. 1942. *Napoleon's Invasion of Russia, 1812.* London: Allen and Unwin.
Tulard, Jean. 1985. *Napoleon: the Myth of the Saviour.* London: Methuen.

Murat, Caroline

See Bonaparte, Caroline, Queen of Naples

Murat, Joachim (1767–1815)

*G*rand duke of Berg, king of Naples, marshal of France, "The First Horseman of Europe," and Napoleon's finest cavalry commander, the daring and impetuous Murat came to embody the extravagance and dash of the Napoleonic armies. The youngest of twelve children of a prosperous innkeeper from Guyenne, he was originally intended for the Church but instead joined the army in 1787. In the early years of the Revolution Murat saw action on the Rhine and was commissioned as a sub-lieutenant of cavalry in 1792.

Murat's destiny became entangled with that of Napoleon in October 1795 when he secured the cannon used for Bonaparte's "whiff of grapeshot" of 13 Vendémiaire. He became Napoleon's chief aide in the Italian campaign of 1796–1797, showing for the first time his conspicuous though often foolhardy courage in leading cavalry charges, a quality he continued to show in the Egyptian campaign, where at Aboukir he engaged in single combat with the Turkish commander, Saïd Mustapha Pasha. Murat returned with Napoleon from Egypt with the rank of general of division, provided valuable support in the coup of 18 Brumaire, and in January 1800 married the new first consul's sister, Caroline Bonaparte. She was sixteen years old, he was thirty.

In Napoleon's second Italian campaign Murat again fought with manifest courage at Marengo (14 June 1800), remaining in Italy until 1804, when he was created a marshal of the empire and began to accumulate the innumerable orders, titles, and honors of which he was inordinately fond. Although Napoleon continued to criticize his rashness, the new Prince Murat's cavalry screen at Austerlitz secured the French victory, and he was the first to occupy Vienna in November 1805. Now grand duke of Berg and Cleves, Murat was accepted as the finest cavalry commander in Europe, serving at Jena-Auerstädt in 1806 and even maintaining his dashing presence during the brutal battle of Eylau.

When Napoleon made his fateful decision to intervene in Spain in 1808 Murat became his deputy in Madrid, responsible

Joachim Murat came to embody the extravagance and dash characteristic of the Napoleonic armies. Although Théodore Géricault's **Charging Chasseur** *(1812) features an unnamed rider in an unknown battle, it displays all the panache of the ideal horseman as set forth by Murat. (Giraudon/Art Resource)*

for the savage repression of the rebellion of 2 May, before succeeding Joseph Bonaparte as king of Naples. He resided in his kingdom until 1812, mounting a failed attack on Sicily in 1809, but showing the first signs of independence from Napoleon by turning a blind eye to breaches of the Continental System and spending as much time as possible with his four children. Murat had to be cajoled by Napoleon into commanding the cavalry and the advance guard in the invasion of Russia in 1812, but he performed with his usual spirit at Smolensk and Borodino and was the first to enter Moscow as he had been at Vienna. During the retreat from Moscow he was given command of the army when Napoleon left for Paris, but once the survivors reached Prussia he passed command to the more suitable hands of Eugène de Beauharnais and departed, without authority, for Naples.

Murat fought beside Napoleon again at Leipzig (17–18 October 1813), but the defeat convinced him that the Napoleonic empire in Europe was doomed. In 1814 he and Caroline came to an agreement with the Austrians and the more reluctant British and so preserved their kingdom after Napoleon's first abdication. When Napoleon escaped from Elba in 1815, however, Murat attacked the Austrians in Italy. Distrusting the British and believing that Napoleon could regain power in France, he called on the Italian people to fight behind him for a united Italy, but his naive crusade ended in defeat. Fleeing to France Murat offered his services to Napoleon for what became the Waterloo campaign, but the emperor ignored him. In a desperate last adventure he tried to recapture Naples from the restored Bourbon rulers with a tiny expeditionary force; he was captured in the village of Pizzo, tried by court-martial, and executed by firing squad on 13 October 1815.

With his extravagant uniforms, bedecked with feathers and medals, Murat epitomizes the romantic side of the Napoleonic legend. Idolized by his troops, whom he had helped to make the best cavalry in Europe, and feared by his enemies, his military skills and personal bravery were never in question. But in politics he seemed to be from another age. He could not command an army in retreat and showed great naïveté in Italy; his wife Caroline was the better administrator and negotiator. Their numerous descendants included several who played prominent roles in the raising to power of Napoleon's nephew as Napoleon III.

Related entries: Austerlitz, Battle of; Berg, Grand Duchy of; Bonaparte, Caroline, Queen of Naples; Borodino, Battle of; Brumaire, Coup of Year VIII; Danube Campaigns; Egyptian Campaign; Eylau, Battle of; Hundred Days; Italian Campaigns; Jena-Auerstädt, Battles of; Leipzig, Battle of; Marengo, Battle of; Naples, Kingdom of; Russian Campaign; Spain; Vendémiaire, Rising of Year IV

Suggestions for further reading:
Atteridge, Andrew Hilliard. 1918. *Joachim Murat, Marshal of France and King of Naples.* London: T. Nelson and Sons.
Cole, Hubert. 1972. *The Betrayers: Joachim and Caroline Murat.* London: Eyre Methuen.
Connelly, Owen. 1965. *Napoleon's Satellite Kingdoms.* New York: Free Press.
Pickles, Tim. 1987. "Murat," in David G. Chandler, ed., *Napoleon's Marshals.* New York: Macmillan.

Musée Napoléon

The old royal palace of the Louvre was transformed into a museum during the Revolution, and the cultural treasures seized by Napoleon during his Italian campaigns and Egyptian campaign made a major contribution to the new collections. In 1802 Dominique Vivant Denon suggested that the new art gallery be renamed the *Musée Napoléon,* which now served as the central depot for works of art looted from occupied Europe. Architectural modifications to the Louvre caused the museum to be closed between 1808 and

1810, but it was reopened with a grand ceremony coinciding with Napoleon's religious marriage to Marie-Louise. The widely admired collection was dismantled on Napoleon's fall, despite Denon's best efforts to keep it all together.

Related entries: Denon, Dominique-Vivant

Suggestions for further reading:
Gould, Cecil H. M. 1965. *Trophy of Conquest: The Musée Napoléon and the Creation of the Louvre.* London: Faber & Faber.

N

Naples, Kingdom of

French armies had first entered Naples and expelled the ruling branch of the Bourbon dynasty in 1799, but King Ferdinand IV was restored by the British and ruled until 1806, when he was banished again and Napoleon created the Kingdom of Naples, with Joseph Bonaparte as king. Having put together a ministry made up of Frenchmen, including Pierre Louis Roederer, and reformist Neapolitans, Joseph introduced radical social and economic reforms, but delayed the introduction of a constitution. Feudal rights and dues were abolished; new crops, including cotton and sugar, were introduced to replace those excluded by the Continental System; French-style administration and courts were set up; and the school and university system considerably improved.

When Napoleon made Joseph king of Spain in 1808, he was replaced on the throne of Naples by Joachim Murat, and the new kingdom eventually succumbed to Murat's desire to become independent of Napoleon. He continued many of Joseph's reforms, but refused to implement his predecessor's constitution. Together with his right-hand man, Antonio Marghella, police prefect of Naples and an ardent Italian nationalist, Murat began creating his own army, which by 1812 numbered some 80,000 men. However, when he was persuaded by Napoleon to take part in the Russian campaign of 1812 any chance Murat may have had of saving his throne became extremely remote.

Although Murat negotiated with the Austrians in 1814, the British stood by their commitments to Ferdinand IV, who had spent the years since his overthrow under their protection in Sicily. Murat's conduct in 1815 mixed miscalculation with naïveté and cost him his throne and his life. With Napoleon's final overthrow Ferdinand returned to Naples, where he ruled until 1825. Naples and Sicily became part of a united Italy in 1860.

Related entries: Bonaparte, Caroline, Queen of Naples; Bonaparte, Joseph, King of Naples, King of Spain; Calabria, Revolt in; Murat, Joachim; Roederer, Pierre Louis

Suggestions for further reading:
Connelly, Owen. 1965. *Napoleon's Satellite Kingdoms.* New York: Free Press.
Davis, John A. 1990. "The Impact of French Rule on the Kingdom of Naples, 1806–1815," *Ricerche Storiche* 20, pp. 367–405.
Noether, Emiliana. 1988. "Change and Continuity in the Kingdom of Naples, 1806–1815," *Consortium on Revolutionary Europe 1988,* pp. 605–618.
Woolf, Stuart. 1979. *A History of Italy, 1700–1860: The Social Constraints of Political Change.* London: Methuen.

Napoleon II, King of Rome (1811–1832)

Born in the Tuileries, Napoleon François Charles Joseph, the only son of Napoleon and Marie-Louise, was adulated from birth by his father and given the title of King of Rome, a city he never visited during his short life. In 1813 Napoleon began preparations for his coronation by the pope, a ceremony which never took place. Napoleon tried to abdicate in his favor in 1814 and again in 1815, but without serious support. The emperor saw his son for the last time on 24 January 1814 at a military parade outside the Tuileries.

The three-year-old prince was taken to Vienna by his doting grandfather, Francis I, and given the new title of duke of Reichstadt. He matured into a handsome and charming young man, fully aware of his inheritance. He could be used as a threat by the Austrians against the post-Napoleonic regimes in France, but after Napoleon's death Bonapartist propaganda portrayed the *aiglon,* the "little eagle," as the "prisoner of Vienna," and his picture could be found adorning the homes of the peasantry. Napoleon's letters to him, presenting Bonapartism in an idealized form, became part of the Napoleonic legend. However, Napoleon II died of tuberculosis at the age of twenty-one, after participating too enthusiastically in Austrian army maneuvers. It was his cousin, Napoleon III, swept to power in 1848, who was to benefit from the legend of the *aiglon.* His remains were brought back to lie with those of his father in the Invalides in December 1940 on the personal orders of Adolf Hitler and interred in a lavish ceremony that was highly embarrassing for the government of Marshal Pétain.

Related entries: Bonapartism; Marie-Louise von Habsburg, Empress; Napoleonic Legend

Suggestions for further reading:
Arnold, Eric A., ed. 1994. *A Documentary Survey of Napoleonic France.* Lanham, MD: University Press of America, pp. 316–317.

In the Cradle of the King of Rome the infant lies under the Roman olive leaves of victory, while a Napoleonic eagle, his father's emblem, protectively watches over his sleep. (Erich Lessing / Art Resource)

Castelot, André. 1960. *Napoleon's Son: The King of Rome.* London: Hamish Hamilton.

Napoleonic Legend

Living he lost the world, dead he conquers it," wrote François René de Chateaubriand (Connelly 1985, p. 298). But the legend of Napoleon, described by the distinguished historian, Jean Tulard, as "the first of the modern myths," was originally deliberately created during Napoleon's life. The legend was forged during the first Italian campaign by newspapers designed to praise the army and its leader, who "flies like lightning and strikes like a thunderbolt. He is everywhere and sees everything." The young Bonaparte marched "accompanied by the god of War and the god of Fortune." Under the empire the figure of the em-

Jean Auguste Dominique Ingres created an almost godlike image of Napoleon seated like Jupiter on his throne with the sword of Charlemagne by his side. A cold and distant portrayal of the emperor in all his majesty, it hangs today in Les Invalides, a suitable companion piece for Napoleon's tomb. (Giraudon/Art Resource)

peror was central to imperial propaganda, exalted in army bulletins, prints, medals, and paintings. This early image was to develop after his downfall and death into a legend that persists to this day.

Under the Bourbon Restoration between 1815 and 1830 admiration for Napoleon was a way of expressing opposition to the restored regime. The regime attempted to eradicate all reference to Napoleon, but popular opinion came to look upon him more favorably as the Bourbons grew more unpopular, and liberals portrayed him as a martyr who had died for the egalitarian principles of the Revolution. The publication in 1823 of the *Mémorial de Sainte-Hélène* consolidated the image of the martyr dying on his lonely rock. Romantic writers like Victor Hugo, Alexandre Dumas, and Stendhal praised the Napoleonic epic, while on a more mundane level old officers retired on half pay, peasants alarmed by the return of old landowners, and officials excluded from offices by the restored regime all looked back with nostalgia on the days of glory.

After 1830, under the July Monarchy of Louis Philippe, dramatic renditions of Napoleon's life and career flooded the Parisian stage, while popular prints portrayed him as the "little corporal" in greatcoat, boots, and cocked hat, the image which is still familiar today. Napoleon became not so much a ruler, conqueror, and legislator, as a soldier caring for his men, going back to the image forged in Italy and Egypt. The Napoleonic war veteran or *grognard* became a stock figure in novels and plays. The "little corporal" and his men were not only participants in a glorious epic, but also part of a heroic and romanticized French people. Louis Philippe tried to appropriate the legend, bringing Napoleon's remains back to France, and Napoleon came to represent military prowess and the militant defense of liberty for all shades of political opinion, not only Bonapartist.

The Napoleonic legend played a part in enabling his nephew, Napoleon III, to become president of the Second Republic in 1848 and then to proclaim the Third Empire in 1852, using Napoleon's favorite device of a plebiscite to legitimize his position as emperor. Even Napoleon III's defeat in the Franco-Prussian War of 1870 did no harm to the legend of his uncle. Napoleon, who had beaten the Prussians at Jena, now became a powerful symbol for the movement of "revenge," expressed in popular novels and by nationalist writers such as Maurice Barrès.

In the twentieth century the legend has been conveyed most effectively in film. Napoleon made his first appearance on screen as early as 1897–1898 in *Bonaparte au Pont d'Arcole*, directed by Alice Guy. Since then he has been portrayed by, among others, Marlon Brando, Rod Steiger, Charles Boyer, and Sacha Guitry, though in most cases with more attention to his love life than to his conquest of Europe. The greatest and most self-consciously heroic depiction is in Abel Gance's ideologically dubious masterpiece *Napoléon vu par Abel Gance* (1925), with Albert Dieudonné as a young Bonaparte who truly "is everywhere and sees everything." Napoleon's tomb in the Invalides is no longer, as it once was, the most visited monument in Paris, but it is still an obligatory stop on the tourist trail, taken in by many thousands of people every year.

Related entries: Bonapartism; *Mémorial de Sainte-Hélène;* Personality, Cult of; Propaganda

Suggestions for further reading:
Connelly, Owen, ed. 1985. *Historical Dictionary of Napoleonic France, 1799–1815.* Westport, CT: Greenwood.
Harvey, A. D. 1998. "Napoleon—the Myth," *History Today* 48 (January 1998), pp. 27–32.
Holtman, Robert B. 1950. *Napoleonic Propaganda.* Baton Rouge: Louisiana State University Press.
Jones, R. Ben. 1977. *Napoleon, Man and Myth.* London: Hodder and Stoughton.
Tulard, Jean. 1985. *Napoleon: The Myth of the Saviour.* London: Methuen.

Nationalism

The relationship between Napoleon, his empire, and emergent nationalism in Europe is complex and inevitably controversial. It is tempting but arguably too easy to hold him responsible for the emergence or strengthening of movements and ideas that only reached maturity later in the nineteenth century. For example, the part played by resistance to Napoleon in the development of nationalism in Germany has been exaggerated both by German nationalist historians and by anti-Napoleon historians who hold him responsible for Prussian militaristic dominance of united Germany. The situation in each country was unique. The nineteenth-century British historian Lord Acton wrote that "Napoleon called a new power into existence by attacking nationality in Russia, by delivering it in Italy, by governing in defiance of it in Germany and Spain." Poland, Switzerland, Illyria, Belgium, and even Great Britain may be added to Acton's formula to create even greater complication.

Napoleon himself had abandoned his youthful Corsican nationalism for commitment to the universal ideals of the Revolution. But once he was in power his policies combined pragmatism and opportunism with his obsession with the supranational empire of Charlemagne. Napoleon's basic lack of belief in "natural" nations is shown by the way he made and unmade new states in Germany, Italy, and eastern Europe without regard to incipient national feelings. In France itself nationalistic feeling under Napoleon was dependent on victory and glory and by 1812 had been worn down, although revived briefly during the Allied invasion of 1814. In Italy and Poland Napoleon encouraged nationalist feeling, but was willing to betray it when it clashed with his own interests. Opposition to Napoleonic rule in Spain and Germany took on a nationalistic tinge, but was more tied to the past than looking to the future: those who believed in revolution against Napoleon rule were a minority compared to those who saw the goal as restoration.

Only in the *Mémorial de Sainte-Hélène* did Napoleon claim that he had wished to preside over a "Europe of the nations." This pretence became part of the Napoleonic legend and was to inspire his nephew, Napoleon III. And it is true that Napoleonic rule had breathed life into moribund state structures while at the same time arousing opposition which would pass into nationalistic myth. In the words of Hans Kohn, "at the beginning of the age of nationalism stands its denial in Napoleon's universal empire" (Kohn 1950, p. 26), but the experience of the Napoleonic Wars and empire in Europe helped to provide some of the myths and nostalgia necessary for the creation of authentic nationalism.

Related entries: Belgium; Bonapartism; Confederation of the Rhine; Corsica; Germany, Campaigns in; Great Britain; Holland, Kingdom of; Illyria; Italy, Kingdom of; *Mémorial de Sainte-Hélène;* Napoleonic Legend; Poland; Prussia; Romanticism; Spain; Switzerland; Warsaw, Duchy of

Suggestions for further reading:
Anderson, Eugene N. 1939. *Nationalism and the Cultural Crisis in Prussia, 1806–1815.* New York: Farrar and Rinehart.
Dann, Otto, and John Dinwiddy, eds. 1988. *Nationalism in the Age of the French Revolution.* London: Hambledon.
Davies, Norman. 1981. *God's Playground: A History of Poland.* 2 vols. Oxford: Clarendon Press.
Kohn, Hans. 1950. "Napoleon and the Age of Nationalism," *Journal of Modern History* 22, pp. 21–37.
Kohn, Hans. 1967. *Prelude to Nation States: The French and German Experience, 1789–1815.* Princeton: Van Nostrand.
Langsam, Walter C. 1930. *The Napoleonic Wars and German Nationalism in Austria.* New York: Columbia University Press.
Schulze, Hagen. 1991. *The Course of German Nationalism: from Fichte to Bismarck, 1763–1867.* Cambridge: Cambridge University Press.
Sheehan, James J. 1989. *German History, 1770–1866.* Oxford: Clarendon Press.
Snyder, Louis L. 1978. *Roots of German Nationalism.* Bloomington: Indiana University Press.

Woolf, Stuart. 1989. "French Civilization and Ethnicity in the Napoleonic Empire," *Past & Present*, no. 124 (August 1989), pp. 96–120.

———. 1991. *A History of Italy, 1700–1860: the Social Constraints of Political Change.* London: Routledge.

Naval Warfare

*T*he inescapable facts of geography dictated that the struggle between Napoleon's France and Britain would take place more at sea than on land. However, British naval superiority had already been established in the 1790s, and as long as the Royal Navy adopted a basically defensive posture the French could never challenge its dominance of the seas. The battle of Trafalgar, though one of the most celebrated sea battles in history, was the only major sea battle of the Napoleonic Wars. Thereafter minor engagements between individual squadrons took the place of epic clashes between the rival fleets. France's main strength lay in attacking British maritime trade through the privateer war.

Napoleon apparently never appreciated the difficulties of naval warfare and how much it was governed by the elements: the weather and the sea itself. Far more sailors perished from disease and the perils of the sea than through enemy action. Winds and tides plunged the best-planned naval campaigns into chaos, which worked to Napoleon's advantage to the extent that British amphibious operations against the Continent were rendered almost impossible. Ships had to be virtually self-sufficient in water and supplies, and ship-to-ship communications were effectively limited to the range of the human eye. Warships doubled as transport vessels for men and horses, so voyages had to be kept as short as possible.

British ships spent longer times at sea than their French or Spanish opponents, losing many ships in the process. But the Spanish fleet had been destroyed at Trafal-gar, and Napoleon's plans to rebuild a formidable French fleet remained perpetually in the future. Despite his confident assertion in 1811 that within five years he would have a navy capable of challenging the British and invading England, the ultimate result of the Napoleonic Wars was to confirm British naval supremacy for a century thereafter.

Related entries: Navy, British; Navy, French; Privateer War

Suggestions for further reading:

Lloyd, Christopher. 1965. "Navies," in C. W. Crawley, ed., *New Cambridge Modern History. Vol. 9: War and Peace in an Age of Upheaval, 1793–1830.* Cambridge: Cambridge University Press.

Mahan, Alfred Thayer. 1892. *The Influence of Seapower upon the French Revolution and Empire, 1793–1812.* 2 vols. London and Cambridge, MA: Sampson Low.

Navy, British

*D*uring the eighteenth century the British or Royal Navy had gained dominance of the seas, and Napoleon was never able to challenge this superiority. Whereas the great French heroes of the Napoleonic Wars were army commanders, the British heroes, principally Horatio Nelson, were seamen. Nevertheless, the struggle against Napoleon did place great strains on British sea power as the fleet was enlarged and its tasks increased. At the height of Napoleon's power between 1805 and 1809 the Royal Navy not only maintained a constant vigil over enemy naval bases throughout Europe, but also patrolled the Baltic, Mediterranean, and Atlantic, mounted colonial expeditions, and escorted convoys under threat from French privateers. British ships therefore spent too much time at sea: of 317 ships lost during the wars, no fewer than 223 were wrecked or foundered rather than being destroyed by enemy action.

British naval superiority was confirmed at the battle of the Nile in 1798 and consecrated at Trafalgar in 1805, where Nelson crippled the French and Spanish fleets. The superior maneuverability, gunnery, and training of the British ships was backed up by the greater daring and initiative shown by British naval commanders such as Admirals Cornwallis, Collingwood, and Keith as well as Nelson. While its successes were counterbalanced by Napoleon's victories on land, the Royal Navy contained any French naval threat to Britain and its colonies.

But the cost of maintaining and repairing the fleet and obtaining naval supplies, threatened by Napoleon's Continental System, stretched the naval budget to over 20 million by 1813. In addition, as the wars dragged on Britain faced a constant shortage of manpower. While the theoretical strength of the Royal Navy reached 145,000 by 1810, the service faced a perpetual shortfall of between 3,000 and 16,000 personnel. The brutal discipline, boredom, low pay, and poor rations of life at sea had sparked off mutinies in 1797, and desertion and disease remained serious problems. The government was forced to rely ever more on the callous practice of impressing throughout the British Isles (about one-quarter of lower-deck seamen at Trafalgar were Irish) and recruitment of foreigners. Even for practiced seafarers service in the privateer war or in the merchant fleet was better paid and less dangerous. The debt owed by the British people to these prisoners within the "wooden walls" of the Royal Navy was immeasurable, and the Napoleonic Wars confirmed British naval superiority for the next century.

Related entries: Continental System; Copenhagen, Battle of; Naval Warfare; Navy, French; Nelson, Horatio, Lord; Nile, Battle of the; Privateer War; Trafalgar, Battle of

Suggestions for further reading:
Horward, Donald D. 1978. "The Influence of British Seapower upon the Peninsular War, 1808–1814," *Naval War College Review* 31, pp. 54–71.
Kennedy, Paul. 1991. *The Rise and Fall of British Naval Mastery.* 3rd ed. London: Fontana.
Pope, Dudley. 1991. *Life in Nelson's Navy.* London: Allen and Unwin.

Navy, French

Napoleon inherited a navy that had been shorn of its officer corps by the Revolution and was no match for its British counterpart. And although he gave more attention to the war at sea than he is sometimes given credit for, he could never make up for crucial defects in personnel and infrastructure or restore the morale weakened by British victories. The French navy under Napoleon remained permanently on the brink of major improvement. In 1811 Napoleon predicted that in five years he would have a fleet capable of taking on the British and that "before ten years are passed, I shall have conquered England." Time was to provide no opportunity to prove whether his optimism was justified.

When hostilities resumed with Britain in 1803 the French navy, dispersed in its principal bases at Rochefort, Brest, Lorient, and Toulon, was unready for action. Appreciating Horatio Nelson's maxim that "only numbers can annihilate," Napoleon and his minister of the marine, Denis Decrès, commissioned new warships, some superior in design and construction to their British opposite numbers, and improved training and discipline. Despite the disaster of Trafalgar, by 1813 he had eighty battleships ready for the sea and thirty-five under construction. But only the Toulon flotilla posed any serious threat to British control of the Mediterranean. The rebirth of French sea power remained more a threat than a reality.

French naval doctrine, inherited from the eighteenth century, suppressed initiative and emphasized the husbanding of resources rather than seeking decisive attacks on the opponent's fleet. The demoralized officer corps was in a slow process of regeneration, and basic training in gunnery was markedly inferior to the British. The problem was that the French were denied the opportunity to improve their seamanship or emulate superior British tactics. The conditions of blockade, meaning that the fleet spent most of its time bottled up in port, deprived commanders and men of essential experience at sea. The quality of ships and dockyards improved through Napoleon's and Decrès's efforts, but French commanders could never match the professionalism and discipline of the British. Without this experience they could never confront the British in another full-scale battle after Trafalgar. British maritime supremacy remained unchallenged.

Related entries: Decrés, Denis; Naval Warfare; Navy, British; Nile, Battle of the; Privateer War; Trafalgar, Battle of; Villeneuve, Pierre de

Suggestions for further reading:
Glover, Richard. 1967. "The French Fleet, 1807–1814: Britain's Problem and Madison's Opportunity," *Journal of Modern History* 39, pp. 233–252.
Rose, J. H. 1924. "Napoleon and Seapower," *Cambridge Historical Journal* 1, pp. 138–157.

Nelson, Horatio, Lord (1758–1805)

*O*f all the figures of the Napoleonic age, Nelson is the only male to have exerted a fascination equal to that of Napoleon himself. His victories, turbulent private life, and heroic death ensure him a secure place in both history and romantic legend.

The son of a village rector from Norfolk, Nelson went to sea at the age of twelve and served (mainly in the West Indies, where he met and married Frances Nisbet, the young widow of a doctor) until 1787, when he retired from active service for five years. When war broke out with revolutionary France in 1793, Nelson was sent to convey reinforcements from Naples for British forces in the siege of Toulon, and made the acquaintance of Sir William Hamilton, British minister to Naples, and his wife Emma. He also took part in the British capture of Corsica in 1794, where he lost his right eye at the siege of Calvi. Nelson was promoted to rear admiral and knighted after winning the battle of Cape St. Vincent in February 1797 and lost his right arm during a raid on Santa Cruz in the Canary Isles in July of the same year.

Between 1798 and 1800 Nelson commanded HMS *Vanguard* in the Mediterranean. He was unable to prevent the ships of Napoleon's Egyptian campaign from reaching their destination, but he destroyed the French fleet in the battle of the Nile. When the British fleet put into Naples for repairs Nelson renewed acquaintance with Lady Hamilton, who nursed him during his recovery from a wound received in Egypt, and became embroiled in Neapolitan politics. The Admiralty in London grew increasingly impatient with Nelson and ordered him home. He returned with the Hamiltons, acclaimed as a popular hero, but shunned by polite society. In 1801 Emma Hamilton gave birth to his daughter Horatia. His next naval duty was as second in command at the battle of Copenhagen, after which he was ennobled as a viscount. Then the peace of Amiens gave him a respite from command, which he spent with Emma at their new country house, Merton Place.

When the war broke out anew Nelson commanded the blockade of Toulon for eighteen months, and when the French fleet under Pierre de Villeneuve broke out he pursued it across the Atlantic to the West Indies and back again to the Bay of Biscay. He eventually succeeded in bringing the combined Franco-Spanish fleet to battle at Trafalgar on 21 October 1805. Nelson hoisted his famous signal, "England expects that every man will do his duty," and in conjunction with Admiral Collingwood brought off a famous victory. But Nelson was wounded by a musket shot and spent three hours below decks giving his commands until he died at 4:30 in the afternoon with the last words: "Now I am satisfied, I have done my duty." Having secured the supremacy of the British navy for the duration of the Napoleonic Wars, Nelson was buried in Saint Paul's Cathedral, London, on 9 January 1806.

Related entries: Copenhagen, Battle of; Corsica; Egyptian Campaign; Navy, British; Nile, Battle of the; Revolutionary Wars; Toulon, Siege of; Trafalgar, Battle of; Villeneuve, Pierre de

Suggestions for further reading:
Bennett, Geoffrey M. 1972. *Nelson, the Commander.* New York: Charles Scribner's Sons.
Howarth, David Armine. 1969. *Trafalgar: The Nelson Touch.* London: Collins.
Oman, Carola. 1954. *Lord Nelson.* London: Collins.
Waller, David. 1978. *Nelson.* London: Hamilton.
White, Colin. 1996. *The Nelson Companion.* Gloucester: Alan Sutton.

Netherlands

*T*he arrival of French troops in the United Provinces of the Netherlands in 1795 brought to power the Patriot party, united only by their opposition to the political ambitions of the House of Orange. During the period of the French "sister" Batavian Republic between 1795 and 1806 Patriot burghers attempted to impose a unitary structure on the traditionally decentralized Dutch state, abolishing the estates, which had previously wielded effective political power, and sponsored social and economic reform. But reforms came to an end after 1801, and the aristocracy recaptured political power with the help of Napoleon. The Napoleonic regimes in the Netherlands created no new group of notables such as emerged in France.

The Netherlands continued to flourish as a world financial center, as it had been since the seventeenth century. The United States borrowed money from the Dutch firm of Hope & Co. to help finance the Louisiana Purchase in 1803. But under the Kingdom of Holland, despite the efforts of King Louis Bonaparte to protect Dutch interests, the trading economy on which the power of the United Provinces had been built was hit hard by Napoleon's Continental System. Agriculture, however, on which half the population depended for their livelihoods, prospered and was even stimulated by the blockade.

Any move toward greater social equality and support for French ideas was brought to an end when Napoleon deposed Louis and incorporated the Netherlands into France in 1810. In 1815 the Netherlands became a monarchy under the house of Orange and expanded to rule Belgium until 1830.

Related entries: Batavian Republic; Belgium; Bonaparte, Louis, King of Holland; Continental System; Holland, Kingdom of

Suggestions for further reading:
Connelly, Owen. 1965. *Napoleon's Satellite Kingdoms.* New York: Free Press.
Kossmann, E. H. 1978. *The Low Countries 1780–1940.* Oxford: Clarendon Press.
Schama, Simon. 1977. *Patriots and Liberators: Revolution in the Netherlands, 1780–1813.* New York: Knopf.

Ney, Michel (1769–1815)

*E*ventually to become prince of Moscow, duke of Elchingen, and marshal of France, Ney was born at Sarrelouis in Lorraine, the son of a cooper. He joined the army in 1787, was commissioned in 1792, and was promoted rapidly during the revolutionary wars, when he fought with the

Army of the North in the Rhineland. In 1799–1800 he served as a light cavalry commander in Switzerland under Jean Moreau, helping to win the vital battle of Hohenlinden, and was minister plenipotentiary in Switzerland in 1802–1803. When Napoleon named him among the first marshals of the empire in 1804, therefore, they had never worked together in the field, and Ney always smarted at serving under veterans of the Italian campaigns such as André Masséna or Joachim Murat.

Ney displayed his tactical prowess in 1805 when he won the victory of Elchingen over the Austrians, which earned him his ducal title in 1808. His corps played a vital role in Napoleon's victory at Ulm in 1805, and though he had to be rescued by Jean Lannes at Jena, he distinguished himself at both Eylau and Friedland in 1807. But when he was dispatched to Spain in 1808 and posted to the Army of Portugal his bad relations with Masséna contributed to the disastrous outcome of the invasion of Portugal. Despite performing well in a difficult campaign, Ney was dismissed for insubordination by Masséna in March 1811.

Ney's finest hour was the retreat from Russia in 1812. He had been in the thick of the fighting as commander of the Third Corps at Borodino, but as commander of the rear guard he became a legend. Cut off during the retreat, he held his troops together, leading by example. Reputedly the last French soldier to leave Russian soil, he was hailed by Napoleon as "the bravest of the brave" and named prince of Moscow. During Napoleon's last campaign in Germany Ney commanded the left wing at Bautzen and was wounded twice at Lützen and at Leipzig. But by now he had become deeply critical of Napoleon.

Ney led the group of marshals who secured Napoleon's first abdication in April 1814 and as a reward was given command of the cavalry by Louis XVIII. During the Hundred Days, however, after promising Louis to bring Napoleon back to Paris in

an iron cage, he defected to Napoleon. He engaged Wellington in the battle of Quatre Bras and was given overall battle command at Waterloo, a role for which he was probably not suited. He nevertheless fought with insane bravery, and he was surprised to be arrested by the restored Bourbons. Charged with treachery, he was tried by a Court of Peers and executed by firing squad on 7 December 1815.

Temperamental, quarrelsome, proud, and touchy, Ney showed energy and great courage on the battlefield, but off it was liable to be led by other people's opinions. During the Hundred Days Napoleon, who clearly did not trust him, only employed him at the last moment. Ney had spent his career mostly disagreeing with everyone, especially his fellow marshals. But he showed typical courage at his execution, himself giving the command to fire and ordering the soldiers to fire straight at the heart.

Related entries: Abdication, First; Bautzen, Battle of; Borodino, Battle of; Eylau, Battle of; Friedland, Battle of; Germany, Campaigns in; Hohenlinden, Battle of; Hundred Days; Jena-Auerstädt, Battles of; Leipzig, Battle of; Lützen, Battle of; Masséna, André; Peninsular War; Portugal; Quatre Bras, Battle of; Revolutionary Wars; Russian Campaign; Switzerland; Ulm, Battle of; Waterloo, Battle of

Suggestions for further reading:
Compton, Piers. 1937. *Marshal Ney.* London: Methuen.
Horricks, Raymond. 1982. *Marshal Ney, the Romance and the Real.* Tunbridge Wells, England: Midas.
Kurtz, Harold. 1957. *The Trial of Marshal Ney.* London: Hamish Hamilton.
Young, Peter. 1987. "Ney," in David G. Chandler, ed., *Napoleon's Marshals.* New York: Macmillan.

Nile, Battle of the (1 August 1798)

*T*he destruction of the French fleet at Aboukir Bay by the British fleet under Horatio Nelson cut off Napoleon's Egyptian expedition, contributing decisively to its ultimate failure. When news reached London of Napoleon's sailing from Toulon the British Admiralty had no definite idea of his destination. Nelson, however, guessed that Napoleon intended to strike at India by way of Egypt. He first reached Alexandria before the French, but not finding them there, sailed north. Returning to Egypt at the end of 1798, he found Napoleon's fleet anchored at Aboukir Bay. As he was later to do in the battle of Copenhagen, Nelson exploited superior British seamanship and lighter vessels by sailing some of his ships of the line on the landward side, taking the French by surprise. Only two of thirteen French ships of the line avoided capture or destruction, and while the French lost over 8,900 men the British suffered less than 900 casualties. Napoleon's Army of the East was stranded in Egypt, and Nelson's victory helped to encourage other powers, starting with the Ottoman Empire, to declare war on France.

Related entries: Egyptian Campaign; Nelson, Horatio, Lord

Suggestions for further reading:
Lloyd, Charles C. 1973. *The Nile Campaign: Nelson and Napoleon in Egypt.* Newton Abbot, England: David & Charles.
Warner, Oliver. 1960. *The Battle of the Nile.* London: Batsford.

Nobility

The Revolution had sought to destroy the power of the French nobility by removing their titles and privileges and confiscating the property of those who emigrated. Many *émigrés,* however, had kept their land by various devices such as using front men to purchase their own property, and when most returned under Napoleon they repossessed unsold land and repurchased much of what had been sold. In many instances the wealthiest noble families once again came to dominate "their" countryside. While some refused to recognize the new political order and lived secluded in their châteaux, others collaborated willingly with the Napoleonic regime, holding office at the local and national level, in the armed forces, and in the diplomatic corps. Many families broke with the old caste mentality and intermarried with the bourgeoisie or Napoleon's new imperial nobility.

The new nobility was created step by step from 1802 onward. The creation of the Legion of Honor was followed in 1804 by that of an imperial court, with the Grand Dignitaries of the Empire and civil officers of the imperial household. The military conquests of 1806–1807 allowed the creation of hereditary fiefs, which were mostly granted to marshals and generals, in the conquered lands. Finally a series of decrees in 1808 created a new noble hierarchy of princes, dukes, counts, barons, and chevaliers. Titles were granted for service in office or by letters patent issued by Napoleon. Between 1808 and 1814, according to the researches of Louis Bergeron, some 3,600 personal titles were conferred by letters patent, and about 200 heads of family received hereditary titles.

But Napoleon's new nobility was not the old nobility in new guise. They had no legal privileges, nor were they imbued with a specifically aristocratic mentality or code of honor. As the regime consolidated, the chances for ambitious young men of the lower or middle classes to achieve a noble title diminished. The top positions in the army had been filled early in the empire, and after his marriage to Marie-Louise Napoleon increasingly gave appointments and honors to members of the old nobility. This bias caused resentment against an ever more rigid social order and frictions within noble families. When the regime collapsed in 1814 neither the new nor the old nobility had any reason to rush to save it.

Related entries: Diplomatic Service; *Émigrés;* Grand Dignitaries of the Empire; Legion of Honor

Suggestions for further reading:
Bergeron, Louis. 1981. *France under Napoleon.* Princeton: Princeton University Press.
Forster, Robert. 1967. "The Survival of the Nobility during the French Revolution," *Past & Present,* no. 37 (July 1967), pp. 71–86.

Notables

The 100,000 *notables* made up the "masses of granite" on whom Napoleon based his regime and from whose numbers he drew his governing elite. In his philosophy the rich who had a stake in society should form the backbone of the state. As he expressed it: "I have made the fortunes of those who have worked with me to found the Empire. I will do the same for their children, it is my duty; and after that I will employ only people who have fifty thousand *livres* a year in landed rents. I am not rich enough to pay everybody, and those who have the most interest in supporting the state should do so for nothing" (Bergeron 1981, p. 152).

In 1802 Napoleon instructed the prefects to compile lists of men of wealth, fame, and local influence, who could mold opinion in the departments and be recruited for the administration. By 1810 these lists of notables provided detailed information on the wealth and lives of the approximately 100,000 men designated to be the leading citizens in the 130 departments of the empire in France and the annexed territories. The honor of being so selected was sup-

posed to imbue the notables with a sense of identity and public service apart from class, family, or ancestry. They were mostly landowners and professional men, an amalgam of old and new landlords, noble and nonnoble, bound together by common outlook and habits, a new elite united in the service of the country and the state.

Essentially the rule of the notables meant the substitution of wealth for birth as the basis of power: what the nineteenth-century writer Hippolyte Taine called the "modern regime" replacing the ancien régime (Tulard 1985, p. 348). They came to see themselves as a service elite, men whose wealth, education, professionalism, and disciplined respectability made them peculiarly fit to rule the land and lead opinion. And although the continuing influence of the old nobility should not be forgotten, it was essentially this elite that was to dominate French life for the best part of a century after 1815.

Related entries: Local Government; Nobility

Suggestions for further reading:
Bergeron, Louis. 1981. *France under Napoleon.* Princeton: Princeton University Press.
Collins, Irene. 1979. *Napoleon and his Parliaments.* London: Edward Arnold.
Ellis, Geoffrey. 1983. "Rhine and Loire: Napoleonic Elites and Social Order," in Gwynne Lewis and Colin Lucas, eds., *Beyond the Terror: Essays in French Regional and Social History, 1794–1815.* Cambridge: Cambridge University Press.
Lyons, Martyn. 1994. *Napoleon Bonaparte and the Legacy of the French Revolution.* London: Macmillan.
Tulard, Jean. 1985. *Napoleon: The Myth of the Saviour.* London: Methuen.
Whitcomb, Edward A. 1974. "Napoleon's Prefects," *American Historical Review* 79, pp. 1089–1118.

O

Oldenburg, Duchy of

This small north German state on the left bank of the river Weser, ruled by the Holstein-Gottorp family, into which Catherine the Great had been born, became an indirect cause or excuse for war between Russia and Napoleon in 1812. The tsars tended to treat Oldenburg as a fief of Russia, and the link was strengthened by the marriage in October 1809 of the Grand Duchess Catherine Pavlovna, Alexander I's favorite sister, to the son of the reigning duke of Oldenburg. Therefore, when Napoleon annexed the duchy along with the rest of the north German coast, December 1810–January 1811, Alexander took it as a personal and family insult, and he made it one of his chief complaints against him. Oldenburg became part of the new German Confederation in 1815.

Related entries: Russian Campaign

Suggestions for further reading:
Cate, Curtis. 1985. *The War of the Two Emperors: The Duel between Napoleon and Alexander, Russia, 1812.* New York: Random House.

Opera Plot (24 December 1800)

This attempt on Napoleon's life by the explosion of an "infernal ma-chine" took place in the Rue Saint-Niçaise, not far from the Tuileries. As the first consul was on his way to the opera to hear Haydn's *Creation* he found a wagon with a large barrel on it blocking the way. Napoleon's escort pushed it aside but it exploded, killing twenty-two onlookers and wounding fifty-six. The passengers in a second carriage, including Joséphine, her daughter Hortense, and Caroline Bonaparte had a lucky escape. The plot was the work of royalists, two of whom were arrested in January 1801 and guillotined on 21 April. Napoleon ordered the area to be razed as part of a project to improve the approaches to the Tuileries.

Related entries: Cadoudal, Georges; Royalists

Suggestions for further reading:
Arnold, Eric A. 1979. *Fouché, Napoleon and the General Police.* Washington, DC: University Press of America.
———, ed. 1996. *A Documentary Survey of Napoleonic France: A Supplement.* Lanham, MD: University Press of America, pp. 41–44.

Opposition Movements

Taking into account the effectiveness of Napoleon's police and his all-pervasive propaganda, the overall extent of domestic opposition to his rule is difficult to determine. In addition to the more-or-less organized movements of republicans and royalists, a kind of opposition was manifested in plots, assassination attempts, strikes by workers, and individual acts of nonconformity. The police were well informed about any such incidents, and their reports may exaggerate the extent of opposition among a French people in all probability mostly resigned to accepting Napoleon's rule. The persistence of Jacobinism showed the survival of a doctrine which Napoleon thought he had appropriated for himself, whereas royalists were the most successful in maintaining clandestine movements hidden from the prying eyes of the state.

But arguably the greatest threat to Napoleon came not from those who opposed him on principle but from the lukewarm or faltering support of his advisers or those charged with carrying out his orders. The first doubts probably arose in the army, first among those of his officers who retained republican sympathies and then among those who opposed the Russian campaign and Napoleon's foolish continuation of a struggle that was as good as lost in 1813–1814. As Marshal François Joseph Lefebvre remarked when it was all over: "That little bugger wouldn't have been happy until he had every last one of us killed" (Vidalenc 1989, p. 136). The general public as well probably tired of military bravado. The veteran soldier of the Revolution, General Noguès, observed after Waterloo: "Napoleon destroyed victories in the mind of the public" (Vidalenc 1989, p. 137).

Of course, it would be a mistake to accept as active opponents of Napoleon all those who, after his downfall, claimed to have opposed him. The administration was well populated with trimmers like the prefect of the Eure, who listed with equal precision the number of conscripts sent to the military depots and the number of draft dodgers and deserters: he sent the first list to Napoleon in February 1814, and the second to the restored Louis XVIII two months later. Indeed, the extent of avoidance of conscription is in its own way as significant as the occasional cry of "Long Live the Republic!" or "Long Live the King!" from arrested "malcontents and fanatics." By the time of his first abdication Napoleon's government enjoyed little prestige, and it took the blunders of the restored Bourbons to restore it briefly to public favor during the Hundred Days.

Related entries: Cadoudal, Georges; Conscription; Counter-Revolution; Fouché, Joseph; *Idéologues;* Imperial Police; Jacobinism; Opera Plot; Pichegru, Jean-Charles; Royalists; Tribunate

Suggestions for further reading:
Lyons, Martyn. 1994. *Napoleon Bonaparte and the Legacy of the French Revolution*. London: Macmillan.
Vidalenc, Jean. 1989. "A Survey," in Frank A. Kafker and James M. Laux, eds., *Napoleon and His Times: Selected Interpretations*. Malibar, FL: Krieger. pp. 122–138.

Organic Articles

Napoleon added three Articles or Titles to the Concordat of 1801 with the Catholic Church, viewing them as supplementary regulations strengthening the Church's dependence on the state. They amounted to concessions to the anticlericals in the Senate and the Tribunate. The articles asserted government control over papal documents entering France, required government authorization for all Church councils and synods, gave the state limited control over seminaries, allowed the government to regulate clerical dress and religious holidays, and provided for state regulation of clerical salaries and parish boundaries. The Organic Articles were never accepted by the papacy, which saw them as violations of the spirit of the Concordat, but they were implemented by Napoleon and remained in force after his downfall and through the nineteenth century.

Related entries: Catholic Church; Concordat; Papacy; Pius VII, Pope

Suggestions for further reading:
Arnold, Eric A., ed. 1994. *A Documentary Survey of Napoleonic France.* Lanham, MD: University Press of America. pp. 90–98.
Dansette, Adrien. 1961. *Religious History of Modern France.* 2 vols. London: Nelson.
Hales, Edward Elton Young. 1962. *Napoleon and the Pope.* London: Eyre and Spottiswoode.
Walsh, Henry Horace. 1933. *The Concordat of 1801: A Study of the Problems of Church and State.* New York: Columbia University Press.

induced the Russians to make peace in 1812. The peace settlements of 1815 left the Ottoman Empire intact, but already on the way to becoming the "sick man of Europe."

Related entries: Coalitions; Danubian Principalities; Egyptian Campaign

Suggestions for further reading:
Shaw, Stanford J. 1971. *Between Old and New: The Ottoman Empire under Sultan Selim III, 1789–1807.* Cambridge: Harvard University Press.
———. 1976–77. *History of the Ottoman Empire and Modern Turkey.* Cambridge: Cambridge University Press.

Ottoman Empire

*I*n the age of Napoleon the slow decline of the once mighty Ottoman Empire, which had struck fear into the heart of Christendom for 300 years, was already starting to pose the Eastern Question of the nineteenth century. Nevertheless, the sultan in Constantinople was still sovereign of lands from the Balkans through Asia Minor to North Africa. But the governors of the different territories, such as the Mamelukes in Egypt, acted as independent rulers in their own right. The deposition and murder in 1807 of the reforming Sultan Selim III, who had attempted to create a Western-style army, weakened an empire particularly vulnerable to Russian expansion in the Danube region and the Black Sea.

Napoleon's Egyptian campaign plunged the Ottomans into war against France between 1798 and 1802. Thereafter, however, relations were mostly friendly, due to Ottoman fear of Russia. Ottoman trade concessions to France led to war with Britain and Russia in 1806, during which a British naval squadron stormed through the Dardanelles. Peace was made with Britain in 1809, but the Ottomans remained at war with Russia until the threat from Napoleon

Oudinot, Nicolas Charles (1767–1847)

*D*uke of Reggio, marshal of France, Napoleon's most wounded marshal nevertheless outlived all the others, dying as a much decorated governor of Les Invalides at the age of eighty-one. The irascible Oudinot sustained thirty-six wounds in twenty-two campaigns, not counting others suffered in bars and theaters. Born at Bar-Le-Duc, the son of a brewer, he enlisted in the army in 1784, beginning a military career that lasted for four decades. During the revolutionary wars he fought mostly in the Rhineland, and in July 1799 he replaced Louis Gabriel Suchet as chief of staff to André Masséna in Switzerland and at the siege of Genoa.

Oudinot took part in the campaign of 1805, when he was wounded at Austerlitz and left incapacitated for over a year. He played a key role in the victory of Friedland in 1807, for which he was given the rank of count, and was wounded again at Essling; at Wagram in 1809 he helped secure victory for Napoleon despite disobeying orders. He was created a marshal in July 1809 and duke of Reggio in April 1810. His rigorous military occupation of the Kingdom of

Holland in 1810 was instrumental in forcing the abdication of King Louis Bonaparte. As commander of the Second Corps in the Russian campaign of 1812 Oudinot was wounded twice and forced to return to France. He nevertheless joined Napoleon for the campaign of 1813 in Germany as commander of the Twelfth Corps and led the right wing in a crucial enveloping movement at Bautzen before being defeated by Jean-Baptiste Bernadotte at Gross-Beeren on 23 August.

Oudinot was one of the marshals who forced Napoleon's first abdication in March 1814 and was to remain loyal to the restored Bourbons thereafter. During the Hundred Days he traveled to Paris to tell Napoleon personally why he could not support him, and Napoleon, with uncharacteristic magnanimity but probably remembering Oudinot's numerous sufferings in his service, allowed him to retire to his country estate. In later life Oudinot was a member of Louis XVIII's Privy Council and fought his last campaign when France intervened in Spain in 1823.

Oudinot was lucky in not fighting in Spain under Napoleon, allowing him to retain his reputation intact. His rough-hewn manners got him into numerous scrapes, but he was popular with his staff. Napoleon thought him "a decent fellow, but not very bright" (Austin 1987, p. 184). He was, however, bright enough to realize when Napoleon was fighting a losing battle in 1813–1814. Oudinot had eleven children by his two wives and his sons continued the military tradition of their father.

Related entries: Abdication, First; Austerlitz, Battle of; Bautzen, Battle of; Danube Campaigns; Essling, Battle of; Friedland, Battle of; Genoa; Germany, Campaigns in; Holland, Kingdom of; Russian Campaign; Switzerland; Wagram, Battle of

Suggestions for further reading:
Austin, Paul Britten. 1987. "Oudinot," in David G. Chandler, ed., *Napoleon's Marshals*. New York: Macmillan.

Steigler, Gaston, ed. 1897. *Memoirs of Marshal Oudinot, duc de Reggio, Compiled from the Hitherto Unpublished Souvenirs of the Duchesse de Reggio.* New York: D. Appleton and Co.

Ouvard, Gabriel Julien (1770–1846)

The scandalous reputation and brazen behavior of the most notorious financier of his age did not stop successive French regimes, including Napoleon's, from making use of his services. Ouvard had made a considerable fortune as the principal handler of naval contracts under the Directory, but his dubious methods led to his imprisonment in 1800. Napoleon had him released in 1802, and under the protection of Joseph Fouché in 1804 he came up with a complicated scheme to supply provisions for the French and Spanish armed forces by bringing Mexican and Cuban bullion through the British blockade to Spain on British ships. The scheme was supposed to profit the French treasury, the Dutch bank of Hope-Labouchère, the British Barings Bank, the East India Company, merchants in the United States, and Ouvard himself. However, it depended on acquiring funds from the Bank of France, which the bank could not afford to provide. The minister of the treasury, François Barbé-Marbois, was dismissed for having believed Ouvard's assurances.

Napoleon threatened to have Ouvard shot, but the financier lived to become bankrupt again. He was imprisoned for debt in 1809, but released thanks to Fouché. In 1810 Ouvard acted as go-between in Fouché's attempt to come to an agreement with Britain, the act which resulted in Fouché being dismissed and Ouvard being sent back to prison, from which he only emerged in 1813. Undaunted, in 1814 Ouvard secured the contract to supply the Allied armies occupying France.

His banking concerns continued to flourish under the Restoration and the July Monarchy.

Related entries: Bank of France; Finance; Fouché, Joseph

Suggestions for further reading:
Bergeron, Louis. 1981. *France under Napoleon.* Princeton: Princeton University Press.
Buist, Marten G. 1974. *At Spes non Fracta: Hope & Co., 1770–1815: Merchant Bankers and Diplomats at Work.* The Hague: Nijhoff.

P

Paoli, Pasquale (1725–1807)

The Corsican patriot, at one time the toast of the salons of Enlightened Europe, was Napoleon's boyhood hero. Proclaimed as governor of Corsica, then struggling for independence from Genoa, in 1755, Paoli won a high degree of autonomy for the island and promoted economic and educational advance. When Genoa ceded Corsica to France in 1768 Paoli led a heroic defense against overwhelming odds, but with defeat at Ponte Nuovo in May 1769 began twenty years of exile. Most of his followers, including Carlo Bonaparte, accepted amnesty from the French, and Napoleon was born a subject of the king of France.

In exile in London, Paoli frequented the company of Samuel Johnson, James Boswell, and other eminent figures in British cultural life, while remaining a legend in Corsica. He seems to have possessed a remarkable presence and impressive character: Johnson thought that he had "the loftiest port of any man he had ever seen." In 1789 Paoli expressed support for the constitutional monarchy established by the Revolution, and on 30 November the National Assembly on the initiative of Antonio Cristoforo Saliceti invited him to return to Corsica. Though by now sixty-five years old and in poor health, he was welcomed as a hero as royal governor, but he still clung to his dream of an independent Corsica under either French or British protection.

With the execution of Louis XVI and the establishment of the Republic Paoli began to turn toward Britain. A clash with Corsican Jacobins, including Napoleon and Lucien Bonaparte, was inevitable. Lucien denounced Paoli as a traitor to the revolutionary club of Toulon, but Paoli's supporters were in the majority on Corsica: the entire Bonaparte family was forced to flee to France in June 1793. In 1795 Paoli, now aged seventy, turned Corsica over to a British viceroy, but in 1796 the French retook the island, and Paoli once again found refuge in England.

Related entries: Corsica

Suggestions for further reading:
Thrasher, Peter A. 1970. *Pasquale Paoli: An Enlightened Hero, 1725–1807.* London: Constable.

Papacy

The papacy under Pius VI (Gianangelo Braschi) had not immediately condemned the Revolution in France for fear of jeopardizing the position of Louis XVI. But in 1791 with the introduction of the Civil Constitution of the Clergy, which demanded that churchmen take an oath of loyalty to the state, the pontiff declared the Revolution anathema. However, he could do little to influence events in France. Napoleon invaded the Papal States in 1797, and the French occupied Rome in February 1798. After taking refuge in Florence, Pius VI was arrested when the French invaded Tuscany and taken to France. He died a prisoner on 29 August 1799 in Valence, where the mayor recorded the death of "Jean Ange Braschi, exercising the profession of pontiff."

Napoleon as first consul needed better relations with the papacy for domestic political reasons: to end divisions within the French clergy and the revolt in the Vendée. The result was the Concordat of 1801, negotiated with the new pope, Pius VII. Relations between Napoleonic France and the Vatican deteriorated from 1805 onward, culminating in the excommunication of Napoleon in 1809 and the imprisonment of Pius VII in 1812. Napoleon's cynical attitude toward the pope helped to raise the prestige of the papacy among conservative French Catholics, laying the foundations for the influence of the propapal Ultramontane party after the Restoration.

Related entries: Catholic Church; Concordat; Papal States; Pius VII, Pope

Suggestions for further reading:
Hales, Edward Elton Young. 1960. *Revolution and Papacy, 1769–1846*. London: Eyre and Spottiswoode.
———. 1962. *Napoleon and the Pope*. London: Eyre and Spottiswoode.

Papal States

The territories in central Italy ruled by the papacy were invaded by Napoleon during his first Italian campaign. By the Treaty of Tolentino in February 1797, Bologna, Ferrara, and the Romagna were ceded to the Cisalpine Republic. In 1798 the assassination of the French general

Léonard Duphot in Rome led to occupation of the Eternal City by French troops under Louis Alexandre Berthier and the reorganization of the Papal States as the Roman Republic. This ephemeral state collapsed when Austrian troops occupied most of the Papal States, but not Rome itself, in 1799. By the Treaty of Lunéville (1801) the northern states, including Bologna, Ferrara, and Ravenna, formed part of the Italian Republic, subsequently the Kingdom of Italy, while Pope Pius VII retained possession of the lands around Rome and of the port of Ancona. The latter, however, was seized by the French in 1805 and incorporated into the Kingdom of Italy in 1808. Rome and what remained of the Papal States were annexed by Napoleon in June 1809. The pope's possessions were restored to him by the Congress of Vienna in 1814–1815.

Related entries: Cisalpine Republic; Italian Campaigns; Italy, Kingdom of; Papacy; Pius VII, Pope

Suggestions for further reading:
Hales, Edward Elton Young. 1960. *Revolution and Papacy, 1769–1846*. London: Eyre and Spottiswoode.
Woolf, Stuart. 1991. *A History of Italy, 1700–1860: The Social Constraints of Political Change*. London: Routledge.

Paris, Treaties of

The first Treaty of Paris (30 May 1814), imposed by the Allies after Napoleon's first abdication, treated France leniently in an attempt to bolster the authority of the restored Louis XVIII. France returned to its borders of 1792, including territory that had not been French in 1789 such as the former papal enclave of Avignon and the Comtat Venaissin and parts of the Rhineland, Belgium, and Savoy. France retained all its colonies except Mauritius, Tobago, and Saint Lucia, and no claims were made for war indemnity.

The second Treaty of Paris (20 November 1815), made after the Hundred Days, was more severe. France was returned to the boundaries of 1790, meaning those of 1789 with the sole addition of Avignon and the Comtat. Seventeen fortresses in northern and northeastern France were to be garrisoned by the Allies for five years, and France had to pay reparations of 700 million francs and restore the artistic treasures taken from other countries by the revolutionary and Napoleonic armies.

Related entries: Abdication, First; Hundred Days

Suggestions for further reading:
Arnold, Eric A., ed. 1994. *A Documentary Survey of Napoleonic France.* Lanham, MD: University Press of America, pp. 331–345, 358–363.
Ross, Steven T. 1981. *European Diplomatic History, 1789–1815.* Malabar, FL: Krieger.

Paul I, Tsar of Russia (1754–1801)

Succeeding his mother, Catherine the Great, in 1796, Paul I brought Russia into the wars against revolutionary France for the first time, and despite personal eccentricities which led to rumors of madness, pursued policies designed to strengthen Russia both at home and abroad. At first he kept Russia out of the wars, concentrating on consolidating its position in Poland and improving state finances, but Napoleon's Egyptian campaign changed his mind. The invasion of Egypt marked French incursion into an area long considered by Russia as its own sphere of influence, and Napoleon's seizure of Malta seemed to threaten Russian interests in the Mediterranean. At the end of 1798, therefore, Paul concluded an alliance with the Ottoman Empire and joined the Second Coalition against France. His ultimate aims were the same as those of the British: to re-store France to its frontiers of 1792 and to restore the pre-1789 situation in Italy, but he was more insistent than was William Pitt on the overthrow of the republic in France and the restoration of the Bourbons.

Russian armies were sent to Italy, Switzerland, and Holland, and the campaigns of 1799 saw several Russian successes under Paul's favorite general, Alexander Suvorov. However, Austria, the third member of the Coalition, deserted its allies in pursuit of its own aims in Italy and Belgium. The Russian army in Switzerland was isolated and crushed by the French at the battle of Zurich. Angered by the course of events, Paul left the Coalition at the end of 1799. In 1800 he formed the League of Armed Neutrality in the Baltic against British commerce and even planned an invasion of India. But a clique of nobles in Russia allied themselves with Paul's son, Alexander, and Paul was assassinated on 23 March 1801.

Related entries: Alexander I, Tsar of Russia; Armed Neutrality; Coalitions; Italian Campaigns; Malta; Ottoman Empire; Revolutionary Wars; Switzerland

Suggestions for further reading:
Ragsdale, Hugh. 1970. "A Continental System in 1801: Paul I and Bonaparte," *Journal of Modern History* 42, pp. 70–89.
———, ed. 1979. *Paul I: A Reassessment of his Life and Reign.* Pittsburgh: University of Pittsburgh Center for International Studies.
———. 1988. *Tsar Paul and the Question of Madness: An Essay in History and Psychology.* New York and Westport, CT: Greenwood Press.

Peasants

The peasantry made up the vast majority of the French population under Napoleon, but as always in French history, it is difficult to make generalizations about their condition for the whole of France. The Revolution had freed them from the burdens of "feudalism," a liberation which meant a lot in some regions, but which in the more advanced areas of northern and eastern France merely meant the removal of some minor and anachronistic irritants. Peasants no longer paid seignorial dues or ecclesiastical tithes and were no longer subject to seignorial justice. All these gains were maintained by Napoleon.

However, the economic status of peasants varied enormously. More substantial proprietors, the *coqs de village* of regions of consolidated agrarian property, profited from the purchase of noble and church lands. Below them lived a solid class of those who owned or leased enough land to maintain their families in reasonable comfort by the standards of the day. These were the leaders in the move toward "agrarian individualism," the domination of agriculture by independent peasant proprietors, which has been such a marked feature of French society until very recent times. But wherever the use of common land and collective agricultural practices were essential to the functioning of the rural economy, as over broad areas of the south, poor peasants lost out. And day laborers, owning nothing but the strength of their bodies, were still dependent on landowners and better-off peasants for their livelihoods.

In general it is safe to say that, apart from the crisis years of 1810–1811, the Napoleonic era was one of relative comfort for the peasantry. The Continental System sheltered those peasants producing for the market rather than merely for subsistence from foreign competition. Peasants ate better and dressed better then ever before. They were to look back on the empire as a "golden age," helping to explain the cult of Napoleon and Bonapartist sympathies among the people of the countryside in the nineteenth century.

Related entries: Bonapartism; Continental System; Economy; Rural Code; Taxation

Suggestions for further reading:
Agulhon, Maurice. 1982. *The Republic in the Village: The People of the Var from the French Revolution to the Second Republic.* Cambridge: Cambridge University Press.
Jones, Peter M. 1985. *Politics and Rural Society: The Southern Massif Central, c. 1750–1880.* Cambridge: Cambridge University Press.
———. 1988. *The Peasantry in the French Revolution.* Cambridge: Cambridge University Press.
Le Goff, T. J. A., and D. M. G. Sutherland. 1991. "The Revolution and the Rural Economy," in Alan Forrest and Peter Jones, eds., *Reshaping France: Town, Country and Region during the French Revolution.* Manchester: Manchester University Press.

Pelet, Jean-Jacques (1777–1858)

An experienced soldier and competent line officer, Pelet was also one of the founders of France's military archives and wrote vivid accounts of the Wagram campaign and the invasion of Portugal in 1810–1811. In 1805 Pelet joined the staff of Marshal André Masséna and fought with him in Italy and Poland, before playing a vital role in the victory at Wagram (2 July 1809). He was the ailing Masséna's chief aide-de-camp in Portugal, but transferred to Louis Davout's corps for the invasion of Russia. He took command of the Forty-eighth Regiment in Russia, and during the retreat joined with Michel Ney in ensuring the escape of the rear guard. Pelet continued his distinguished service in Germany in 1813 and all the major battles of the 1814 campaign in France. He ended his active military career commanding the Young Guard at Waterloo. Although at first considered suspect by the restored Bourbons, Pelet pursued his career in military administration, becoming head of the General Staff School in 1830.

Related entries: Germany, Campaigns in; Portugal; Russian Campaign; Wagram, Battle of; Waterloo, Battle of

Suggestions for further reading:
Chandler, David G. 1974. *The Campaigns of Napoleon: The Mind and Method of History's Greatest Soldier.* New York: Macmillan.

Horward, Donald D., ed. and trans. 1973. *The French Campaign in Portugal, 1810–11: An Account by Jean-Jacques Pelet*. Minneapolis: University of Minnesota Press.

Penal Code

Napoleon's Penal Code of 1810 replaced the revolutionary Code of 25 September 1791 and was much harsher. It restored branding, the iron collar, and fetters, the deprivation of civil rights, and other penalties abolished by the more enlightened penal thought of the Revolution. However, it was also much clearer in language than its predecessor and introduced the idea of "extenuating circumstances," which allowed a better adaptation of punishments to individual crimes.

Related entries: Law, Codification of

Suggestions for further reading:
Bergeron, Louis. 1981. *France under Napoleon*. Princeton: Princeton University Press.
Holtman, Robert B. 1967. *The Napoleonic Revolution*. Philadelphia: Lippincott.

Peninsular War

Napoleon's intervention in Spain and the subsequent popular uprising that began in May 1808 led to a war, Napoleon's "Spanish ulcer," which sapped French resources and morale through to 1813. "It was that miserable Spanish affair," he later declared, "that killed me" (Connelly 1985, p. 385). In 1807 Spain was nominally an ally of Napoleon, but he considered the Spanish Bourbon ruling house unreliable and decided to install his brother Joseph as king of Spain. His real aim was the conquest of Portugal, an ally of Britain in all but name, which was violating the Continental System.

Following the Treaty of Tilsit in eastern Europe Napoleon was free to act. In November 1807 he dispatched troops into the Iberian Peninsula: an army under Andoche Junot marched into Portugal, forcing the royal family into exile in Brazil, and another under Joachim Murat occupied Madrid virtually unopposed. Shortly before, the Spanish crown prince had overthrown his father, Charles IV, and declared himself Ferdinand VII. Napoleon responded by calling both kings and a Spanish national junta to meet him in Bayonne, where he forced both Charles and Ferdinand to abdicate in favor of Joseph Bonaparte. Their departure was followed by an uprising in Madrid, the famous *Dos de Mayo* (2 May 1808), which was viciously suppressed by Murat and immortalized in the painting by Francisco Goya.

Joseph, crowned king at Burgos, briefly took possession of Madrid, but was isolated in his new capital. News of the reverse at Bailen and the landing of a British army under Arthur Wellesley, later duke of Wellington, in Portugal, where it defeated Junot at Vimiero, led to his retreat and determined Napoleon to intervene personally. In November 1808 he advanced on and took Madrid, defeated the Spanish forces sent against him, and set about restoring order, with the utmost brutality where necessary. Only Saragossa, under its heroic commander, José Palafox, withstood the French siege until February 1809. Napoleon made Joseph commander in chief in Spain and departed for Paris. The French hold over Spain, however, turned out to be an illusion.

Meanwhile a British force under Sir John Moore had fought an indecisive battle against Marshal Nicolas Soult at La Coruña and been forced to escape on Royal Navy ships. But Soult's advance into Portugal was repulsed by Wellington. The marshals had no confidence in Joseph as a commander and missed the chance to destroy Wellington in the indecisive battle of Talavera (27–29 July 1809). The British commander was able to secure control of Portugal, from

Napoleon ordered **The Crossing of the Guadarrama in December 1808** *(1812) by Nicolas-Antoine Taunay to celebrate the heroism of his troops in the Peninsular War at a time when the outcome of the conflict was still in doubt. (Giraudon/Art Resource)*

which he eventually emerged at the head of British, Portuguese, and Spanish forces to attack the French in Spain.

During 1810 and 1811 the French managed to gain apparent control over Spain, though still engaged in constant combat with guerrilla bands. Joseph and Soult conquered Andalusia, and Marshal Louis Suchet occupied Aragon and Valencia. Joseph was king, but the marshals ruled the provinces: Spain became, in the words of the historian Pieter Geyl, "a training ground in disobedience for the marshals."

But Wellington remained secure in Portugal. In September 1810 André Masséna secured a victory at Bussaco, but was forced to retreat after failing in the siege of Torres Vedras, where Wellington gathered his forces. Auguste Marmont, replacing Masséna, was similarly incapable of penetrating into Portugal, and in early 1812 Wellington took Ciudad Rodrigo and Badajoz. As the duke prepared to drive into Spain, Napoleon departed on the Russian campaign, leaving Joseph as commander in Spain presiding over the unruly marshals.

Wellington, marching into Spain as Napoleon marched into Russia, defeated Marmont at the battle of Salamanca (22 July 1812) and advanced on Madrid. Joseph fled to Valencia, and although, after combining forces with Soult, he was able to retake the capital, the unperturbed Wellington went into winter quarters at Ciudad Rodrigo, emerging in the spring of 1813 as *generalissimo* of Allied forces in the peninsula. Napoleon ordered Joseph to establish his headquarters at Valladolid, placing his force of some 250,000 troops between Wellington and the French border. By June Joseph had reluctantly abandoned Madrid for good, and his forces were scattered between Valladolid and Bayonne.

Wellington's forces of 95,000 British, Portuguese, and Spanish troops accompanied by swarms of guerrillas materialized northwest of Valladolid on 4 June, threatening Joseph's communications with France. Joseph managed to assemble some 70,000 troops at Vitoria, but his army was shattered irrevocably in the battle of 21 June. The war was all but over. Soult fought a delaying action in the Pyrenees, while Suchet evacuated eastern France. In October 1813 Wellington invaded southern France.

The Peninsular War had cost France in the region of 300,000 casualties and untold sums of money and material. Once Napoleon had abdicated, Ferdinand VII was restored to the throne of Spain, but his people's rejoicing was short-lived. Ferdinand reneged on his promises of constitutional government and Spain descended into an era of reaction and oppression.

Related entries: Bailen, Battle of; Bonaparte, Joseph, King of Naples, King of Spain; Bussaco, Battle of; Corunna, Battle of; Ferdinand VII, King of Spain; Goya y Lucientes, Francisco de; Guerrilla Warfare; Junot, Andoche; Marmont, Auguste Frédéric Louis Viesse de; Masséna, André; Moore, Sir John; Murat, Joachim; Portugal; Salamanca, Battle of; Soult, Nicolas Jean de Dieu; Spain; Suchet, Louis Gabriel; Vitoria, Battle of; Wellington, Duke of

Suggestions for further reading:
Berkeley, Alice D., ed. 1991. *New Lights on the Peninsular War.* Lisbon: British Historical Society of Portugal.
Connelly, Owen, ed. 1985. *Historical Dictionary of Napoleonic France, 1799–1815.* Westport, CT: Greenwood.
Esdaile, Charles J. 1988. *The Spanish Army in the Peninsular War.* Manchester: Manchester University Press.
Gates, David. 1986. *The Spanish Ulcer: A History of the Peninsular War.* London: Allen and Unwin.
Glover, Michael. 1974. *The Peninsular War, 1807–14.* Hampden, CT: Archon Books.
Lovett, Gabriel H. 1965. *Napoleon and the Birth of Modern Spain.* 2 vols. New York: New York University Press.
Oman, Charles W. C. 1902–1930. *A History of the Peninsular War.* 7 vols. Oxford: Clarendon Press.
Read, Jan. 1977. *War in the Peninsula.* London: Faber.

Personality, Cult of

Napoleon has been described by the historian Jean Tulard as "the first of the modern myths." Much of his propaganda and image-making centered on his own personality, but this cult was only semi-modern, in that he self-consciously harked back to the cults surrounding the French monarchs of the ancien régime, especially Louis XIV. The exaltation of the image of Napoleon began with the military bulletins of the first Italian campaign, but reached its height under the empire. Artists, writers, and musicians were employed to celebrate every notable event in his career and also for the mass production of prints, paintings, and busts of Napoleon. And buildings, monuments, and decorations in the Empire style were adorned with the Napoleonic "N" or the bee symbol.

While popular prints exalted the "little corporal," military hero, and man of the people, the heroic image of Napoleon shaped by artists steeped in classical antiquity could reach ludicrous proportions, with the emperor looking nothing like himself, clothed (or unclothed) as Jupiter or Apollo. In similar vein were the Feast of the previously nonexistent "Saint Napoleon," replacing the Feast of the Assumption on 15 August, and the quasi-religious canonization of the emperor in the Imperial Catechism.

In fairness to Napoleon, these extremes were combined with less absurdly overblown imagery: he wanted to be an emperor, an equal among the crowned heads of Europe, over whom a shadow of divinity still lingered, but also the hardworking reformer dedicated to the good of his people. He was curiously unwilling to have statues of himself erected in public places. Napoleon's ideal was that every lower-class household should have a print depicting him on its walls and every bourgeois salon should be adorned with his bust. As for the public domain, the whole of France was to be his monument and a reflection of his personality.

Related entries: Coronation; David, Jacques-Louis; Empire Style; Gros, Antoine Jean; Imperial Catechism; Napoleonic Legend; Propaganda; Vernet, Émile Jean Horace

Suggestions for further reading:
Holtman, Robert B. 1950. *Napoleonic Propaganda.* Baton Rouge: Louisiana State University Press.
Mathews, Joseph J. 1950. "Napoleon's Military Bulletins," *Journal of Modern History* 22, pp. 137–144.

Wilson-Smith, Timothy. 1996. *Napoleon and His Artists.* London: Constable.

Pichegru, Jean-Charles (1761–1804)

A respected general in the early years of the revolutionary wars, Pichegru had nevertheless been in contact with royalists and British agents since 1795 and resigned from the army in 1796. Elected to the Directory's Council of Five Hundred in April 1797, Pichegru was still suspected of treason and vaguely involved in royalist plots. Deported to Guyana, he escaped in June 1798. From London he became involved in the Cadoudal conspiracy of 1803, following Georges Cadoudal to Normandy and trying to gain the support of Jean-Victor Moreau. But the plot was betrayed and Pichegru arrested on 28 February 1804. He was found dead in his cell on 5 April, having either hanged himself or been strangled on Napoleon's orders.

Related entries: Cadoudal, Georges; Royalists

Suggestions for further reading:
Godechot, Jacques. 1981. *The Counter-Revolution: Doctrine and Action, 1789–1804.* Princeton: Princeton University Press.
Mitchell, Harvey. 1965. *The Underground War against Revolutionary France: The Missions of William Wickham, 1794–1800.* Oxford: Clarendon Press.

Pitt, William the Younger (1759–1806)

The second son of William Pitt, first earl of Chatham, who had led Britain against France in the Seven Years War, the younger Pitt abandoned many of his Whig principles in his unyielding fight against revolutionary France and

Napoleon. In 1784 as the youngest prime minister in British history, he had favored independence for the colonies, the abolition of slavery and the slave trade, religious toleration, concessions to Ireland, and above all reform of government and administration. But with the outbreak of the Revolution in France he abandoned reform, advocated all-out resistance to France and French ideas, and introduced a succession of repressive measures against British radicals.

The shock of rebellion in Ireland in 1798 made him advocate Union with England, but combined with emancipation for Irish Catholics. When King George III refused concessions on the religious question, Pitt first carried through the Act of Union but then resigned on 14 March 1801. His resignation made possible the negotiation of the Peace of Amiens with Napoleon, but the breakdown of this settlement in 1804 led to his recall as prime minister. Pitt successfully negotiated the alliances with Russia and Austria, making possible the Third Coalition of 1805, but he died on 13 January 1806, shortly after hearing the news of Napoleon's victory at Austerlitz, which had shattered the alliance.

Pitt's policy was based on keeping Britain out of direct military engagement in Europe, instead providing substantial subsidies for Napoleon's enemies and directing British efforts toward robbing France of its colonies. A great orator and shrewd politician, he confessed to ignorance of military affairs, declaring that he "distrusted extremely any Ideas of my own on Military Subjects" (Ehrman 1996, p. 380). Pitt was buried with great public ceremony in Westminster Abbey and commemorated in popular song as "the pilot who weathered the storm."

Related entries: Coalitions; Great Britain

Suggestions for further reading:
Ehrman, John. 1969. *The Younger Pitt: The Years of Acclaim.* London: Constable.

———. 1983. *The Younger Pitt: The Reluctant Transition.* London: Constable.
———. 1996. *The Younger Pitt: The Consuming Struggle.* London: Constable.

Pius VII, Pope (Gregorio Barnaba Chiaramonti) (1742–1823)

A Benedictine who had been Cardinal-Archbishop of Imola since 1785, Chiaramonti was elected pope in 1800 after three months of voting at an enclave held in Venice rather than Rome. This unusual venue indicates that the question of relations with Napoleon, fresh from his victory at Marengo, would dominate Pius's papacy. In negotiating the Concordat of 1801 Pius's aims were to retain possession of the Papal States and increase papal influence in France. But as long as Napoleon remained in power these accomplishments were to remain beyond the pope's grasp.

By attending Napoleon's coronation in 1804 Pius hoped to win concessions from the emperor, but he was to be disappointed. Relations remained uneasy, and when French troops occupied Rome in 1808 and the rest of the Papal States in 1809, Pius excommunicated Napoleon. The pope was arrested and imprisoned, albeit in great comfort, first at Savona and then between June 1812 and January 1814 at Fontainebleau. As Napoleon's empire in Europe began to crumble, he sought a new agreement with Pius. After visiting the pope in his gilded cage for a week in January 1813, he extracted the Fontainebleau Concordat, but Pius refused to ratify it.

Pius was taken back to Italy in January 1814 and slowly made his way to Rome. He reentered his capital in triumph on 24 May 1814, a few days after Napoleon's arrival on Elba. The Papal States were restored in the peace settlements of 1814–1815. Pius treated Maria Letizia Bonaparte and her

Thomas Lawrence's **Pope Pius VII** *(ca. 1818–1819) includes in the background Roman works of art looted by Napoleon's armies and returned to the papal city on his downfall. (Royal Collection Enterprises, Windsor Castle)*

half-brother, Joseph Fesch, generously during their exile in Rome after Napoleon's final defeat, but he could afford to be benevolent. He emerged from the Napoleonic era as a respected elder statesman and with an aura of martyrdom conferred by Napoleon's contemptuous treatment of him. In France and throughout Catholic Europe the Church enjoyed a new level of respect and dignity.

Related entries: Bernier, Abbé Etienne; Catholic Church; Concordat; Coronation; Fesch, Joseph; Organic Articles; Papacy; Papal States

Suggestions for further reading:
Hales, Edward Elton Young. 1962. *Napoleon and the Pope.* London: Eyre and Spottiswoode.
O'Dwyer, Margaret M. 1985. *The Papacy in the Age of Napoleon and the Restoration: Pius VII, 1800–1823.* Lanham, MD: University Press of America.

Plebiscites

The repeated use of plebiscites to confer an apparent popular legitimacy on the constitutions of 1800, 1802, and 1804 was one of the original features of the Napoleonic regime. But the results cannot be taken as a reliable guide to public opinion. Officially the plebiscite of February 1800 on the establishment of the consulate produced 3,011,007 votes in favor and 1562 votes against. But the voting was not secret; it was easily open to intimidation and manipulation; the rate of abstention was extremely high; and half a million votes were added to the "Yesses" for soldiers and sailors unable to vote in their home communes. Votes in the later plebiscites were uncannily similar to those of 1800.

Napoleon was the first figure to use "plebiscitary democracy" to legitimize dictatorship, a practice which has become all too familiar in the modern world. While theoretically acknowledging the fundamental principle of the Revolution that

sovereignty resided in the people, the plebiscite became the means by which the people abdicated its sovereignty. Napoleon could identify himself with "the will of the people" and brand opposition as "antinational." And the recognized organs of government and representation could be bypassed, creating a direct link between the dictator and the people similar to the mystical union supposed to exist in an absolute monarchy. Numerous dictators in the twentieth century have claimed a similar connection. Napoleon's statement as first consul, "In France there is but a single party and a single will," has a chilling sound to modern ears.

Related entries: Constitutions; Consulate; Empire

Suggestions for further reading:
Bergeron, Louis. 1981. *France under Napoleon.* Princeton: Princeton University Press.
Lyons, Martyn. 1994. *Napoleon Bonaparte and the Legacy of the French Revolution.* London: Macmillan.

Poland

Of all European countries Poland is probably where Napoleon's memory is most revered. The Poles are certainly the only people to sing about him in their national anthem, evoking the tragic adventure of Jan Henryk Dabrowski's Polish Legion: "We shall pass Vistula and Warta / We shall be Polish / Bonaparte has shown us how to win." This admiration is only partly deserved. Napoleon did establish the Duchy of Warsaw in 1807, encourage Polish exiles in 1806–1807 and again in 1812, and inspire the creation of the Polish Legions by Dabrowski and Jozef Poniatowski. But his attitude toward Polish national aspirations was governed by the state of his relations with Russia. Thus in 1806, while at war with Alexander I, he declared that: "It is in the interest of Europe, it is in the interest of

France that Poland should exist." But while allied with Russia in 1810 he wrote: "Poland exists only in the imagination of those who want to use it as a pretext for spinning dreams." However, he had changed his mind again when preparing for war with Russia in 1812, telling his ministers with some convenient amnesia: "It has always seemed to me that the restoration of Poland is desirable for all the Western powers" (Herold 1983, p. 118).

After the old kingdom of Poland finally ceased to exist following the Third Partition of 1795 between Austria, Prussia, and Russia, many Polish patriots in exile looked to revolutionary France for help. Dabrowski's Polish Legion fought under Napoleon in his first Italian campaign and as a Polish division of the *Grande Armée* against the Prussians at Jena and Friedland. Poniatowski's men freed Cracow from the Austrians in 1809, uniting the city to the Duchy of Warsaw. Other Poles, however, notably Alexander I's minister and confidant Prince Adam Czartoryski, hoped for a recognition of Polish nationality under Russian patronage.

The military events of 1813 left Russia in occupation of most of Poland, and Alexander wanted to proclaim a Kingdom of Poland, of which he would be sovereign. The matter of Poland was debated heatedly for three months at the Congress of Vienna. Eventually Austria retained Polish Galicia and Prussia recovered Poznania. Cracow became a "free city," and the rest of the Duchy of Warsaw, including the capital itself, became a kingdom to be ruled in perpetuity by the tsar of Russia. Alexander I issued a Constitutional Charter for "Congress Poland" in November 1815, providing for internal self-government, but the Poles were rapidly disillusioned. The first major anti-Russian revolt broke out in 1830, after which many Polish patriots once more sought refuge in France.

Related entries: Alexander I, Tsar of Russia; Austria; Poniatowski, Jozef, Prince; Prussia; Warsaw, Duchy of

Suggestions for further reading:
Davies, Norman. 1981. *God's Playground: A History of Poland.* 2 vols. Oxford: Clarendon Press.
Herold, J. Christopher. 1983. *The Horizon Book of the Age of Napoleon.* New York: American Heritage Publishing Co./Bonanza Books.
Nieuwazny, Andrzej. 1998. "Napoleon and Polish Identity," *History Today* 48 (May 1998), pp. 50–55.
Wandycz, Piotr. 1975. *The Lands of Partitioned Poland, 1795–1918.* Seattle: University of Washington Press.

Poniatowski, Jozef, Prince (1763–1813)

Napoleon's only non-French marshal is remembered as an enlightened patriotic reformer and Polish national hero. Born in Vienna, Poniatowski entered the Austrian army in 1780 and was then commissioned in the Polish army in 1789. But these were the years when Russia, Austria, and Prussia were engaged in the partition of Poland, and Poniatowski resigned from the army and was banished from Poland in 1792. In 1794 he joined Tadeusz Kosciuszko's rebellion against the Russians and went into retirement after its defeat.

There followed for Poniatowski years devoted to extravagant living and affairs of the heart, brought to an end by Napoleon's destruction of the Prussian army at Jena-Auerstädt. He commanded one of the three Polish divisions of the *Grande Armée* in the campaign of 1806–1807, and after the Treaty of Tilsit was made minister of war of the Duchy of Warsaw. His seizure of Galicia and liberation of Cracow in July 1809 made him a national hero. Poniatowski led the Fifth Corps in Napoleon's Russian campaign in 1812, where his Poles fought with a fervor motivated by national hatred. They took part in the storming of Smolensk and the battle of Borodino, but Poniatowski was seriously wounded during the retreat from Moscow when crossing the river Berezina.

On his recovery Napoleon named Poniatowski commander of the Eighth Corps in March 1813. He was wounded again in the actions preceding the battle of Leipzig and was given his marshal's baton on the first morning of this fateful "Battle of the Nations." On 18 October 1813, the final day of the battle, with half of his army dead or wounded, Poniatowski covered Napoleon's retreat. Twice wounded, he attempted to cross the river Elster on his horse, but was shot again and killed. In 1816 his remains were returned to Poland and buried in Cracow cathedral next to those of Kosciuszko.

Poniatowski's motto of "God, Honor, Fatherland" had forced him to serve Napoleon. Encouraged from childhood, despite a cosmopolitan ancestry, to think of himself as a prince of Poland, he showed great talent as a light cavalry officer, but was temperamentally unsuited for the subtleties of politics. Napoleon at first thought him an "inconsequential lightweight," later changed his opinion of his military capabilities, but still regarded him as potentially dangerous politically. He died in Napoleon's service, but his posthumous renown was as a champion of Poland.

Related entries: Borodino, Battle of; Leipzig, Battle of; Poland; Russian Campaign; Warsaw, Duchy of

Suggestions for further reading:
Davies, Norman. 1981. *God's Playground: A History of Poland*. 2 vols. Oxford: Clarendon Press.
De Lee, Nigel. 1987. "Poniatowski," in David G. Chandler, ed., *Napoleon's Marshals*. New York: Macmillan.

Population

When Mme. de Staël asked Napoleon: "What kind of woman would you love the most?" he replied: "The one who would have the most children" (McLynn 1997, p. 163). But Napoleon's wish for increasing numbers of young Frenchmen to swell his armies turned out to be an illusion. The total population of France rose from about 28 million in 1789 to about 30 million in 1815, but its share of the total European population was falling, as other countries grew faster.

The age of marriage had begun to fall during the Revolution, helped by more liberal legislation on family matters, but without any corresponding rise in the number of births. The rule of equal inheritance in Napoleon's Civil Code did not encourage large families, whereas in the longer term knowledge of contraception and detachment from Catholicism in many regions helped to promote smaller families. As the birth rate fell, so did the death rate, but this was a European phenomenon aided by advances in medicine and by the fact that food shortages, although they still occurred, were less deadly than they had been under the ancien régime. The fall in the birth rate, on the other hand, was as yet specifically French, only occurring later in other countries.

The geographical distribution of the population remained unchanged in the Napoleonic period. The urban growth of the eighteenth century continued, but places with more than 2,000 inhabitants still accounted for less than a fifth of the total population, and the French people were still not very mobile, most migration being purely seasonal in pursuit of work.

War losses under Napoleon, probably amounting to between 900,000 and a million men, had the effect of reducing demographic vitality in the long term by reducing the numbers of men of an age to have children. The emperor's wish for large numbers of patriotically fertile women could neither make up for this lack, nor hold back ineluctable long-term changes.

Related entries: Civil Code; Peasants

Suggestions for further reading:
Bergeron, Louis. 1981. *France under Napoleon*. Princeton: Princeton University Press.

McLynn, Frank. 1997. *Napoleon*. London: Jonathan Cape.

Portalis, Jean Étienne Marie (1745–1807)

*O*ne of the most distinguished lawyers in his native Provence before the Revolution, the pious and learned Portalis was an outstanding example of how Napoleon aimed to use the best available talents regardless of their political past. Returning from exile in Switzerland after the coup of 18 Brumaire, Portalis was a member of the commission that drafted the Civil Code and participated in the negotiations with Pope Pius VII leading to the Concordat of 1801. Napoleon appointed him to the Council of State, charged with church affairs, and in 1804 made minister of ecclesiastical affairs, presiding over a full-blown bureaucratic department enforcing Napoleon's desire to subject all religions in France to his will while restoring normal life for worshipers. Portalis died in office in 1807, having done much to reconcile the Catholic faithful to Napoleon's domineering rule.

Related entries: Catholic Church; Civil Code; Concordat; Council of State

Suggestions for further reading:
Church, Clive H. 1981. *Revolution and Red Tape: The French Ministerial Bureaucracy 1770–1850*. Oxford: Clarendon Press.

Portugal

*T*he Kingdom of Portugal maintained its independence from Spain and Napoleon at great human cost, and Portuguese armies played a crucial role in his defeat in the Peninsular War. Napoleon viewed Portugal as a satellite of Great Britain, and indeed the Anglo-Portuguese alliance had helped considerably in preserving national independence in the late eighteenth century. The Portuguese regent, Dom João, ruling for his mother, the insane Queen Maria I, was forced into war against a Spain supported by France in 1801. In the peace settlement the French plenipotentiary, Jean Lannes, extracted lucrative trade concessions and subsidies from Portugal.

When in 1807 Portugal refused to apply Napoleon's Continental System in full, France and Spain agreed on a plan for the partition of "England's oldest ally." A Franco-Spanish army under Andoche Junot occupied Lisbon and central Portugal, and João and the rest of the royal family escaped to Brazil, Portugal's richest colony. However, following the Spanish uprising of May 1808, Portuguese nationalists rose against French rule. A British expeditionary force landed at Mondego Bay in August 1808. Junot was defeated at Vimeiro and forced to evacuate the country by the Convention of Cintra. The regency was re-established, a British army remained in Portugal, and a new Portuguese army raised with British finance and expertise, supervised by a British commander in chief, William Carr Beresford.

A second French invasion in 1809 led by Nicolas Soult was driven out by the Anglo-Portuguese forces. But Napoleon's most determined effort to subdue Portugal in 1810–1811 was only repulsed at great cost. A scorched earth policy, guerrilla warfare, and the lines of Torres Vedras, constructed to protect Lisbon, allowed the duke of Wellington as supreme commander of the armies to repel French forces led by Soult in the south and André Masséna in the north. Anglo-Portuguese collaboration continued until the French were driven out of the peninsula in 1813, but the struggle left Portugal impoverished. The country remained under the effective control of a Council of Regency headed by Beresford until 1820, when a liberal revolt led to the return of the regent as King João VI.

Related entries: Guerrilla Warfare; Junot, Andoche; Masséna, André; Peninsular War; Soult, Nicolas Jean de Dieu; Spain; Wellington, Duke of

Suggestions for further reading:
Gates, David. 1986. *The Spanish Ulcer: A History of the Peninsular War.* London: Allen and Unwin.
Horward, Donald D. 1989. "Wellington and the Defence of Portugal," *International History Review* 11, pp. 55–67.
Livermore, Harold V. 1966. *A New History of Portugal.* Cambridge: Cambridge University Press.

Prefects

Appointed to impose the will of central government in the departments, prefects were also the eyes and ears of the government in the localities they administered and the keystone of Napoleonic administration in France and the annexed territories. The rule that prefects would never be appointed to the department of their birth was only rarely ignored, though many came from the same region and locals were recruited in conquered lands. The first ninety-seven prefects were appointed in 1800, from a list supervised by Lucien Bonaparte, and their number reached 130 under the empire at its largest in 1810. The original appointees were mostly experienced administrators of bourgeois origin, though over time more nobles were appointed, being especially preferred in the conquered territories.

The creation of the prefectoral corps was one of Napoleon's most lasting achievements. Within a short period of time the new system provided stable, experienced, and increasingly professional administration. A bureaucratic hierarchy was established, and prefects could advance from smaller to more important departments: those with major population centers were considered the top class, and the prefect of the most important department, the Seine (which included Paris) enjoyed quasi-ministerial status. The prefects also represented the Napoleonic ideal of a fusion of noble and bourgeois into a new elite of notables. The prefectoral system survives in France to this day, and paradoxically, although a number of Napoleon's appointees owed their positions to the patronage of prominent ministers or the Beauharnais family, under successive regimes since 1815 the corps has usually been more politicized than it was in Napoleon's day.

Related entries: Centralization; Empire; Local Government; Nobility; Notables

Suggestions for further reading:
Bergeron, Louis. 1981. *France under Napoleon.* Princeton: Princeton University Press.
Chapman, Brian. 1955. *The Prefects and Provincial France.* London: George Allen and Unwin.
Holtman, Robert B. 1967. *The Napoleonic Revolution.* Philadelphia: Lippincott.
Whitcomb, Edward A. 1974. "Napoleon's Prefects," *American Historical Review* 79, pp. 1089–1118.

Press

Napoleon recognized the power of newspapers, made use of them for his own propaganda, and controlled them through rigorous censorship. As emperor he demanded loyalty, discipline, and obedience from the Parisian political press, and in 1811 eliminated all but four newspapers: the *Moniteur, Journal de l'Empire, Gazette de France,* and *Journal de Paris.* Publications in all areas under his control were subject to similar restrictions, and journalism as a profession had nothing to thank him for.

However, nonpolitical publishing thrived under Napoleon's rule in France. Scientific and literary journals, mostly in Paris, were left unmolested so long as they concentrated narrowly on their particular interests. At the same time, Napoleon's insistence that his proclamations and various legal actions should be recorded provided a source of revenue for new publications in the provinces. The provincial papers, authorized and kept under surveillance by the prefects, published biased versions of political events to the glory of the imperial family and the empire. This function diluted their local character, but helped to lay the foundations for a more genuine provincial press to emerge in the nineteenth century.

Related entries: Censorship; Propaganda

Suggestions for further reading:
Allen, James Smith. 1992. *In the Public Eye: A History of Reading in Modern France, 1800–1940.* Princeton: Princeton University Press.
Arnold, Eric A. 1979. *Fouché, Napoleon and the General Police.* Washington, DC: University Press of America.
Holtman, Robert B. 1950. *Napoleonic Propaganda.* Baton Rouge: Louisiana State University Press.

Pressburg, Treaty of (26 December 1805)

*T*his treaty imposed on Austria by Napoleon after his victory at Austerlitz recognized French possession of the Italian territories of Piedmont, Parma, and Piacenza. Austria also ceded Venice, Istria, and Dalmatia to the Kingdom of Italy and recognized Napoleon as king of Italy. The Habsburgs lost their western possessions. France's ally Bavaria gained the Tyrol, Vorarlberg, the bishoprics of Brixen and Trent, Eichstädt, Passau, Lindau, and Augsburg, while Württemberg became a kingdom and Baden a grand duchy.

Related entries: Bavaria, Kingdom of; Italy, Kingdom of

Suggestions for further reading:
Arnold, Eric A., ed. 1994. *A Documentary Survey of Napoleonic France.* Lanham, MD: University Press of America. pp. 207–215.

Ross, Steven T. 1981. *European Diplomatic History, 1789–1815.* Malabar, FL: Krieger.

Privateer War

*G*iven the Royal Navy's dominance of the seas, commerce raiding by privateers, privately owned vessels licensed by government authorities, also known as corsairs, became Napoleon's principal weapon against British maritime power. In conjunction with the Continental System, privateer raids operating from the western ports of France had a significant effect on British international trade. Apart from the Channel, the areas most at risk from privateers included the Baltic, the coasts of Spain, and the Caribbean. In response the Royal Navy organized escort convoys and patrolled home waters with "Q-ships," armed vessels disguised as merchantmen.

In theory privateering was governed by complex international conventions, but these were largely ignored, and the consequent abuses and lawlessness of the corsairs led to persistent accusations of piracy on all sides. French privateers recruited seamen from all over Europe and became popular heroes of the war, even if Napoleon himself seemed to give the impression that recognition of their piratical activities was rather beneath his dignity. He did, however, try to appease neutrals by declaring that French actions against neutral shipping were exceptional measures for which claims of indemnity could be entered after the return of peace. The privateer war played a vital role in ensuring that France was never completely cut off from supplies such as northern European naval stores, and privateers remained active right up to the end of the wars. In the absence of a serious French challenge to British naval superiority, they were essential in keeping Napoleon's war machine operating, even if this was apparently not always appreciated by the emperor himself.

Related entries: Continental System; Naval Warfare

Suggestions for further reading:
Crowhurst, Patrick. 1989. *The French War on Trade: Privateering, 1793–1815*. Aldershot, England: Scolar.

Propaganda

In 1812 a British *Memorial Respecting the Present State of the British Press* lamented, "There is just one circumstance in which the little Corsican usurper has got the start of us." This was Napoleon's propaganda use of the press: "It is a mortifying truth that he has done more mischief by means of the *Moniteur of Paris* than he has ever effected by the united efforts of the cannon and the sword." As well as stringent censorship, Napoleon used all possible media to shape public opinion.

From the days of his Italian campaigns he used army bulletins to inform public opinion of his triumphs and build up his own image. The military bulletins became his major propaganda instrument, castigating the enemy and strengthening morale on the home front. They "might, with not too much imagination," writes the historian Geoffrey Best, "be seen as the start of the practice which in course of time, as media development made it possible, produced President Roosevelt's fireside chats and the dictators' radio speeches" (Best 1982, p. 119). They enabled Napoleon to be the first sovereign to speak directly and frequently to his subjects.

Newspapers were inevitably Napoleon's main propaganda instrument, with the *Moniteur universel* as the official paper for political affairs. Subsidies and news bulletins given to other papers and orders to provincial papers to copy the *Moniteur* completed the news management. He did not hesitate to use the "big lie," most notoriously in the failure of the Russian campaign, and had rumors circulated in an attempt both to influence opinion and to determine its condition.

Napoleon used all available media to supplement his newspaper propaganda. Pamphlets were used more than handbills or posters. The theater, festivals, and church services helped communication with the illiterate. Napoleon frequently selected personally the topics to be dealt with, and a great deal of the propaganda centered on the emperor himself and the creation of the Napoleonic legend. Musicians, artists, and writers were employed with an eye to history to celebrate the outstanding events of his career. Images of Napoleon and the emblems of the empire flooded the country from drawing rooms to humble peasant dwellings.

Assessing the effectiveness of Napoleonic propaganda is difficult if not impossible. His first appeal was to his soldiers and here he remained a master. But whether it was as efficacious among the mass of the people is a thorny question. Certainly his enemies would not have been so concerned about his propaganda if they had not been worried about its effectiveness. With France almost constantly at war the heightened emotional temperature probably worked in Napoleon's favor. But he was unwilling to delegate authority in this area, and the conditions of the age did not allow the kind of blanket propaganda we are familiar with in the twentieth century or the sophisticated activities of modern "spin-doctors." And in the long run events overtake even the best propaganda: from 1812 onward they turned irrevocably against Napoleon.

Related entries: Censorship; Empire Style; Imperial Catechism; Napoleonic Legend; Personality, Cult of; Press

Suggestions for further reading:
Best, Geoffrey. 1982. *War and Society in Revolutionary Europe, 1770–1870*. London: Fontana.

François Gérard's **Portrait of Napoleon in Coronation Robes** *(1805) presents Napoleon as emperor in all his majesty. He wears the coronation robes designed by Jacques–Louis David and is surrounded by the emblems of power: the orb, the scepter, and the hand of justice. (Giraudon/Art Resource)*

Holtman, Robert B. 1950. *Napoleonic Propaganda.* Baton Rouge: Louisiana State University Press.

Mathews, Joseph J. 1950. "Napoleon's Military Bulletins," *Journal of Modern History* 22, pp. 137–144.

Roberts, Warren. 1989. *Jacques-Louis David: Revolutionary Artist.* Chapel Hill: University of North Carolina Press.

Wilson-Smith, Timothy. 1996. *Napoleon and His Artists.* London: Constable.

Protestants

France's Protestant, predominantly Calvinist, minority had been granted equal rights in 1787 in the dying days of the ancien régime, and during the Revolution were mostly identified with the revolutionary cause, leading to hostility and religious conflict, especially in southern France. Napoleon, having signed the Concordat of 1801 ordering the lives of French Catholics, wished for a similar agreement with the Protestants. The Organic Articles for the Protestants, negotiated between Jean Portalis and a selection of Protestant notables, were promulgated on 8 April 1802.

As with Catholics and Jews, the legislation for Protestants sought to regularize the churches and religious worship under state supervision. The Calvinist community was divided into congregations of 6,000 souls, each to be governed by a pastor in collaboration with elders chosen from among the highest paying taxpayers. The traditional Calvinist church order was thereby modified to bring it into line with Napoleon's centralized, notable-dominated France. The less numerous Lutheran congregations, mostly to be found in Alsace and Lorraine, were to be supervised by directories, most of whose members were named by Napoleon. The government reserved a right of veto over the appointment of new pastors and over alterations in religious doctrine. In 1804 Protestant pastors were salaried by the state. Protestants gladly accepted their new position within Napoleon's state, which seemed to guarantee them against persecution and granted them an official and equal status within French society. They were to be found in numbers in the Napoleonic elite as generals, bankers, and senators.

Related entries: Portalis, Jean Étienne Marie

Suggestions for further reading:
Arnold, Eric A., ed. 1994. *A Documentary Survey of Napoleonic France.* Lanham, MD: University Press of America, pp. 98–104.

Poland, B. C. 1957. *French Protestantism and the French Revolution: A Study in Church and State, Thought and Religion, 1685–1815.* Princeton: Princeton University Press.

Prussia

The Kingdom of Prussia had risen to great power status under Frederick the Great between 1740 and 1786 and had challenged the hegemony of the Austrian Habsburgs in Germany. The basis of Prussian strength lay in the army created by Frederick and in his enlightened reforms, including an independent judiciary, religious toleration, and an honest and effective civil service. But he had not changed a rigid class system that erected insurmountable barriers between the nobility and the rest of the population and left many peasants living in hereditary subjection to their landlords.

Frederick's successor, his nephew Frederick William II (reigned 1786–1797) joined the First Coalition against revolutionary France in 1792, but the war exposed unsuspected weaknesses in the Prussian army. After making peace in 1795, Frederick William showed more zeal in completing the partition of Poland with Austria and Russia than he did in fighting France. The Prussian state reached its greatest extension to that date and secured eleven years of peace with France, but the new king, Frederick William III, found his halfhearted attempts at reform blocked by the all-powerful nobility. He did, however, seal a new friendship with Russia by the Potsdam Oath of 1805.

It was evident that sooner or later Prussia would have to stand up against Napoleon's expansionism. But when the country belatedly went to war in 1806 the weaknesses of the Prussian state and army were cruelly exposed. Defeat in the battles of Jena-Auerstädt was followed in 1807 by the virtual dismemberment of the kingdom in the Treaty of Tilsit. Only Alexander I's desire to maintain a buffer state between Russia and Napoleon's empire saved Prussia from extinction. But the disaster did provide reformers with the opportunity to regenerate the Prussian state and army. Ministers led by Karl vom Stein and K. A. von Hardenberg created properly functional ministries, replacing government through personal advisers. Legal distinctions between classes were removed, serfdom was abolished, and the educational system modernized. Gerhard von Scharnhorst, August von Gneisenau, and their supporters rebuilt an army with careers open to talent, conscription, and promotion based on merit. But Frederick William still hesitated about committing himself against Napoleon until the emperor met his nemesis in Russia in 1812.

A Prussian corps under Yorck von Wartenburg was attached to Napoleon's forces during the campaign in Russia, but on 30 December 1812 Yorck concluded his own peace with the Russians by the Convention of Tauroggen. The new alliance was sealed by the Treaty of Kalisch, and the revitalized Prussian army proved its value in the campaign of 1813 and the battle of Leipzig before advancing into France in 1814. Then the presence of Gebhard von Blücher's army at Waterloo gave Prussia additional bargaining power at the Congress of Vienna.

In the peace settlement Prussia recovered the territories lost in 1807 except those in Poland and acquired parts of Saxony, Westphalia, and various smaller territories along the Rhineland frontier with France. Prussia was thus well prepared for industrialization and for becoming the nucleus of German nationalism in the nineteenth century. However, its eventual success in opposing Napoleon put an end to further social and political reforms. There was no move toward representative government, and Prussia retained its image as a caste-ridden society dominated by the military.

Related entries: Blücher, Gebhard Leberecht von; Coalitions; Frederick William III, King of Prussia; Germany, Campaigns in; Gneisenau, August Wilhelm Anton Neidhardt von; Jena-Auerstädt, Battles of; Kalisch, Treaty of; Leipzig, Battle of; Louise of Mecklenburg, Queen of Prussia; Nationalism; Quadruple Alliance; Revolutionary Wars; Scharnhorst, Gerhard Johann David von; Tilsit, Treaty of; Vienna, Congress of; Yorck von Wartenburg, Johann David Ludwig, Count

Suggestions for further reading:
Craig, Gordon A. 1955. *The Politics of the Prussian Army.* New York: Oxford University Press.
Gray, Marion W. 1986. *Prussia in Transition: Society and Politics under the Stein Reform Ministry of 1808.* Philadelphia: American Philosophical Society.
Haffner, Sebastian. 1980. *The Rise and Fall of Prussia.* London: Weidenfeld and Nicolson.
Shanahan, William O. 1945. *Prussian Military Reforms 1786–1813.* New York: Columbia University Press.
Sheehan, James J. 1989. *German History, 1770–1866.* Oxford: Clarendon Press.
Simon, Walter M. 1955. *The Failure of the Prussian Reform Movement.* Ithaca, NY: Cornell University Press.

Pyramids, Battle of the (21 July 1798)

The victory over the Mamelukes, which secured Napoleon's control of the Lower Nile during his Egyptian campaign, was a thoroughly one-sided affair. The Mameluke cavalry under Murad Bey were totally ineffective against the four French divisions drawn up in squares by Napoleon. Unable to break the squares and suffering heavy losses from French artillery and musket fire, the Mamelukes retired to the south, leaving their irregular infantry to be routed by superior French organization and firepower. Cairo surrendered to Napoleon the next day.

Related entries: Egyptian Campaign

Suggestions for further reading:
Barthorp, Michael. 1978. *Napoleon's Egyptian Campaigns, 1798–1801.* London: Osprey.
Herold, J. Christopher. 1962. *Bonaparte in Egypt.* New York: Harper and Row.

Quadruple Alliance

Signed on the same day as the second Treaty of Paris (20 November 1815) the Quadruple Alliance pledged Britain, Austria, Russia, and Prussia to come to each other's assistance if the treaty were violated. The members of the Alliance, joined by France in 1818, would meet in conference to safeguard the peace and stability of Europe whenever they were threatened. It is an indication of the kind of new thinking imposed on diplomats by the failure to unite consistently in opposition to Napoleon.

Related entries: Paris, Treaties of

Suggestions for further reading:
Ross, Steven T. 1981. *European Diplomatic History, 1789–1815*. Malabar, FL: Krieger.

Quatre-Bras, Battle of (16 June 1815)

In this preliminary engagement to the battle of Waterloo, fought on the same day as the battle of Ligny, Marshal Michel Ney fought an indecisive encounter against the duke of Wellington, who was attempting to concentrate his British and Dutch forces. Ney failed to receive the reinforcements necessary to do more than dispute the ground around the crossing of the Namur-Nivelles road and the main route from Brussels to Charleroi. Wellington, on hearing of Napoleon's victory at Ligny, withdrew toward Brussels and the defensive position of Waterloo.

Related entries: Hundred Days; Ney, Michel; Waterloo, Battle of; Wellington, Duke of

Suggestions for further reading:
Brett James, Antony. 1966. *The Hundred Days: Napoleon's Last Campaign from Eyewitness Accounts*. New York: Macmillan.
Chandler, David G. 1980. *Waterloo: The Hundred Days*. London: Osprey.

R

Récamier, Jeanne Françoise Julie Adélaïde (1777–1849)

Juliette Bernard, daughter of a notary of Lyon, married Jean Récamier, a rich banker and friend of her parents, in 1793 at the age of fifteen. It was a marriage in name only, and rumor had it that Récamier was really her father. As hostess of a literary and political salon under the Directory she came into contact with the leading figures of the day, a connection strengthened in 1798 by her friendship with Germaine de Staël. But her rejection of the advances of Lucien Bonaparte and friendship with opposition figures led to problems with the Napoleonic regime. Napoleon ordered her to leave Paris in 1805, and she went into exile in Italy, returning to Paris to reopen her salon after the Restoration. The German-born Marie-Anne de Gérando said of her: "The French want only youth, charm, pleasures and vivacity in the sex they so spoil. Madame Récamier is the very embodiment of this sort of person" (Woolf 1991, p. 216).

Related entries: Empire Style

Suggestions for further reading:
Trouncer, Margaret. 1949. *Madame Récamier.* London: Macdonald.
Williams, Hugh Noel. 1907. *Madame Récamier and Her Friends.* London and New York: Harper & Bros.

Woolf, Stuart. 1991. *Napoleon's Integration of Europe.* London and New York: Routledge.

Regnaud de Saint Jean d'Angély, Michel, Comte (1762–1819)

As president of the section of the interior of Napoleon's Council of State, Regnaud was at the center of power for over fourteen years. A moderate politician in the early years of the Revolution, he first met Napoleon when acting as administrator of the hospitals of the Army of Italy in 1796. In 1799 after the coup of 18 Brumaire he became a member of the Council of State, president of its section of the interior in 1801, and in 1804 *procureur* of the imperial high court and secretary to the imperial family.

Widely seen as the most accomplished orator of the age, Regnaud was also skilled in recognizing the essentials of a problem and proposing a rational solution. He could present Napoleon's arguments, no matter how specious, persuasively. Thus he drafted the speeches given by Napoleon and Joséphine when their divorce was proclaimed to the world. But his relentless administrative activity was mostly concerned with getting laws, decrees, and regulations drafted and put into practice effectively. As a member of the special Council of Adminis-

François Gérard portrays **Madame Récamier** *modeling the perfect Empire style, at once tantalizing and demure. Amid classical décor she reclines in a simple white dress and a golden shawl, with feet and shoulders uncovered. She combines studied perfection with coquetry as the perfect society hostess. (Giraudon/Art Resource)*

tration of the Interior, he knew more about the functioning of the Ministry of the Interior than any of his successive ministers and kept a watchful eye on its work. And if necessary he could use his oratorical skills to defend draft laws before the Legislative Body and the Tribunate.

Regnaud also personally reviewed the annual budgets of the departments of France and of all the towns, several thousand in all, whose annual revenue exceeded 10,000 francs. Napoleon's success in tight budgetary control owed much to his indefatigable exertions. At the same time he came to be seen as the most influential member of the Council of State, calmly considering all the affairs that came before its regular twice- or thrice-weekly meetings. As a proponent of well-informed moderate government Regnaud provided a counterweight to more conspicuous but slippery figures such as Joseph Fouché or Charles Maurice de Talleyrand. In this role he played an essential part in the relatively smooth functioning of Napoleon's internal administration.

Related entries: Centralization; Council of State; Finance; Local Government

Suggestions for further reading:
Freedeman, Charles E. 1961. *The Conseil d'Etat in Modern France.* New York: Columbia University Press.

Régnier, Claude (1736–1814)

As minister of justice between 1802 and 1813 and president of the commission of claims of the Council of State between 1806 and 1813, Régnier did much to ensure that the rule of law and impartial justice remained a reality in Napoleon's France. He had been president of the Council of Ancients under the Directory but supported the coup of 18 Brumaire and was subsequently involved in the drafting of the Civil Code. As minister of justice his freedom of action was circumscribed by the watchful eye of arch-chancellor Jean-Jacques-Régis de Cambacérès, but on the Council of State he ensured that citizens with a grievance against the state officials or courts got a fair hearing and that the facts of each case were correctly established. This kind of oversight helped to ensure that Napoleon's highly centralized administration could not act in an arbitrary fashion with impunity. Thanks to Régnier's probity and effectiveness, the role of court of appeal for citizens was to become the chief function of the Council of State under post-Napoleonic French regimes. Régnier retired as minister of justice in 1813 and died a few months after Napoleon's first abdication.

Related entries: Centralization; Council of State; Law, Codification of

Suggestions for further reading:
Church, Clive H. 1981. *Revolution and Red Tape: The French Ministerial Bureaucracy 1770–1850.* Oxford: Clarendon Press.
Freedeman, Charles E. 1961. *The Conseil d'Etat in Modern France.* New York: Columbia University Press.

Revolutionary Wars

Conflict between revolutionary France and the monarchies of Europe began when France declared war on Austria, soon joined by the partners of the First Coalition, in 1792. The victories of the mass French armies (large armies made up of conscripts or volunteers, as opposed to the usual small professional armies) at Valmy and Jemappes amazed Europe and ensured the survival of the Revolution. Prussia, Spain, and the Netherlands made peace with France in 1795, leaving Austria and Piedmont-Sardinia to sustain the fight on the Continent. Napoleon's first Italian campaign of 1796–1797 forced Piedmont to withdraw, and he compelled Austria to accept the terms of the Treaty of Campo Formio.

Napoleon's Egyptian campaign of 1798, designed to strike at British interests in the East, compelled William Pitt the Younger to organize a new coalition, with Britain allied with Russia, Austria, Naples, Portugal, and the Ottoman Empire. Fighting resumed in Italy, with the coalition forces commanded by Alexander Suvorov, but quarrels among the Allies led to Russia's withdrawal. Napoleon, as first consul after the coup of 18 Brumaire, had to bring the war to a conclusion. His victory at Marengo on 14 June 1800 and that of Jean Moreau at Hohenlinden on 3 December led to the collapse of the coalition. Austria made peace by the Treaty of Lunéville in 1801 and Britain by the Peace of Amiens in 1802. It would not be long, however, before Napoleon's ambitions led to a renewal of conflict, and the new series of wars would bear his name, rather than that of the Revolution.

Related entries: Amiens, Peace of; Austria; Campo Formio, Treaty of; Coalitions; Directory; Egyptian Campaign; Great Britain; Italian Campaigns; Lunéville, Treaty of; Ottoman Empire; Prussia; Spain; Switzerland

Suggestions for further reading:
Bertaud, Jean-Paul. 1988. *The Army of the French Revolution.* Princeton: Princeton University Press.
Lefebvre, Georges. 1967. *The French Revolution from 1793 to 1799.* London: Routledge and Kegan Paul.

Rivoli, Battle of (14 January 1797)

The last major battle of Napoleon's first Italian campaign prevented the Austrians from relieving their large force trapped under siege in Mantua. Despite the French victories at Bassano and Arcola, the Austrians, coming south from Germany, launched a two-pronged attack toward Mantua. Napoleon, ignoring the weaker of the two forces, turned against the larger contingent and defeated it at Rivoli before turning on the smaller force near Padua. The starving Austrian garrison in Mantua surrendered early in February 1797.

Related entries: Italian Campaigns; Mantua

Suggestions for further reading:
Marshall-Cornwall, Sir James. 1987. "Massena," in David G. Chandler, ed., *Napoleon's Marshals.* New York: Macmillan.

Roederer, Pierre Louis (1754–1835)

Journalist, economist, financier, political theorist, and administrator, Roederer was the only *idéologue* to support Napoleon consistently, even though he found many of his own ideas thwarted. Born in Metz, the son of a magistrate, Roederer had sat in the National Assembly between 1789 and 1791, gone into hiding during the Terror, and emerged under the Directory as editor of the *Journal de Paris* and a member of the *Institut National.* During this period he elaborated the liberal political and economic ideas to which he always adhered. Roederer supported the coup of 18 Brumaire, and during the consulate Napoleon confided in him frequently, most often after dinner; he defended the regime before his fellow *idéologues.*

Roederer's respect for constitutional forms made him the natural choice to draft the resolution inviting Napoleon to assume the life consulate with due care and attention. He was appointed president of the Section of the Interior of the Council of State and director general of public instruction, but his ambitious plans for secondary education were never implemented. Roederer's disagreements with Jean Antoine

Chaptal and open and justified distrust of Joseph Fouché led to his dismissal from his posts in 1802, though he was appointed to the Senate by way of compensation.

Roederer was given more scope for implementing his ideas as minister of finance in the Kingdom of Naples under Joseph Bonaparte between 1806 and 1808. He instituted a proper tax-collecting bureaucracy to replace tax-farming, replaced numerous direct taxes with a single one on land and industrial property, simplified indirect taxes, established a national bank, and began liquidating the public debt. The essence of his reforms remained in place after the restoration of the Bourbon rulers of Naples in 1815.

Roederer continued to serve Napoleon as administrator of the Grand Duchy of Berg from 1810 to 1813, imperial commissioner in Strasbourg in 1813–1814, and during the Hundred Days as commissioner in southeast France. He retired from public life in 1815, devoting himself to writing histories and his memoirs, in which he recorded a number of his conversations with Napoleon for posterity.

Related entries: Council of State; Education; *Idéologues;* Naples, Kingdom of

Suggestions for further reading:
Connelly, Owen. 1965. *Napoleon's Satellite Kingdoms.* New York: Free Press.
Margerison, Kenneth. 1983. *P.-L. Roederer, Political Thought and Practice during the French Revolution.* Philadelphia: American Philosophical Society.
Roederer, Pierre Louis. 1989. *The Spirit of the Revolution of 1789 and Other Writings on the Revolutionary Epoch.* Ed. and trans. Murray Forsyth. Aldershot, England: Scolar.

Romanticism

At first sight, the revolt against classical formality and restraint and the unbridled expression of the emotions represented by the Romantic movement in the arts stands in violent opposition to the neoclassicism favored under Napoleon. Yet the turbulence and drama of Napoleon's career and his apparent "shaking of the world" by the force of his imagination complicated his relationship to an inconsistent cultural creed whose relationship to politics depended very much on circumstance. The example of Jacques-Louis David exemplifies how the Romantic revolt could be harnessed for Napoleonic propaganda. As David moved away from the cool neoclassicism of his revolutionary works, the figure of Napoleon provided an ideal subject for a more imaginative, even fantastic form of expression.

Romanticism as the expression of the deepest emotions of the human soul could take many forms, but it was clearly opposed to the ordered rationality of the Napoleonic state and Napoleon's imperialism in Europe. The principal early exponents of literary Romanticism in France, Mme. de Staël and François René de Chateaubriand, both opposed Napoleon vehemently. In Germany the main current of Romanticism became associated with emotional nationalism, harking back to an idealized Middle Ages and hoping to sway German feeling against Napoleonic domination. Neither Romantic individualism nor the medievalism of Walter Scott nor the Catholicism of Chateaubriand would have much appeal to supporters of the last of the Enlightened Despots.

Yet Napoleon's defeat and exile and the blanket of conformity imposed upon Europe after 1815 helped to turn Romanticism against the traditional established order. The growing Napoleonic legend held a particular appeal to French Romantics like Stendhal and Victor Hugo, for whom Bonaparte's towering ambition became a symbol of opposition to mediocrity and the "conquering bourgeoisie" of the Restoration period. The fact that the ruling class of notables was largely Napoleon's creation seemed to pass them by. An idealized

Anne-Louis Girodet's extraordinary painting **Ossian Receiving the Spirits of French Heroes** *(1802) shows the bard Ossian greeting Jean-Baptiste Kléber, Louis Desaix, and other French soldiers killed in Napoleon's Egyptian and Italian campaigns into the Celtic "Morren," home of immortal heroes. (Erich Lessing/Art Resource)*

image of the exiled Napoleon, brooding godlike on his Atlantic rock, came to have a singular appeal, turning Romantics from royalism to Bonapartism. When allied, as in Hugo's case, to a growing awareness of social injustice, Romantic Bonapartism could become a potent force, but one likely in time to move in a more democratic or socialistic direction and away from the myth of the Great Man.

Related entries: Chateaubriand, François René, Vicomte de; David, Jacques-Louis; Napoleonic Legend; Staël, Germaine de; Stendhal

Suggestions for further reading:
Bainbridge, Simon. 1995. *Napoleon and English Romanticism.* Cambridge: Cambridge University Press.
Friedlaender, Walter. 1952. *David to Delacroix.* Cambridge: Harvard University Press.
Harvey, A. D. 1998. "Napoleon—the Myth," *History Today* 48 (January 1998), pp. 27–32.

Honour, Hugh. 1979. *Romanticism*. London: Allen Lane.

Porter, Roy, and Mikulás Teich, eds. 1988. *Romanticism in National Context*. Cambridge: Cambridge University Press.

Talmon, J. L. 1967. *Romanticism and Revolt: Europe 1815–1848*. London: Thames and Hudson.

Roustan Raza (1780–1845)

Napoleon's Mameluke bodyguard was born in Tbilisi; he was kidnapped and sold into slavery before being recruited to the Mamelukes and in 1799 given to Bonaparte in Cairo. He slept on a mattress outside Napoleon's bedroom and accompanied him on campaign as his personal gun bearer, sleeping at the entrance of his tent. After the first abdication in April 1814 Roustan refused to follow Napoleon to Elba, and during the Hundred Days was imprisoned at Vincennes. Under the July Monarchy after 1830 he was given the position of postmaster at Dourdan, where he spent the rest of his days.

Royalists

Moderate royalist opinions were doubtless widespread in Napoleonic France, including within the heart of the administration, as Napoleon was determined to use the most talented people available, regardless of their politics. The absolutely irreconcilable, those who never saw Napoleon as anything other than another upstart general, were either in exile or reduced to shadowy plots and intrigues. Popular royalism could find little expression except in *chouannerie*. Napoleon's reconciliation with the Catholic Church through the Concordat reduced royalism among the clergy to support for draft dodgers and deserters or for the *chouan* bands of western France.

The effectiveness of the police under Joseph Fouché and later A. J. M. R. Savary kept a lid on royalist plotting after the failure of the Opera Plot of 1800, the conspiracy around Georges Cadoudal in 1804, and the subsequent kidnapping and execution of the duke of Enghien. Royalist would-be conspirators could hold clandestine meetings in their drawing rooms and transmit political news while on apparent social calls, but moving to the stage of taking action was much more difficult. The only really organized royalist body, the Chevaliers de la Foi (Knights of the Faith), had members throughout the administration and in the National Guard, and avoided detection by creating their own courier system, safe from the prying eyes of the police. But their activities never went beyond some discreet propaganda and attempts to curb the enthusiasm of zealous Bonapartist or republican colleagues. Napoleon's downfall was the result of military defeat and the changing of sides by his former closest allies, not of the shadowy actions of his permanent enemies.

Related entries: Cadoudal, Georges; Catholic Church; *Chouannerie; Émigrés;* Louis XVIII, King of France; Opera Plot; Opposition Movements

Suggestions for further reading:
Godechot, Jacques. 1981. *The Counter-Revolution: Doctrine and Action, 1789–1804*. Princeton: Princeton University Press.

Lewis, Gwynne. 1978. *The Second Vendée: The Continuity of Counter-Revolution in the Department of the Gard, 1789–1815*. New York: Oxford University Press.

Lyons, Martyn. 1994. *Napoleon Bonaparte and the Legacy of the French Revolution*. London: Macmillan.

Sutherland, D. M. G. 1985. *France, 1789–1815: Revolution and Counter-Revolution*. London: Fontana.

Rural Code

Napoleon wished to complete his codification of the law with a Rural

Code, but it was only ever published in incomplete form in 1814. The most influential changes in rural society, the abolition of feudalism and consolidation of private property rights, had been achieved under the Revolution and by Napoleon's Civil Code. However, the absence of a Rural Code meant that the legal and customary framework of peasant life continued to vary widely in the different regions of France.

Related entries: Law, Codification of; Peasants

Suggestions for further reading:
Holtman, Robert B. 1967. *The Napoleonic Revolution*. Philadelphia: Lippincott.

Russian Campaign (1812)

*T*his decisive event, which was to jeopardize all that Napoleon had gained in the previous eight years, had its origins in worsening relations between France and Russia ever since the Treaty of Tilsit of 1807. The deep and irreconcilable differences between Napoleon and Tsar Alexander I culminated in a Russian ultimatum in April 1812 virtually ordering Napoleon to evacuate Pomerania and Prussia. On 22 June Napoleon replied with a stirring proclamation claiming that Russia had broken the promises made at Tilsit, that he had to choose between dishonor and war, and that the coming conflict would "put an end to the fatal influence which Russia has exercised over Europe for the past fifty years" (Gates 1997, p. 206).

Contrary to popular myth Napoleon was fully aware of the immense problems involved in the invasion of Russia and took meticulous care in preparing for the campaign. "We can hope for nothing from the countryside," he told Marshal Davout, "and accordingly must take everything with us" (Gates 1997, p. 206). Nevertheless, the sheer size of his forces and their attendant supplies meant that he would have to engage the Russians as quickly and as far west as possible. He hoped by a series of marches to concentrate 400,000 troops against the two Russian armies commanded by Prince Barclay de Tolly and Prince Bagration and eliminate them in a decisive battle. But the Russians retreated eastward, abandoning Smolensk to Napoleon's multinational forces and imposing a scorched-earth strategy on the unfortunate peasantry, who were forced to abandon their homes and villages. Ignoring the opinions of some of his advisers, Napoleon pressed on toward Moscow, still hoping for the climactic battle. But while the cavalry could advance quickly, the rest were held up by poor roads, stifling heat, and lack of food. Finding little to drink, men and horses died in hundreds.

Finally the Russian army, now commanded by Mikhail Kutuzov, turned to bar the road to Moscow at Borodino, and in the resulting bloody battle on 7 September 1812 was defeated but not destroyed. Napoleon moved on and occupied Moscow but found little comfort there. While Alexander rejected all peace overtures, fire destroyed much of the ancient Russian capital. In October Napoleon began his retreat. Delayed by the battle of Maloyaroslavets (24 October), the retreat through the same devastated country they had crossed earlier turned into a nightmare for the *Grande Armée*. Harassed by bands of mobile Russian light troops, slowed down by overstretched supplies, and weighed down by loot, Napoleon's forces faced the full rigor of the Russian winter in a sorry state. As a final disaster, they were forced to cross the river Berezina under heavy Russian fire and assailed on both banks. By the time Napoleon left the army to return to Paris on 8 December the exhausted Russians had stopped their pursuit, but only a fragment of his forces remained alive.

The precise extent of the catastrophe is impossible to calculate. The military historian David G. Chandler estimates that some 570,000 personnel, 200,000 horses, and

1,050 cannon were lost (Kafker and Laux 1989, p. 136). An eyewitness who saw some of the survivors stagger wretchedly into Berlin recalled: "One saw no guns, no cavalry, only suffering men crippled by frightful wounds, men with hands, arms or feet missing or else completely destroyed by frostbite." Napoleon in a bulletin of 3 December presented a distorted account of the campaign to the French people, ending with an assurance that his health had never been better.

But the extent of the disaster could not be concealed. Prussia immediately began diplomatic moves to disengage herself from her alliance with Napoleon, and during the early months of 1813 most of the Napoleonic satellites in Germany followed suit. The campaign had ended by placing Russia at the heart of a new coalition against Napoleon. Carl von Clausewitz, who was attached to the Russian army during the campaign, observed: "The highest wisdom could never have devised a better strategy than the one the Russians followed unintentionally."

Related entries: Alexander I, Tsar of Russia; Bagration, Pyotr Ivanovich, Prince; Barclay de Tolly, Mikhail Andreas, Prince; Beauharnais, Eugène Rose de; Borodino, Battle of; Davout, Louis Nicolas; Moscow; Murat, Joachim; Ney, Michel

Suggestions for further reading:
Brett James, Antony. 1966. *1812: Eyewitness Accounts of Napoleon's Invasion of Russia.* New York: Macmillan.
Cate, Curtis. 1985. *The War of the Two Emperors: The Duel between Napoleon and Alexander, Russia, 1812.* New York: Random House.
Chandler, David G. 1974. *The Campaigns of Napoleon: The Mind and Method of History's Greatest Soldier.* New York: Macmillan.
Collins, Irene. 1976. "Variations on the Theme of Napoleon's Moscow Campaign," *History* 81, pp. 39–53.
Duffy, Christopher. 1972. *Borodino and the War of 1812.* London: Seeley.
Gates, David. 1997. *The Napoleonic Wars, 1803–15.* London: Edward Arnold.
Kafker, Frank A., and James M. Laux, eds. 1989. *Napoleon and His Times: Selected Interpretations.* Malibar, FL: Krieger.
Palmer, Alan. 1967. *Napoleon in Russia.* London: André Deutsch.
Riehn, Richard K. 1991. *1812: Napoleon's Russian Campaign.* New York: John Wiley.
Tarle, E. 1942. *Napoleon's Invasion of Russia, 1812.* London: Allen & Unwin.

S

Saint Helena

Napoleon's final place of exile is a volcanic island in the South Atlantic, a British colony occasionally used as a port of call in voyages to and from India. After his second abdication Napoleon had requested asylum in England, but the decision to send him to Saint Helena was taken while he was still aboard ship in Torbay, and he arrived on the island on 15 October 1815. He settled with a small group of French companions in the sprawling residence of Longwood, where he held court with the same formal etiquette as if he were still in power in Paris. Napoleon was frequently unwell, possibly with hepatitis and certainly with cancer of the stomach. The Irish naval surgeon Barry O'Meara was replaced as his personal physician in 1818 by the incompetent Francesco Antommarchi, sent by Napoleon's mother.

Napoleon's life on Saint Helena was marked by squabbles among his attendants and a running feud with the governor, Sir Hudson Lowe. But he exaggerated his miseries so as to build up the legend of his martyrdom. The publication of O'Meara's *A Voice from St. Helena* in 1822 and especially of Las Cases's *Mémorial de Sainte-Hélène*, dictated by Napoleon, in 1823 fabricated a legendary account of his life in which his fight for peace, liberty, and democracy was foiled by the unyielding hatred of the British. Through such means Napoleon's life became an epic that has become folklore.

Related entries: Las Cases, Emmanuel Augustin, Comte de; Lowe, Sir Hudson; *Mémorial de Sainte-Hélène;* Napoleonic Legend

Suggestions for further reading:
Korngold, Ralph. 1960. *The Last Years of Napoleon: His Captivity at St. Helena.* London: Victor Gollancz.
Martineau, Gilbert. 1968. *Napoleon's St. Helena.* London: John Murray.
———. 1976. *Napoleon's Last Journey.* London: John Murray.
Masson, Frédéric. 1949. *Napoleon at St. Helena, 1815–1821.* Oxford: Pen-in-Hand Publishing Co.
Thornton, M. J. 1968. *Napoleon after Waterloo: England and the Saint Helena Decision.* Stanford, CA: Stanford University Press.

Salamanca, Battle of (22 July 1812)

This important victory for the duke of Wellington was one of the most significant engagements of the Peninsular War and destroyed French power in northern and central Spain. With Napoleon in Russia, French military authority in Spain was divided between Joseph Bonaparte and Marshal Louis Marmont, enabling Wellington to take the city of Salamanca on 27

June 1812. After several weeks of stalemate, Marmont's dangerously extended forces were fooled by Wellington's pretence that he was ordering a retreat toward Ciudad Rodrigo. The French forces were caught by heavy artillery fire and an exceptional British cavalry charge. Marmont was badly wounded, and only the failure of Wellington's Spanish troops to secure a vital bridge over the river Tormes allowed the French to escape a total disaster. Wellington was now free to march on Madrid.

Related entries: Marmont, Auguste Frédéric Louis Viesse de; Peninsular War; Wellington, Duke of

Suggestions for further reading:
Pimlott, John L. 1987. "Marmont," in David G. Chandler, ed., *Napoleon's Marshals.* New York: Macmillan.
Young, Peter, and J. P. Lawford. 1972. *Wellington's Masterpiece: The Battle and Campaign of Salamanca.* London: Allen & Unwin.

Saliceti, Antonio Cristoforo (1757–1809)

A prominent Corsican revolutionary and patron of the young Napoleon, Saliceti served the Napoleonic empire in Italy but remained a Jacobin at heart. As a deputy to the Estates General at Versailles in 1789–1790, Saliceti secured Corsica's annexation to France but also gained pardons for Corsican patriots who had opposed the French in 1769 and a decree allowing the return of Pasquale Paoli from exile. But his Jacobin opinions came to override his Corsican loyalties. Elected to the Convention in 1792, Saliceti voted for the execution of Louis XVI. As representative on mission to the army during the siege of Toulon in 1793 he was instrumental in Napoleon's promotion to command the artillery, thus helping the young general's rapid rise to fame.

Saliceti, having demonstrated his capacity for brutality in presiding over the reduc-

tion of Toulon, became supplier to Napoleon's Army of Italy in 1796 and helped organize the Cisalpine Republic. In the coup of 18 Brumaire he helped obtain Jacobin support for Napoleon and was rewarded by not being sent into the exile reserved for his fellow radicals. After serving in various missions in Italy, Saliceti organized the annexation of the Ligurian Republic to France in 1805 and in 1806 was sent to be minister of police in Joseph Bonaparte's new Kingdom of Naples. Acting largely behind Joseph's back, he developed a repressive system that made short work of enemies of the regime, and on becoming minister of war in 1807, he set about cultivating support among the Neapolitans.

Saliceti's position and his capacity for intrigue were seen as a threat by Joachim Murat when he replaced Joseph as king of Naples. Murat cut Saliceti down to size and removed him from the war ministry. Saliceti presented his case to Napoleon, who sent him back to Italy to assist in the seizure of the Papal States and the arrest of Pope Pius VII. Saliceti died suddenly in Naples on 23 December 1809, but rumors that he had been poisoned by his successor as minister of police, Antonio Marghella, proved to be unfounded.

Related entries: Cisalpine Republic; Corsica; Jacobinism; Naples, Kingdom of

Suggestions for further reading:
Connelly, Owen. 1965. *Napoleon's Satellite Kingdoms.* New York: Free Press.
Lyons, Martyn. 1975. *France under the Directory.* Cambridge: Cambridge University Press.
Morton, John B. 1948. *Brumaire: The Rise of Bonaparte.* London: T. Werner Levine.

Savary, Anne Jean Marie René (1774–1833)

A s a soldier and then as minister of the police between 1810 and 1814,

Savary was valued by Napoleon as an obedient and unscrupulous servant. If there was dirty work to be done, Savary was the man to do it, and Napoleon expressed his appreciation by saying: "I like this fellow very much; he would kill his own father if I ordered it" (Kafker and Laux 1989, p. 136).

The son of a cavalry officer, Savary served in the revolutionary wars, becoming aide-de-camp to General Louis Desaix. When Desaix was killed at the battle of Marengo, Savary joined Napoleon's staff. In 1803 he was assigned to counterintelligence work, to which his blind obedience and moral insensitivity made him well suited. He took charge of the abduction and execution of the duke of Enghien and helped to dupe Charles IV and Ferdinand VII of Spain into the meeting at Bayonne that resulted in their both losing the crown. Savary was rewarded for his work by being promoted to general of division in 1805 and created duke of Rovigo in 1808.

As minister of police after 1810, he tightened press censorship and acted vigorously against unrest caused by high bread prices. But he lacked the subtlety of his predecessor, Joseph Fouché; was heavy-handed and obtuse; and committed the cardinal sin for a policeman when he was made to look ridiculous during the Malet conspiracy in 1812. His laxity toward the opposition salons in Paris was thus rewarded by his becoming a laughingstock, while his brutal methods contributed to the growing unpopularity of the Napoleonic regime. Savary's devotion to Napoleon remained total. After rallying during the Hundred Days, he tried to accompany his master into exile on Saint Helena, but was prevented by the British. After exile in Malta and Turkey, Savary lived for several years in Rome before briefly returning to military service in 1831–1832 in command of the French army pacifying newly conquered Algiers.

Related entries: Censorship; Enghien, Louis Antoine de Condé, Duc d'; Malet Conspiracy; Opposition Movements

Suggestions for further reading:
Arnold, Eric A. 1979. *Fouché, Napoleon and the General Police.* Washington, DC: University Press of America.
Artom, Guido. 1970. *Napoleon is Dead in Russia: The Extraordinary Story of One of History's Strangest Conspiracies.* London: Allen & Unwin.
Bergeron, Louis. 1981. *France under Napoleon.* Princeton: Princeton University Press.
Kafker, Frank A., and James. M. Laux, eds. 1989. *Napoleon and His Times: Selected Interpretations.* Malibar, FL: Krieger.

Saxony

Saxony, with its capital in Dresden, was in a weakened condition but of great strategic significance during the Napoleonic Wars. Elector Frederick Augustus of Saxony, though officially allied with Prussia, remained neutral until 1806, when he was inveigled into providing 20,000 troops to aid the Prussian army in the Jena campaign. After this crushing defeat Saxony made peace with Napoleon by the Treaty of Posen (11 December 1806). The territorial integrity of Saxony was guaranteed, Frederick Augustus became king, and Saxony joined the Confederation of the Rhine.

In 1807 Napoleon placed Frederick Augustus at the head of the new Duchy of Warsaw, created out of Prussia's possessions in Poland. The alliance with Napoleon forced Saxony to pay a heavy price in the lives of her soldiers. A Saxon corps of 19,000 men suffered heavy casualties at Wagram in 1809, and of the 20,000 who marched with Napoleon into Russia in 1812 only 2,500 returned home. Frederick Augustus remained loyal to Napoleon in 1813, but during the battle of Leipzig large numbers of his troops deserted to the Allies, and his kingdom was devastated by the campaign.

At the Congress of Vienna in 1815 Saxony was reduced to less than half its former size, but Frederick Augustus retained the title of king and the cities of Dresden and Leipzig. Prussian ambitions to seize the whole of Saxony were thwarted by the other Allies. The kingdom survived in some form until 1918, but after 1871 as an integral part of the German Empire.

Related entries: Confederation of the Rhine; Germany, Campaigns in; Leipzig, Battle of; Wagram, Battle of

Suggestions for further reading:
Sheehan, James J. 1989. *German History, 1770–1866*. Oxford: Clarendon Press.

Scharnhorst, Gerhard Johann David von (1755–1813)

As the Prussian reformer who best understood the reasons behind French success in the revolutionary and Napoleonic Wars, Scharnhorst deserves the main credit for establishing a mass Prussian army (a large army made up of conscripts and volunteers instead of the more usual small professional army) to oppose Napoleon in 1813–1814. As early as 1797 he had emphasized the political and psychological advantages enjoyed by the French republican armies, and from 1801, while a colonel in the artillery, had devoted himself to the discussion and publication of new ideas about military affairs. Only after the Prussian disaster of 1806, however, was Scharnhorst able to put his ideas into practice, replacing caste with merit in the selection and promotion of officers, modernizing organization, discipline, and tactics, and laying the foundations for a mass army capable of engaging Napoleon in an equal struggle. His death in 1813 while serving as chief of staff to Gebhard von Blücher deprived the Prussians of probably their best commander, but his work was carried on by August von Gneisenau.

Related entries: Prussia

Suggestions for further reading:
Craig, Gordon A. 1955. *The Politics of the Prussian Army.* New York: Oxford University Press.
White, Charles Edward. 1989. *The Enlightened Soldier: Scharnhorst and the Militarische Gesellschaft in Berlin, 1801–1805.* New York: Praeger.

Schönbrunn, Treaty of (14 October 1809)

The humiliating treaty imposed by Napoleon on Austria after his victory at Wagram forced the Habsburgs to pay a crippling indemnity, limit the size of their army, and cede territory to France and her allies. France received the Austrian territories on the Adriatic that became the provinces of Illyria, and Salzburg and other Alpine territories were ceded to Bavaria, West Galicia to the Duchy of Warsaw, the southern Tyrol to the Kingdom of Italy, and a section of East Galicia to Russia. Austria also joined the Continental System. For all its harshness, however, the treaty did preserve the Habsburg dynasty, whose alliance with Napoleon was to be cemented by his marriage to Marie-Louise.

Related entries: Austria; Bavaria, Kingdom of; Illyria

Suggestions for further reading:
Arnold, Eric A., ed. 1994. *A Documentary Survey of Napoleonic France.* Lanham, MD: University Press of America. pp. 288–296.
Ross, Steven T. 1981. *European Diplomatic History, 1789–1815.* Malabar, FL: Krieger.

Senate

When created by the Constitution of the Year VIII in December 1799, the Senate was meant to ensure stability of government under the consulate and to curb Napoleon's evident dictatorial ambitions. Under the presidency of Emmanuel

Sieyès it comprised sixty members, thirty-one named directly by the first consul and the rest by Sieyès and his associates. The Senate chose, from lists submitted to it, the members of the Tribunate and the Legislative Body, and until 1802 possessed certain rights of appointment in the appeal courts and financial administration. However, in 1801 Napoleon instituted the *sénatus consulte,* a form of decree issued by him and "witnessed" by the Senate. Initially used for important political matters, such as the amnesty for *émigrés* in 1802, these decrees gave a basis in law for the drift to the empire, established by *sénatus-consulte* in May 1804.

Princes and grand dignitaries of the empire were added to the Senate in 1804, and many other members were named by the emperor, so that by 1814 there were 141 senators. The method of recruitment and the advantages conferred by membership in the Senate, including a considerable basic salary of 250,000 francs a year, turned it into a docile, even servile body. As its powers diminished, its attraction as a social institution increased. Membership, which included representatives from annexed territories, was the sure sign of belonging to the social elite of the empire. It comes as no surprise, however, to learn that the august senators turned against Napoleon in April 1814.

Related entries: Constitutions; Consulate; Empire; *Sénatoreries;* Sieyès, Emmanuel Joseph

Suggestions for further reading:
Arnold, Eric A., ed. 1994. *A Documentary Survey of Napoleonic France.* Lanham, MD: University Press of America. pp. 148–150.
Bergeron, Louis. 1981. *France under Napoleon.* Princeton: Princeton University Press.
Collins, Irene. 1979. *Napoleon and His Parliaments.* London: Edward Arnold.

Sénatoreries

From 1804 onward a certain number of members of the Senate were pro-moted to act as super-prefects in the regions of France. Holders of such *sénatoreries* were given a residential palace and an urban seat, while their senatorial salaries were doubled. Appointed to the part of the country from which they came, these privileged personages personified Napoleon's aristocratic ideal of public service associated with appropriately large landed property and income.

Related entries: Local Government; Senate

Suggestions for further reading:
Arnold, Eric A., ed. 1994. *A Documentary Survey of Napoleonic France.* Lanham, MD: University Press of America. pp. 148–150.

Sieyès, Emmanuel Joseph (1748–1836)

The abbé Sieyès has been described by the historian François Furet as "the best symbol of the French Revolution" and "its most profound political thinker" (Furet 1992, p. 45). In his famous pamphlet of 1789, *What is the Third Estate?* he used his reading of Enlightenment thinkers to attack the privileges of the nobility and clergy and promote the cause of popular sovereignty. Throughout the turmoil of the Revolution Sieyès followed a moderate popular line, going into eclipse during periods of Jacobin domination. Asked later what he did during the Terror, he simply asserted: "I survived." He took the lead in drawing up the Constitution of the Year III (1795), served on the Directory's Council of Five Hundred, and became a Director himself in June 1799 along with Roger Ducos.

Ever fearful of a return to the Terror, Sieyès was worried by Jacobin domination of the Directory's legislative councils, and to counter this secured the appointment of his allies Joseph Fouché as minister of police and François Lefebvre as commander of the Army of the Interior. Firmly convinced of the necessity of a stronger executive, Sieyès became the prime mover in the coup of 18 Brumaire, but made a major mistake in selecting Napoleon for what he saw as a primarily ceremonial role as head of government. Once ensconced in power alongside Sieyès and Ducos, Napoleon changed the complicated system devised in Sieyès's draft of the Constitution of the Year VIII and concentrated power in his own hands.

After resigning as temporary consul, Sieyès was relegated to the Senate, where he continued to be influential and again proved his talents as a survivor. He was named a grand officer of the Legion of Honor in 1804 and given the title of count of the empire in 1808. Banished as a regicide in 1815, Sieyès lived in exile in Brussels until 1830, when he returned to Paris, where he died on 20 June 1836. Sieyès was a great deviser of systems, and his casting aside of tradition and history made him an ideal target for counterrevolutionary thinkers, who believed that his disregard of tradition and attempt to create an ideal constitution from nothing would lead to disaster. Napoleon also had rejected his careful accumulation of checks and balances in favor of personal power of a kind Sieyès himself would never have thought of wielding.

Related entries: Brumaire, Coup of Year VIII; Constitutions; Consulate; Directory

Suggestions for further reading:
Clapham, John H. 1912. *The Abbé Sieyès: An Essay in the Politics of the French Revolution.* London: P. S. King and Son.
Furet, François. 1992. *Revolutionary France, 1770–1880.* Oxford: Basil Blackwell.
Van Deusen, Glyndon G. 1932. *Sieyès: His Life and His Nationalism.* New York: Columbia University Press.
Woloch, Isser. 1970. *Jacobin Legacy: The Democratic Movement under the Directory.* Princeton: Princeton University Press.

Soult, Nicolas Jean de Dieu (1769–1851)

Duke of Dalmatia, marshal of France, born the son of a notary from Gascony, Soult joined the royal army in 1785 and rose rapidly through the ranks during the early revolutionary wars, fighting mainly in the Rhineland and Belgium. By 1799 he was a general of division serving in Switzerland under André Masséna. Soult was seriously wounded and taken prisoner while fighting alongside Masséna in the siege of Genoa in 1800, the action which allowed the launch of Napoleon's victorious second Italian campaign. From this point on Soult was less willing to expose his person in battle, but he had won the admiration of Napoleon for his tactical acumen and the iron discipline he imposed on his troops.

Soult was created a marshal in 1804, and as commander of the Fourth Corps led the attack on the Pratzen Heights at Austerlitz and fought with distinction at Jena and Eylau. Given the title of duke of Dalmatia in 1808, he led a corps to Spain, where he was to remain with only one brief interruption until 1814. In 1809 as "major-general" to King Joseph Bonaparte, Soult was responsible for the pursuit of Sir John Moore to Corunna, and he invaded Portugal, reaching Oporto before being checked by the duke of Wellington. In 1810 he conquered Andalusia and remained there as uncrowned king of the province until 1812, when he was forced to withdraw in the face of Wellington's victories in the north. After briefly joining Napoleon in Germany in early 1813, he returned to take charge of French forces in Spain. In the last phase of the Peninsular War Soult fought a tenacious delaying action in the Pyrenees and southern France, but was often outmaneuvered by Wellington. When the two faced each other in the battle of Toulouse Napoleon had already abdicated.

Soult rallied to Napoleon during the Hundred Days, but proved an ineffective chief of staff during the Waterloo campaign. Exiled until 1819, he returned to public office as minister of war under Louis Philippe in 1830 and was prime minister between May 1832 and February 1836 and again from May 1839 to March 1840. Like Wellington, he had become a grand old man and the two old rivals met at the coronation of Queen Victoria in June 1838. He continued to serve as minister of war and briefly prime minister again until 1847, when he was made marshal-general of France, an honor only ever held by two other men. When he died on 26 November 1851 he was survived by Louise Berg, his wife of fifty-five years, whom he had met while fighting in the revolutionary army near Düsseldorf in 1796.

Soult was widely admired, not least by Napoleon, for his organizational gifts and understanding of strategic situations, but he was also as avaricious as he was energetic, prone to self-indulgence, and seen by the more cultured marshals as retaining the manners of the drill-sergeant he had once been. One of his staff officers observed, a trifle unfairly: "In war he loved vigorous enterprises, but only on condition that he did not expose his own person too far. . . . This defect came to him with the great fortune he had amassed" (Griffith 1987, p. 467). Soult was unequal to the burden imposed on him in Spain by Napoleon and quarreled with all the other commanders. His feud with Michel Ney was longstanding and of grave consequence for the French in the peninsula. But he showed great resilience in postponing the moment of final defeat and died as one of France's most honored soldiers of all time.

Related entries: Austerlitz, Battle of; Corunna, Battle of; Eylau, Battle of; Genoa; Hundred Days; Italian Campaigns; Jena-Auerstädt, Battles of; Moore, Sir John; Peninsular War; Portugal; Toulouse, Battle of; Waterloo, Battle of; Wellington, Duke of

Suggestions for further reading:
Griffith, Paddy. 1987. "Soult," in David G. Chandler, ed., *Napoleon's Marshals.* New York: Macmillan.
Oman, Charles W. C. 1902–1930. *A History of the Peninsular War,* 7 vols. Oxford: Clarendon Press.

Souper de Beaucaire, Le

The most substantial of the young Napoleon's political pamphlets was intended to record the success of the campaign of 1793 against the federalist revolt in southern France and to persuade the people of Marseille to submit to the armies of the Republic. It demonstrates his appreciation of the importance of artillery, soon to be shown at the siege of Toulon, and looks forward to a repentant and republican Marseille becoming the "centre of gravity of liberty." Publication of the pamphlet was secured for Napoleon by Antonio Saliceti.

Related entries: Federalism; Jacobinism; Saliceti, Antonio Cristoforo; Toulon, Siege of

Suggestions for further reading:
De Chair, Somerset, ed. 1992. *Napoleon on Napoleon.* London: Cassell.

South America

The separation between Spain and her colonies created by Napoleon's interference in Spanish affairs and the intrusion of British naval power into the southern Atlantic contributed to the complex development of independence movements in South America, but their greatest successes only came after 1816. The British made attempts to gain footholds in Buenos Aires and Montevideo in 1806–1807, but plans in 1808 to send military support to Francisco de Miranda in Venezuela were abandoned. In 1811 Napoleon instructed his minister in Washington to "encourage the independence of all the Americas" (Herold 1983, p. 306), hoping that this would strengthen the United States at Britain's expense. This turned out to be a half-correct prophecy. Independence for Latin America was to open up markets for British goods that would have remained closed if the colonies had remained under Spanish rule. South American leaders faced the unusual situation of being encouraged, albeit mostly from afar, by both sides in the Napoleonic Wars, while having to rely on their own efforts to attain their goals.

Related entries: Great Britain; Spain; United States of America

Suggestions for further reading:
Esdaile, Charles J. 1992. "Latin America and the Anglo-Spanish Alliance against Napoleon, 1808–1814," *Bulletin of Hispanic Studies* 49, pp. 55–70.
Herold, J. Christopher. 1983. *The Horizon Book of the Age of Napoleon*. New York: American Heritage Publishing Co./Bonanza Books.
Lynch, John. 1986. *The Spanish American Revolution, 1808–1826*. 2nd ed. New York: Norton.
———, ed. 1994. *Latin American Revolutions, 1808–26, Old and New World Origins*. Norman: University of Oklahoma Press.

Spain

By the time of the French Revolution Spain, once the most powerful country in Europe, had declined into being a second-class power. The Bourbon kings were tied by the "family pact" to France and financially dependent on their American colonies. King Charles IV declared war on the French Republic in 1793, but peace was concluded by Manuel Godoy in 1795, a peace that would last until 1808. The Spanish fleet shared in the French disaster at Trafalgar in 1805, and the British seized Trinidad from Spain and cut off communications with South America.

After Napoleon ordered the occupation of Spain by French troops in 1808 the country's history is inseparable from that of the Peninsular War. Both Charles IV and his son Ferdinand VII, who had overthrown him, were deposed and replaced by Joseph Bonaparte. All Joseph's good intentions and attempts at reform were hindered by the unpopularity of French rule and the fact that rebels against him always held some territory, even if only Cadiz, in the name of Ferdinand VII. For five years Joseph, aided by Spanish ministers, tried to give Spain the benefits of enlightened government. He tried to rule according to the Constitution of Bayonne, which provided for a Cortes with a majority elected indirectly by universal manhood suffrage, introduced laws based on the Napoleonic codes, and brought in such educational and liberal economic reforms as were compatible with his permanent financial problems.

But even most Spanish liberals opposed Joseph's rule, preferring to support the rebel government in Cadiz. Joseph, perpetually at war but leaving its prosecution to the marshals, might have done much valuable work for Spain if he had not been imposed on the country by his conquering brother. The Constitution of Cadiz, proclaimed by liberal rebels in 1812 and later a model for liberal constitutions in Europe, was an attempt to improve on the Constitution of Bayonne. Meanwhile, Spanish regular troops joined with the Anglo–Portuguese forces of the duke of Wellington in driving Joseph from his throne in 1813. Ferdinand VII returned from exile in France in March 1814 and on his return to Madrid disavowed the Cadiz constitution. His persecution of his liberal erstwhile supporters drove many, ironically, into exile in France.

Although Spain regained her independence from France, the rule of the reactionary and authoritarian Ferdinand soon dashed any hope for national revival and progress. Crucially, the loss of her American colonies put the country on the road

Francisco Goya's **El Dos de Mayo** *(1814) is a dramatic depiction of the events of 2 May 1808 in Madrid, marking the beginning of the Spanish uprising against Napoleonic Rule. Goya emphasizes the confused melée of men and horses, doing nothing to alleviate the savagery of hand-to-hand conflict. (Alinari/Art Resource)*

to bankruptcy. Within eight years France was again interfering in Spain, this time to aid the restored monarchy against its liberal opponents.

Related entries: Bonaparte, Joseph, King of Naples, King of Spain; Charles IV, King of Spain; Ferdinand VII, King of Spain; Godoy, Manuel; Peninsular War; South America; Trafalgar, Battle of

Suggestions for further reading:

Callahan, William J. 1984. *Church, Politics and Society in Spain, 1750–1874.* Cambridge: Harvard University Press.

Carr, Raymond. 1982. *Spain: 1808–1975.* 2nd ed. Oxford: Clarendon Press.

Connelly, Owen. 1968. *The Gentle Bonaparte: A Biography of Joseph, Napoleon's Elder Brother.* New York: Macmillan.

Glover, Michael. 1971. *Legacy of Glory: The Bonaparte Kingdom of Spain, 1808–1813.* New York: Scribners.

Lovett, Gabriel H. 1965. *Napoleon and the Birth of Modern Spain,* 2 vols. New York: New York University Press.

Lynch, John. 1989. *Bourbon Spain, 1700–1808.* Oxford: Basil Blackwell.

Staël, Germaine de (1766–1817)

*T*he only child of Jacques Necker, the celebrated finance minister of the last days of the ancien régime, Mme. de Staël was one of the great figures in the salons of Paris between 1797 and 1803 and became a determined and irritating intellectual opponent of Napoleon. Along with her lover, Benjamin Constant, she had initially welcomed the coup of 18 Brumaire, but within a year she was helping to write Constant's speeches in the Tribunate advocating civil and political liberties. In intermittent exile after 1804, Mme. de Staël turned the

Necker family home at Coppet in Switzerland into a residential salon opposed to what she called Napoleon's "chattering tyranny."

Napoleon's anger at her arose initially from her links with Jean Moreau and from the feminist and pro-English sentiments of her novel *Delphine* (1803). Her other works included *On Literature* (1800), which associated liberty with human perfectibility, and the relatively innocuous novel *Corinne* (1807), the success of which annoyed Napoleon overmuch. The first edition of *On Germany* (1810), her great and positive critical study of German literature and life, was destroyed by Napoleon's police. De Staël's mature political position favored constitutional monarchy, but in 1814 she foolishly supported Jean-Baptiste Bernadotte for the French throne before rallying to the Bourbons. Her hesitant approval of Constant's *Acte Additionel* during the Hundred Days was also somewhat embarrassing.

Mme. de Staël's belief in humankind's advance toward moral perfection through material progress places her close to the *idéologues,* but her circle remained distinct from them or any other party. Her acute and hostile assessment of Napoleon's personality as dominated by the will to command and pragmatic pursuit of power was probably the main reason for his implacable hostility toward her.

Related entries: Constant, Benjamin; Romanticism

Suggestions for further reading:
Herold, J. Christopher. 1959. *Mistress to an Age: A Life of Madame de Staël.* London: Hamish Hamilton.
Staël, Germaine de, trans. Vivien Folkenflik. 1987. *Major Writings of Germaine de Staël.* New York: Columbia University Press.

Statistics

A great effort was made under the consulate and empire to revive and intensify the collection of demographic and economic statistics begun during the eighteenth century, but the results were sketchy. The demographic historian Jacques Dupâquier has called the supposed statistical excellence of the Napoleonic period a "legend" (Bergeron 1981, p. 116). But given the circumstances a large amount of data was accumulated, which has turned out to be more useful to historians than it was to Napoleon's government.

The Bureau of Statistics was established in the Ministry of the Interior by Lucien Bonaparte and Jean Antoine Chaptal, and in 1801 it launched a massive statistical description of France. However, despite the enthusiastic efforts of the Bureau's chief, Alexandre de Ferrière, reports were slow to come in and were often incomplete or inaccurate. While overworked staffs in prefectures and communes struggled to answer primitive questionnaires, personal rivalries and conflicting ideas under successive ministers of the interior hampered the bureau's work. It continued, however, to produce statistical investigations of various sectors of the economy until it was closed down in 1812.

Outside official circles, local learned societies, concerned with the perennial problem of British industrial supremacy, became interested in statistics, and statistical periodicals were published. Napoleon's interest, based on a desire to control and predict the movement of the population and economic activity, undoubtedly helped to stimulate interest in statistics, but it was not until 1835 that the modern French statistical service was launched.

Related entries: Centralization; Chaptal, Jean Antoine; Economy

Suggestions for further reading:
Bergeron, Louis. 1981. *France under Napoleon.* Princeton: Princeton University Press.
Perrot, Jean-Claude, and Stuart Woolf. 1984. *State and Statistics in France, 1789–1815.* London: Harwood Academic.

Stendhal (Henri Beyle) (1783–1842)

The great novelist made a successful career in the military administration under Napoleon and took part in the retreat from Moscow in 1812. He was a critic of Napoleon's policies, the waste of war, and lost liberties, but his major works in the 1820s and 1830s indicate how under the conservative, noble-dominated, and ultra-religious restored monarchy many looked back with nostalgia on the Napoleonic period. Julien Sorel, the hero of Stendhal's masterpiece *Le rouge et le noir, or Scarlet and Black* (1830), idolizes Napoleon, looking back to a time when talented men of humble origins could rise to glory and greatness. His other great novel, *La Chartreuse de Parme, or The Charterhouse of Parma* (1839), praises Napoleonic policy in Italy and contains a famous description of the battle of Waterloo, when the hero, Fabrice del Dongo, wanders in confusion through a part of the battlefield, having no idea what is going on.

Related entries: Napoleonic Legend; Romanticism

Suggestions for further reading:
May, Gita. *Stendhal and the Age of Napoleon.* New York: Columbia University Press.

Suchet, Louis Gabriel (1770–1826)

Duke of Albufera, marshal of France, Suchet was born the son of a prosperous Lyon silk merchant. Full of revolutionary fervor, he volunteered for the army in 1791, and first met Napoleon at the siege of Toulon in 1793. He subsequently fought, always with distinction, in the first Italian campaign, but at this time was suspicious of General Bonaparte and doubtful about his abilities. As a result he was never a member of Napoleon's intimate circle and had to wait longer than some less deserving soldiers to get the rewards he merited. While Napoleon was in Egypt in 1798–1799, Suchet served in Holland and Switzerland, reaching the rank of major general, and in the second Italian campaign of 1800 acted brilliantly as second in command to André Masséna. He also served in the Austerlitz and Jena-Auerstädt campaigns, but gained no promotion despite performing creditably.

By 1808 Suchet had garnered great experience in all kinds of warfare and showed particular skill as a military organizer and administrator. But his true reputation was made in Spain between 1808 and 1814. Uniquely among French commanders in the Peninsular War, Suchet not only organized his forces into a disciplined and effective fighting force but also gained a deserved popularity among the Spanish people. As military governor of Aragon and then Catalonia, he won his marshal's baton by victories over the Anglo-Spanish forces and guerrilla bands and employed Spanish officials in an administration that respected local religion and customs. He was given the title of duke of Albufera for his capture of Valencia in 1812.

When the French position in Spain became untenable in 1814, Suchet conducted an orderly retreat into France and transferred his allegiance to Louis XVIII on patriotic rather than opportunistic grounds. During the Hundred Days, however, he rallied to Napoleon and successfully defended southeastern France against Austrian or Piedmontese invasion. This was Suchet's last act in public life. He was pardoned for his support of Napoleon in 1819 and died at his château near Marseille on 3 January 1826.

Suchet's attitude and conduct in Spain was in sharp contrast to that of the French soldiery in general. Partly this was due to his exhaustive care for his own men, ensuring that they were treated fairly, fed properly, given proper medical attention, and even paid on time. Suchet and his beloved wife Honorine, a niece of Julie and Désirée Clary, were held in great respect by the Aragonese and Catalans. On his death a requiem mass was held in Saragossa, an honor it is difficult to imagine being granted to any of Napoleon's other Peninsular commanders. Napoleon remarked: "Had I been served by two marshals like Suchet, I would have conquered Spain and kept it" (Palmer 1984, p. 264).

Related entries: Danube Campaigns; Germany, Campaigns in; Hundred Days; Italian Campaigns; Peninsular War

Suggestions for further reading:
Ojala, Jeanne A. 1987. "Suchet," in David G. Chandler, ed., *Napoleon's Marshals.* New York: Macmillan.
Palmer, Alan. 1984. *An Encyclopaedia of Napoleon's Europe.* London: Weidenfeld and Nicolson.

Suvorov, Alexander (1729–1800)

*T*he immensely experienced and ruthless Russian field marshal Suvorov was recalled to arms in 1799 to lead the Russo-Austrian army charged with winning back the gains of Napoleon's first Italian campaign. He successfully drove the French forces from Milan and Turin, but the victories of André Masséna against his subordinate commanders in Switzerland forced the Russians to withdraw to Austria. The discredited Suvorov returned to Saint Petersburg, broken in health, and died a few weeks later, admired by all who served under him but suffering under the petulant hostility of Tsar Paul I.

Related entries: Italian Campaigns; Switzerland

Suggestions for further reading:
Longworth, Philip. 1965. *The Art of Victory: The Life and Achievements of Generalissimo Suvorov, 1729–1800.* London: Constable.

Switzerland

*T*he Swiss Confederation, made up of a mosaic of thirteen virtually independent cantons, was invaded by France in 1798 and remained a French protectorate, in reality if not in name, until the fall of Napoleon. Swiss liberals exiled in France had stirred up revolutionary agitation in favor of a unified state, and in November 1797 Napoleon had been greeted as a hero when he visited Switzerland to test public opinion. But the Directory's aims in invading the cantons were far from altruistic: the French seized the treasury of Berne to finance Napoleon's Egyptian campaign and secured control of the strategically important mountain passes. A unified Helvetic Republic was proclaimed and all resistance crushed ruthlessly.

The republic introduced a liberal constitution based on that of the Directory, but the strong and tenacious persistence of federalist sentiment led to chronic political instability. Napoleon wanted to disengage from Switzerland, leaving it neutral, but political chaos threatened. In 1803, therefore, the republic was replaced under his guidance by a new Helvetic Confederation of nineteen cantons with a federal Diet effectively subservient to Paris. The new system, which put an end to popular sovereignty but satisfied neither federalists nor centralists, remarkably produced eleven years of peace, as well as economic and cultural progress. Switzerland was bound to France by a defensive alliance, and the Continental System damaged her trade. Napoleon was able to use the Confederation as a source of troops, about 10,000 of whom died during the Russian campaign.

Napoleon ended the French occupation of Switzerland in 1813, and the country regained its independence without a struggle. Austrian troops violated Swiss neutrality in support of cantons which opposed the liberals, while the British diplomat Stratford Canning tried to secure agreement for a new constitution which would preserve some aspects of the Napoleonic centralization. All nineteen cantons sent representatives to the Congress of Vienna, while Geneva, Neuchâtel, and the Valais, which had been annexed to France, were readmitted to the Confederation. After prolonged negotiations, Stratford Canning failed to persuade the cantons to accept greater unity, and the enlarged Confederation consisted of twenty-two cantons, all with their own currencies, weights and measures, and armies. The Federal Compact, ratified by the cantons and guaranteed by the major European powers, pledged Switzerland to permanent international neutrality.

Related entries: Helvetic Republic

Suggestions for further reading:
Ellis, Geoffrey. 1991. *The Napoleonic Empire.* Atlantic Highlands, NJ: Humanities Press International.
Oechsli, Wilhelm. 1922. *History of Switzerland.* Cambridge: Cambridge University Press.
Woolf, Stuart. 1991. *Napoleon's Integration of Europe.* London and New York: Routledge.

Syria, Campaign in

See Egyptian Campaign

T

Talleyrand-Périgord, Charles Maurice de (1754–1838)

One of the most remarkable figures in the international politics of his day, Talleyrand acted as Napoleon's foreign minister before betraying him. In his own eyes Talleyrand's personal interests always seemed to coincide with those of France, and he may well have been right. Born into a leading aristocratic family, he was crippled by an accident in childhood, and instead of the military career toward which his birth impelled him, he entered the Church, rising to become bishop of Autun in 1789. But after being elected to the Constituent Assembly he identified himself with the cause of the Revolution and renounced his clerical state in 1791.

Talleyrand entered his natural environment of international politics when he was sent on a diplomatic mission to London in July 1792, largely because he had previously made the acquaintance of William Pitt. During the Terror he was condemned as a traitor and spent three years in exile in the United States, mainly in Philadelphia. Returning to France late in 1796, he became foreign minister of the Directory in July 1797. Talleyrand first met Napoleon in December 1797 and joined with him in proposing the Egyptian expedition of 1798–1799, but he resigned as foreign minister in July 1798 after failing to prevent the formation of the Second Coalition against France. He strongly backed the coup of 18 Brumaire and returned to the Foreign Ministry in November 1799, remaining until August 1807.

Napoleon called Talleyrand "the most capable minister I ever had" (Connelly 1985, p. 465), and indeed Talleyrand used all his talent even in promoting policies of which he disapproved, including the Continental System and the alliance with Russia sealed by the Treaty of Tilsit. Talleyrand became the voice of moderation, consistently advocating an end to conquest and agreements with Britain and Austria against the rising threats of Prussia and Russia. At the same time, however, he connived in the execution of the duke of Enghien and the establishment of the empire. He enriched himself with imperial titles and demanded and received huge sums of money from the governments with which he negotiated, meaning that he could be justly accused of unbridled cupidity even as he pursued a consistent and sensible policy. After leaving the Foreign Ministry after Tilsit, he saw that Napoleon's ambitions would ultimately lead to disaster and established secret contacts with Saint Petersburg and Vienna. Yet Napoleon continued to consult him and use him for special missions. The opportunities for patriotic treason against the "imperial madman" were many.

James Gillray's satirical **Tiddy-Doll, the Great French Gingerbread Baker, drawing out a new Batch of Kings** *(1806) shows the old kingdoms of Europe being pushed into the ash-hole by the "Corsican besom of destruction." While Napoleon pulls out his newly baked kingdoms and duchies, Talleyrand prepares more dough from Hungary, Poland, Turkey, and Hanover. (The British Museum, London)*

From 1809 onward Talleyrand informed the Austrian ambassador, Klemens von Metternich, of the secret orders sent to French army commanders. And in 1814, for all his suspicions, Napoleon does not seem to have realized that Talleyrand was in close contact with the advancing Allied commanders. Having helped to force Napoleon's first abdication, Talleyrand became president of the provisional government and negotiated an agreement with Louis XVIII by which he became "Prince de Talleyrand" and foreign minister. The Congress of Vienna saw Talleyrand in his element and at his best, exploiting differences among the Allies to secure recognition of France as a great power.

Talleyrand's sure eye for a sinking ship never deserted him. After relaxing through the Restoration in his magnificent château of Valençay, he returned to Paris in 1830 to help in the overthrow of Charles X and the succession of Louis Philippe. His last official position was as ambassador to London between 1830 and 1834, a fitting conclusion to his own peculiar pursuit of the entente cordiale. In all Talleyrand served six regimes and betrayed four of them. But his insistence that he had always served the interests of France was not mere self-justification. Talleyrand's achievements were as remarkable as his unscrupulousness in exploiting situations for his personal gain. Napoleon might have been better off if he had taken more notice of both his wise counsels and his capacity for treachery.

Related entries: Austria; Brumaire, Coup of Year VIII; Consulate; Directory; Fouché, Joseph; Great Britain; Vienna, Congress of

Suggestions for further reading:
Bernard, Jack F. 1973. *Talleyrand: A Biography.* London: Collins.
Brinton, Crane. 1936. *The Lives of Talleyrand.* New York: George Allen and Unwin.
Connelly, Owen, ed. 1985. *Historical Dictionary of Napoleonic France, 1799–1815.* Westport, CT: Greenwood.

Cooper, A. Duff. 1932. *Talleyrand*. London: Jonathan Cape.

Norman, Barbara. 1976. *Napoleon and Talleyrand: The Last Two Weeks.* New York: Stein and Day.

Whitcomb, Edward A. 1979. *Napoleon's Diplomatic Service.* Durham, NC: Duke University Press.

Talma, François Joseph (1763–1826)

The greatest French actor of his day became friends with the little-known General Bonaparte after the end of the Terror and was reputedly one of the few people whom Napoleon took into his confidence. Talma coached Napoleon in oratory, adapting the more natural style he had introduced into the highly formal world of French theater, causing Chateaubriand to remark that Talma had taught Napoleon how to act like an emperor. Talma performed before the assembled crowned heads at the Congress of Erfurt in 1808 and in the last play Napoleon attended on 21 April 1815. Talma continued his career after Napoleon's fall, only retiring shortly before his death in 1826.

Suggestions for further reading:

Carlson, Marvin A. 1966. *The Theater of the French Revolution.* Ithaca, NY: Cornell University Press.

Collins, Herbert F. 1964. *Talma.* New York: Faber & Faber.

Taxation

For the most part Napoleon preserved the tax system he inherited from the Directory, but from the first days of the consulate introduced more rigorous collection by appointing specialist collectors at communal, district, and departmental level. The governments of the Revolution had preferred direct to indirect taxes, considering them more socially just. The three direct taxes, on land, personal property, and business licenses, were kept at a moderate level until forced upward by the disasters of 1812–1813, but they could not provide sufficient income to sustain Napoleon's government and armed forces. He sharply increased indirect taxes, adding new duties on alcohol, salt, and tobacco to the existing minor duties such as registration fees, stamp duties, and the Directory's tax on doors and windows. The new duties, administered by an office known as the *droits réunis,* were violently detested, and were either greatly reduced or abolished after the Restoration. The tax system put in place by the Directory and Napoleon remained largely unchanged until 1914, and Napoleon's new organization of tax collection has remained essentially unchanged to the present day.

Related entries: Centralization; Economy; Finance; Local Government

Suggestions for further reading:

Bergeron, Louis. 1981. *France under Napoleon.* Princeton: Princeton University Press.

Lyons, Martyn. 1994. *Napoleon Bonaparte and the Legacy of the French Revolution.* London: Macmillan.

Teplitz, Treaties of (9 September 1813)

The formalization of the alliance between Russia, Prussia, and Austria against Napoleon committed the signatories not to make a separate peace with France and to fight for "the re-establishment of a just equilibrium between the Powers." Austria and Prussia were to recover all territories lost since 1805, while the Confederation of the Rhine and the Duchy of Warsaw were to be abolished. Most issues concerning Germany and Poland, however, were shirked, and the status of the intermediate states between Prussia and Austria was left deliberately vague.

Related entries: Coalitions

Suggestions for further reading:
Ross, Steven T. 1981. *European Diplomatic History, 1789–1815*. Malabar, FL: Krieger.

Tilsit, Treaty of (7–9 July 1807)

Signed after the French victory at the battle of Friedland at a somewhat theatrical meeting between Napoleon and Alexander I on a raft in the middle of the river Niemen, the various Tilsit documents transformed the map of central-eastern Europe. Frederick William III of Prussia saw his kingdom lose about half its territory. Its Polish provinces became the Duchy of Warsaw and its lands west of the Elbe formed the bulk of the Kingdom of Westphalia, with Jérôme Bonaparte as king. Russia and Prussia both joined the Continental System, and Russia by secret articles ceded the Dalmatian coast and the Ionian Islands to France. By way of some return, Napoleon encouraged Russia in her designs against the Ottoman Empire. The results of Tilsit were that Prussia ceased to be a great power and that Britain was left without an ally on the Continent except for Sweden, itself vulnerable to Russian attack. Louis Antoine Bourrienne was moved to write of the meeting at Tilsit: "One of the culminating points of modern history. . . . The waters of the Niemen reflected the image of Napoleon at the height of his glory" (Horne 1996, p. 5).

Related entries: Alexander I, Tsar of Russia; Continental System; Prussia

Suggestions for further reading:
Arnold, Eric A., ed. 1994. *A Documentary Survey of Napoleonic France*. Lanham, MD: University Press of America, pp. 231–246.
Butterfield, Herbert. 1929. *The Peace Tactics of Napoleon, 1806–1808*. Cambridge: Cambridge University Press.

Gioacchino Giuseppe Serangeli's 1807 painting is a somewhat romanticized image of Napoleon bidding Alexander I a fond farewell after the signing of the Treaty of Tilsit. (Giraudon/Art Resource)

Horne, Alistair. 1996. *How Far from Austerlitz? Napoleon 1805–1815.* London: Macmillan.
Ragsdale, Hugh. 1980. *Détente in the Napoleonic Era: Bonaparte and the Russians.* Lawrence, KS: Regents Press.

Ratcliffe, Bertram. 1981. *Prelude to Fame: An Account of the Early Life of Napoleon up to the Battle of Montenotte.* London: Warne.

Toulon, Siege of (September–December 1793)

After some years of frustration and false starts, Napoleon's part in the recapture of Toulon, the chief French naval base in the Mediterranean, first brought him fame and promotion to the rank of brigadier-general. The city, in revolt against the government of the Terror in Paris, had been taken over by royalists, and in August 1793 the British admiral Samuel Hood reinforced the rebels with an Anglo-Spanish force of 17,000 troops. When the siege began on 7 September the artillery commander, General Cousin de Dommartin, was wounded, and the government's representatives on mission, led by Paul Barras and Antonio Cristoforo Saliceti, replaced him with the young Napoleon Buonaparte, as he was still known. Rightly or wrongly, Napoleon's plan, involving the capture of fortifications on the heights above the harbor, was credited with forcing the city to capitulate. After a two-day artillery barrage from Napoleon's batteries, Hood withdrew on 18 December, and Toulon fell the next day. The republican authorities took terrible vengeance on the royalist defenders of Toulon. "There is a high incidence of mortality among the subjects of Louis XVII," wrote the representative Louis Fréron (Herold 1983, p. 28). Napoleon was a witness to the massacre, but in later reminiscences always minimized its extent.

Related entries: Artillery; Barras, Paul François Jean Nicholas, Vicomte de; Federalism; Saliceti, Antonio Cristoforo

Suggestions for further reading:
Herold, J. Christopher. 1983. *The Horizon Book of the Age of Napoleon.* New York: American Heritage Publishing Co./Bonanza Books.

Toulouse, Battle of (10 April 1814)

This pointless engagement may be considered as the last battle of the Peninsular War. Neither the duke of Wellington nor Nicolas Soult was aware that Napoleon had abdicated when the British commander attacked Soult around the city of Toulouse. Soult made good use of the barrier provided by the river Garonne, and the Anglo-Spanish forces suffered heavily in storming Toulouse's outer defenses. Soult withdrew his inadequate and demoralized forces northward on the night of 11–12 April and learned of Napoleon's downfall on the following morning.

Related entries: Peninsular War; Soult, Nicolas Jean de Dieu; Wellington, Duke of

Toussaint-L'Ouverture, François Dominique (1743–1803)

By the time Napoleon assumed power in France the fame of Toussaint-L'Ouverture as a black revolutionary leader in the colony of Saint-Domingue, the French part of Haiti, was widespread in the West Indies and Europe; he was idolized by blacks and respected by whites. Born a slave, Toussaint was legally freed in 1777, participated in the slave revolt of 1791, fought with the Spanish against the French in 1793, and switched sides in 1794 when the French National Convention abolished slavery. But fighting between Toussaint's forces and French governors had by 1800 caused great devastation in Saint-Domingue from which the colony never recovered.

In firm control of Saint-Domingue, in 1801 Toussaint, ignoring Napoleon's orders, invaded the Spanish colony of Santo Domingo, where slavery still operated. Now in command of the entire island of Haiti, Toussaint drew up a new constitution that made him governor-general for life with near dictatorial powers, including the right to name his successor. He declared that Saint-Domingue was "a colony forming part of the French empire, but governed by its own laws." These laws were based in part on the principles of the Revolution, but with Catholicism as the official state religion. Toussaint declared himself a good Frenchman, loyal to Napoleon, but there was no provision for any French official in the colony.

Toussaint's position and reputation was seen by Napoleon as a threat to himself and his political projects. The first consul was irritated by what he called the "pretensions of gilded Africans," while Toussaint's conquest of Santo Domingo threatened his plans for alliance with Spain and the restoration of slavery in Saint-Domingue and Guadeloupe. In January 1802, therefore, a French invasion force under Charles Leclerc began a systematic campaign to remove Toussaint from power. Many of Toussaint's supporters deserted him, bringing their bands of followers into French service. Toussaint was captured by trickery and transported to France, where he was confined at Fort de Joux in the Alps. He died there on 7 April 1803.

Related entries: Haiti

Suggestions for further reading:
Bryan, Patrick E. 1984. *The Haitian Revolution and Its Effects.* London: Heinemann.
James, C. L. R. 1938. *The Black Jacobins: Toussaint L'Ouverture and the San Domingo Revolution.* London: Secker & Warburg.

Trafalgar, Battle of (21 October 1805)

*T*he celebrated engagement that confirmed British naval superiority and thwarted Napoleon's ambitions in the Mediterranean was the culmination of a long campaign in which the British admirals Horatio Nelson and Cuthbert Collingwood had sought to bring the Franco-Spanish fleet under Pierre de Villeneuve to a decisive battle. As Villeneuve was attempting to sail from Cadiz into the Mediterranean Nelson intercepted him off Cape Trafalgar, some thirty miles south of Cadiz at the approaches to the Straits of Gibraltar.

Although Nelson, with twenty-seven ships of the line, faced superior numbers, including thirty-three ships of the line and seven frigates, morale on the British ships was high, whereas Villeneuve was convinced that he was doomed to defeat. On the gray and squally morning of 21 October Nelson hoisted his famous signal: "England expects that every man will do his duty." Nelson's boldness in piercing the enemy line allowed the superior British ships to engage in close combat, but his plan to annihilate the Franco-Spanish fleet was foiled when he was mortally wounded. Nevertheless, eighteen French and Spanish ships were sunk or captured, whereas no British vessels were lost. The Franco-Spanish losses in men were staggering, running to many thousands, and some 1,500 British seamen also perished.

Contrary to legend, Trafalgar did not save Britain from invasion by Napoleon. The *Grande Armée* had already left the Channel coast for the Danube more than a month earlier. Although Trafalgar confirmed British domination of the seas, the death of Nelson cast a pall over celebrations in London, especially as it was followed closely by news of Napoleon's victories at Ulm and Austerlitz. Neither the British nor Napoleon immediately grasped the significance of Trafalgar. Only in retrospect did it come to be seen as decisive, marking as it did the end of any serious attempt on Napoleon's part to challenge British naval supremacy.

Related entries: Naval Warfare; Navy, British; Navy, French; Nelson, Horatio, Lord; Spain; Villeneuve, Pierre de

Suggestions for further reading:
Bennett, Geoffrey M. 1977. *The Battle of Trafalgar.* London: Batsford.
Harbron, John D. 1988. *Trafalgar and the Spanish Navy.* London: Conway Maritime.
Howarth, David Armine. 1969. *Trafalgar: The Nelson Touch.* London: Collins.

Tribunate

Under the Constitution of the Year VIII, the Tribunate, a house of one hundred members, was supposed to discuss draft laws sent down to it by the Council of State and recommend their acceptance or rejection. It came to represent the only real opposition to Napoleon's accumulation of power under the consular regime. The *idéologue* Pierre Cabanis, presenting the Constitution to the citizenry, had claimed that the role of the Tribunate would be to appeal to public opinion, censure the acts of government and its agents, and act as "one of the principal guarantees of public liberty." Much to Napoleon's irritation, some members took this seriously.

The original members of the Tribunate included Benjamin Constant, Pierre Daunou, the poet and dramatist Marie-Joseph Chénier, and the liberal economist Jean-Baptiste Say. This group organized a "Committee of Enlightenment," where preparations were made for debates, and as early as January 1800 made detailed criticisms of government proposals on a wide variety of issues. Their audacity sometimes rubbed off on the Legislative Body, even if only rarely to the point of securing a negative vote. Napoleon purged

twenty tribunes in 1802, replacing them with more pliant nominees, including Lucien Bonaparte and Pierre Daru. But the opposition continued to make itself heard over the Concordat, the creation of the Legion of Honor, and the restoration of slavery in the colonies. The Constitution of the Year X finally emasculated the Tribunate by reducing it to fifty members and dividing it into sections, each associated with a section of the Council of State. It was thereby reduced to a mere collection of committees, incapable of organizing any real opposition to Napoleon's dictatorial plans.

Related entries: Constant, Benjamin; Constitutions; Consulate; Council of State; Daunou, Pierre Claude François; *Idéologues;* Opposition Movements

Suggestions for further reading:
Arnold, Eric A., ed. 1994. *A Documentary Survey of Napoleonic France.* Lanham, MD: University Press of America, pp. 247–249.
Collins, Irene. 1979. *Napoleon and His Parliaments.* London: Edward Arnold.

Tuscany, Grand Duchy of

The former Habsburg Grand Duchy of Tuscany was ceded by Austria to France in the Treaty of Lunéville in 1801 and became the core of the Kingdom of Etruria, ruled by the duke of Parma under French protection. However, Napoleon did not consider the new kingdom servile enough, principally because it continued to trade with the British, and in October 1807 Tuscany was annexed to the French Empire and transformed into three departments governed from Paris. This arrangement proved both inefficient and unpopular, and in 1809 Napoleon tried to placate local opinion by turning Tuscany into a grand duchy with his sister Elisa Bonaparte as grand duchess.

Elisa's state remained technically part of France, but she acted independently, keeping her brother happy by supplying him with an army of 10,000 men. Under her enlightened rule the Napoleonic law codes were introduced in Tuscany; new schools and public works were inaugurated; the state became financially independent; a brilliant court was created in Florence; the streets and public buildings of Florence were restored; and local administration improved by a French-trained civil service and judiciary. But Elisa was forced to withdraw from Tuscany in 1813 by Joachim Murat's defection to the Allies, and the grand duchy reverted to the Habsburgs in 1814. Nevertheless, the reforms introduced by Napoleon's most talented sister had made a considerable contribution to the future of Italy.

Related entries: Bonaparte, Elisa, Grand Duchess of Tuscany

Suggestions for further reading:
Hearder, Harry. 1983. *Italy in the Age of the Risorgimento, 1790–1870*. London and New York: Longman.
Woolf, Stuart. 1991. *Napoleon's Integration of Europe*. London and New York: Routledge.
———. 1991. *A History of Italy, 1700–1860: the Social Constraints of Political Change*. London: Routledge.

Tyrol, Revolts in

The Austrian province of the Tyrol was ceded to Bavaria, Napoleon's closest German ally, by the Treaty of Pressburg in December 1805, but it rapidly became evident that Bavarian rule was unacceptable to the people. A French general who served there in 1809 wrote: "The country can be compared to a natural fortress whose belligerent population constitutes an equally natural garrison" (Broers 1996, p. 169). The Tyrolese found a leader and folk hero in Andreas Hofer, who, in collusion with the Austrians, launched a successful revolt in the Innsbruck region. French intervention was necessary to suppress the guerrilla bands, causing Napoleon to complain: "I think the German Tyrol will always be badly governed, that it will never be subdued, and will cause us serious trouble" (Broers 1996, p. 170).

In February 1813 survivors of Hofer's rising planned a second insurrection in an attempt to force Austria to turn against Napoleon. The plan was supported by the Habsburg Archduke John, but opposed by Klemens von Metternich, who feared it would limit his freedom of action in bargaining with Napoleon. Emperor Francis I placed the archduke under house arrest, and the rising never took place. Metternich's approach proved the wiser, and Austria regained the Tyrol in 1814.

Related entries: Guerrilla Warfare; Hofer, Andreas

Suggestions for further reading:
Broers, Michael G. 1996. *Europe under Napoleon 1799–1815*. London: Edward Arnold.
Eyck, F. Gunther. 1986. *Loyal Rebels: Andreas Hofer and the Tyrolean Uprising of 1809*. Lanham, MD: University Press of America.

Ulm, Battle of
(8–20 October 1805)

This series of engagements, forming a kind of prologue to the battle of Austerlitz, eliminated thousands of Austrian troops from further participation in the war against Napoleon. The Austrians under the command of General Karl Mack were taken by surprise in the city of Ulm when the entire *Grande Armée,* ordered to the Danube from the English Channel, materialized between Ulm and Munich. Joachim Murat was given temporary command for the attack on Ulm, but it was the gallant action of Michel Ney on 14 October that saved General Pierre Dupont's division when it was left isolated on the north side of the Danube. The squabbling Austrian commanders were trapped in Ulm as it was bombarded and further French forces arrived. On 17 October an armistice was signed, followed three days later by Mack's surrender. Some 24,000 Austrian troops tramped out of Ulm under the eyes of Napoleon himself. When a French officer asked one of the Austrians to point out their commander to him, the reply came, "You see before you the miserable Mack" (Gates 1997, p. 25).

Related entries: Danube Campaigns

Suggestions for further reading:
Gates, David. 1997. *The Napoleonic Wars, 1803–15.* London: Edward Arnold.
Maude, Frederic N. 1912. *The Ulm Campaign, 1805.* London: Special Campaign Series.

United States of America

The political and commercial development of the young United States was strongly influenced by its relations with revolutionary and Napoleonic France and with Great Britain. American opinion about Napoleon was divided throughout his career. Federalists saw him as a despot who endangered the world and incidentally American trade with Britain and her colonies, while the majority Republicans tended to view Britain as their chief trading rival and on occasions still harbored the illusion that Napoleon was fighting for the Enlightenment values embodied in the early Revolution and in the founding principles of the American Republic. Napoleon probably had few enthusiastic admirers in the United States, but his career was followed with passionate interest.

When Thomas Jefferson became president in 1801 concern for American national security was being heightened by Napoleon's inexorable rise to power. But the first consul's erratic colonial policy and the failure of General Charles Victor Leclerc's expedition to Haiti was to have momentous consequences in the purchase of the Louisiana Territory from France in 1803. For a sum amounting to around $15 million, the United States doubled in size. The extent of the purchase was somewhat vague, but included, besides the present-day state of Louisiana, all of Missouri, Kansas, Arkansas, Oklahoma, Nebraska, North and South Dakota, Iowa, Minnesota, and parts of Montana, Wyoming, and Colorado. "By this increase in territory," declared Napoleon, "the power of the United States will be consolidated forever, and I have just given England a seafaring rival which, sooner or later, will humble her pride" (Herold 1983, pp. 291–292).

As Napoleon's maritime war against Britain increased in intensity, America, as the leading neutral carrier, was caught between the Continental System and Britain's response in its Orders in Council. But Britain's dominance of the seas meant that she imposed the greater damage on American trade and treated American concerns lightly. Jefferson attempted pragmatically to deal with the British and French restrictions through the Embargo Act of 1807, replaced by the Non-Intercourse Act of 1809, while similar measures were enacted by his successor, James Madison. British obstinacy resulted in the War of 1812, declared by Congress on 18 June, unaware that the Orders in Council had been revoked two days earlier. The war may have been unnecessary, but its impact on the United States was enormous, making her stronger and contributing to the developing idea of America's special destiny among the nations.

By the time of Napoleon's downfall the American Republic had proved its durability as an independent country and completed its conquest of economic independence for Britain. Jefferson later described Napoleon as a "wretch" who had caused "more misery and suffering to the world than any other being who ever lived before him." For most Americans the cause of liberty and self-government would henceforth be upheld in their own land rather than in Europe.

Related entries: Continental System; Great Britain; Haiti

Suggestions for further reading:

Egan, Clifford L. 1983. *Neither Peace nor War: Franco-American Relations, 1803–1812.* Baton Rouge: Louisiana State University Press.

Herold, J. Christopher. 1983. *The Horizon Book of the Age of Napoleon.* New York: American Heritage Publishing Co./Bonanza Books.

Kaplan, Lawrence S. 1987. *Entangling Alliances with None: American Foreign Policy in the Age of Jefferson.* Kent, OH: Kent State University Press.

Lyon, Elijah Wilson. 1934. *Louisiana in French Diplomacy, 1759–1804.* Norman: University of Oklahoma.

Shulim, Joseph I. 1952. *The Old Dominion and Napoleon Bonaparte: A Study in American Opinion.* New York: Columbia University Press.

Vendée Revolt

The Catholic and royalist popular revolt in western France had begun in 1793 and been ruthlessly suppressed in 1796–1797. However, unrest, supplied with weapons provided by royalist agents and the British, continued and flared up while the Directory was in crisis during the summer of 1799. General Gabriel d'Hedouville was instructed to negotiate a truce with the rebels, and after the coup of 18 Brumaire Napoleon at first maintained this policy. But his real plan was to end the running sore of the Vendée rebellion by harsh repression followed by concessions to the rebels' Catholic beliefs.

General Guillaume Brune undertook the repression, and by February 1800 organized resistance was at an end, though unorganized *chouannerie* was never to be eliminated. Following the Concordat of 1801, which satisfied most of the rebels' religious demands, the remaining leaders laid down their arms. Napoleon also spared the Vendée the full rigor of the conscription laws. The principal town of the Vendée department, La Roche-sur-Yon, was rebuilt by Napoleon as a center of surveillance for the region. Laid out geometrically, it was rechristened Napoléon-Vendée. The *Place Napoléon* in the center of La Roche boasts an equestrian statue of the emperor that has survived all changes of regime, which is re-

markable for a region that remains deeply conservative to this day.

Related entries: Bernier, Abbé Étienne; Brune, Guillaume Marie Anne; Cadoudal, Georges; Catholic Church; *Chouannerie;* Concordat; Counter-Revolution; Royalism

Suggestions for further reading:
Paret, Peter. 1961. *Internal War and Pacification: The Vendée, 1789–1796.* Princeton: Woodrow Wilson School of Public and International Affairs.
Sutherland, D. M. G. 1985. *France, 1789–1815: Revolution and Counter-Revolution.* London: Fontana.
Tilly, Charles. 1976. *The Vendée.* Cambridge: Harvard University Press.

Vendémiaire, Rising of Year IV

The royalist revolt of 13 Vendémiaire Year IV (5 October 1795) in Paris marked Napoleon's arrival on the Parisian political scene. The first counterrevolutionary rising in the capital, it was directed against constitutional chicanery by the Thermidorian Convention to prevent a possible royalist advance in forthcoming elections. Seven Parisian sections declared themselves to be in a state of insurrection on 11 Vendémiaire, and the Convention named a commission for its defense, with Paul Barras as its leading member. Barras called upon Napoleon, whom he had encountered at the siege of Toulon. The Convention had at its disposal only 5,000 men, without artillery or munitions, but Napoleon sent Joachim Murat to the camp of Les Sablons to seize its cannons. Skillfully deploying his new artillery in the streets so as to prevent the rebels from gathering en masse, Napoleon's victory was also aided by his opponents' lack of combativeness. Nevertheless, Napoleon's "whiff of grapeshot" saved the Thermidorians from the royalist threat, and as a reward he received command of the Army of Italy.

Related entries: Barras, Paul François Jean Nicolas, Vicomte de; Counter-Revolution

Suggestions for further reading:
Fryer, Walter R. 1965. *Republic or Restoration in France, 1794–1797*. Manchester: Manchester University Press.
Lyons, Martyn. 1975. *France under the Directory*. Cambridge: Cambridge University Press.
Sydenham, M. J. 1974. *The First French Republic, 1792–1804*. London: Batsford.

Venice

The Venetian Republic remained neutral in the wars against revolutionary France until Napoleon unilaterally declared war on 1 May 1797 and easily occupied the city. By the Treaty of Campo Formio Napoleon handed over the Venetian territories in Italy and Dalmatia to Austria, but as emperor in 1805 he took them back in the Treaty of Pressburg. Between 1806 and 1814 Venice formed part of the Kingdom of Italy, before returning to Austrian hands, where it remained until 1866. Napoleon and Joséphine had been sumptuously received there in September 1797, but he only visited the city on the lagoon once again, making a spectacular state entry up the Grand Canal on 29 November 1807. He famously described St. Mark's Square as "a cathedral open to the skies."

Related entries: Illyria; Italian Campaigns; Italy, Kingdom of

Suggestions for further reading:
Woolf, Stuart. 1991. *A History of Italy, 1700–1860: The Social Constraints of Political Change*. London: Routledge.

Vernet, Émile Jean Horace (1789–1863)

Horace Vernet gained his principal fame as a war painter under the July Monarchy after 1830, but his early work provides some graphic and evocative images of the Napoleonic Wars. His anecdotal paintings and lithographs of soldiers' lives and deaths stand in contrast to the battle paintings of Antoine Jean Gros, although he also attempted some grander scenes such as the *Battle of Sorno-Sierra* (1816). As a full-blooded Romantic in the 1820s, Vernet also contributed to the Napoleonic legend with his *Apotheosis of Napoleon* (1823).

Related entries: Napoleonic Legend

Suggestions for further reading:
Wilson-Smith, Timothy. 1996. *Napoleon and His Artists*. London: Constable.

Victor, Claude (1764–1841)

Duke of Belluno, marshal of France, Claude Victor Perrin was born of humble parents in the Vosges. His career is one of the few to justify the saying that in Napoleon's army every soldier "carried a marshal's baton in his knapsack." But he was not in the front rank of the Napoleonic marshals. Victor had enlisted in the Royal Army at the age of seventeen, but his military career began in earnest in 1791, and thanks to the Revolution he rose from sergeant to general in three years. He owed his

Jean Emile Horace Vernet's depiction of Napoleon as he defeats the Austrians in the Battle of Wagram, July 1809. (Corbis-Bettmann)

final promotion to his heroic conduct at the siege of Toulon, when he led a nocturnal assault on a British redoubt.

Victor fought in both of Napoleon's Italian campaigns and in Egypt. He distinguished himself at the battle of Marengo (14 June 1800), but Napoleon refused to share the credit for this notable victory that did so much for his reputation. Victor missed the Austerlitz campaign, but fought against the Prussians in 1806 and led the First Corps superbly at the battle of Friedland (14 June 1807). For his leadership he received his marshal's baton and the meaningless title of duke of Belluno (beautiful moon), apparently the result of a joke by Pauline Bonaparte about his short fat legs. He had hoped to become duke of Marengo.

In Spain between 1808 and 1811 Victor acquitted himself better than some French commanders, but shared the responsibility for Joseph Bonaparte's defeat at Talavera in June 1809. He did not figure prominently in the Russian campaign of 1812 until he helped to impose order on the retreat from Moscow, and he became demoralized at the French defeats of 1813 and 1814. Napoleon angrily remarked, "The duke of Belluno's conduct has been dreadful" (Arnold 1987, p. 519). The humiliated Victor refused to support Napoleon during the Hundred Days and, having transferred his allegiance to Louis XVIII, became "more royalist than the king," as the French saying goes. His attitude toward his former colleagues, with whom he had never been friends, was spiteful. A grateful Louis made him a peer of France and major general of the Royal Guard, and he served as minister of war between 1821 and 1823. He retired from public life after the Revolution of 1830.

Victor's character remains puzzling. Ambitious and jealous, he was unfortunate in that the battles he served at with most distinction, Marengo and Friedland, were victories Napoleon refused to share with others. He continued to serve Napoleon well despite the insults he received, then served Louis XVIII with even greater zeal. The exiled Napoleon, referring to his conduct during the retreat from Russia, said enigmatically, "Victor was better than one might suppose" (Arnold 1987, p. 519).

Related entries: Friedland, Battle of; Germany, Campaigns in; Italian Campaigns; Marengo, Battle of; Peninsular War; Russian Campaign

Suggestions for further reading:
Arnold, James R. 1987. "Victor," in David G. Chandler, *Napoleon's Marshals.* New York: Macmillan.

Victor Emmanuel I, King of Piedmont-Sardinia (1759–1824)

Piedmont had been forced to withdraw from the war against revolutionary France when Napoleon imposed the Treaty of Cherasco in 1796. Victor Emmanuel, younger son of King Victor Amadeus III, had led the Piedmontese forces against the French, and he became king in October 1798 when his brother, Charles Emmanuel IV, was forced to abdicate. Between 1799 and 1814 mainland Piedmont was annexed to France, but Sardinia, protected by the British fleet, remained in Allied hands. Victor Emmanuel returned to his capital of Turin in 1814, recovering Nice and Savoy from France and gaining Genoa. However, the returned king aroused resentment among a population that had benefited from religious toleration and the Napoleonic law codes. Liberal revolt forced him to abdicate in March 1821.

Related entries: Italian Campaigns

Suggestions for further reading:
Woolf, Stuart. 1991. *A History of Italy, 1700–1860: The Social Constraints of Political Change.* London: Routledge.

Vienna, Congress of

The meeting of the representatives of European states at Vienna between 15 September 1814 and 9 June 1815 was designed to create a new stable order in Europe following the defeat of Napoleon, an order based on the principles of monarchical legitimacy and the balance of power. The main decisions were made by Austria, Great Britain, Russia, and Prussia, but Charles-Maurice de Talleyrand managed to exploit differences between the victorious Allied powers, and on 9 January 1815 the Council of Four became the Council of Five, including France. The lengthy meeting of the Congress, marked by innumerable balls, receptions, parades, concerts, and gala performances, earned it a reputation for frivolity. But behind the scenes committees worked to untangle the knotty problems left behind by Napoleon's redrawing of the map of Europe. Also Napoleon's return from Elba in March concentrated minds further, and the final act with 121 articles was signed on 9 June 1815.

The Congress of Vienna created a new conservative order. It restored France, Spain, and Portugal to their former positions; it created a Kingdom of the Netherlands uniting Belgium to the United Provinces of the northern Low Countries; Sweden received Norway in compensation for Finland, lost to Russia; and it created a German Confederation of thirty-nine states. Prussia expanded westward into Westphalia, Saxony, and Pomerania, and Austria was compensated for losses in eastern central Europe by the new Kingdom of Lombardy-Venetia in northern Italy. Austria now dominated Italy. The Bourbons returned to Naples and Sicily, and the Papal States were restored. Russia emerged as the dominant power in eastern Europe, enlarged by Finland and by Bessarabia, gained from the Ottoman Empire. The tsar also ruled the new Kingdom of Poland. Britain retained Malta and other overseas possessions conquered during the wars.

The Congress recommended an extension of the rights of Jewish communities in Europe and condemned the slave trade. But it was a disappointment to liberals everywhere, and challenges to the new order would not be slow to appear, in Germany, Belgium, Poland, and elsewhere.

Related entries: Castlereagh, Robert Stewart, Viscount; Metternich, Klemens Wenceslas Lothar, Fürst von; Talleyrand-Périgord, Charles-Maurice de

Suggestions for further reading:
Dakin, Douglas. 1979. "The Congress of Vienna, 1814–15, and its Antecedents," in Alan Sked, ed., *Europe's Balance of Power, 1815–1848*. London: Macmillan.
Kraehe, Enno Edward. 1983. *Metternich's German Policy, Vol. 2: The Congress of Vienna, 1814–1815*. Princeton: Princeton University Press.
Nicolson, Harold. 1946. *The Congress of Vienna*. London: Constable.
Webster, Charles K. 1934. *The Congress of Vienna, 1814–1815*. London: G. Bell and Sons.

Villeneuve, Pierre de (1763–1806)

An experienced seaman who had seen service in the Caribbean before the Revolution, Rear Admiral Villeneuve commanded the outer division of the French fleet at the battle of the Nile, from which he escaped with four vessels and sailed to Malta. In late 1804 the new admiral Villeneuve took command of the Toulon squadron and, joined by the Span-

ish fleet, began the cat-and-mouse game with the British navy that was to culminate in the battle of Trafalgar on 21 October 1805. One reason for his decision to engage the British off Cadiz was that he knew that Napoleon, with his poor understanding of naval warfare, thought him a coward and intended to replace him. Captured during the battle, Villeneuve was held prisoner for six months by the British. Jane Austen's brother, Frank, an admiral in the Royal Navy, met Villeneuve after Trafalgar and found him "so much of a Frenchman as to bear his misfortunes with cheerfulness" (Horne 1996, p. 44). Six months later Villeneuve committed suicide.

Related entries: Navy, French; Nile, Battle of the; Trafalgar, Battle of

Suggestions for further reading:
Bennett, Geoffrey M. 1977. *The Battle of Trafalgar*. London: Batsford.
Horne, Alistair. 1996. *How Far from Austerlitz? Napoleon 1805–1815*. London: Macmillan.
Howarth, David Armine. 1969. *Trafalgar: The Nelson Touch*. London: Collins.

Vitoria, Battle of (21 June 1813)

The decisive defeat inflicted by the duke of Wellington on the French army commanded by Joseph Bonaparte and Jean-Baptiste Jourdan effectively marked the end of the Peninsular War. Joseph was in full flight from Madrid with 50,000 men and an endless train of plundered loot, munitions, supplies, and refugees. They faced Wellington's Anglo-Portuguese army of 75,000 men on a twelve-mile front west of the town of Vitoria, thirty-two miles southeast of Bilbao. Although not all of Wellington's complex maneuvers worked, the French were thrown back on Vitoria itself and then forced to scatter to the east. The abandoned loot was too great a temptation for Wellington's army, which disintegrated into a plundering mob, and nearly 42,000 French soldiers escaped to fight again in southern France. The victory, though far from glorious, signaled the end of Napoleon's rule in Spain, and it was celebrated lavishly in the Allied capitals.

Related entries: Bonaparte, Joseph, King of Naples, King of Spain; Jourdan, Jean-Baptiste; Peninsular War; Wellington, Duke of

Suggestions for further reading:
Glover, Michael. 1987. "Jourdan," in David G. Chandler, ed., *Napoleon's Marshals.* New York: Macmillan.

W

Wagram, Battle of (5–6 July 1809)

Napoleon's victory over the Austrian army commanded by Archduke Charles, which ended the campaign of 1809, was fought between the largest armies yet seen in European history. 173,000 French and their allies faced some 155,000 Austrians along a long front to the east of Vienna. Having failed to cross the Danube at the battle of Essling, Napoleon withdrew his forces onto the island of Lobau in the great river, facing a ring of Austrian forces on the north bank. The ensuing battle involved Napoleon launching various corps from the Lobau in the shape of an arrowhead pointing at the Austrian center at Wagram.

The inexperience of Saxon and Bavarian conscripts and the problems encountered by his commanders against the stubborn Austrian contingents meant that Napoleon had to deploy all his skill in what developed into a two-day bludgeoning match. In particular, the failure of Jean-Baptiste Bernadotte's Saxons in a thrust at Wagram caused Napoleon to dismiss his marshal from the army. However, the attacks of Louis Davout on the Austrian left and Jacques Macdonald on the center allowed Napoleon to execute a bold march across the front and reinforce his own left

under André Masséna when they had been forced to retreat. By the end of the second day most of Macdonald's units, formed into a massive column, had lost half their strength, while batteries of artillery inflicted heavy casualties on both sides.

Napoleon claimed that he could have won a quick victory if his commanders had been more efficient, and on the morning of 7 July was convinced that he faced a third day of fighting. But he did not understand that Charles's main priority was to preserve as much of the Austrian army as possible. Rather than risk total destruction the archduke withdrew toward Bohemia. Napoleon, with exhausted troops and depleted cavalry, was in no position to pursue the Austrians. Charles had been beaten but not routed, and he had no intention of risking the remainder of his forces in another battle. About one-quarter of the strengths of both armies had been killed, wounded, or taken prisoner. The slaughter of Wagram ensured that resuming the war was an impractical proposition for the Austrians and made peace, eventually to be signed at Schönbrunn, essential.

Related entries: Bernadotte, Jean-Baptiste Jules; Charles, Archduke of Austria; Danube Campaigns; Davout, Louis Nicolas; Macdonald, Jacques Étienne Joseph Alexandre; Masséna, André

Suggestions for further reading:
Gates, David. 1997. *The Napoleonic Wars, 1803–15.* London: Edward Arnold.

Hankinson, Alan. 1987. "Macdonald," in David G. Chandler, ed., *Napoleon's Marshals*. New York: Macmillan.

Rothenberg, Gunther E. 1982. *Napoleon's Great Adversaries: The Archduke Charles and the Austrian Army, 1792–1814*. London: Batsford.

Walcheren Expedition (July–December 1809)

The largest amphibious operation of the Napoleonic Wars, this British attack on the estuary of the Scheldt River in the Low Countries was supported by Viscount Castlereagh but opposed by George Canning, and it turned into an unmitigated disaster. Planned as a diversion for Austria's benefit, it only took place after the defeat at Wagram. A British army of over 44,000 men, supported by 266 ships, was intended to destroy naval establishments at Flushing on the island of Walcheren and make the river Scheldt unnavigable for warships. However, stormy weather, the navy's inability to blockade Flushing, and the indecisive leadership of John Pitt, second earl of Chatham, slowed progress, and over 12,000 British soldiers were laid low by "Walcheren fever," a lethal mixture of malaria, dysentery, typhus, and typhoid. The French naval facilities at Flushing were destroyed, but the debilitated British troops had to be withdrawn. Austria, which had delayed making peace after Wagram, finally signed the Treaty of Schönbrunn in October 1809.

Related entries: Canning, George; Castlereagh, Robert Stewart, Viscount; Naval Warfare

Walewska, Marie (1786–1817)

Napoleon's most celebrated lover was born Marie Laczinska in Warsaw. In 1804 at the age of seventeen she was forced by family arrangement to marry the much older Count Anastazy Walewski. Bold and beautiful, she was presented to Napoleon in January 1807 during his winter campaign in Poland and later captivated him at a ball in Warsaw. She only yielded to his advances, however, when persuaded by Polish patriots that it was her national duty. After spending the spring with Napoleon at the château of Finkenstein, she visited him in Paris in 1808 and at Schönbrunn in 1809. Their son, Alexandre Walewski, was born at Walewice in Poland in May 1810 and acknowledged by Napoleon as his child.

After his marriage to Marie-Louise, Napoleon stopped seeing Marie, but she lived in Paris between 1810 and 1813 and was well provided for. She visited him during his exile on Elba in 1814 and saw him again during the Hundred Days. In 1816, with Napoleon exiled on Saint Helena, Marie married his distant cousin, General Philippe Antonio d'Ornano, and died in childbirth on 15 December 1817. Alexandre Walewski served Napoleon III as foreign minister between 1850 and 1855 and presided over the Congress of Paris that ended the Crimean War. He died in 1868.

Related entries: Poland

Suggestions for further reading:
Sutherland, Christine. 1979. *Marie Walewska, Napoleon's Great Love*. London: Weidenfeld and Nicolson.

Warsaw, Duchy of

Formed in 1807 from Prussian territory in Poland ceded by the Treaty of Tilsit, the Duchy of Warsaw, under the nominal rule of Frederick Augustus of Saxony, marks the beginning of modern Polish national identity. It included all the lands taken by Prussia from Poland since 1772, and it was enlarged in 1809 to include western Galicia, taken from Austria. The

Napoleonic law codes were introduced, and a bicameral Diet, comprising a Senate and a House of Representatives, dominated by the Polish nobility, provided active opposition to many government measures. Serfdom was abolished and civil rights guaranteed to Jews, although these were suspended for ten years in 1809.

As a result of the duchy's existence Poland was one of the few regions of Europe where the advantages of Napoleonic rule outweighed the burdens. Its very presence on the map proved that the Poles still existed as a nation despite the destruction of the old Polish state in the Partitions of 1772, 1793, and 1795. The introduction of French-style administration and the Napoleonic codes was of permanent benefit, as were the educational reforms by Stanislaw Potocki, under which Polish replaced German as the language of instruction in elementary and secondary schools. Similarly the duchy's army, reorganized by Jozef Poniatowski, especially the Polish Legions that fought for Napoleon from Italy to Russia, was to gain an almost mythic status within Polish nationalism.

Following Napoleon's defeat in Russia in 1812, Warsaw was occupied by the Russians in February 1813, and Alexander I installed a provisional government in the duchy. It officially came to an end in 1815, and Warsaw became the capital of the "Congress Kingdom" of Poland under Russian control. But many of the Napoleonic changes in administration, law, and the army were retained, and no attempt was made to reimpose serfdom. Napoleon had unwittingly strengthened Polish nationalism and given it a more populist and even democratic content. Although it existed for less than ten years, the Duchy of Warsaw changed the future of Poland and still enjoys a legendary status in Polish history.

Related entries: Poland

Suggestions for further reading:
Davies, Norman. 1981. *God's Playground: A History of Poland.* 2 vols. Oxford: Clarendon Press.
Wandycz, Piotr. 1975. *The Lands of Partitioned Poland, 1795–1918.* Seattle: University of Washington Press.

Waterloo, Battle of (18 June 1815)

Napoleon's final defeat was a "close-run thing," as the duke of Wellington described it, and arguments about what might have been have continued to this day, but the result was as decisive as any of his former victories. Waterloo is a village ten miles south of Brussels on the road to Charleroi. Here Wellington established his headquarters in a strong defensive position on a ridge at Mont-Saint-Jean. His Anglo-Dutch army of 68,000 could thereby hold up the march of Napoleon's 72,000 men toward the Belgian capital, while Gebhard von Blücher's 72,000 strong Prussian force advanced from the east to attack the French right flank. The battle took place on a small plateau, which made Napoleon's room for maneuver smaller than in any of his major battles since Marengo.

Heavy rain on the night of 17 June meant that the ground was sodden on the morning of the eighteenth, and Napoleon delayed his attack until the sun had begun to dry it out. The main French infantry attack on Wellington's position around a fortified farmhouse at Hougoumont was beaten off with heavy losses on both sides, while French advances up the ridge, lacking cavalry support, were repulsed. Michel Ney's cavalry engaged in gallant charges against the Anglo-Dutch squares, but met with stubborn resistance, especially from the British, and with concentrated artillery fire. "Never did I see such a pounding match," observed Wellington (Herold 1983, p. 371). Ney finally dislodged the British and Hanoverians defending Wellington's central position at about half past six in the evening, but his cavalrymen were too exhausted to exploit their advantage, and in any case by now Blücher's Prussians had arrived and the French were caught between two fires.

Napoleon's final gamble was to throw his Imperial Guard into the fight, something he had refused to do at Borodino, but it was thrown back by murderous fire from the Allies. According to the famous but apocryphal story, General Cambronne, when called upon to surrender, replied, "The Guard dies but does not surrender." The other version of his answer often quoted, "Merde!" is probably closer to the truth. All the Guard could do was to try and cover Napoleon's retreat as the army disintegrated into a mass of retreating refugees. Napoleon had lost some 41,000 men in the battle, while Allied casualties were about 22,000. Within four days of the defeat Napoleon had signed his second abdication.

The union of the Prussians with Wellington's multinational force sealed Napoleon's fate at Waterloo. He himself tried to blame the disaster on Emmanuel Grouchy's failure to stop Blücher's advance or to join the main French army in time, but Grouchy had only been following his orders to the best of his ability, if somewhat unimaginatively. Blücher's arrival was not providential. Wellington had been expecting it all day, and if anything his lateness almost turned what should have been certain victory into defeat. That it did not was due as much as anything to the persistence and staying power of the British infantry. But Napoleon's own miscalculations about the whereabouts and abilities of the Prussians reveal the extent of his own responsibility for his defeat.

Related entries: Blücher, Gebhard Leberecht von; Grouchy, Emmanuel, Marquis de; Hundred Days; Imperial Guard; Ney, Michel; Wellington, Duke of

Suggestions for further reading:
Brett James, Antony. 1964. *The Hundred Days: Napoleon's Last Campaign from Eyewitness Accounts.* New York: Macmillan.
Chandler, David G. 1980. *Waterloo: The Hundred Days.* London: Osprey.
Hamilton-Williams, David. 1993. *Waterloo: New Perspectives: The Great Battle Reappraised.* London: Arms and Armour.
Herold, J. Christopher. 1983. *The Horizon Book of the Age of Napoleon.* New York: American Heritage Publishing Co./Bonanza Books.
Hibbert, Christopher. 1998. *Waterloo.* London: Wordsworth Military Library.
Howarth, David Armine. 1968. *A Near-Run Thing: The Day of Waterloo.* London: Collins.
Keegan, John. 1976. *The Face of Battle.* London: Cape.
Parker, Harold T. 1983. *Three Napoleonic Battles.* Durham, NC: Duke University Press.

Wellington, Duke of (Arthur Wellesley) (1769–1852)

The "Iron Duke" was already an experienced soldier and politician when he played his most important parts in the defeat of Napoleon, first as the leading British commander in the Peninsular War and then as Allied commander at Waterloo. Born in Dublin and educated in part at a French military school, Wellesley first served in Flanders in 1794, where he learned "what one ought not to do," and then in India, where his brother was governor-general. He returned from India in 1805 and for the next three years was more involved in politics, serving as chief secretary for Ireland, than in military affairs.

Wellesley's first command in the Iberian Peninsula came in 1808, where as commander of the British expeditionary force he defeated the French under Andoche Junot. He returned to Portugal after the death of Sir John Moore in 1809, drove Marshal Nicolas Soult out of Oporto, and fought the indecisive battle of Talavera against the French under Joseph Bonaparte, but he was forced to retreat from Spain in the face of the numerical superiority of the

Thomas Lawrence's flattering portrait of the Duke of Wellington (c. 1815) bears little resemblance to the image found in hostile caricatures of Napoleon's great adversary. (Victoria & Albert Museum, London / Art Resource)

French. In September 1809 he was created Viscount Wellington of Talavera.

Wellington was British commander in Iberia from 1809 to 1814, marshal-general of the Portuguese army in July 1809, and generalissimo of the armies in Spain in September 1812. But he was forced to adopt a patient strategy. In the campaign on 1811, despite successive victories over André Masséna, including the battle of Bussaco, he again had to retreat into Portugal. And even the more successful campaign in 1812, which saw Wellington advance into central Spain and capture Madrid after the battle of Salamanca, had the same outcome.

In 1813 Wellington, now an earl and a knight of the garter, advanced again into Spain, this time with decisive results. While the French forces concentrated on Valladolid to protect southern France, Wellington forced them back with a series of brilliant flanking maneuvers and gained a crushing victory at the battle of Vitoria (21 June 1813). After overcoming a deter-

mined French counterattack in the Pyrenees, he took San Sebastian on 31 August and Pamplona on 31 October and defeated Soult at Nivelle on 10 December. By the time of his victory at Toulouse on 10 April 1814 the war was over. Wellington was created a duke, and named ambassador to Paris in July.

Wellington was attending the Congress of Vienna when on 7 March 1815 news arrived of Napoleon's escape from Elba. He was immediately named commander in chief of the Anglo-Hanoverian and Dutch armies, based in Brussels. His troops successfully held back the forces of Michel Ney at Quatre-Bras on 16 June, and two days later he gained his greatest victory at Waterloo. He contained all Napoleon's attacks until the arrival of the Prussians under Gebhard von Blücher gave the Allies numerical superiority and French resistance collapsed.

Waterloo was Wellington's last battle. He was commander in chief of the allied army of occupation in France until November 1818, but thereafter devoted himself to politics. As prime minister in 1828–1829 he carried through the law for Catholic Emancipation, but his hostility to parliamentary reform in 1832 made him politically unpopular. When he died Victorian Britain mourned a great military hero but a less than popular politician.

Related entries: Bussaco, Battle of; Hundred Days; Peninsular War; Portugal; Quatre-Bras, Battle of; Salamanca, Battle of; Toulouse, Battle of; Vitoria, Battle of; Waterloo, Battle of

Suggestions for further reading:
Esdaile, Charles J. 1990. *The Duke of Wellington and the Command of the Spanish Army, 1812–14.* London: Macmillan.
Gash, Norman, ed. 1990. *Wellington: Studies in the Military and Political Career of the First Duke of Wellington.* Manchester: Manchester University Press.
Glover, Michael. 1968. *Wellington as Military Commander.* London: Batsford.
James, Lawrence. 1992. *The Iron Duke: A Military Biography of Wellington.* London: Weidenfeld and Nicolson.

Westphalia, Kingdom of

Created from lands formerly held by Prussia, Hanover, and a dozen smaller states, Westphalia was the largest state founded by Napoleon on German territory and was a member of the Confederation of the Rhine. Jérôme Bonaparte was installed as king and turned out to be not unpopular with his subjects. But Napoleon wanted Westphalia to be a model state, serving as the advanced bastion for the moral conquest of Germany by French ideals. It was, declared an official of the new regime, "a creation, like the universe itself, in which the creator turns primary materials into a finished object" (Sheehan 1989, p. 260). In November 1807, therefore, the kingdom was given a constitution promising civil equality and religious liberty, the abolition of guilds, serfdom, and aristocratic privilege, and the adoption of Napoleon's legal codes, open courts, and trial by jury.

Unfortunately, the proclaimed liberty and liberalism was incompatible with Napoleon's foreign policy and military demands. The representative Diet met only twice, in 1808 and 1810, and the structure of rural society remained virtually unchanged. Instead of liberty and prosperity the people of Westphalia were faced by the tax collectors, military recruiters (taking some 600,000 men, more per head of population than anywhere else in Europe), and greedy land-grabbing politicians of an increasingly dictatorial and exploitative regime. When Napoleon was defeated in 1813 the kingdom fell apart, and the majority of the population greeted its demise with relief. However, Jérôme's short-lived kingdom had in some respects served as an example to the reformers of Prussia, and some of its successor states, especially Prussia, allowed some of his liberal legislation to remain in effect.

Related entries: Bonaparte, Jérôme, King of Westphalia; Confederation of the Rhine

Suggestions for further reading:
Connelly, Owen. 1965. *Napoleon's Satellite Kingdoms.* New York: Free Press.
Sheehan, James J. 1989. *German History, 1770–1866.* Oxford: Clarendon Press.

Y

Yorck von Wartenburg, Johann David Ludwig, Count (1759–1830)

Born in Potsdam of English descent, General Yorck became a rather unlikely Prussian national hero in 1812–1813. He had fought in the Jena-Auerstädt campaign of 1806, and he became an important figure in the revival of the Prussian army defeated by Napoleon, advocating conscription and improved treatment of rank-and-file troops. In the Russian campaign of 1812, however, he commanded the Prussian corps attached to the French left wing under Marshal Jacques Macdonald. During the retreat in December 1812 he succumbed to Russian pleas for separate negotiations. On 30 December, acting on his own initiative, he signed the Convention of Tauroggen, withdrawing the Prussian troops from the campaign. This act provided the impetus for Prussia's declaration of war on France in March 1813 and came to be seen as the signal for the start of the German War of Liberation.

Related entries: Prussia; Russian Campaign

Suggestions for further reading:
Paret, Peter. 1966. *Yorck and the Era of Prussian Reform, 1807–15*. Princeton: Princeton University Press.

DOCUMENTS

This selection of documents is intended to provide insights into Napoleon's character, the major events of his career, and his style of government. Excerpts from his memoirs and proclamations are interspersed with others providing different and complementary perspectives, ending with assessments of his personality by two of his most determined opponents.

CORSICA

In his exile on Saint Helena Napoleon recalled his native island, glossing over his early nationalism, but also betraying a degree of nostalgia and affection for its inhabitants.

Corsica lies twenty leagues from the coast of Tuscany, forty from that of Provence, and sixty from that of Spain. It belongs, geographically, to the Italian peninsula, but as Italy is not a nation, Corsica naturally forms an integral part of France. . . .

The isle is woody. The plains and hills are, or may be, covered with olives, mulberry, orange, lemon, and other fruit trees. The mountainsides are clothed with chestnut trees, among which are villages naturally fortified by their position, and on the mountain-tops are forests of pines, firs, and evergreen oaks. The olive trees are as large as those of the Levant. The chestnut trees are enormous, and of the largest species. The pines and firs are not inferior to those of Russia in height and bulk. . . . Oil, wine, silk, and timber are the four major exports that enrich the island. . . .

Corsica is a beautiful country in the months of January and February. In the dog-days, though, it becomes dry and water grows scarce, especially in the plains. The inhabitants then like to take up residence on the sides of the hills, whence they descend into the low grounds in winter, either to graze their flocks or to cultivate the plains. . . .

In the course of twenty years, from 1769 to 1789, the island of Corsica was greatly improved. But all those benefits of French rule had no effect on the hearts of the inhabitants, who were anything but French at the time of the Revolution. A lieutenant-general of infantry, who was crossing the mountains, once talked with a shepherd about the ingratitude of his fellow Corsicans. Enumerating the benefits of the French administration, he said: "In your Paoli's time you paid double what you pay now." "That is true, Signor," the shepherd replied, "but then we gave it, and now you take it."

Napoleon on Napoleon, ed. Somerset de Chair (London: Cassell, 1992), pp. 50–52, 54.

THE SIEGE OF TOULON

In his account of the siege of Toulon Napoleon denies any role to Paul Barras, Antonio Saliceti, or any of the politicians in securing his promotion. Everything connected with the French victory and his advance was due to his own genius.

For a month I had been carefully reconnoitring the ground and I had made myself perfectly acquainted with the whole terrain. It was I who proposed the plan of attack that resulted in the reduction of Toulon. I regarded all the proposals of the committee of fortifications as totally useless and was of the opinion that a regular siege was simply not necessary. If from fifteen to twenty mortars, thirty or forty pieces of cannon, and furnaces for red-hot balls could be positioned where they could maintain fire upon every point of the greater and lesser roadsteads, then it was evident that the combined squadron would be obliged to withdraw. The garrison would then be placed in a state of blockade, being unable to communicate with the squadron, which would be forced to stand out to sea. That being so, I was convinced that the combined forces would prefer to withdraw the garrison, and burn the French vessels and magazines, rather than leave in the fortress 15,000 or 20,000 men who sooner or later would be obliged to surrender, but who would then have no bargaining power to ensure terms of capitulation for themselves.

In short, I said that there was no need to march against the town at all, but only to occupy the position I proposed. This was at the extreme point of the promontory of Balagnier and l'Eguillette. I had discovered this position a month before, and had pointed it out to the General-in-Chief, assuring him that if he would occupy it with three battalions he would take Toulon in four days. But the English had become, since I first observed it, so sensible of its importance, that they had disembarked 4,000 men there, had cut down all the wood that covered the promontory of Le Caire, which commanded the whole position, and had employed all the resources of Toulon, even the galley-slaves, to entrench themselves there, making of it, in their words, "a little Gibraltar." Now, therefore, the point, which a month ago might have been seized and occupied without opposition, required a serious attack. It would not be advisable to risk a direct assault. Instead, batteries of 24-pounders and mortars should destroy the breastworks, which were built of wood, break down the palisades, and throw a shower of shells into the interior of the fort. Then, after forty-eight hours of vigorous fire, the fort should be stormed by picked troops. Two days after the fort had been taken, I judged, Toulon would belong to the Republic. This plan of attack was much discussed and the engineer officers who were present at the council were of the opinion that my project was a necessary preliminary to a regular siege, the first principle of all sieges being the establishment of a strict blockade. From this time on there was unanimity of opinions. . . .

It was at Toulon that my reputation began. All the generals, representatives and soldiers who had heard me give my opinions in the different councils, three months before the taking of the town, anticipated my future military career. From that moment I won the confidence of all the soldiers of the Army of Italy. Dugommier wrote to the Committee of Public Safety soliciting the rank of brigadier-general for me, and using these words: "Reward this young man and promote him, for if he is ungratefully treated he will promote himself."

Napoleon on Napoleon, ed. Somerset de Chair (London: Cassell, 1992), pp. 75–76, 83.

ITALY AND THE NAPOLEONIC LEGEND

Napoleon's success as a commander owed much to the high morale of his troops and their personal devotion to him. During the Italian campaign of 1796–1797 army newspapers, distributed to the soldiers and circulated in France helped to create the myth of Bonaparte as an invincible, almost superhuman figure.

He moves at the speed of light and strikes like a thunderbolt. He is everywhere at once and misses nothing. . . . If one examines his domestic life, one finds a man who happily divests himself of all grandeur when with his family; he has the constant air of a man preoccupied with some grand scheme, which frequently interrupts his meals and his sleep. He says with simple dignity to those whom he respects: "I have seen kings at my feet; I could have amassed fifty millions in my coffers; I could easily have claimed to be someone other than what I am; but I am a citizen of France, I am the leading general of *La Grande Nation;* I know that posterity will do me justice."

Le Courrier de l'armée d'Italie, 23 October 1796; quoted in D. G. Wright, *Napoleon and Europe* (London and New York: Longman, 1984), pp. 98–99.

The testimony of Laure Permon, the future Laure Junot, duchess of Abrantès, demonstrates that the new cult of personality had its effect in France. Only Napoleon's masters in the Directory remained immune to adoration of the Republic's new star general and self-styled savior.

The Army of Italy surprised us every day by the prodigies communicated in its bulletins. The Directory, which disliked General Bonaparte, would have liked to have thrown a veil over the glory of the young hero; but the country, which he had saved from Austrian invasion, the soldiers, whom he led to victory, had thousands of voices to proclaim it.

It would be very difficult to convey even a slight idea of the enthusiasm with which Bonaparte was received when he arrived in Paris. The French people are volatile, not very capable of constancy in their affections, but keenly alive to the sentiment of glory. Give them victories, and they will be more than content, they will be grateful. . . .

Had Bonaparte's vanity been ever so great, it must have been satisfied; for all classes joined . . . to give him a cordial welcome on his return to his country. The populace shouted, "Long live General Bonaparte! Long live the conqueror of Italy, the peace-maker of Campo Formio!" The shopkeepers said, "May God preserve him for our glory, and deliver us from the yoke of the Directors!" The higher class, ungagged and unbastilled, ran with enthusiasm to meet a young man who in a year had advanced from the battle of Montenotte to the Treaty of Leoben, and from victory to victory. He may have committed errors, and even very grave ones, since that time, but he was then a Colossus of great and pure glory.

At the Court of Napoleon: Memoirs of the Duchesse d'Abrantès, ed. Olivier Bernier (New York: Doubleday, 1989), pp. 44–45.

EGYPT

In Napoleon's retrospective account of the Egyptian campaign he places the motives behind it in a global context, justifies his own behavior, and provides a curious insight into his attitude toward religion. He typically puts the blame for failure on others and as always accuses Britain of perfidy.

The expedition to Egypt had three aims: to establish on the Nile a French colony which would prosper without slaves and serve France in place of the republic of Santo Domingo and all the sugar islands; to open a market for our manufactures in Africa, Arabia, and Syria and supply our commerce with all the production of those vast countries, and to gain Egypt as a base from which an army of 60,000 men would set out to the Indus to excite the Mahrattas and oppressed people of those extensive regions to insurrections. . . .

The first two of these aims were fulfilled, and notwithstanding the loss of Admiral Brueys's squadron at Alexandria, the intrigue by which Kléber was induced to sign the Convention of El-Arisch, and the landing of from 30,000 to 35,000 English commanded by Abercrombie at Aboukir and Cosseir, the third aim also would have been attained—a French army would have reached the Indus in the winter of 1801–2—had not the command of the army devolved, as a result of the murder of Kléber, on a man [General Menou] who, although abounding in courage, business talent, and goodwill, was temperamentally wholly unfit for military command. . . .

After Alexandria and Cairo had been taken and the Mamelukes defeated at the Pyramids, the question of conquest was still undecided, unless the *ulemas* and all the ministers of the Muslim religion could be conciliated. Ever since the Revolution, the French army had exercised no worship— even in Italy it never attended church. Advantage was taken of this circumstance —the army was presented to the Muslims as an army of converts, disposed to embrace Mohammedanism. The Coptic, Greek, Latin, and Syrian Christians were numerous; they wanted to avail themselves of the presence of the French army to escape the restrictions imposed on their worship. I opposed this proceeding, and took care to keep religious affairs on the footing on which I found them. Every morning at sunrise, the sheiks of the Grand Mosque of Gemil-Azar (a sort of Sorbonne) used to come to my levee. I had all possible respectful attentions shown them and I discoursed with them at length on the various circumstances of the Prophet's life and on the chapters of the Koran. . . .

After the battle of Aboukir, on 3 August 1799, the English commodore sent to Alexandria the English newspapers and the French Gazette of Frankfurt for the months of April, May, and June, which communicated the news of the reverse sustained by the Armies of the Rhine and of Italy. We heard of the war of the second coalition at the camp at Acre.

I returned to France for three reasons: first, because my instructions authorized me to do so (I had carte-blanche in all respects); secondly, because my presence was necessary to the Republic; thirdly, because the Army of the East, which was victorious and numerous, would not, for a long time, have any enemy to contend with. The first object of the Egyptian expedition had been accomplished; the second could not be attained so long as the frontiers of the Republic were under threat and anarchy prevailed in its interior. . . . When . . . I left the command to Kléber, it [the French army] must have had 28,000 men, of whom 25,000 were in a condition to take the field. It is notorious that, when I left Egypt in August 1799, I thought that country forever secured to France and hoped one day to be able to realize the second object of the expedition. As to the ideas I then entertained on the affairs of France, I communicated them to Menou, who has often repeated them: I planned the revolution of 18 Brumaire.

Napoleon on Napoleon, ed. Somerset de Chair (London: Cassell, 1992), pp. 107–112.

18 BRUMAIRE

Napoleon's proclamation justifying his role in the coup of 18 Brumaire manages to give the impression that he had been the victim of unprovoked hostility and acted purely for the good of his country. By skilfully using half-truths and playing upon popular feelings, he constructs a clever piece of propaganda while again demonstrating his own courage, foresight, and position "above party."

On my return to Paris, I found all authorities divided, and agreement only on one truth: that the Constitution was half destroyed and could not save liberty.

All the parties came to me, and confided in me their plans, revealed their secrets, and asked me for help, but I refused to be the man of a party.

The Council of Ancients called me; I responded to its call. A plan of restoration had been put together by men whom the nation is accustomed to see as defenders of liberty, equality, and property: This plan demanded scrutiny, calm, free, exempt from all influence and fear. Accordingly, the Council of Ancients decided to move the legislative body to St Cloud, and charged me with commanding the force necessary for its independence. I believed it my duty to my fellow citizens, to the soldiers perishing in our armies, and the national glory bought with their blood, to accept the command.

The Councils assembled at St Cloud. Republican troops guaranteed their security outside, but murderers created terror inside. Several deputies from the Council of 500, armed with daggers and pistols, circulated death threats.

The plans which should have been developed were restrained, the majority disorganized, the most courageous speakers disconcerted, and the uselessness of every wise proposition evident.

I took my indignation and grief to the Council of Ancients. I demanded assurance of the execution of its generous plans; I showed it the evils of the fatherland, which they understood; it united with me, showing new evidence of its constant will.

I presented myself at the Council of 500, alone, unarmed, head uncovered, just as the Ancients had received and applauded me. I came to remind the majority of its wishes and to assure it of its power.

The daggers which threatened the deputies were immediately raised against their liberator. Twenty murderers threw themselves on me and aimed at my chest. The grenadiers of the legislative body, whom I had left at the door of the hall, hearing, interposed themselves between the murderers and myself. One of the grenadiers had his clothes pierced by a dagger blow. He was carried out.

At the same instant, cries of "outlaw!" were raised against the defender of the law. This was the fierce cry of murderers against the force destined to put them down.

They pressed around the President, with threats in their mouths and arms in their hands. They ordered him to proclaim "outlaw"; I was warned and ordered him wrested from their fury, and six grenadiers of the legislative body snatched him. Immediately after that, the grenadiers of the legislative body charged into the hall and cleared it.

The factions, intimidated, dispersed and withdrew. The majority, safe from their attacks, returned freely and peacefully to the meeting hall, heard the propositions which were put before them of public safety, discussed and prepared the salutary resolution which will become the new provisional law of the Republic.

Frenchmen, without doubt you will recognize in this conduct the zeal of a soldier of liberty. Conservative, tutelary, liberal ideas are returned to their rights by the dispersal of the factions oppressing the

Councils and who, having become the most odious of men, have not ceased to be the most contemptible.

Eric A. Arnold, ed., *A Documentary Survey of Napoleonic France* (Lanham, MD: University Press of America, 1994), pp. 20–22.

MARENGO

A.-C. Thibaudeau, prefect in Bordeaux, noted in his memoirs how the victory of Marengo, which brought Napoleon's second Italian campaign to a triumphant conclusion, was greeted with huge popular enthusiasm throughout France. The first consul had, it appeared, brought peace and glory to French arms through another masterstroke.

The victory at Marengo decided the fate of Italy and proved a happy omen for France. The Cisalpine Republic was re-established, the Ligurian Republic liberated, the annexation of Piedmont secretly prepared. The First Consul and the Catholic Church formed an alliance at Milan. The Church sang his triumphs and treated him as a sovereign. The victory anthems and the mood of triumphant joy spread to Paris, to Bordeaux and throughout the Republic. A campaign so short, so brilliant and so decisive had never previously been witnessed. Covered in laurels, the First Consul swiftly travelled across Italy, laid the foundation stone of the restoration of the Place de Bellecoeur at Lyon, and then returned to Paris, able to say, with justice, like Caesar: *veni, vidi, vici*. He arrived on the 13 Messidor (2 July) 1800 at two o'clock, with a slight wound from an accident to his carriage. The whole population flowed into the courtyard and garden of the Tuileries palace. Everyone's face expressed a joy which had not been seen for a long time.

Mémoires de A.-C. Thibaudeau 1799–1815, quoted in D. G. Wright, *Napoleon and Europe* (London and New York: Longman, 1984), pp. 101–102.

THE RELIGIOUS SETTLEMENT

The Concordat of 1802, reconciling the Catholic Church to the Consular regime, was of prime importance in securing Napoleon's position and resolving the religious conflict in France. In his proclamation of 17 April, Napoleon as always emphasizes his personal role in ending the divisions that had tormented France for a decade, but he suggests wrongly that the initiative came from Pope Pius VII.

Frenchmen! From the bosom of a revolution inspired by the love of the fatherland suddenly exploded in your midst religious dissensions, which became the plague of your families, the nourishment of factions, and the hope of your enemies.

An insane policy tried to stifle them under the debris of the altars, under the very ruins of religion. By its commands, pious solemnities ceased where citizens were called by the sweet name of brothers, all were recognized as equal under the hand of God who created them. The dying, alone with their grief, no longer heard that consoling voice which calls Christians to a better life, and even God seemed exiled from nature.

But public conscience, the sentiment of the independence of opinion, rose up and soon, distracted by external enemies, their explosion brought devastation into our departments. Frenchmen forgot that they were French and became the instruments of foreign hatred.

On the other hand, passions were unchained, morals were without support, hope in the future was denied, all were united to bring confusion into society.

To put an end to this confusion, it was necessary to set up religion on its base again and to take only measures accepted by religion itself.

It was the sovereign Pontiff who the example of centuries and reason directed to appeal to unite opinions and reconcile hearts.

The head of the Church pondered in his wisdom and in the interest of the Church the proposition that the interest of the state had dictated.

His voice was heard by the pastors; what he approved, the Government agreed to, and the Legislators passed a law of the Republic. Thus vanished all the elements of confusion; thus faded all qualms which could alarm consciences, and all obstacles that malevolence could oppose to the return of internal peace.

Ministers of a religion of peace, may the most profound forgetfulness cover your dissensions, your woes, and your faults, may this religion that unites you attach you by the same ties, by indissoluble ties, to the interest of your fatherland.

Exert for it all the force and ascendancy of spirit that your ministry gives you; that your lessons and examples may form in young citizens the love of our institutions, respect for and attachment to the tutelary authorities which have been created to protect them; may they learn from you that the God of peace is also the God of armies, and that He fights alongside those who defend the independence and liberty of France.

Citizens who profess Protestant religions, the law equally extends to you its care. Let this morality, common to all Christians, this morality so holy, so pure, so fraternal, unite them all in the same love of the fatherland, in the same respect for its laws, in the same affection for all the members of its great family.

Never let doctrinal struggles alter the sentiments inspired and commanded by religion.

Frenchmen, let us all be united for the happiness of the fatherland and humanity; let this religion, which civilized Europe, still be the bond which brings humanity together, and let the virtue it demands always be associated with the light that illuminates us.

Proclamation of 17 April 1802, in Eric A. Arnold, ed., *A Documentary Survey of Napoleonic France* (Lanham, MD: University Press of America, 1994), pp. 118–120.

THE IMPERIAL CATECHISM

Not the least advantage of the religious settlement from Napoleon's point of view was that the Church could be incorporated into the effort to inculcate young French people with the ideals of the Napoleonic state. The Imperial Catechism shows the cult of the emperor and the strong state in its most extreme and almost caricatural form.

Q. What are the duties of Christians in respect to the Princes who govern them, and what in particular are our duties to Napoleon I, our Emperor?

A. Christians owe to the Princes who govern them, and in particular we owe to Napoleon I, our Emperor, love, respect, obedience, loyalty, military service, the taxes levied for the preservation and defence of the Empire and of his throne; we also owe him our prayers for his safety and the spiritual and temporal well-being of the state.

Q. Why are we obliged to all of these duties to our Emperor?

A. First, because God, who created empires and distributes them according to His will, in heaping on our Emperor gifts, both in peace and war, has established him as our sovereign and rendered him the minister of His power and image on earth. To honor and serve our Emperor is thus to honor and serve God himself. Second, because our Lord Jesus Christ, both by His teaching and example, has Himself taught us what we owe our sovereign: He was born according to the law of Caesar Augustus; He paid the prescribed tax, and He even ordered us to render unto God that which belongs to God, and He ordered us to render unto Caesar that which belongs to Caesar.

Q. Are there not particular reasons which should attach us more strongly to Napoleon I, our Emperor?

A. Yes, because it is he whom God raised in difficult circumstances to re-establish public worship of the holy religion of our fathers and to be the protector of it. He has restored and preserved public order by his profound and active wisdom; he defends the state by his powerful arm; he has become the anointed of the Lord by the consecration which he received from the sovereign Pontiff, Head of the Church Universal.

Q. What should one think of those who fail in their duty to the Emperor?

A. According to the Apostle Saint Paul, they would be resisting the order established by God Himself, and would render themselves worthy of eternal damnation.

Q. Are the duties that we owe to our Emperor equally binding on us to his legitimate successors, in the order established by the Constitutions of the Empire?

A. Yes, without doubt, because we read in Holy Scripture that God, Lord of Heaven and Earth, by a command of His supreme will and by His providence, gives empires not only to one person in particular, but also to his family.

Q. What are our obligations to his civic officers?

A. We owe them honor, respect and obedience, because they are agents of the authority of our Emperor.

Q. What is forbidden to us by the Fourth Commandment?

A. We are forbidden to be disobedient to our superiors, to injure them, or to speak ill of them.

Excerpt from Imperial Catechism: Lesson VII, Continuation of the Fourth Commandment, from Eric A. Arnold, ed., *A Documentary Survey of Napoleonic France* (Lanham, MD: University Press of America, 1994), pp. 222–224.

PERFIDIOUS ALBION

Napoleon always sought to portray the outbreak of war as the fault of the other side. In a long tirade he wrote for the official government newspaper, *Le Moniteur,* in 1803, the breakdown of the Peace of Amiens is entirely due to British greed and ambition.

If France had possessed ambitious schemes and ideas of aggrandizement, would she not have kept all Italy under her direct influence? Would she not have annexed the Batavian Republic, Switzerland and Portugal? Instead of these easy acquisitions, she wisely offers to limit her territory and power, and she accepts the loss of the huge territory of Santo Domingo as well as of the large sums of money and the armies which have been sent to recover that colony. She makes every sacrifice so that peace may continue. . . . For the sake of indulging her malignant and all too powerful passions, England disturbs the peace of the world, wantonly violates the rights of nations, tramples on the most solemn treaties, and breaks her pledged faith—that ancient and eternal faith which even savage hordes acknowledge and religiously respect.

One sole obstacle stands in the way of her policies and her ambitions—victorious, moderate, prosperous France; her vigorous and enlightened government; her illustrious and magnanimous leader. These are the targets of England's delirious envy, of her constant attacks, of her implacable hatred, of her diplomatic intrigues, of her maritime conspiracies, and of the official denunciations of France to her Parliament and subjects. But Europe is watching; France is arming. History writes: Rome destroyed Carthage!

Le Moniteur, May 1803, in D. G. Wright, *Napoleon and Europe* (London and New York: Longman, 1984), p. 103.

ENLIGHTENED GOVERNMENT IN THE EMPIRE

Napoleon's letter to his brother Jérôme, newly installed as king of Westphalia, demonstrates how authoritarian rule in the satellite states ideally was to be combined with rational and progressive ideals. The people would be grateful for a new reign of liberty, replacing the obscurantism and tyranny of the old regime. Napoleon's demands for taxes and soldiers for his armies in fact destroyed the efforts of even a relatively popular ruler like Jérôme, but many of the beneficial aspects of imperial rule were retained after 1815.

My Brother, you will find enclosed with this letter the constitution of your kingdom. . . . This constitution comprises the conditions on which I renounce all my rights of conquest and the rights I have acquired over your country. You must follow it faithfully. The wellbeing of your people is important to me not only for the influence that it will have on your glory and mine, but also for the prospect of Europe as a whole. Do not listen to those who say that your people, accustomed to slavery, will receive our kindness ungratefully. There is more understanding in the Kingdom of Westphalia than one would lead you to believe, and your throne will only be established on the confidence and love of your population. What the people of Germany impatiently want is individuals of no noble rank whatsoever, but who have great talent and who will have equal right to your consideration and employment, and that every sort of servitude or of intermediaries between the sovereign and the lowest class of people will be totally removed. The benefits of the *Code Napoléon,* public trials, the establishment of juries, will be, above all, the distinctive characteristics of your rule. And, if I must tell you my thoughts, I count more on their effects for the extension and consolidation of your rule than on the greatest military victories. It is essential that your people enjoy a liberty, an equality, a wellbeing unknown to the people of Germany, and that this liberal government produces, one way or another, the most salutary changes to the system of the Confederation of the Rhine and the power of your rule. This manner of governing will be a more powerful barricade between you and Prussia than the Elbe, fortresses, and the protection of France. What people would wish to return to arbitrary Prussian government when it will have tasted the benefits of a wise and liberal administration? The people of Germany, like those of France, Italy, and Spain, want equality and liberal values. I have guided European affairs for some time and I have become convinced that the burden of privileges was contrary to general opinion. Be a constitutional king. If reason and the spirit of the age do not suffice, in your position good sense dictates it. You will find that having public support is a natural advantage over your neighbors who are absolute kings.

Letter to Prince Jérôme Bonaparte, 15 November 1807, in Eric A. Arnold, ed., *A Documentary Survey of Napoleonic France* (Lanham, MD: University Press of America, 1994), pp. 250–251.

THE NATIONALIST RESPONSE

What Napoleon showed in his instructions to Jérôme that he did not understand was that the power of nationalism could be stronger than forms of government and could be directed against both the absolute monarchs and himself. As Friedrich von Schiller wrote in 1804: "The German Empire and the German nation are two different things. The glory of the Germans has never been based upon the power of its princes." Johann Gottlieb Fichte's *Addresses to the German Nation,* a series of lectures given in occupied Berlin in 1807–1808, are among the founding texts of a culturally based German nationalism.

It is only by means of the common characteristic of being German that we can avert the downfall of our nation, which is threatened by its fusion with foreign peoples, and win back again an individuality that is self-supporting and quite incapable of any dependence on others. . . . We alone must help ourselves if help is to come to us. . . . By means of the new education we want to mold the Germans into a corporate body. It is the general aim of these addresses to bring courage and hope to the suffering, to proclaim joy in the midst of deep sorrow, to lead us gently and softly through the hour of deep affliction. . . . The German, if only he makes use of all his advantages, can always be superior to the foreigner. . . . Only the German really has a people and is entitled to count as one; he alone is capable of real and rational love for his nation.

In D. G. Wright, *Napoleon and Europe* (London and New York: Longman, 1984), pp. 115–116.

THE PENINSULAR WAR

Napoleon's views on the war in Spain and Portugal show him at his most egotistical. If only he had been able to take command himself, he tells us, and if only his policy had been followed by his subordinates, then the war could have been won. But there is also a kind of grudging recognition that Napoleon's style of swift decisive action could not deal with a national uprising and guerrilla warfare.

The Spanish war ended in 1809. In three months I had beaten and dispersed the four Spanish armies of 160,000 men, taken Madrid and Saragossa, and forced General Moore to re-embark, after losing half his army, his stores, and military chests. Spain was conquered. When the war with Vienna obliged me to return to France, the war of Spain recommenced. King Joseph was not competent to direct it. England made unheard-of efforts and her armies obtained some success in Portugal. Spain was surrounded by seas on three sides and English fleets unexpectedly carried new forces into Catalonia, Biscay, Portugal, the Kingdom of Valencia, and Cadiz.

The error committed in Spain was not that of proceeding too rapidly, but that of proceeding too slowly after my departure. Had I remained there a few months, I would have taken Lisbon and Cadiz, united all parties, and pacified the country. My armies never lacked military stores, clothing, or provisions. . . . The guerrillas were not formed until two years later, when they arose as a result of the disorders and abuses which had crept into the whole army, except the corps of Marshal Suchet, which occupied the Kingdom of Valencia. The Anglo-Portuguese became as skillful in maneuvers as the French army; the latter was afterwards defeated through the accidents of war, maneuvers, and strategical errors, at Talavera, Salamanca, and Vitoria. Spain was lost after a struggle of five years. The argument on the lack of fortresses is extremely misplaced—the French Army had taken them all. The Spaniards formerly offered the same resistance to the Romans.

The people of conquered nations become the subjects of the victor only through a mixture of policy and severity and by being amalgamated with the army. These points were not successfully managed in Spain. . . .

After the re-embarkation of the English army, the King of Spain remained inactive, wasting four months. He should have marched on Cadiz, Valencia, and Lisbon—political means would then have done the rest. No-one can deny that had the Court of Austria not declared war and I had been able to remain four months longer in Spain, all would have been over. The presence of a general is indispensable—he is the head, the whole of an army. It was not the Roman army that subdued Gaul, but Caesar himself: nor was it the Carthaginian army that made the Republic tremble at the gates of Rome, but Hannibal himself; neither was it the Macedonian army which reached the Indus, but Alexander; it was not the French army which carried the war to the Weser and the Inn, but Turenne; nor was it the Prussian army which, for seven years, defended Prussia against the three greatest powers of Europe, it was Frederick the Great.

Napoleon on Napoleon, ed. Somerset de Chair (London: Cassell, 1992), pp. 216–217.

1812: THE RUSSIAN CAMPAIGN

In his exile on Saint Helena Napoleon persisted in looking back on the Russian campaign as a glorious episode and justifying his decision to undertake the invasion in terms of the containment of Russia.

The history of the campaign in Russia will never be well known, because the Russians either do not write at all or write without the slightest regard for truth, while the French are afflicted by a strange mania for dishonoring and decrying their own

glory. The Russian war became a necessary consequence of the Continental System the moment the Emperor Alexander violated the conventions of Tilsit and Erfurt, but a consideration of much greater importance determined me to begin it. I thought that the French Empire, which I had created by so many victories, would be dismembered at my death and the scepter of Europe would pass into the hands of a tsar, unless I drove back the Russians beyond the Dnieper and raised up the throne of Poland, the natural barrier of the empire. In 1812 Austria, Prussia, Germany, Switzerland and Italy marched under the French eagles. Was it not natural that I should think the moment had come to consolidate the immense edifice I had raised, but on which Russia would lean with all her weight as long as she could send her numerous armies, at pleasure, to the Oder? Alexander was young and vigorous, like his empire; it was to be presumed that he would survive me. This is the whole secret of that war. No personal feeling was ever concerned in it, as pamphleteers have pretended. The campaign of Russia was the most glorious, the most difficult, and the most honorable to the Gauls of all that are recorded in ancient and modern history. The Russians are very brave troops and their whole army was united. At the battle of Moskva [Borodino] they had 170,000 men, including the Moscow troops. Kutuzov had taken up a fine position, and occupied it judiciously. All advantages were on his side—superiority in infantry, cavalry and artillery, an excellent position, and a great number of redoubts. Nonetheless he was vanquished. Intrepid heroes—Murat, Ney, Poniatowski—it is to you that the glory of the victory is due! What great, what brilliant actions might history cull from these events!

Napoleon on Napoleon, ed. Somerset de Chair (London: Cassell, 1992), pp. 219–220.

Those who took part were entitled to take a slightly different view. Eugénie de Coucy, wife of Marshal Oudinot, en route to join her wounded husband in Vilnius in September 1812, met her friend General Jean-François Jacqueminot, who voiced the doubts within the army.

"What a strange circumstance," he said, "is your presence in the midst of this desert, madame la duchesse! Oh, that all-devouring ambition which leads us to the end of the world, which disorganizes every existence and paralyzes every industry! And to what will it bring us? We are all done for."

This diatribe, the first I had heard uttered against the Emperor since my marriage, this violent discontent on the part of a man who was as brave as he was enthusiastic, petrified me with surprise. I listened in silence.

"Yes," he continued, "misfortunes without end have already reached and are increasingly threatening our army, and I do not know which of us will ever see France again."

Memoirs of Marshal Oudinot, duc de Reggio, compiled from the hitherto unpublished souvenirs of the duchesse de Reggio by Gaston Steigler (New York: D. Appleton and Co., 1897), pp. 154–155.

Lieutenant-General de Fezensac described the horrors of the retreat from Moscow, showing something of the reality behind Napoleon's vainglory.

The sufferings which we were destined to undergo in places, the destruction of which had been equally the object of Russians and French, may be easily conceived. Where we found a few houses still standing, the inhabitants were absent. We had now nothing to look forward to before Smolensk, which was eighty leagues distant. Until our arrival there, we would seek in vain for either flour, meat, or forage for our horses. We were reduced to those provisions we had brought from Moscow, and these, trifling as they were, like all plunder, most unequally distributed. One regiment had preserved its oxen, and was in want of bread. Another had flour, and was without meat. This inequality prevailed even in the same regiment. Some companies had abundance, while others were starving; and though commanding officers endeavoured to effect something like an equal distribution, egotism and selfishness succeeded in evading their superintendence and evading their authority. Moreover, to preserve our provisions, the horses that drew them also had to be preserved, but these perished in numbers every day for lack of food. The soldiers who strayed from their ranks to seek wherewith to relieve their hunger fell into the hands of the Cossacks and armed peasants. The route was covered with ammunition wagons condemned to be blown up, with cannons and carriages left to their fate, their teams having no longer the strength to draw them. From the very first day, our retreat had the semblance of a rout. The Emperor continued to wreak his vengeance on all buildings. Marshal d'Eckmühl [Davout], commanding the rearguard, was ordered to burn everything, and never was an order carried out so literally. Detachments were sent as far as the proximity of the enemy would permit, to the right and left, to burn the chateaux and villages. Yet even the sight of these conflagrations was not the most distressing which we encountered. A column of Russian prisoners marched immediately in our front, escorted by troops of the Confederation of the Rhine. They barely received a little horse flesh for food, and their guards massacred those who could no longer march. We came across some of their corpses, which, without exception, had their skulls knocked in. I must do the soldiers of my regiment the justice to record their indignation on beholding these evidences of so dark a deed. Moreover they were not insensible to the cruel reprisals which this conduct exposed them to, should they chance to fall into the hands of the enemy.

A Journal of the Russian Campaign of 1812, translated from the French of Lieut.-General de Fezensac (London, 1852; rept. Cambridge: Ken Trotman Ltd., 1988), pp. 75–77.

In a speech to the Senate on his return to Paris, Napoleon emphasizes how he has always acted in the interests of peace and stability at home, justifies his monarchy, manages to imply that he invaded Russia for her own good, and adopts a rather casual attitude to the sufferings of his soldiers.

Senators, what you have said is most pleasing to me. I have at heart the glory and power of France, but my first thoughts are solely for that which could perpetuate internal calm and always shelter my people from the discords of factions and the horrors of anarchy. It is upon these enemies of the happiness of the people that I have, with the will and love of the French, built this throne, to which the fate of the Fatherland is henceforth tied.

Some timid and cowardly soldiers lose the independence of nations, but faint-hearted magistrates destroy the authority of the laws, the rights of the throne, and the social order itself.

The most beautiful death would be that of a soldier who dies on the battlefield, if the death of a magistrate dying in the defense of his sovereign, the throne, and the laws, would not be even more glorious.

When I undertook the regeneration of France, I requested of Providence a fixed number of years. One destroys in an instant, but one can only rebuild with the aid of time. The greatest need of the state is that of courageous magistrates.

Our fathers had a rallying cry: "The King is dead, long live the King!" These few words comprise the principal advantages of the monarchy. I think that I have studied well the spirit that my peoples have shown throughout the centuries; I have thought about what has made the difference between epochs of our history; I will think on it again.

The war that I am waging against Russia is a political war. I have waged it without hatred. I could have wished to spare her the ills which she has done to herself. I could have armed a great part of the population against her, by proclaiming the liberty of the serfs, as a great number of villages demanded of me. But, when I learned of the degradation of this numerous class of the Russian people, I rejected this measure which would have condemned many families to death, devastation, and the most horrible torments.

My army has sustained losses, but that is due to the harshness of the season.

I accept the wishes that you express to me.

Speech to Senate, 20 December 1812, in Eric A. Arnold, ed., *A Documentary Survey of Napoleonic France* (Lanham, MD: University Press of America, 1994), pp. 104–105.

FRANCE IN 1814

Eugénie de Coucy, Mme. Oudinot, records the widespread disillusion and war-weariness as Napoleon's regime tottered toward collapse following defeat in Germany and the campaign of France.

France had long since been exhausted, not so much of money, for the countries conquered by us still supplied this, but of men. This last scarcity, which it was endeavoured to remedy by every kind of conscription, threw whole families into despair and want. They were really bled to the uttermost. The poor man had to give his last son and in him lost his support; and in the fields it was often the women and girls who led the plough. Husbandry suffered as much as individuals. And the same disasters occurred in the towns. Numerous families condemned themselves perpetually to cripple their fortunes in order to save the young man whom other measures ended by reaching. Great names, great fortunes, in short, all that might have hoped for independence were compelled to assist at least in the recruiting of guards of honor.

In any case, the young man serving under the flag, whatever the feeling of repulsion with which his antecendents might inspire him for the government, saw nothing but honor before him, and served with courage and loyalty. But it was in the families that resentment was felt. The crape with which the Russian and Leipzig campaigns had covered France had not yet disappeared. Bitter tears were still being shed. People realized that, by yielding a certain number of his conquests of preceding years, the Emperor might have saved France from this invasion. . . . Peace! The cry was in every heart: for of glory, the everyday food of the country, France had had a sufficient share.

Memoirs of Marshal Oudinot, duc de Reggio, compiled from the hitherto unpublished souvenirs of the duchesse de Reggio by Gaston Steigler (New York: D. Appleton and Co., 1897), pp. 252–253.

1815: THE FINAL GAMBLE

Ignoring the kinds of feeling recorded by Mme. Oudinot, Napoleon in his Proclamation to the French People on his escape from Elba blames others for the defeats of 1813–1814. He identifies himself with the people and calls upon them to reject any government imposed by foreigners. Anyone who opposes him is a traitor.

Napoleon, by the grace of God and the constitutions of the state, Emperor of the French, etc., etc.

Frenchmen, the defection of the duke of Castiglione [marshal Augereau] delivered Lyon defenseless to our enemies. The army, of which I had confided command to him, was, by the number of its battalions, the bravery and patriotism of the troops which composed it, able to fight the Austrian army which opposed it, and to arrive at the rear of the left wing of the enemy threatening Paris.

The victories of Champaubert, Montmirail, Château Thierry, Vauchamp, Mormans, Montereau, Caronne, Reims, Arcis-sur-Aube, and St-Dizier, the insurrection of the brave peasants of Lorraine, Champagne, Alsace, Franche-Comté and Burgundy and the position that I had taken in the rear of the enemy army, separating it from its supply dumps, from its reserves, from its convoys and all its equipment, placed it in a desperate situation. It would have found its grave in those vast regions that it had so pitilessly plundered, when the treason of the duke of Ragusa [marshal Marmont] surrendered the capital and disorganized the army.

The unexpected behaviour of these two generals, who betrayed at the same time their fatherland, their Prince and their benefactor, changed the outcome of the war. The disastrous situation of the enemy was such that at the end of the incident which took place before Paris, he was without ammunition and separated from his reserve supplies.

In these great and new circumstances, my heart was torn, but my spirit remained resolute. I consulted only the interest of the fatherland. I exiled myself on a rock in the middle of the sea. My life was and still had to be useful to you. I did not allow the great number of citizens who wished to accompany me to share my fate: I thought their presence would be useful in France, and I only took with me a handful of brave fellows necessary as my guard.

Raised to the throne by your choice, all that has been done without you is illegitimate. For twenty-five years France has had new interests, new institutions, a new glory, which could only be guaranteed by a national government and by a dynasty born in these new circumstances. A prince who would reign over you, who would sit on my throne thanks to the very armies which ravaged our territory, would seek in vain to bolster himself by the principles of feudal rights; he could only assure the honor and the rights of a small number of individuals, enemies of the people who, for twenty-five years, have condemned them in all our national assemblies. Your peace at home and respect abroad would be lost forever.

Frenchman, in my exile I heard your complaints and wishes. You were clamouring for a government of your choice, which alone is legitimate. You were blaming me for my long sleep, you were reproaching me for sacrificing the great interests of the state to my own comfort.

I crossed the sea in the midst of all sorts of perils. I arrived among you to regain my rights, which are yours.

Everything that certain individuals have done, written, or said since the taking of Paris, I will ignore forever. It will have no influence on the memory that I retain of the important services that they have rendered, because there are events of such a nature that they are beyond human comprehension.

Frenchmen, there is no nation, however small it might be, which does not have the right to reject the dishonor of obeying a prince imposed by a temporarily victorious enemy. When Charles VII re-entered Paris and overthrew the ephemeral throne of Henry VI, he recognized that he held his throne by the valor of his brave men and not from a prince-regent of England. It is

likewise to you alone and to the courageous soldiers of the army that I give and will always dedicate every duty.

Proclamation of 1 March 1815, in Eric A. Arnold, ed., *A Documentary Survey of Napoleonic France* (Lanham, MD: University Press of America, 1994), pp. 345–348.

THE FINAL ACT

Napoleon's second abdication, with its masterly understatement that "circumstances appear to have changed," sees the emperor regretting nothing and posing as a sacrificial victim to foreign hatred.

Frenchmen, in beginning the war to maintain national independence, I counted on the joining of all efforts, of all wills, and on the co-operation of all national authorities. I was justified in hoping for success, and I defied all the declarations of the powers against me.

Circumstances appear to have changed.

I offer myself as a sacrifice to the hatred of the enemies of France. May they be sincere in their declarations of only wishing for my person!

My political life is ended, and I proclaim my son, under the title Napoleon II, Emperor of the French.

The present ministers will temporarily form the Government Council. The interest that I have in my son binds me to invite the Chambers to recognize, without delay, the urgency of the law.

Unite for the public safety, and to remain an independent nation.

At the Elysée, 22 June 1815.

From Eric A. Arnold, ed., *A Documentary Survey of Napoleonic France* (Lanham, MD: University Press of America, 1994), pp. 357–358.

In these general reflections recorded on Saint Helena, Napoleon gives his advice on gaining success in war, based on unity of command, concentration of forces, and decisive action. Any aspiring Napoleon should also, he advises, study the great commanders of ancient and modern times. Napoleon also betrays his reading of the classics by using the old cliché of Fortune as a woman, so stressing the importance of seizing favorable opportunities when they present themselves.

Every war ought to be methodical, because every war ought to be conducted in conformity with the principles and rules of the art and without an object. It should be carried on with forces proportional to the obstacles that are foreseen. There are therefore two sorts of offensive war—one that is well understood and conformable to the principles of the science and one that is ill understood and which violates those principles. . . .

There should be only one army, for unity of command is of the first necessity in war. The army must be kept united. The greatest possible number of forces must be concentrated on the field of battle. The favourable opportunity must be seized, for fortune is female—if you balk her today, you must not expect to meet with her again tomorrow.

Make offensive war like Alexander, Hannibal, Gustavus Adolphus, Turenne, Prince Eugene, and Frederick the Great. Read again and again the history of their eighty-eight campaigns and model yourself on them: that is the only way to become a great commander and to attain the secrets of the art. Your genius, when thus enlightened, will lead you to reject maxims contrary to the principles of these great men.

Napoleon on Napoleon, ed. Somerset de Chair (London: Cassell, 1992), pp. 208–209.

Although she gives the wrong impression when she implies that she was the only one to see through Napoleon from the beginning, Mme. de Staël's unremittingly hostile views on Napoleon are among the most acute of his contemporaries. They also shed unflattering light on Napoleon's misogynistic, "Mediterranean" attitude toward women.

During the twelve years of exile to which Napoleon condemned me, I often thought that he would be unable to bear the misery of being deprived of France, having no memory of France in his heart. Nothing but the rocks of Corsica retraced his childhood days; Necker's daughter was more French than he. . . .

I guessed Napoleon's character and political schemes more quickly than most people, and I am proud of that. An infallible instinct enlightens all real friends of liberty about such things. But my position at the beginning of the Consulate was dreadful, because good society in France at the time thought Bonaparte the very man to save them from anarchy or Jacobinism. As a result, my spirit of opposition earned me a lot of disapproval. Anyone who can see as far as tomorrow in politics arouses the wrath of people who can see no further than today. I must say it took even more strength to bear the persecution of society than to expose myself to the persecution of power.

I have always kept the memory of one of those society tortures (if it is all right to speak that way) that French aristocrats are so good at inflicting whenever it suits them on people who do not share their opinions. A large part of the old nobility had rallied to Napoleon; some, as we have seen since then, trying to recapture their former habits as courtiers, others hoping that the first consul would bring back the old monarchy. Everyone knew I was strongly against the system of government Napoleon was preparing, and the supporters of arbitrary government followed their usual custom of calling opinions that tended to elevate the dignity of nations "antisocial." If anyone were to remind the *émigrés* who came back under Bonaparte how furiously they blamed the friends of liberty who were still loyal to the same theory, they might learn indulgence from remembering their mistakes.

I was the first woman exiled by Napoleon, though he banished many women of opposing opinions soon afterward. One of the most interesting was the Duchess of Chevreuse, who died of the heart condition brought on by her exile. As she lay dying, she could not get Napoleon's permission to come back to Paris one last time to consult her doctor and see her friends again. Where could such luxuriating in evil come from, if not from a hatred of all independent beings? Women annoyed Napoleon as rebels; they were of no use to his political designs, on the one hand, and were less susceptible than men to the hopes and fears dispensed by power. As a result, he took pleasure in saying hurtful and vulgar things to women. His pursuit of etiquette was matched by his hatred of chivalry: a bad choice to make from the manners of former times. From his early habits of Revolutionary days he also retained a certain Jacobin antipathy to brilliant Paris society, which was greatly influenced by women; he was afraid of the art of teasing which we must admit is characteristic of Frenchwomen. If Bonaparte had been willing to keep the proud role of great general and first magistrate of the Republic, he would have floated with the height of genius above all the little stinging barbs of salon wit. Once he decided to become a parvenu king, the bourgeois gentleman on the throne, he was exposing himself to the kind of society satire which can only be repressed

by the use of espionage and terror: and that is how, in fact, he repressed it. . . .

Shortly after the Eighteenth Brumaire, Bonaparte was given a report that I had spoken out in private society against the burgeoning oppression whose growth I could foretell as clearly as if I could see into the future. Joseph Bonaparte, whose wit and conversation I liked, came to see me saying: "My brother is complaining about you. Only yesterday he asked me: 'Why isn't Mme. de Staël supporting my government? What does she want? Payment on her father's account? I will order it. To live in Paris? I will give my permission.'" "Good Lord," I replied. "It's a question of what I think, not what I want." I do not know if that answer was ever reported to Bonaparte, but I am convinced at any rate that he made no sense of it if he did hear it, because he doesn't believe anybody can have sincere opinions about anything. Bonaparte considers every kind of morality a formula which has no more significance than the complimentary close of a letter. After you have assured your correspondent that you are his humble servant, he has no right to require anything of you. In the same way, Bonaparte believes that anyone who says he loves liberty, or believes in God, or prefers a clear conscience to self-interest, is just a man following the forms of etiquette to explain his ambitious pretensions or selfish calculations. The only kind of human being he does not understand is people who are sincerely attached to an opinion, whatever the consequences. Bonaparte considers such men either fools or shopkeepers trying to raise their own prices. As we shall see, the only mistakes he has ever made in this world have been about decent people, whether as individuals or, even more, as nations. . . .

I do not think that Bonaparte had already made his plan for universal monarchy when he first took charge of things. I believe his system was, as he told one of his friends shortly after the Eighteenth Brumaire, to do "something new every three months, so as to capture the imagination of the French nation. In France, anyone who does not move ahead is lost." He had promised himself to stamp out French liberty and European independence day by day; he did not lose sight of this goal, but he was able to adapt to circumstances. If the obstacle was too big, he would go around it; if the wind was blowing too strongly in the opposite direction, he stopped short. He is a most impatient man at heart, but he has a talent for standing still when necessary. He gets this from the Italians, who are capable of controlling themselves to reach their heart's desire exactly as if they had picked out this goal in cold blood. It was by alternating trickery and force that he conquered Europe. Europe is a big word, though. What was Europe? At the time, it consisted of a few ministers, none of whom had as much wit as one would find in a random sample of the men they governed.

Major Writings of Germaine de Staël, trans. Vivian Folkenflik (New York: Columbia University Press, 1987), pp. 370–371, 375, 376–377.

BENJAMIN CONSTANT

In his *The Spirit of Conquest and Usurpation and their Relation to European Civilization* (1814), Benjamin Constant considers Napoleon as usurper and conqueror. It is usurpation itself that explains Napoleon's "evil," more than the fatal flaws in his character. He also, interestingly, sees Napoleon as a man out of his time, a throwback to an age before international communications and commerce and the growth of public opinion. Within a year of writing this assessment, it is worth remembering, Constant was col-laborating with Napoleon by drawing up the Additional Act to the constitutions of the empire during the Hundred Days. . . .

I shall not be accused of trying to justify someone whom I never wished to acknowledge. But I believe that those who attribute his enterprises, his crimes and his fall to a perversity or folly peculiar to him, are in the wrong. On the contrary, he seems to me to have been powerfully affected both by his position as usurper and by the spirit of his century. Indeed, it was in his nature to be more affected by these causes than any other man would have been. What characterized him was the absence of all moral sense, that is of all sympathy, all human emotion. He was self-interest personified; if that self-interest produced results which were disastrously odd, it is because it rested upon two opposed and irreconcilable terms, usurpation, which made despotism necessary, and a degree of civilization which made it impossible. From this there resulted contradictions, incoherences, a violent double reaction which have been wrongly taken for individual eccentricities. . . .

Had France remained at peace, her peaceful citizens, her idle warriors would have observed the despot, would have judged him, and would have communicated their judgments on him. Truth would have passed through the ranks of the people. Usurpation would not have long withstood the influence of truth. Thus Bonaparte was compelled to distract public attention by bellicose enterprises. War flung onto distant shores that part of the French nation that still had some real energy. It prompted the police harassment of the timid, whom it could not force abroad. It struck terror into men's hearts, and left there a certain hope that chance would take responsibility for their deliverance: a hope agreeable to fear and convenient to inertia. How many times have I heard men who were pressed to resist tyranny postponing this, during wartime till the coming of peace, and in peacetime until war commences!

I am right therefore in claiming that a usurper's sole resource is uninterrupted war. Some object what if Bonaparte had been pacific? Had he been pacific, he would never have lasted for twelve years. Peace would have re-established communication among the different countries of Europe. These communications would have restored to thought its means of expression. Works published abroad would have been smuggled into the country. The French would have seen that they did not enjoy the approval of the majority of Europe: their prestige could not have been sustained. Bonaparte perceived this truth so well that he broke with England in order to escape the British newspapers. Yet even this was not enough. While a single country remained free, Bonaparte was never safe. Commerce, active, adroit, invisible, indefatigable, capable of overcoming any distance and of insinuating itself through a thousand roundabout means, would sooner or later have reintroduced into the empire those enemies whom it was so important to exile from it. Hence the Continental blockade and the war with Russia.

What I assert about the means of usurpation, I assert also about its fall. I claimed that it must fall by the inevitable effect of the wars which it requires. Some have objected that, had Bonaparte not made such and such a military error, he would not have been overthrown. Not this time but some other time; not today but tomorrow. It is only too natural that a gambler, who every day takes a new risk, should some day meet with the one which must ruin him. . . .

I confess that I believe it is more important to show that the evils inflicted by Bonaparte on France derived from the fact that his power had degenerated into usurpation, and thus put the blame on usurpation itself, rather than on some individual as a unique being, made for evil, and committing crimes out of neither necessity nor self-interest. The first perspective teaches us great lessons for the future; the second transforms history into a sterile study of isolated phenomena, and into the mere enumeration of effects without causes.

Benjamin Constant, *Political Writings,* trans. and ed. Biancamaria Fontana (Cambridge: Cambridge University Press, 1988), pp. 161, 163, 164, 165.

CHRONOLOGY

1769 *15 August* Birth of Napoleone Buonaparte at Ajaccio, Corsica.

1779 *January* Napoleon enters school at Autun.

April Napoleon enters the Military Academy of Brienne.

1784 *30 October* Napoleon enters the *École Militaire* in Paris.

1785 *September–October* Napoleon graduates from the *École Militaire* and is assigned to La Fère Artillery Regiment at Valence.

1788 *June* Napoleon is attached to the School of Artillery at Auxonne.

1789 *May* Beginning of the French Revolution with the meeting of the Estates General.

14 July Storming of the Bastille.

1791 *1 April* Napoleon promoted to first lieutenant.

1 October Constitution of 1791 establishes constitutional monarchy.

1792 *February* First Coalition against France formed by Prussia and Austria.

20 April France declares war on Austria.

28 May Napoleon promoted to captain.

10 August Louis XVI overthrown.

September Napoleon and his brother Lucien active in Jacobin clubs in Corsica.

22 September Proclamation of the French Republic.

1793 *March* The Buonaparte family is forced to flee from Corsica.

July Beginning of the Terror.

August–September Napoleon at siege of Toulon.

16 September Napoleon appointed commander of the French artillery.

22 December Napoleon promoted to general of brigade.

1794 *6 February* Napoleon assigned to Army of Italy.

28 July / 10 Thermidor Year II End of Terror and execution of Robespierre.

9–20 August Napoleon jailed at Antibes as a Jacobin.

1795 *March–May* Napoleon transferred to Paris; he turns down assignment to the Vendée.

21 August Napoleon assigned to *Bureau Topographique.*

5 October / 13 Vendémiaire Year IV Suppression of revolt in Paris by Napoleon's "whiff of grapeshot."

16 October Napoleon promoted to general of division.

26 October Napoleon appointed commander of the Army of the Interior.

3 November/12 Brumaire Year IV Beginning of Directory.

1796 *2 March* Napoleon appointed commander of the Army of Italy.

9 March He marries Joséphine de Beauharnais.

6 April Beginning of Napoleon's first Italian campaign.

10 May Battle of Lodi.

15 May Napoleon enters Milan.

15–17 November Battle of Arcola.

1797 *14 January* Battle of Rivoli.

2 February Surrender of Mantua.

18 April Preliminary peace of Leoben marks end of first Italian campaign.

17 October Treaty of Campo Formio.

1798 *19 May* Napoleon's expedition sails from Toulon for Alexandria and beginning of the Egyptian campaign.

21 July Battle of the Pyramids.

1 August Battle of the Nile.

29 December Second Coalition formed against France.

1799 *20 February* Napoleon invades Syria.

19 March–20 May Siege of Acre.

18 June Purge of Directory; Napoleon's ally, Paul Barras, consolidates his power.

24 August Napoleon sails for France.

16 October Napoleon in Paris.

9–10 November Coup of 18 Brumaire; Napoleon, Sieyès, and Ducos appointed temporary consuls.

12 December Constitution of Year VIII. Napoleon is first consul; Cambacérès

and Lebrun are second and third consuls.

1800 *7 February* Constitution approved by plebiscite.

15–23 May Napoleon crosses the Alps.

Early June Beginning of second Italian campaign.

14 June Battle of Marengo. End of second Italian campaign.

5 November Negotiations for Concordat open with the papacy.

3 December Battle of Hohenlinden.

24 December "Opera Plot" attempt to assassinate Napoleon.

1801 *9 February* Treaty of Lunéville with Austria.

15 July Concordat signed with Pope Pius VII.

30 August French army in Egypt surrenders to the British.

1802 *26 January* Napoleon becomes president of the Republic of Italy.

25 March Treaty of Amiens with Britain.

1 May New education system launched with creation of *lycées.*

19 May Legion of Honor established.

2 August Napoleon named Consul for Life.

4 August Constitution of Year X.

1803 *11 March* Camps established at Boulogne to train army for invasion of England.

18 May Rupture of Treaty of Amiens leads to resumption of war between France and Britain.

1804 *February–March* Royalist plot to kidnap Napoleon—arrests of Generals Moreau and Pichegru and Georges Cadoudal.

20 March Execution of the duke of Enghien.

21 March Civil Code promulgated.

18 May Proclamation of the French Empire.

19 May Marshals of the empire created.

2 December Coronation of Napoleon as emperor.

1805 *26 May* Napoleon becomes king of Italy.

7 June Eugène de Beauharnais named viceroy of Italy.

9 August Third Coalition formed—Austria joins Britain and Russia against France.

25 August The *Grande Armée* leaves Boulogne for Germany.

20 October Battle of Ulm.

21 October Battle of Trafalgar.

14 November Napoleon enters Vienna.

2 December Battle of Austerlitz.

26 December Treaty of Pressburg with Austria.

1806 *30 March* Joseph Bonaparte becomes king of Naples.

4 April Publication of Imperial Catechism.

May–June Creation of Kingdom of Holland with Louis Bonaparte as king.

12 July Napoleon establishes the Confederation of the Rhine.

July Formation of Fourth Coalition led by Prussia, Russia, and Britain.

25 September Prussian army invades the Confederation of the Rhine.

6 October Napoleon takes command of the *Grande Armée* in Germany.

14 October Battles of Jena-Auerstädt.

27 October Napoleon enters Berlin.

21 November Continental System inaugurated by Berlin Decrees.

18 December Napoleon enters Warsaw.

1807 *7 February* Battle of Eylau.

14 June Battle of Friedland.

7–9 July Treaty of Tilsit between France, Russia, and Prussia.

30 November Occupation of Lisbon by General Junot marks the beginning of the Peninsular War.

1808 *1 March* Organization of the imperial nobility.

18 March Ferdinand VII proclaimed king of Spain.

2 May Revolt in Madrid against Joachim Murat's troops marks beginning of Spanish revolt against French rule.

7 July Joseph Bonaparte crowned king of Spain; Murat and Caroline Bonaparte become king and queen of Naples.

30 July Joseph evacuates Madrid.

8 October Napoleon meets Alexander I at Erfurt.

5 November Napoleon assumes command of the army of Spain.

13 December Napoleon recaptures Madrid.

1809 *16 January* Battle of Corunna; Napoleon leaves Spain.

6 April Fifth Coalition formed by Britain, Austria, and rebel Spain.

22 April Battle of Eckmühl.

26 April British army under Arthur Wellesley (later duke of Wellington) lands at Lisbon.

17 May France annexes the Papal States.

21–22 May Battle of Essling (Aspern).

5–6 July Battle of Wagram.

14 October Treaty of Schönbrunn between France and Austria.

30 November Napoleon announces intention to divorce Joséphine.

15 December The divorce is pronounced.

1810 *17 February* Rome annexed to French Empire.

1 April Napoleon marries Marie-Louise of Austria.

1 July Holland annexed to France; Louis abdicates as king.

29 September Battle of Bussaco.

13 December North German territories annexed to French Empire.

31 December Alexander I breaks with Continental System.

1811 *January–December* Preparations for Russian campaign.

20 March Birth of Napoleon II, king of Rome.

1812 *30 May* Sixth Coalition formed by Russia and Sweden with support from Britain and rebel Spain; Napoleon takes command of *Grande Armée* in East Prussia and Poland.

24–25 June The *Grande Armée* crosses the Niemen, beginning the Russian campaign.

22 July Battle of Salamanca.

7 September Battle of Borodino.

14 September Napoleon enters Moscow.

October Duke of Wellington (then Viscount Wellington) made allied commander in Spain.

19 October French begin retreat from Moscow.

23 October Malet conspiracy in Paris.

26–28 November Remnants of *Grande Armée* cross the Berezina.

5 December Napoleon leaves his army; Murat takes command.

19 December Napoleon reaches Paris.

1813 *January–April* The *Grande Armée* completes its retreat into Germany under Eugène de Beauharnais after Murat returns to Naples.

26 February Treaty of Kalisch between Prussia and Russia.

16 March Prussia declares war on France.

2 May Battle of Lützen.

21 May Battle of Bautzen.

21 June Wellington defeats Joseph Bonaparte at Vitoria.

26–27 August Battle of Dresden.

16–19 October Battle of Leipzig ("Battle of the Nations").

October–November Collapse of the Confederation of the Rhine and Napoleon's power in Germany.

1814 *January–March* Campaign of France.

11 January Murat defects to Allies.

10–18 February Napoleon scores a series of victories against the invading Allies in eastern Europe.

12 March Wellington's Allied army enters Bordeaux.

31 March Marshals Marmont and Mortier surrender Paris to the Allies.

2–3 April The Senate and the Legislative Body proclaim the deposition of Napoleon.

6 April Napoleon abdicates in favor of his son.

11 April Napoleon abdicates unconditionally.

1 May Treaty of Paris; Louis XVIII proclaimed king of France.

4 May Napoleon starts his exile on Elba.

29 May Death of Joséphine at Malmaison.

1814–
1815 *September–June* Congress of Vienna

1815 *25 February* Napoleon sails from Elba.

1 March Napoleon lands in France near Cannes.

20 March Napoleon arrives in Paris; beginning of the Hundred Days.

16 June Battles of Ligny and Quatre-Bras.

18 June Battle of Waterloo.

22 June Napoleon's second abdication.

7 July Allies enter Paris.

2 August Napoleon declared prisoner by the Allies.

7 August Napoleon leaves Plymouth for exile on Saint Helena.

16 October Napoleon's exile begins.

20 November Second Treaty of Paris.

1821 *5 May* Death of Napoleon on Saint Helena.

1840 *15 December* Napoleon's remains are returned to Paris and interred in the Invalides.

BIBLIOGRAPHY

Agulhon, Maurice. 1982. *The Republic in the Village: The People of the Var from the French Revolution to the Second Republic.* Cambridge: Cambridge University Press.

Alexander, R. S. 1991. *Bonapartism and the Revolutionary Tradition in France: The Fédérés of 1815.* Cambridge: Cambridge University Press.

Allen, James Smith. 1992. *In the Public Eye: A History of Reading in Modern France, 1800–1940.* Princeton: Princeton University Press.

Anderson, Eugene N. 1939. *Nationalism and the Cultural Crisis in Prussia, 1806–1815.* New York: Farrar and Rinehart.

Aretz, Gertrude. 1929. *Queen Louise of Prussia.* New York: G. P. Putnam's Sons.

Arnold, Eric A. 1966. "Some Observations on the French Opposition to Napoleonic Conscription, 1804–1806," *French Historical Studies* 4, pp. 452–462.

———. 1979. *Fouché, Napoleon and the General Police.* Washington, DC: University Press of America.

———, ed. 1994. *A Documentary Survey of Napoleonic France.* Lanham, MD: University Press of America.

———, ed. 1996. *A Documentary Survey of Napoleonic France: A Supplement.* Lanham, MD: University Press of America.

Arnold, James R. 1991. *Crisis on the Danube: Napoleon's Austrian Campaign of 1809.* London: Arms and Armour.

Aronson, Theo. 1965. *The Golden Bees: The Story of the Bonapartes.* London: Oldbourne.

Artom, Guido. 1970. *Napoleon is Dead in Russia: The Extraordinary Story of One of History's Strangest Conspiracies.* London: Allen and Unwin.

Atteridge, Andrew Hilliard. 1909. *Napoleon's Brothers.* London: Methuen.

———. 1918. *Joachim Murat, Marshal of France and King of Naples.* London: T. Nelson and Sons.

Austin, Paul Britten. 1987. "Oudinot," in David G. Chandler, ed., *Napoleon's Marshals.* New York: Macmillan.

Bainbridge, Simon. 1995. *Napoleon and English Romanticism.* Cambridge: Cambridge University Press.

Barnard, Howard C. 1969. *Education and the French Revolution.* Cambridge: Cambridge University Press.

Barthorp, Michael. 1978. *Napoleon's Egyptian Campaigns, 1798–1801.* London: Osprey.

Bear, Joan. 1972. *Caroline Murat: A Biography.* London: Collins.

Beauharnais, Hortense de. 1927. *Memoirs of Queen Hortense.* 2 vols. New York: Cosmopolitan.

Beck, Thomas D. 1974. *French Legislators, 1800–1834.* Berkeley: University of California Press.

Bennett, Geoffrey M. 1972. *Nelson, the Commander.* New York: Charles Scribner's Sons.

———. 1977. *The Battle of Trafalgar.* London: Batsford.

Bérenger, Jean. 1994. *A History of the Habsburg Empire.* London and New York: Longman.

Bergeron, Louis. 1981. *France under Napoleon.* Princeton: Princeton University Press.

Berkeley, Alice D., ed. 1991. *New Lights on the Peninsular War.* Lisbon: British Historical Society of Portugal.

Bernard, Jack F. 1973. *Talleyrand: A Biography.* London: Collins.

Bertaud, Jean-Paul. 1986. "Napoleon's Officers," *Past & Present,* no. 112 (August 1986), pp. 99–111.

———. 1988. *The Army of the French Revolution.* Princeton: Princeton University Press.

Best, Geoffrey. 1982. *War and Society in Revolutionary Europe, 1770–1870.* London: Fontana.

Bjelovuc, Harriet. 1970. *The Ragusan Republic: Victim of Napoleon and Its Own Conservatism.* Leiden: E. J. Brill.

Black, Jeremy. 1998. "Napoleon's Impact on International Relations," *History Today* 48 (February 1998), pp. 48–51.

Blanning, T. C. W. 1995. *The Napoleonic Wars 1803–1815.* London: Edward Arnold.

Boime, Albert. 1990. *Art in an Age of Bonapartism, 1800–15.* Chicago: University of Chicago Press.

Bowden, Scott. 1990. *Napoleon's Grande Armée of 1813.* Chicago: The Emperor's Press.

Brauer, Kinley, and William E. Wright, eds. 1990. *Austria in the Age of the French Revolution, 1789–1815.* Minneapolis: Center for Austrian Studies, University of Minnesota.

Brett James, Antony. 1964. *The Hundred Days: Napoleon's Last Campaign from Eyewitness Accounts.* New York: Macmillan.

———. 1966. *1812: Eyewitness Accounts of Napoleon's Invasion of Russia.* New York: Macmillan.

———. 1970. *Europe Against Napoleon: The Leipzig Campaign, 1813, from Eyewitness Accounts.* New York: Macmillan.

Brinton, Crane. 1930. *The Jacobins.* New York: Macmillan.

———. 1936. *The Lives of Talleyrand.* New York: George Allen and Unwin.

Britt, Albert Sidney, III. 1986. *Campaign Atlas to the Wars of Napoleon.* Wayne, NJ: Avery.

Broers, Michael G. 1996. *Europe under Napoleon 1799–1815.* London: Edward Arnold.

Brookner, Anita. 1980. *Jacques-Louis David.* London: Chatto and Windus.

Bruce, Evangeline. 1995. *Napoleon and Josephine: An Improbable Marriage.* New York: Scribner.

Bruun, Geoffrey. 1983. *Europe and the French Imperium.* Westport, CT: Greenwood Press.

Bryan, Patrick E. 1984. *That Haitian Revolution and Its Effects.* London: Heinemann.

Buist, Marten G. 1974. *At Spes non Fracta: Hope & Co., 1770–1815: Merchant Bankers and Diplomats at Work.* The Hague: Nijhoff.

Burton, Reginald George. 1912. *Napoleon's Campaigns in Italy, 1796–97 and 1800.* London and New York: G. Allen.

Butterfield, Herbert. 1929. *The Peace Tactics of Napoleon, 1806–1808.* Cambridge: Cambridge University Press.

Callahan, William J. 1984. *Church, Politics and Society in Spain, 1750–1874.* Cambridge: Harvard University Press.

Carlson, Marvin A. 1966. *The Theater of the French Revolution.* Ithaca, NY: Cornell University Press.

Carr, Raymond. 1982. *Spain: 1808–1975.* 2nd ed. Oxford: Clarendon Press.

Carrington, Dorothy. 1971. *Granite Island: A Portrait of Corsica.* London: Longman.

———. 1988. *Napoleon and His Parents: On the Threshold of History.* London: Viking.

Carter, Francis W. 1972. *Dubrovnik (Ragusa): a Classic City-State.* London: Seminar Press.

Castelot, André. 1960. *Napoleon's Son: The King of Rome.* London: Hamish Hamilton.

Cate, Curtis. 1985. *The War of the Two Emperors: The Duel between Napoleon and Alexander, Russia, 1812.* New York: Random House.

Caulaincourt, Armand Augustin Louis de. 1930. *Memoirs of General de Caulaincourt, Duke of Vicenza,* ed. Jean Hanoteau. 3 vols. London: Cassell.

———. 1935. *With Napoleon in Russia,* ed. George Libaire. New York: William Morrow.

Chambers, George L. 1910. *Bussaco.* London: Sonnenschein.

Chandler, David G. 1974. *The Campaigns of Napoleon: The Mind and Method of History's Greatest Soldier.* New York: Macmillan.

———. 1979. *Dictionary of the Napoleonic Wars.* London: Arms and Armour.

———. 1980. *Waterloo: The Hundred Days.* London: Osprey.

———. 1989. "Napoleon as Man and Leader," *Consortium on Revolutionary Europe, Proceedings.*

———. 1994. *On the Napoleonic Wars: Collected Essays.* London: Greenhill.

———, ed. 1987. *Napoleon's Marshals.* New York: Macmillan.

Chapman, Brian. 1955. *The Prefects and Provincial France.* London: George Allen and Unwin.

Charles-Roux, François. 1937. *Bonaparte: Governor of Egypt.* London: Methuen.

Chastenet, Jacques. 1953. *Godoy: Master of Spain.* London: Batchworth Press.

Chateaubriand, François René de. 1965. *The Memoirs of Chateaubriand,* ed. Robert Baldick. 1965. Harmondsworth, England: Penguin.

Christie, Ian R. 1982. *Wars and Revolutions: Britain, 1760–1815.* London: Edward Arnold.

Church, Clive H. 1981. *Revolution and Red Tape: The French Ministerial Bureaucracy 1770–1850.* Oxford: Clarendon Press.

Clapham, John H. 1912. *The Abbé Sieyès: An Essay in the Politics of the French Revolution.* London: P. S. King and Son.

Clausewitz, Carl von. 1993. *On War.* Ed. and trans. Michael Howard and Peter Paret. London: Everyman's Library.

Clough, Shepherd B. 1939. *France: A History of National Economics, 1789–1939.* New York: Charles Scribner's Sons.

Cobb, Richard C. 1970. *The Police and the People, 1789–1820.* New York: Oxford University Press.

Cobban, Alfred. 1960. *In Search of Humanity: The Role of the Enlightenment in Modern History.* New York: G. Braziller.

Cole, Hubert. 1963. *Josephine.* New York: Viking Press.

———. 1971. *Fouché: The Unprincipled Patriot.* London: Eyre and Spottiswoode.

———. 1972. *The Betrayers: Joachim and Caroline Murat.* London: Eyre Methuen.

Collins, Herbert F. 1964. *Talma.* New York: Faber & Faber.

Collins, Irene. 1976. "Variations on the Theme of Napoleon's Moscow Campaign," *History* 81, pp. 39–53.

———. 1979. *Napoleon and His Parliaments.* London: Edward Arnold.

———. 1986. *Napoleon: First Consul and Emperor of the French.* London: Historical Association Pamphlet.

Compton, Piers. 1937. *Marshal Ney.* London: Methuen.

Connelly, Owen. 1965. *Napoleon's Satellite Kingdoms.* New York: Free Press.

———. 1968. *The Gentle Bonaparte: A Biography of Joseph, Napoleon's Elder Brother.* New York: Macmillan.

———. 1987. *Blundering to Glory: Napoleon's Military Campaigns.* Wilmington, DE: Scholarly Resources.

———, ed. 1985. *Historical Dictionary of Napoleonic France, 1799–1815.* Westport, CT: Greenwood.

Constant, Benjamin. 1988. *Political Writings*, trans. and ed. Biancamaria Fontana. Cambridge: Cambridge University Press.

Cookson, J. E. 1997. *The British Armed Nation 1793–1815*. Oxford: Clarendon Press.

Cooper, A. Duff. 1932. *Talleyrand*. London: Jonathan Cape.

Craig, Gordon A. 1955. *The Politics of the Prussian Army*. New York: Oxford University Press.

———. 1966. "Problems of Coalition Warfare: The Military Alliance against Napoleon," in *War, Politics and Diplomacy*. London: Weidenfeld and Nicolson.

Cronin, Vincent. 1972. *Napoleon*. New York: Morrow.

Crosland, Maurice Pierre. 1967. *The Society of Arcueil: A View of French Science at the Time of Napoleon*. London: Heinemann.

Crouzet, François. 1964. "Wars, Blockades and Economic Change in Europe, 1792–1815," *Journal of Economic History* 24, pp. 567–588.

Crowhurst, Patrick. 1989. *The French War on Trade: Privateering, 1793–1815*. Aldershot, England: Scolar.

Cubberley, R. E. 1969. *The Role of Fouché during the Hundred Days*. Madison: Wisconsin University Press.

Dakin, Douglas. 1979. "The Congress of Vienna, 1814–15, and its Antecedents," in Alan Sked, ed., *Europe's Balance of Power, 1815–1848*. London: Macmillan.

Dann, Otto, and John Dinwiddy, eds. 1988. *Nationalism in the Age of the French Revolution*. London: Hambledon.

Dansette, Adrien. 1961. *Religious History of Modern France*. 2 vols. London: Nelson.

Davies, David William. 1974. *Sir John Moore's Peninsular Campaign, 1808–1809*. The Hague: Nijhoff.

Davies, Norman. 1981. *God's Playground: A History of Poland*. 2 vols. Oxford: Clarendon Press.

Davis, John A. 1990. "The Impact of French Rule on the Kingdom of Naples, 1806–1815," *Ricerche Storiche* 20, pp. 367–405.

De Chair, Somerset, ed. 1992. *Napoleon on Napoleon*. London: Cassell.

Derry, John W. 1976. *Castlereagh*. London: Allen Lane.

Deutsch, Harold C. 1938. *The Genesis of Napoleonic Imperialism*. Cambridge: Harvard University Press.

Dible, James H. 1970. *Napoleon's Surgeon*. London: William Heinemann.

Dixon, Peter. 1976. *Canning: Politician and Statesman*. London: Weidenfeld and Nicolson.

Dixon, Pierson. 1966. *Pauline: Napoleon's Favourite Sister*. New York: D. McKay.

Dowd, D. L. 1957. *Napoleon: Was He the Heir of the Revolution?* New York: Krieger.

Duffy, Christopher. 1972. *Borodino and the War of 1812*. London: Seeley.

———. 1977. *Austerlitz*. Hampden, CT: Archon Books.

Dufraisse, Roger. 1992. *Napoleon*. New York: McGraw-Hill.

Egan, Clifford L. 1983. *Neither Peace nor War: Franco-American Relations, 1803–1812*. Baton Rouge: Louisiana State University Press.

Ehrman, John. 1969. *The Younger Pitt: The Years of Acclaim*. London: Constable.

———. 1983. *The Younger Pitt: The Reluctant Transition*. London: Constable.

———. 1996. *The Younger Pitt: The Consuming Struggle*. London: Constable.

Ellis, Geoffrey. 1981. *Napoleon's Continental Blockade: The Case of Alsace*. Oxford: Clarendon Press.

———. 1991. *The Napoleonic Empire*. Atlantic Highlands, NJ: Humanities Press International.

———. 1996. *Napoleon*. London and New York: Longman.

———. 1997. "Religion According to Napoleon: The Limitations of Pragmatism," in Nigel Aston, ed., *Religious Change in Europe 1650–1914: Essays for John McManners*. Oxford: Clarendon Press.

Elting, John R. 1988. *Swords around a Throne: Napoleon's Grande Armée.* New York: Free Press.

Emsley, Clive. 1979. *British Society and the French Wars.* New York: Macmillan.

———. 1993. *The Longman Companion to Napoleonic Europe.* London and New York: Longman.

Epstein, Robert M. 1994. *Napoleon's Last Victory and the Emergence of Modern War.* Lawrence, KS: University Press of Kansas.

Epton, Nina. 1975. *Josephine: The Empress and her Children.* London: Weidenfeld and Nicolson.

Esdaile, Charles J. 1988. *The Spanish Army in the Peninsular War.* Manchester: Manchester University Press.

———. 1988. "Heroes or Villains? The Spanish Guerrillas and the Peninsular War," *History Today* 48 (April 1988), pp. 29–35.

———. 1990. *The Duke of Wellington and the Command of the Spanish Army, 1812–14.* London: Macmillan.

———. 1991. "The Problem of the Spanish Guerrillas," in Alice D. Berkeley, ed. *New Lights on the Peninsular War.* Lisbon: British Historical Society of Portugal.

———. 1992. "Latin America and the Anglo-Spanish Alliance against Napoleon, 1808–1814," *Bulletin of Hispanic Studies* 49, pp. 55–70.

———. 1995. *The Wars of Napoleon.* London and New York: Longman.

Esposito, Vincent J., and John R. Elting. 1964. *A Military History and Atlas of the Napoleonic Wars.* New York: Praegar.

Eyck, F. Gunther. 1986. *Loyal Rebels: Andreas Hofer and the Tyrolean Uprising of 1809.* Lanham, MD: University Press of America.

Feldbaek, Ole. 1980. *Denmark and the Armed Neutrality 1800–1801.* Copenhagen: Akademisk Forlag.

———. 1986. "The Foreign Policy of Tsar Paul I, 1800–1801: An Interpretation." *Jahrbücher für Geschichte Osteuropas* 30, pp. 16–36.

Ferrero, Guglielmo. 1961. *The Gamble: Bonaparte in Italy (1796–1797).* London: G. Bell.

Finley, Milton. 1989. "The Most Monstrous of Wars: Suppression of Calabrian Brigandage, 1806–1811," *Consortium on Revolutionary Europe: Proceedings* 18, pp. 251–266.

———. "Patriots or Brigands? The Calabrian Partisans, 1806–1812," *Consortium on Revolutionary Europe, Proceedings 1991,* pp. 161–170.

Forrest, Alan, 1989. *Conscripts and Deserters: the Army and French Society during the Revolution and Empire.* New York: Oxford University Press.

Forrest, Alan, and Peter Jones, eds. 1991. *Reshaping France: Town, Country and Region during the French Revolution.* Manchester: Manchester University Press.

Freedeman, Charles E. 1961. *The Conseil d'Etat in Modern France.* New York: Columbia University Press.

Fregosi, Paul. 1989. *Dreams of Empire: Napoleon and the First World War, 1792–1815.* London: Hutchinson.

Friedlaender, Walter. 1952. *David to Delacroix.* Cambridge: Harvard University Press.

Furet, François. 1992. *Revolutionary France, 1770–1880.* Oxford: Basil Blackwell.

Fryer, Walter R. 1965. *Republic or Restoration in France, 1794–1797.* Manchester: Manchester University Press.

Gallagher, John G. 1976. *The Iron Marshal: A Biography of Louis N. Davout.* Carbondale: Southern Illinois University Press.

Gash, Norman. 1984. *Lord Liverpool: The Life and Political Career of Robert Banks Jenkinson, Second Earl of Liverpool, 1770–1828.* London: Weidenfeld and Nicolson.

———, ed. 1990. *Wellington: Studies in the Military and Political Career of the First Duke of Wellington.* Manchester: Manchester University Press.

Gassier, Pierre. 1985. *Goya: A Witness of his Times.* New York: Alpine Fine Arts Collection.

Gates, David. 1986. *The Spanish Ulcer: A History of the Peninsular War*. London: Allen and Unwin.

———. 1997. *The Napoleonic Wars, 1803–15*. London: Edward Arnold.

Geer, Walter. 1928–1929. *Napoleon and his Family: The Story of a Corsican Clan*. 3 vols. London: George Allen and Unwin.

Geyl, Pieter. 1949. *Napoleon: For and Against*. New Haven: Yale University Press.

Gibson, Ralph. 1989. *A Social History of French Catholicism 1789–1914*. London: Routledge.

Gildea, Robert. 1994. *The Past in French History*. New Haven: Yale University Press.

Gill, John H. 1992. *With Eagles to Glory: Napoleon and His German Allies in the 1809 Campaign*. Novato, CA: Presidio Press.

Glover, Michael. 1963. *Wellington's Peninsular Victories: Busaco, Salamanca, Victoria, Nivelle*. London: Batsford.

———. 1968. *Wellington as Military Commander*. London: Batsford.

———. 1971. *Legacy of Glory: The Bonaparte Kingdom of Spain, 1808–1813*. New York: Scribners.

———. 1974. *The Peninsular War, 1807–14*. Hampden, CT: Archon Books.

———. 1980. *Warfare in the Age of Bonaparte*. London: Cassell.

Glover, Richard. 1967. "The French Fleet, 1807–1814: Britain's Problem and Madison's Opportunity," *Journal of Modern History* 39, pp. 233–252.

———. 1973. *Britain at Bay: Defence Against Bonaparte, 1803–14*. New York: Barnes and Noble.

Godechot, Jacques. 1981. *The Counter-Revolution: Doctrine and Action, 1789–1804*. Princeton: Princeton University Press.

Gonzalez-Palacios, Alvar. 1970. *The French Empire Style*. London: Hamlyn.

Goodspeed, Donald James. 1965. *Bayonets at St Cloud: The Story of the 18th Brumaire*. London: Rupert Hart-Davis.

Gottschalk, Louis R., and Margaret Maddox. 1969–1973. *Lafayette in the French Revolution*. 2 vols. Chicago: University of Chicago Press.

Gould, Cecil H. M. 1965. *Trophy of Conquest: The Musée Napoléon and the Creation of the Louvre*. London: Faber & Faber.

Goy, Joseph. 1989. "Civil Code," in François Furet and Mona Ozouf, eds., *Critical Dictionary of the French Revolution*. Cambridge: Harvard University Press.

Grab, Alexander. 1988. "The Kingdom of Italy and Napoleon's Continental Blockade." *Consortium on Revolutionary Europe, Proceedings, 1988*, pp. 587–604.

———. 1995. "State Power, Brigandage and Rural Resistance in Napoleonic Italy," *European History Quarterly* 25, pp. 39–70.

Gray, Marion W. 1986. *Prussia in Transition: Society and Politics under the Stein Reform Ministry of 1808*. Philadelphia: American Philosophical Society.

Greer, Donald M. 1951. *The Incidence of Emigration during the French Revolution*. Cambridge: Harvard University Press.

Gregory, Desmond. 1996. *Malta, Britain and the European Powers, 1793–1815*. Madison, NJ: Fairleigh Dickinson University Press.

Griffith, Paddy. 1987. "Soult," in David G. Chandler, ed., *Napoleon's Marshals*. New York: Macmillan.

Guy, Alan J., ed. 1990. *The Road to Waterloo: The British Army and the Struggle against Revolutionary and Napoleonic France*. London: National Army Museum.

Haffner, Sebastian. 1980. *The Rise and Fall of Prussia*. London: Weidenfeld and Nicolson.

Hahn, Roger. 1971. *The Anatomy of a Scientific Institution: The Paris Academy of Sciences, 1666–1803*. Berkeley: University of California Press.

Hales, Edward Elton Young. 1962. *Napoleon and the Pope*. London: Eyre and Spottiswoode.

Hall, Christopher D. 1992. *British Strategy in the Napoleonic Wars*. Manchester: Manchester University Press.

Hamilton-Williams, David. 1993. *Waterloo: New Perspectives: The Great Battle Reappraised*. London: Arms and Armour.

———. 1994. *The Fall of Napoleon: The Final Betrayal*. London: John Wiley.

Hampson, Norman. 1976. *The First European Revolution 1776–1815*. London: Thames and Hudson.

Harbron, John D. 1988. *Trafalgar and the Spanish Navy*. London: Conway Maritime.

Hartley, Janet. 1994. *Alexander I*. London and New York: Longman.

Harvey, A. D. 1998. "Napoleon—the Myth," *History Today* 48 (January 1998), pp. 27–32.

Haythornwaite, Philip J., et al. 1996. *Napoleon: The Final Verdict*. London: Arms and Armour.

Head, Brian. 1985. *Ideology and Social Science: Destutt de Tracy and French Liberalism*. Dordrecht, Netherlands: Nijhoff.

Hearder, Harry. 1983. *Italy in the Age of the Risorgimento, 1790–1870*. London and New York: Longman.

Hecksher, E. F. 1922. *The Continental System: An Economic Interpretation*. Oxford: Publications of the Carnegie Endowment for International Peace.

Herold, J. Christopher. 1959. *Mistress to an Age: A Life of Madame de Staël*. London: Hamish Hamilton.

———. 1962. *Bonaparte in Egypt*. New York: Harper and Row.

———. 1983. *The Horizon Book of the Age of Napoleon*. New York: American Heritage Publishing Co./Bonanza Books.

———, ed. 1955. *The Mind of Napoleon*. New York: Columbia University Press.

Hibbert, Christopher. 1961. *Corunna*. London: Batsford.

———. 1998. *Waterloo*. London: Wordsworth Military Library.

Hilt, Douglas. 1987. *The Troubled Trinity: Godoy and the Spanish Monarchs*. Tuscaloosa: University of Alabama Press.

Hinde, Wendy. 1981. *Castlereagh*. London: Collins.

———. 1989. *George Canning*. Oxford: Basil Blackwell.

Holmes, Edward Richard. 1971. *Borodino 1812*. London: Batsford.

Holtman, Robert B. 1950. *Napoleonic Propaganda*. Baton Rouge: Louisiana State University Press.

———. 1967. *The Napoleonic Revolution*. Philadelphia: Lippincott.

Honour, Hugh. 1968. *Neo-Classicism*. Harmondsworth, England: Penguin.

———. 1979. *Romanticism*. London: Allen Lane.

Horne, Alistair. 1979. *Napoleon, Master of Europe 1805–1807*. New York: William Morrow.

———. 1996. *How Far from Austerlitz? Napoleon 1805–1815*. London: Macmillan.

Horricks, Raymond. 1982. *Marshal Ney, the Romance and the Real*. Tunbridge Wells, England: Midas.

Horward, Donald D. 1965. *The Battle of Bussaco: Masséna vs Wellington*. Tallahassee: Florida State University.

———. 1978. "The Influence of British Seapower upon the Peninsular War, 1808–1814," *Naval War College Review* 31, pp. 54–71.

———. 1989. "Wellington and the Defence of Portugal," *International History Review* 11, pp. 55–67.

———, ed. and trans. 1973. *The French Campaign in Portugal, 1810–11: An Account by Jean-Jacques Pelet*. Minneapolis: University of Minnesota Press.

Howarth, David Armine. 1968. *A Near-Run Thing: The Day of Waterloo*. London: Collins.

———. 1969. *Trafalgar: The Nelson Touch*, London: Collins.

Hunt, Lynn, et al. 1979. "The Failure of the Liberal Republic in France, 1795–1799: The Road to Brumaire," *Journal of Modern History* 51, pp. 734–759.

Hutt, Maurice. 1983. *Chouannerie and Counter-Revolution.* 2 vols. Cambridge: Cambridge University Press.

Hyman, Paula E. 1991. *The Emancipation of the Jews of Alsace.* New Haven: Yale University Press.

Jackson, Sir William Godfrey Fothergill. 1953. *Attack in the West: Napoleon's First Campaign Re-read Today.* London: Eyre and Spottiswoode.

James, C. L. R. 1938. *The Black Jacobins: Toussaint L'Ouverture and the San Domingo Revolution.* London: Secker & Warburg.

James, Lawrence. 1992. *The Iron Duke: A Military Biography of Wellington.* London: Weidenfeld and Nicholson.

Jedin, Hubert, ed. 1981. *History of the Church, Vol. 7: The Church between Revolution and Restoration.* London: Burns and Oates.

Jewsbury, George F. 1976. *The Russian Annexation of Bessarabia, 1774–1828: A Study of Imperial Expansion.* Boulder, CO: East European Quarterly.

———. 1979. "Nationalism in the Danubian Principalities, 1800–1825: A Reconsideration," *East European Quarterly* 13, pp. 287–296.

Jones, Peter M. 1985. *Politics and Rural Society: The Southern Massif Central, c. 1750–1880.* Cambridge: Cambridge University Press.

———. 1988. *The Peasantry in the French Revolution.* Cambridge: Cambridge University Press.

Jones, R. Ben. 1977. *Napoleon, Man and Myth.* London: Hodder and Stoughton.

Josselson, Michael and Diana. 1980. *The Commander: A Life of Barclay de Tolly.* Oxford University Press.

Kafker, Frank A., and James M. Laux, eds. 1989. *Napoleon and His Times: Selected Interpretations.* Malibar, FL: Krieger.

Kaiser, Thomas E. 1980. "Politics and Political Economy in the Thought of the Ideologues," *History of Political Economy* 12, pp. 141–160.

Kaplan, Lawrence S. 1987. *Entangling Alliances with None: American Foreign Policy in the Age of Jefferson.* Kent, OH: Kent State University Press.

Keegan, John. 1976. *The Face of Battle.* London: Cape.

Kennedy, Emmet. 1978. *A Philosophe in the Age of Revolution: Destutt de Tracy and the Origins of Ideology.* Philadelphia: American Philosophical Society.

Kennedy, Paul. 1991. *The Rise and Fall of British Naval Mastery.* 3rd ed. London: Fontana.

Kircheisen, Friedrich Max. 1932. *Jovial King: Napoleon's Youngest Brother.* London: E. Mathews and Marrot.

Klang, Daniel. 1965. "Bavaria and the War of Liberation, 1813–1814," *French Historical Studies* 4, pp. 22–41.

Knapton, Ernest J. 1964. *Joséphine.* Cambridge: Harvard University Press.

Kohn, Hans. 1950. "Napoleon and the Age of Nationalism," *Journal of Modern History* 22, pp. 21–37.

———. 1967. *Prelude to Nation States: The French and German Experience, 1789–1815.* Princeton: Van Nostrand.

Korngold, Ralph. 1960. *The Last Years of Napoleon: His Captivity at St Helena.* London: Victor Gollancz.

Kossman, E. H. 1978. *The Low Countries, 1780–1940.* Oxford: Clarendon Press.

Kraehe, Enno Edward. 1963. *Metternich's German Policy, Vol. 1: The Contest with Napoleon, 1799–1814.* Princeton: Princeton University Press.

———. 1983. *Metternich's German Policy, Vol. 2: The Congress of Vienna, 1814–1815.* Princeton: Princeton University Press.

Kurtz, Harold. 1957. *The Trial of Marshal Ney.* London: Hamish Hamilton.

Lachouque, Henry. 1966. *Napoleon's Battles.* New York: Dutton.

———. 1997. *The Anatomy of Glory: Napoleon and his Guard.* London: Greenhill.

Langsam, Walter C. 1930. *The Napoleonic Wars and German Nationalism in Austria.* New York: Columbia University Press.

———. 1949. *Francis the Good: The Education of an Emperor, 1768–1792.* New York: Macmillan.

Lawford, James P. 1977. *Napoleon: The Last Campaigns.* New York: Crown.

Lefebvre, Georges. 1965. *The Directory.* London: Routledge and Kegan Paul.

———. 1967. *The French Revolution from 1793 to 1799.* London: Routledge and Kegan Paul.

———. 1970. *Napoleon,* 2 vols. New York: Columbia University Press.

Lewis, Gwynne.1978. *The Second Vendée: The Continuity of Counter-Revolution in the Department of the Gard, 1789–1815.* New York: Oxford University Press.

Livermore, Harold V. 1966. *A New History of Portugal.* Cambridge: Cambridge University Press.

Lloyd, Charles C. 1973. *The Nile Campaign: Nelson and Napoleon in Egypt.* Newton Abbot, England: David & Charles.

Lloyd, Christopher. 1965. "Navies," in C. W. Crawley, ed., *New Cambridge Modern History. Vol. 9: War and Peace in an Age of Upheaval, 1793–1830.* Cambridge: Cambridge University Press.

Longworth, Philip. 1965. *The Art of Victory: The Life and Achievements of Generalissimo Suvorov, 1729–1800.* London: Constable.

Lovett, Gabriel H. 1965. *Napoleon and the Birth of Modern Spain,* 2 vols. New York: New York University Press.

Lynch, John. 1986. *The Spanish American Revolution, 1808–1826.* 2nd ed. New York: Norton.

———. 1989. *Bourbon Spain, 1700–1808.* Oxford: Basil Blackwell.

———, ed. 1994. *Latin American Revolutions, 1808–26, Old and New World Origins.* Norman: University of Oklahoma Press.

Lynn, John A. 1989. "Towards an Army of Honour: The Moral Evolution of the French Army," *French Historical Studies,* 16, pp. 152–182.

Lyon, Elijah Wilson. 1934. *Louisiana in French Diplomacy, 1759–1804.* Norman: University of Oklahoma.

Lyons, Martyn. 1975. *France under the Directory.* Cambridge: Cambridge University Press.

———. 1994. *Napoleon Bonaparte and the Legacy of the French Revolution.* London: Macmillan.

Macdonald, Jacques. 1893. *Recollections of Marshal Macdonald,* ed. Camille Rousset, trans. S. L. Simeon. 2 vols. London: Bentley and Sons.

Macdonell, A. G. 1934. *Napoleon and His Marshals.* London: Macmillan.

Mackenzie, Norman. 1982. *The Escape from Elba: The Fall and Flight of Napoleon, 1814–1815.* New York: Oxford University Press.

MacManners, John. 1969. *The French Revolution and the Church.* London: Society for the Promotion of Christian Knowledge.

Mahan, Alfred Thayer. 1892. *The Influence of Seapower upon the French Revolution and Empire, 1793–1812.* 2 vols. London and Cambridge, MA: Sampson Low.

Malino, Frances. 1978. *The Sephardic Jews of Bordeaux: Assimilation and Emancipation in Revolutionary and Napoleonic France.* University, Alabama: University of Alabama Press.

Mansel, Philip. 1981. *Louis XVIII.* London: Blond and Briggs.

———. 1987. *The Eagle in Splendour: Napoleon I and his Court.* London: George Philip.

Margerison, Kenneth. 1983. *P.-L. Roederer, Political Thought and Practice during the French Revolution.* Philadelphia: American Philosophical Society.

Markham, Felix. 1964. *Napoleon.* New York: New American Library.

Marmont, Louis Viesse de. 1974. *The Spirit of Military Institutions.* Westport, CT: Greenhill.

Marshall-Cornwall, Sir James. 1965. *Marshal Massena.* New York: Oxford University Press.

———. 1967. *Napoleon as Military Commander.* London: Batsford.

Martineau, Gilbert. 1968. *Napoleon's St. Helena.* London: John Murray.

———. 1976. *Napoleon's Last Journey.* London: John Murray.

———. 1978. *Madame Mère: Napoleon's Mother.* London: John Murray.

Masson, Frédéric. 1949. *Napoleon at St. Helena, 1815–1821.* Oxford: Pen-in-Hand Publishing Co.

Mathews, Joseph J. 1950. "Napoleon's Military Bulletins," *Journal of Modern History* 22, pp. 137–144.

Maude, Frederic N. 1912. *The Ulm Campaign, 1805.* London: Special Campaign Series.

May, Gita. *Stendhal and the Age of Napoleon.* New York: Columbia University Press.

McLynn, Frank. 1997. *Napoleon.* London: Jonathan Cape.

Mitchell, Harvey. 1965. *The Underground War against Revolutionary France: The Missions of William Wickham, 1794–1800.* Oxford: Clarendon Press.

Morton, John B. 1948. *Brumaire: The Rise of Bonaparte.* London: T. Werner Levine.

Mowat, R. B. 1924. *The Diplomacy of Napoleon.* London: Edward Arnold.

Muir, Rory. 1996. *Britain and the Defeat of Napoleon.* New Haven: Yale University Press.

———. 1998. *Tactics and the Experience of Battle in the Age of Napoleon.* New Haven: Yale University Press.

Myers, Bernard S. 1964. *Goya.* London: Spring Books.

Nanteuil, Luc de. 1990. *Jacques-Louis David.* London: Thames and Hudson.

Nicolson, Harold. 1946. *The Congress of Vienna.* London: Constable.

Nieuwazny, Andrzej. 1998. "Napoleon and Polish Identity," *History Today* 48 (May 1998), pp. 50–55.

Niven, Alexander C. 1978. *Napoleon and Alexander I.* Washington, DC: University Press of America.

Noether, Emiliana. 1988. "Change and Continuity in the Kingdom of Naples, 1806–1815," *Consortium on Revolutionary Europe 1988,* pp. 605–618.

Norman, Barbara. 1976. *Napoleon and Talleyrand: The Last Two Weeks.* New York: Stein and Day.

O'Dwyer, Margaret M. 1985. *The Papacy in the Age of Napoleon and the Restoration: Pius VII, 1800–1823.* Lanham, MD: University Press of America.

Oakey, Stewart P. 1972. *A Short History of Denmark.* New York: Praeger.

Oddie, E. M. 1931. *Marie Louise, Empress of France, Duchess of Parma.* London: E. Mathews and Marrot.

Oechsli, Wilhelm. 1922. *History of Switzerland.* Cambridge: Cambridge University Press.

Ojala, Jeanne A. 1987. "Suchet," in David G. Chandler, ed., *Napoleon's Marshals.* New York: Macmillan.

Oman, Carola. 1953. *Sir John Moore.* London: Hodder and Stoughton.

———. 1954. *Lord Nelson.* London: Collins.

———. 1966. *Napoleon's Viceroy: Eugène de Beauharnais.* London: Collins.

Oman, Charles W. C. 1902–1930. *A History of the Peninsular War.* 7 vols. Oxford: Clarendon Press.

Ortzen, Len. 1974. *Imperial Venus: The Story of Pauline Bonaparte-Borghese.* New York: Stein and Day.

Palmer, Alan. 1967. *Napoleon in Russia.* London: André Deutsch.

———. 1974. *Alexander I, Tsar of War and Peace.* London: Weidenfeld and Nicolson.

———. 1984. *An Encyclopaedia of Napoleon's Europe.* London: Weidenfeld and Nicolson.

———. 1990. *Bernadotte: Napoleon's Marshal, Sweden's King.* London: John Murray.

Palmer, R. R. 1985. *The Improvement of Humanity: Education and the French Revolution.* Princeton: Princeton University Press.

Paret, Peter. 1961. *Internal War and Pacification: The Vendée, 1789–1796.* Princeton: Woodrow Wilson School of Public and International Affairs.

———. 1966. *Yorck and the Era of Prussian Reform, 1807–15*. Princeton: Princeton University Press.

Parker, Harold T. 1971. "The Formation of Napoleon's Personality," *French Historical Studies* 7, pp. 6–26.

———. 1983. *Three Napoleonic Battles*. Durham, NC: Duke University Press.

Parkinson, Roger. 1975. *The Hussar General: The Life of Blücher, Man of Waterloo*. London: Peter Davies.

———. 1976. *Moore of Corunna*. London: Hart-Davis, MacGibbon.

———. 1976. *The Fox of the North: The Life of Kutuzov, General of War and Peace*. London: Peter Davies.

Perrot, Jean-Claude, and Stuart Woolf. 1984. *State and Statistics in France, 1789–1815*. London: Harwood Academic.

Petre, F. Loraine. 1972. *Napoleon's Conquest of Prussia, 1806*. London: Arms and Armour.

———. 1974. *Napoleon's Last Campaign in Germany, 1813*. London: Arms and Armour.

———. 1984. *Napoleon at War: Selected Writings of F. Loraine Petre*. New York: Hippocrene Books.

Phipps, Ramsay Weston. 1926–1939. *The Armies of the First French Republic and the Rise of the Marshals of Napoleon I*. 5 vols. London: Humphrey Milford.

Pinckney, David H. 1978. *Napoleon, Historical Enigma*. St Louis, MS: Forum.

Pivka, Otto von. 1977. *Armies of 1812*. Cambridge, England: Stephens.

Poland, B. C. 1957. *French Protestantism and the French Revolution: A Study in Church and State, Thought and Religion, 1685–1815*. Princeton: Princeton University Press.

Pope, Dudley. 1991. *Life in Nelson's Navy*. London: Allen and Unwin.

Porter, Roy, and Mikulás Teich, eds. 1988. *Romanticism in National Context*. Cambridge: Cambridge University Press.

Quimby, Robert Sherman. 1957. *The Background to Napoleonic Warfare*. New York: Columbia University Press.

Raeuber, Charles. 1987. "Berthier," in David G. Chandler, ed. *Napoleon's Marshals*. New York: Macmillan.

Ragsdale, Hugh. 1968. "Russian Influence at Lunéville," *French Historical Studies* 5, pp. 274–284.

———. 1970. "A Continental System in 1801: Paul I and Bonaparte," *Journal of Modern History* 42, pp. 70–89.

———, ed. 1979. *Paul I: A Reassessment of his Life and Reign*. Pittsburgh: University of Pittsburgh Center for International Studies.

———. 1980. *Détente in the Napoleonic Era: Bonaparte and the Russians*. Lawrence, KS: Regents Press.

———. 1988. *Tsar Paul and the Question of Madness: An Essay in History and Psychology*. New York and Westport, CT: Greenwood Press.

Rapport, Michael. 1998. "Napoleon's Rise to Power," *History Today* 48 (January 1998), pp. 12–19.

Ratcliffe, Bertram. 1981. *Prelude to Fame: An Account of the Early Life of Napoleon up to the Battle of Montenotte*. London: Warne.

Rath, Reuben J. 1941. *The Fall of the Napoleonic Kingdom of Italy, 1814*. New York: Columbia University Press.

Read, Jan. 1977. *War in the Peninsula*. London: Faber.

Richardson, Robert G. 1974. *Larrey: Surgeon to Napoleon's Imperial Guard*. London: John Murray.

Riehn, Richard K. 1991. *1812: Napoleon's Russian Campaign*. New York: John Wiley.

Roberts, J. M. 1972. *The Mythology of the Secret Societies*. London: Secker and Warburg.

Roberts, Warren. 1989. *Jacques-Louis David: Revolutionary Artist*. Chapel Hill: University of North Carolina Press.

Rodger, A. B. 1964. *The War of the Second Coalition, 1798–1801.* New York: Oxford University Press.

Roederer, Pierre Louis. 1989. *The Spirit of the Revolution of 1789 and Other Writings on the Revolutionary Epoch.* Ed. and trans. Murray Forsyth. Aldershot, England: Scolar.

Rogers, H. C. B. 1974. *Napoleon's Army.* London: Allen.

Rolo, Paul Jacques Victor. 1965. *George Canning: Three Biographical Studies.* London: Macmillan.

Rose, J. H. 1924. "Napoleon and Seapower," *Cambridge Historical Journal,* 1, pp. 138–157.

Ross, Michael. 1976. *The Reluctant King: Joseph Bonaparte, King of the Two Sicilies and Spain.* London: Sidgwick and Jackson.

Ross, Steven T. 1981. *European Diplomatic History, 1789–1815.* Malabar, FL: Krieger.

Rothenberg, Gunther E. 1968. "The Austrian Army in the Age of Metternich," *Journal of Modern History* 40, pp. 155–165.

———. 1980. *The Art of Warfare in the Age of Napoleon.* Bloomington: Indiana University Press.

———. 1982. *Napoleon's Great Adversaries: the Archduke Charles and the Austrian Army, 1792–1814.* London: Batsford.

Rothney, John. 1969. *Bonapartism after Sedan.* Ithaca, NY: Cornell University Press.

Ruppenthal, Roland. 1943. "Denmark and the Continental System," *Journal of Modern History* 15, pp. 7–23.

Saul, Norman E. 1970. *Russia and the Mediterranean, 1797–1807.* Chicago: University of Chicago Press.

Saunders, David. 1992. *Russia in the Age of Reaction and Reform, 1801–1881.* New York: Longman.

Schama, Simon. 1977. *Patriots and Liberators: Revolution in the Netherlands, 1780–1813.* New York: Knopf.

Schmitt, H. A. 1983. "Germany without Prussia: A Closer Look at the Confederation of the Rhine," *German Studies Review* 6, pp. 9–39.

Schom, Alan. 1992. *One Hundred Days: Napoleon's Road to Waterloo.* New York: Oxford University Press.

———. 1997. *Napoleon Bonaparte.* New York: HarperCollins.

Schroeder, Paul W. 1994. *The Transformation of European Politics 1763–1848.* New York: Oxford University Press.

Schulze, Hagen. 1991. *The Course of German Nationalism: From Fichte to Bismarck, 1763–1867.* Cambridge: Cambridge University Press.

Schwarz, Bernard, ed. 1956. *The Code Napoleon and the Common Law World.* New York: New York University Press.

Schwarzfuchs, Simon. 1979. *Napoleon, the Jews and the Sanhedrin.* London: Routledge and Kegan Paul.

Scott, Franklin Daniel. 1933. "Bernadotte and the Throne of France, 1814, *Journal of Modern History* 5, pp. 465–478.

———. 1935. *Bernadotte and the Fall of Napoleon.* Cambridge: Harvard University Press.

Seward, Desmond. 1986. *Napoleon's Family.* London: Weidenfeld and Nicolson.

Shanahan, William O. 1945. *Prussian Military Reforms, 1786–1813.* New York: Columbia University Press.

———. 1981. "A Neglected Source of German Nationalism: The Confederation of the Rhine, 1806–13," in Michael Palumbo and William O. Shanahan, eds., *Nationalism: Essays in Honor of Louis L. Snyder.* Westport, CT.: Greenwood Press, pp. 106–132.

Shaw, Stanford J. 1971. *Between Old and New: The Ottoman Empire under Sultan Selim III, 1789–1807.* Cambridge: Harvard University Press.

———. 1976–77. *History of the Ottoman Empire and Modern Turkey.* Cambridge: Cambridge University Press.

Sheehan, James J. 1989. *German History 1770–1866.* Oxford: Clarendon Press.

Sherwig, John M. 1969. *Guineas and Gunpowder: British Foreign Aid in the War with France.* Cambridge: Harvard University Press.

Shulim, Joseph I. 1952. *The Old Dominion and Napoleon Bonaparte: A Study in American Opinion*. New York: Columbia University Press.

Sieburg, Friedrich. 1961. *Chateaubriand*. London: George Allen and Unwin.

Simon, Walter M. 1955. *The Failure of the Prussian Reform Movement*. Ithaca, NY: Cornell University Press.

Snyder, Louis L. 1978. *Roots of German Nationalism*. Bloomington: Indiana University Press.

Sorkin, David Jan. 1987. *The Transformation of German Jewry, 1780–1840*. New York: Oxford University Press.

Staël, Germaine de, trans. Vivien Folkenflik. 1987. *Major Writings of Germaine de Staël*. New York: Columbia University Press.

Staum, Martin S. 1980. *Cabanis: Enlightenment and Medical Philosophy in the French Revolution*. Princeton: Princeton University Press.

Stearns, Josephine B. 1948. *The Role of Metternich in Undermining Napoleon*. Urbana: University of Illinois Press.

Steigler, Gaston, ed. 1897. *Memoirs of Marshal Oudinot, duc de Reggio, Compiled from the Hitherto Unpublished Souvenirs of the Duchesse de Reggio*. New York: D. Appleton and Co.

Stirling, Monica. 1961. *A Pride of Lions: A Portrait of Napoleon's Mother*. London: Collins.

Stoeckl, Agnes de. 1962. *Four Years an Empress: Marie Louise, Second Wife of Napoleon*. London: John Murray.

Sutherland, Christine. 1979. *Marie Walewska, Napoleon's Great Love*. London: Weidenfeld and Nicolson.

———. 1982. *The Chouans: the Social Origins of Popular Counter-Revolution in Upper Brittany, 1770–1796*. New York: Oxford University Press.

Sutherland, D. M. G. 1985. *France, 1789–1815: Revolution and Counter-Revolution*. London: Fontana.

Sydenham, M. J. 1974. *The First French Republic, 1792–1804*. London: Batsford.

———. 1981. "The Republican Revolt of 1793," *French Historical Studies* 12, pp. 120–138.

Talmon, J. L. 1967. *Romanticism and Revolt: Europe 1815–1848*. London: Thames and Hudson.

Tarle, E. 1942. *Napoleon's Invasion of Russia, 1812*. London: Allen and Unwin.

Thompson, J. M. 1952. *Napoleon Bonaparte, His Rise and Fall*. Oxford: Basil Blackwell.

Thornton, M. J. 1968. *Napoleon after Waterloo: England and the Saint Helena Decision*. Stanford, CA: Stanford University Press.

Thrasher, Peter A. 1970. *Pasquale Paoli: An Enlightened Hero, 1725–1807*. London: Constable.

Tilly, Charles. 1976. *The Vendée*. Cambridge: Harvard University Press.

Tolstoy, Leo. 1982. *War and Peace*. Trans. Rosemary Edmonds. Harmondsworth, England: Penguin.

Trouncer, Margaret. 1949. *Madame Récamier*. London: Macdonald.

Tulard, Jean. 1985. *Napoleon: The Myth of the Saviour*. London: Methuen.

Turnbull, Patrick. 1971. *Napoleon's Second Empress*. London: Joseph.

Van Deusen, Glyndon G. 1932. *Sieyès: His Life and His Nationalism*. New York: Columbia University Press.

Vess, David M. 1975. *Medical Revolution in France, 1789–1796*. Gainesville: University Presses of Florida.

Vidalenc, Jean. 1989. "A Survey," in Frank A. Kafker and James M. Laux, eds., *Napoleon and His Times: Selected Interpretations*. Malibar, FL: Krieger. pp. 122–138.

Waller, David. 1978. *Nelson*. London: Hamilton.

Walsh, Henry Horace. 1933. *The Concordat of 1801: A Study of the Problems of Church and State*. New York: Columbia University Press.

Wandycz, Piotr. 1975. *The Lands of Partitioned Poland, 1795–1918*. Seattle: University of Washington Press.

Warner, Oliver. 1960. *The Battle of the Nile.* London: Batsford.

Watson, Sidney John. 1954. *Carnot.* London: Bodley Head.

———. 1957. *By Command of the Emperor: A Life of Marshal Berthier.* London: Bodley Head.

Webster, Charles K. 1934. *The Congress of Vienna, 1814–1815.* London: G. Bell and Sons.

———. 1950. *The Foreign Policy of Castlereagh.* London: G. Bell.

Weiner, Margery. 1960. *The French Exiles, 1789–1815.* London: John Murray.

———. 1964. *The Parvenu Princesses: Elisa, Pauline and Caroline Bonaparte.* London: John Murray.

Whitcomb, Edward A. 1974. "Napoleon's Prefects," *American Historical Review,* 79 pp. 1089–1118.

———. 1979. *Napoleon's Diplomatic Service.* Durham, NC: Duke University Press.

White, Charles Edward. 1989. *The Enlightened Soldier: Scharnhorst and the Militarische Gesellschaft in Berlin, 1801–1805.* New York: Praeger.

White, Colin. 1996. *The Nelson Companion.* Gloucester: Alan Sutton.

Williams, Gwyn A. 1976. *Goya and the Impossible Revolution.* London: Allen Lane.

Wilson-Smith, Timothy. 1996. *Napoleon and His Artists.* London: Constable.

Woloch, Isser. 1970. *Jacobin Legacy: The Democratic Movement under the Directory.* Princeton: Princeton University Press.

———. 1979. *The French Veteran from the Revolution to the Restoration.* Chapel Hill: University of North Carolina Press.

———. 1986. "Napoleonic Conscription: State Power and Civil Society," *Past & Present,* no. 111, pp. 101–129.

Wood, Dennis. 1993. *Benjamin Constant.* London and New York: Routledge.

Woolf, Stuart. 1979. *A History of Italy, 1700–1860: The Social Constraints of Political Change.* London: Methuen.

———. 1989. "French Civilization and Ethnicity in the Napoleonic Empire," *Past & Present,* no. 124 (August 1989), pp. 96–120.

———. 1991. *A History of Italy, 1700–1860: The Social Constraints of Political Change.* London: Routledge.

———. 1991. *Napoleon's Integration of Europe.* London and New York: Routledge.

Woronoff, Denis. 1984. *The Thermidorian Regime and the Directory, 1794–1799.* Cambridge: Cambridge University Press.

Wright, Constance Choate. 1962. *Daughter to Napoleon: A Biography of Hortense, Queen of Holland.* London: Alvin Redman.

Wright, D. G. 1984. *Napoleon and Europe.* London and New York: Longman.

Young, Peter. 1987. "Ney," in David G. Chandler, ed., *Napoleon's Marshals.* New York: Macmillan.

Young, Peter and J. P. Lawford. 1972. *Wellington's Masterpiece: The Battle and Campaign of Salamanca.* London: Allen & Unwin.

INDEX

Venezuela, 233
Venice, 11, 47, 129, 152, 161, 201, 208, **252**
   History of the Venetian Republic (Daru), 75
   Venetia, 57
Venus Reclining (Canova), 37
Vernet, Horace, **252**, 253
Verona, 6
Versailles, 25
Verviers, 22
Vicenza, 17
Victor Amadeus III, King of Piedmont-Sardinia, 56, 254
Victor, Claude, 157–158, 161, **252–254**
Victor, Emmanuel I, King of Piedmont-Sardinia, **254**
Victoria, Queen of Great Britain, 233
   opinion of Jérôme Bonaparte, 32
Vienna, 1, 23, 53, 55, 73, 74, 82, 95, 128, 159, 171, 176, 204, 257
   Congress of, xx, 11, 18, 48, 50, 104, 124, 165, 194, 204, 212, 229–230, 239, 242, **254–255**, 261
Villanova, 5
Villeneuve, Pierre de, 182, 246, **255**
Vimiero, Battle of, 197, 206
Vincennes, 94, 223
Visconti, Giuseppina, 25
Viterbo, 35

Vitoria, Battle of, 33, 134, 199, **255–256**, 261
Voltaire (François-Marie Arouet), 94
Vorarlberg, 18, 208 Vosges, 252

Wagner, Friedrich, 147
Wagram, Battle of, xviii, 11, 19, 23, 55, 61, 74, 78, 113, 116, 143, 155, 162, 289, 229, 230, **257–258**
   Wagram campaign, 25, 31, 73–74, 85, 95, 134, 161, 196
Walcheren Expedition, 22, 50, 113, **258**
Walewice, 258
Walewska, Marie, 141, **258**
Walewski, Alexandre, 258
Walewski, Anastazy, Count, 258
Wallachia, 74
Warsaw, Duchy of, xvii, 4, 26, 78, 91, 203, 204, 229, 230, 243, 244, **258–259**
   freemasonry in, 105
Waterloo, Battle of, xxi, 2, 3, 21, 22, 27, 31, 38, 61, 65, 113, 125, 143, 148, 170, 196, 212, 237, **259–260**, 261
   Emmanuel Grouchy and, 116
   Waterloo campaign, 78, 90, 110, 116–117, 122, 173, 215, 253

Wavre, 116
Weimar, 48, 108, 132
Wellington, Duke of, xviii, xx, xxi, 33, 43, 50, 58, 116, 118, 122, 134, 161, 162, 184, 197–199, 206, 215, 227–228, 232, 233, 234, 245, 255–256, 259–260, **260–261**
Westphalia, 254
   Jérôme Bonaparte as king of, 31
   Kingdom of, xvii, xx, 63, 85, 212, 244, **262**, 273
Weyrother, Franz Von, 9
What is the Third Estate? (Sieyès), 231
White Terror, 57
William I, Prince of Orange-Nassau, 22
Wilson-Smith, Timothy (historian), 93
Wittgenstein, Prince, 152
Wolfe, Charles, 169
Women
   and Civil Code, 59
   education of, 87–88
   fashion, 92–93
   Napoleon on, 205, 281
Würmser, Dagobert Von, 17, 49, 128
Württemburg, 208

Yorck Von Wartenburg, Johann, 212, **263**

Zurich, Battle of, 162, 195